Making Cars in the New India

Auto manufacturing holds the promise of employing many young Indians in relatively well-paid, high-skill employment, but this promise is threatened by the industry's role as a site of immense conflict in recent years. Conflict between foreign vehicle manufacturers, domestic firms and state institutions has characterised much of the industry's development. Labour relations have been characterised by high levels of industrial, social and political strife in urban manufacturing regions.

This book asks: How do we explain this conflict? What are the implications of conflict for the ambitious economic development agendas of Indian governments? Based upon extensive field research in India's National Capital Region, this book is the first to focus on labour relations in the Indian auto industry. It proposes the theory that conflict in the auto industry has been driven by twin forces: First, the intersection of global networks of auto manufacturing with regional social structures which have always relied on informal and precariously-employed workers; and, second, the systematic displacement of securely-employed 'regular workers' by waves of precariously-employed 'de facto informal workers'.

Drawing upon a range of critical social and economic theories, *Making Cars in the New India* argues that the problem of conflict can be addressed by bringing together key elements of the Global Value Chain (GVC) and Global Production Network (GPN) traditions, which focus on firms and inter-firm relations, with social-relational explanations found in theories of social class, gender and caste.

Tom Barnes is an economic sociologist at the Institute for Religion, Politics and Society at Australian Catholic University in Melbourne. His research primarily focuses on insecure, precarious and informal work in Asia, especially India and Indonesia, and Australia. He has published *Informal Labour in Urban India: Three Cities, Three Journeys* with Routledge in 2015.

Development Trajectories in Global Value Chains

A feature of the current phase of globalisation is the outsourcing of production tasks and services across borders, and increasing organisation of production and trade through global value chains (GVCs), global commodity chains (GCCs), and global production networks (GPNs). With a large and growing literature on GVCs, GCCs, and GPNs, this series is distinguished by its focus on the implications of these new production systems for economic, social, and regional development.

This series publishes a wide range of theoretical, methodological, and empirical works, both research monographs and edited volumes, dealing with crucial issues of transformation in the global economy. How do GVCs change the ways in which lead and supplier firms shape regional and international economies? How do they affect local and regional development trajectories, and what implications do they have for workers and their communities? How is the organisation of value chains changing and how are these emerging forms contested as more traditional structures of North–South trade complemented and transformed by emerging South–South lead firms, investments, and trading links? How does the large-scale entry of women into value chain production impact on gender relations? What opportunities and limits do GVCs create for economic and social upgrading and innovation? In what ways are GVCs changing the nature of work and the role of labour in the global economy? And how might the increasing focus on logistics management, financialisation, or social standards and compliance portend important developments in the structure of regional economies?

This series includes contributions from all disciplines and interdisciplinary fields and approaches related to GVC analysis, including GCCs and GPNs, and is particularly focused on theoretically innovative and informed works that are grounded in the empirics of development related to these approaches. Through their focus on the changing organisational forms, governance systems, and production relations, volumes in this series contribute to on-going conversations about theories of development and development policy in the contemporary era of globalisation.

Series editors

Stephanie Barrientos is Professor of Global Development at the Global Development Institute, University of Manchester.

Gary Gereffi is Professor of Sociology and Director of the Center on Globalization, Governance and Competitiveness, Duke University.

Dev Nathan is Visiting Professor at the Institute for Human Development, New Delhi, and Visiting Research Fellow at the Center on Globalization, Governance and Competitiveness, Duke University.

John Pickles, Earl N. Phillips Distinguished Professor of International Studies at the University of North Carolina, Chapel Hill.

Other titles in the Series

1. *Labour in Global Value Chains in Asia*
   Edited by Dev Nathan, Meenu Tewari and Sandip Sarkar
2. *The Sweatshop Regime: Labouring Bodies, Exploitation, and Garments 'Made in India'*
   Alessandra Mezzadri
3. *The Intangible Economy: How Services Shape Global Production and Consumption*
   Edited by Deborah K. Elms, Arian Hassani and Patrick Low

Making Cars in the New India
Industry, Precarity and Informality

Tom Barnes

CAMBRIDGE
UNIVERSITY PRESS

CAMBRIDGE
UNIVERSITY PRESS

University Printing House, Cambridge CB2 8BS, United Kingdom

One Liberty Plaza, 20th Floor, New York, NY 10006, USA

477 Williamstown Road, Port Melbourne, vic 3207, Australia

314 to 321, 3rd Floor, Plot No.3, Splendor Forum, Jasola District Centre, New Delhi 110025, India

79 Anson Road, #06–04/06, Singapore 079906

Cambridge University Press is part of the University of Cambridge.

It furthers the University's mission by disseminating knowledge in the pursuit of education, learning and research at the highest international levels of excellence.

www.cambridge.org
Information on this title: www.cambridge.org/9781108422130

© Tom Barnes 2018

First published 2018

Printed in India by Rajkamal Electric Press, Kundli, Haryana.

A catalogue record for this publication is available from the British Library

ISBN 978-1-108-42213-0 Hardback
ISBN 978-1-108-43379-2 Paperback

For Dina

Contents

Tables, Figures and Maps   *viii*
Acknowledgments   *ix*
Abbreviations   *xiii*

1. The Limits of Industrialisation   1

2. The Auto Industry in India Today   36

3. Auto Manufacturing and the Evolution of Industrial Policy   77

4. The Transformation of Labour Relations   105

5. Auto Workers in India's National Capital Region   136

6. Work and Life at the Bottom of the Auto Supply Chain   170

7. Driving Down the 'Low Road'?   197

Appendix   *229*
Bibliography   *233*
Index   *253*

Tables, Figures and Maps

Tables

1.1	List of industrial actions reported in Indian auto manufacturing	4
2.1	Top 10 countries for passenger cars and commercial vehicles by production volume, 2014	37
2.2	Annual growth (%), production of passenger cars and commercial vehicles, 2000–2014	38
2.3	Automobile Export Trends, 2010–2016	38
2.4	Main motor vehicle manufacturing regions in India and key OEMs in each region	41
3.1	Mode of entry for key foreign OEMs in Indian auto manufacturing	93
5.1	Tier-1 and Tier-2 Auto Manufacturing Suppliers, National Capital Region	152
6.1	Tier-3 auto manufacturing suppliers, National Capital Region	175
7.1	Main work-based problems encountered by employment configuration	210

Figures

1.1	Employment configurations, regional labour control regimes and global production networks in Indian auto manufacturing	32
4.1	The text of the Good Conduct Bond issued to striking MSIL workers, Manesar, June 2011	115

Maps

2.1	Main auto manufacturing regions of India	40
5.1	Key auto manufacturing and fieldwork sites in the National Capital Region (NCR) of India	142

Acknowledgments

This book is the outcome of a journey which began a decade ago when I shifted careers to return to my alma mater, the University of Sydney, to undertake doctoral research. I was motivated by a fascination with the rising powers of Asia and its implications for Australia's society and economy. This was probably a fashionable thing at the time – Goldman Sachs staffers had, in 2003, declared the rise of the BRIC economies (Brazil-Russia-India-China) as the new shapers of the globe; in 2005, *New York Times* columnist, Thomas Friedman, declared a technology-driven 'flattening' of the world; and, in 2012 in Australia, the then-Federal Government published a white paper titled *Australia in the Asian Century*.

Initially interested in the impact of India as a rising power on Australia, I was later drawn into what I felt – and still feel – was the main story: the radical transformation of economic life in India through the country's gradual integration with the world economy. Thus began seven years of research on informal work in India. This led to my first book, *Informal Labour in Urban India* (Routledge, 2015), which is the first book-length study of the Economic Census, a key measure of 'unorganised sector' activity and employment. Combining an institutional and radical political economy, *Informal Labour* questioned dominant narratives about the supposed tendency of 'informalisation' to shift work away from waged labour towards self-employment and micro-entrepreneurship. On the contrary, this book argued that the economic development of urban regions in the global era produced a tendency towards class differentiation with a growing role for waged work among men and women.

As time went on, I increasingly applied this 'classes of labour' approach (Bernstein, 2010) to work in auto manufacturing. During the time of my field research in India's National Capital Region (NCR), a series of fierce and, at times, violent conflicts emerged in the local auto manufacturing sector. As documented in this book, a conflation of developmental factors – the rise of consumer society, the imposition of global production networks, and enhanced market competition – encouraged industrialists to systematically displace their once-securely, well-paid workers with legions of 'de facto informal workers' – people whose work is formally recognised by the state but who, in practice, are denied the agency to access these formal protections.

This book also represents an intellectual journey from political economy to economic sociology via development studies, with a dose of economic geography for good measure. While focused on economic sociology, the critical importance of genuinely inter-disciplinary research – and a refusal to accept the intellectual silos and 'blinkers' of mainstream academia – has stayed with me. The manuscript was completed as I moved to Australian Catholic University (ACU) in Melbourne to undertake postdoctoral studies on industrial transformation in American and Australian cities. With Australia set to become one of few affluent societies – and the only Group of 20 (G20) member nation other than Saudi Arabia to lack an auto manufacturing industry, this research explores the mirror image of the Asian experience – a rather forlorn picture of industrial decline rather than rapid expansion.

At ACU, my research has formed part of a wider foray, envisaged by the renowned sociologist Bryan Turner, into the link between changes to the economic structure of society, individual flourishing and 'happiness'. The structural factors that shape individual 'success' are complex and include the quality and affordability of housing, healthcare, education and childcare services, mobility and mass public transport, rights *to* and *at* work, physical, economic and social security, and the capacity of civic organisations to unify and organise cross-sections of communities.

Within this catalogue, I have continued to focus on the response of civic and political organisations – above all, trade unions – to the transformation of work, including and especially the prevalence of insecure, precarious and informal work. This core concern with security, work and organisation has transported me between western and Asian societies, including a growing interest in manifestations of industrial transformation in Indonesia and comparisons between South and Southeast Asia.

Despite clear differences, my focus on auto manufacturing has clarified a remarkable similarity between these countries and regions: that the problem of insecure and precarious work is on the rise, regardless of whether regions are undergoing industrial decline or industrial expansion. In the former case, for which Australia is an unfortunate example, many ex-manufacturing workers are threatened with a future of growing labour market uncertainty and insecurity.

In the latter case, dominant institutions in emerging regions have taken advantage of labour market and workforce practices in which precarity, insecurity and informality are pre-established norms. As this book suggests, this is not the straightforward picture of growing prosperity that industry advocates have so enthusiastically pitched, and runs contrary to expectations that automotive expansion would bring about a new era of 'high road' labour standards and employment relations. I hope that this research can contribute, even in a small way, to a new space for international comparative research on industrial transformation and insecure work in Asia and beyond.

This book has benefitted from the indispensable work and support of colleagues and friends. The field research results detailed in Chapter 5 updates my work with Krishna Shekhar Lal Das and Surendra Pratap from 2011 to 2013 (Barnes, Lal Das and Pratap, 2015). Shekhar and Surendra proved to be the perfect research partners and I hope we can resume the partnership when time and circumstance permits.

My work in India also benefitted from the insights and assistance of Alakh N. Sharma, Dev Nathan and the late Preet Rustagi of the Institute for Human Development (IHD) in New Delhi. I also benefited greatly from the counsel of Debal Singha Roy and his colleagues at Indira Gandhi National Open University (IGNOU). Sher Singh of *Faridabad Workers News* was a constant source of advice and debate, as were his comrades, Manibushan and Manu. Marco at *Gurgaon Workers News* provided what is undoubtedly the most thorough English-language account of workers' conditions and struggles in the region. Amit, Shyambir, and comrades were always happy to help, between seemingly-constant bouts of struggle and campaigning. K. R. Shyam Sundar provided valuable commentary on India's institutional and legal framework.

Among many foreign scholars I met in India, I particularly valued Jens Lerche's intellectual input into my earlier work, and learned much from Lorenza Monaco's co-travails in the field. I was also lucky enough to gain wisdom from the late Sharit Bhowmik, whose writings on workers movements remain a major source of inspiration.

In more recent times at ACU, I have benefitted from the advice and friendship of many colleagues. I am especially grateful to Sally Weller's ongoing mentorship. From other Australian institutions, a special mention goes to Bill Dunn and Frank Stilwell for their indispensable work as my PhD supervisors. While my PhD finished several years ago, this research helped to lay foundations for the completion of this book. Thanks also to Anita Chan for her support and encouragement.

Finally, it is a cliché, but none of this would be possible without my (growing!) family. I would like to thank, above all, to Dina Marissa for her constant love and companionship, to Alfie for being a constant source of joy and a marvel of curiosity, and to my parents and parents-in-law. One day, I'm sure, we will repeat this exercise on 'home turf'. Perhaps in Cigaru?

List of Abbreviations

ACMA	Automotive Component Manufacturers Association of India
AGC	Asahi Glass Company
AICCTU	All-India Central Council of Trade Unions
AITUC	All-India Trade Union Congress
AMP-1	Automotive Mission Plan 2006–2016
AMP-2	Automotive Mission Plan 2016–2026
ASAL	Automotive Stampings and Assemblies Limited
ATP	Aathi Thamizhar Peravai
BJP	Bharatiya Janata Party
BKES	Bharatiya Kamdar Ekta Sangh
BMS	Bharatiya Mazdoor Sangh
BMW	Bayerische Motoren Werke
BPO	Business Processing Outsourcing
BRIC	Brazil-Russia-India-China
CEO	Chief Executive Officer
CITU	Centre of Indian Trade Unions
CK Birla	Chandra Kant Birla
CKD	Complete Knockdown
CLARA	*Contract Labour (Abolition and Regulation) Act 1970*
CMA	Chennai Metropolitan Area
CNC	Computer Numerical Control
CTUO	Central Trade Union Organisation
C-SEZ	Chakan Special Economic Zone
DDA	Delhi Development Authority
ESI	Employees' State Insurance
FCA	Fiat Chrysler Automobiles
FDI	Foreign Direct Investment
FERA	*Foreign Exchange Regulation Act 1973*
FIBRO	Fischer-Brodbeck
FIEU	Ford India Employees Union
FIPL	Ford India Private Limited
FMC	Ford Motor Company

FMS	Faridabad Mazdoor Samachar
GCC	Global Commodity Chain
GDP	Gross Domestic Product
GE Capital	General Electric Capital
GKM	Gujarat Kamdar Mandal
GM	General Motors
GOI	Government of India
GPN	Global Production Network
GUF	Global Union Federation
GVC	Global Value Chain
GWN	Gurgaon Workers News
HARTRON	Haryana State Electronics Development Corporation
HMC	Hyundai Motor Company
HMIATS	Hyundai Motor India Anna Thozhilalar Sangam
HMIEU	Hyundai Motor India Employees Union
HMIL	Hyundai Motor India Limited
HMS	Hind Mazdoor Sabha
HMSI	Honda Motorcycle and Scooter India
HMWU	Hero MotoCorp Workers Union
HR	Human Resources
HRM	Human Resource Management
HSIIDC	Haryana State Industrial and Infrastructure Development Corporation
ICT	Information and Communications Technology
IDA	*Industrial Disputes Act 1947*
IKD	Incomplete Knockdown
ILO	International Labour Organisation
IMT	Industrial Model Town
INC	Indian National Congress
INTUC	Indian National Trade Union Congress
ISI	Import Substitution Industrialisation
IT	Information Technology
ITI	Industrial Training Institute
ITES	Information Technology-Enabled Services
JBM	Jay Bharat Maruti
KEPS	Kamgar Ekta Premier Sanghatana
MBA	Master of Business Administration
MBI	Mercedes Benz India
MIT	Massachusetts Institutes of Technology
MOU	Memorandum of Understanding
MRF	Madras Rubber Factory

MRTPA	*Monopolies and Restrictive Trade Practices Act 1969*
MSIL	Maruti Suzuki India Limited
MSWU	Maruti Suzuki Workers Union
MUEU	Maruti Udyog Employees Union
MUKU	Maruti Udyog Kamgar Union
MUL	Maruti Udyog Limited
MSPEU	Maruti Suzuki Powertrain Employees Union
NCEUS	National Commission for Enterprises in the Unorganised Sector
NCR	National Capital Region
NCRPB	National Capital Region Planning Board
NCT	National Capital Territory
NGO	Non-Government Organisation
NREGA	*(Mahatma Gandhi) National Rural Employment Guarantee Act 2005*
NTUI	New Trade Union Initiative
OBC	Other Backward Class
OEM	Original Equipment Manufacturer
PMP	Phased Manufacturing Program
PPP	Public Private Partnership
PSU	Public Sector Undertaking
PF	Provident Fund
R and D	Research and Development
SAIC Motor	Shanghai Automotive Industry Corporation
SAIPL	Skoda Auto India Private Limited
Saket MTC	Saket Metal Technocraft
SEZ	Special Economic Zone
SIAM	Society of Indian Automobile Manufacturers
SMC	Suzuki Motor Corporation
SOE	State-Owned Enterprise
SUV	Sports Utility Vehicle
TACO	Tata AutoComp Systems Limited
TCS	Tata Consultancy Services
TELCO	Tata Engineering and Locomotive Company Limited
TKAPL	Toyota Kirloskar Auto Parts Limited
TKMEU	Toyota Kirloskar Motors Employees Union
TKML	Toyota Kirloskar Motor Limited
TKSA	Toyota Kirloskar Suppliers Association
TMA	Team Member Association
TMEU	Tata Motors Employees Union
TPS	Toyota Production System
TVS	ThirukkurungudiVengaram Sundaram
UAW	United Auto Workers

UNCTAD	United Nations Conference on Trade and Development
UP	Uttar Pradesh
VASI	Visteon Automotive Systems India
VE	Volvo-Eicher
VRS	Voluntary Retirement Scheme
VTSC	Visteon Technical and Services Center
VW	Volkswagen
VWI	Volkswagen India
ZF	Zahnradfabrik

The Limits of Industrialisation

There are few people as famous in contemporary India as sporting great Sachin Tendulkar. So, for German luxury vehicle manufacturer BMW, the decision to hire Tendulkar as a brand ambassador represented a major foray into India's vast and rapidly-expanding automobile market.

While not among the largest vehicle manufacturers in the country, BMW's passenger cars and Sports Utility Vehicles (SUVs) represent an upmarket product range for a small minority of affluent, aspiring buyers. This growing consumer base has emerged in a country where, just a single generation ago, *any* model of passenger car was considered a rare luxury. Even today, cars represent rare opulence for the tens of millions of Indians who continue to live and work in poverty.

Nevertheless, BMW's Indian manufacturing operations and extensive marketing, spearheaded by Tendulkar, signify something important about the transformation of Indian society and its economy over the last quarter of a century. It suggests that there is a growing market for foreign-branded luxury consumption.

BMW has recently taken steps to align itself with the 'Make in India' initiative, which was announced by Prime Minister Narendra Modi in September 2014 to market India as the global 'destination of choice' for Foreign Direct Investment (FDI) in manufacturing. In 2015, BMW announced plans to increase locally-manufactured content in its cars and SUVs from 20 per cent to 50 per cent and openly identified with Modi's industrial policy agenda (Subramaniam, 2015).

To help promote this decision, BMW marketed a video with Sachin Tendulkar, tagged on social media as '#SachinMakingBMW: Legendary sportsman Mr. Sachin Tendulkar marked the occasion in a unique way by assembling a BMW 5 Series using parts from Indian auto component suppliers' (BMW India, 2015). This video encapsulates much of the face of Indian automobile production today, including branded luxury consumption, celebrity glitz and social emulation. It also demonstrates how these features of the industry are complementing efforts by local states to encourage the world to set-up new bases for mass production and consumption across India.

But every story can be interpreted in different ways. Another face of the story of Indian auto manufacturing is the tragic deaths of three managers in the last decade during hostile industrial disputes. In September 2008, the Managing Director of Italian gearbox manufacturer, Graziano Trasmissioni, was killed at the company's Greater Noida plant, on the south-eastern edge of New Delhi, during a confrontation with hundreds of workers who had been angered by a protracted industrial dispute and company lockout (Kumari, 2008). One year later, in September 2009, a Vice President of Indian auto parts manufacturer Pricol Limited, was killed by workers at the company's Coimbatore plant in Tamil Nadu after dozens of workers were dismissed (Allirajani, 2009).

In July 2012, a Human Resources (HR) manager was killed during a factory fire at Maruti's Suzuki auto manufacturing facility in Industrial Model Town (IMT) Manesar, about 40 km south-west of New Delhi. This tragedy marked the culmination of a tumultuous period from June 2011 to August 2012 in which workers and management were engaged in a major dispute. Following the violent events of July 2012, thousands of workers were sacked and dozens imprisoned for criminal offences.

The Maruti Suzuki conflict in 2011/12 was arguably the highest profile industrial dispute to emerge in India since the Mumbai textile workers' strike over 35 years ago (Van Wersch, 1992). This was due, in part, to Maruti's standout role as India's largest passenger car manufacturer, and its historical role as the pioneer of the local industry's modernisation. It is also due to the ferocity and scale of the conflict, with simultaneous strikes occurring in supply firms in the region, and major disruptions to production and profits in the sector.

The immediate roots of the 2011/12 conflict lie in the workplace divisions at the Manesar facility. Prior to the dispute, Maruti management had maintained a decade-long policy of hiring new workers through numerous labour contractors who acted as labour market intermediaries. This practice was transplanted into the Manesar facility after its establishment in 2007. It divided the workforce into a core of permanent or 'regular' workers who received relatively high wages and generous employment benefits and a larger group of 'contract' workers whose employment was managed by labour contractors. These workers received lower wages and far fewer employment benefits.

Tensions at the Manesar site erupted over the treatment of workers and the perception that many who work in these different employment categories were being utilised for similar production-line roles, despite large disparities in wages and conditions between regular and non-regular workers. These tensions led to demands to close these disparities, to convert the roles of many non-regular workers into regular or ongoing employment – that is, to 'regularise' workers' employment – and to form a trade union for all workers at the facility, known as the Maruti Suzuki Workers Union (MSWU).

The campaign, and Maruti's refusal to bargain over several core issues, led to a drawn out process of industrial conflict: a strike in June 2011, which severely disrupted production and led to the reinstatement of workers sacked for their union activities; a second strike in August 2011 lead to a round of mass sackings; a 12-day factory occupation in October 2011 ended in large termination payments for suspended union leaders, large pay rises for all workers, and company recognition of the MSWU membership for regular workers in March 2012; a further round of sackings in April and May 2012; and, finally, a violent clash involving workers and managers which led to the death of HR manager, Awanish Kumar Dev.

This tragedy marked the end of this drawn-out industrial conflict and spelled disaster for the majority of workers at the Manesar facility. Nearly 2,000 workers lost their jobs, 148 workers were imprisoned and awaiting trial for several years; in March 2017, 31 former-Maruti employees were convicted with a range of criminal offences. Thirteen of these workers were handed life sentences for murder.[1]

It is not just the ferocity of conflicts in Indian auto manufacturing industries, but also the *number* of conflicts that took place over the 2000s that is striking. Table 1.1 provides a list of key industrial actions reported in India since 2000. Although not exhaustive, this data provides a strong indication of the volume of industrial conflicts. While strikes also occurred before 2000, the expansion of the industry since then has been met with a notable rise in industrial conflict.

Of the 57 industrial actions recorded in the table from 2000 to 2017, the number of actions began to increase significantly from 2008, following major disputes at Maruti Suzuki (2000–01) and Hero Honda (2005) factories in Gurugram (formerly Gurgaon)[2] near New Delhi, as well as Toyota Kirloskar in Bengaluru (formerly Bangalore) in 2001/02. Ninety-three per cent of the recorded actions occurred after 2007, with a notable spike in actions in 2011. The table records 14 actions for 2011, or one quarter of the total number of actions.

Most of the 2011 actions were connected in some form to the protracted dispute at Maruti Suzuki in Manesar and involved solidarity strike action or similar disputes focused on demands for union recognition at key auto suppliers in the NCR. As this book will outline, Maruti Suzuki radically shifted the focus of its employment relations practices from the 1990s to the 2000s, with profound consequences for employment relations across the auto industry as a whole.

---

[1] See Chapter 2 for details about Maruti's role in the auto industry and Chapter 4 for full details of the 2011/2012 dispute in Manesar and the transformation of company employment relations in the 2000s.

[2] The name of 'Gurgaon' was officially changed to 'Gurugram' by the Government of India in September 2016 following a campaign by the Bharatiya Janata Party (BJP)-led Government of Haryana, which was elected in October 2014.

Table 1.1: List of industrial actions reported in Indian auto manufacturing[3]

Firm	Location (region/ state)	Date
National Capital Region (NCR)[4]		
Maruti Suzuki India Ltd (MSIL)	Gurugram	September 2000–January 2001
Hero Honda	Gurugram	August 2005
Hero Honda	Gurugram	April–May 2008
Hero Honda	Gurugram	October 2008
Bony Polymers	Faridabad	November–December 2008
Sunbeam Auto	Gurugram	May 2009
Honda Motorcycle & Scooter India (HMSI)	Manesar	August–October 2009
Rico Auto	Gurugram	August–October 2009
ShivamAutotech	Gurugram	August–October 2009
Sunbeam Auto	Gurugram	August–October 2009
Hero Honda	Gurugram	October 2009
Sona Koyo Steering Systems	Gurugram	October 2009
Lumax Industries	Gurugram	October 2009
MSIL	Manesar	June–August 2011
MSIL	Manesar	October 2011
Suzuki Powertrain India	Manesar	October 2011
Suzuki Castings	Manesar	October 2011
Suzuki Motorcycle India	Manesar	October 2011
Endurance Auto	Manesar	October 2011
Satyam Auto	Manesar	October 2011

Contd.

[3] This is an indicative, non-exhaustive list of industrial actions in different regional clusters based on the author's field research, media and internet searches. 'Industrial action' denotes all forms of industrial dispute and/or collective action, including employer lockouts, employee strikes, solidarity protests and strikes, factory occupations, sit-down protests (e.g. blocking a site entrance), 'dharnas', go-slows, stop-work meetings, hunger strikes and other forms of unofficial or 'wildcat' industrial action. 'Auto manufacturing' refers to auto components manufacturing and raw materials processing in Tier-1 and Tier-2 firms as well as auto assembly Original Equipment Manufacturing (OEM) in passenger cars, two-wheelers and commercial vehicles, including truck and bus manufacturing. Although there is evidence of industrial action in Tier-3 firms (Chapter 6), these have generally occurred on a smaller scale, and have mostly not been documented or reported in the media.

[4] All locations within the state of Haryana unless otherwise stated.

Firm	Location (region/ state)	Date
Hilex India	Manesar	October 2011
MSIL	Manesar	July 2012
Napino Auto	Gurugram	March 2014
Shriram Pistons and Rings	Alwar (Rajasthan)	April 2014
Asti Electronics India	Manesar	December 2014
Bridgestone Tyres India	Manesar	September 2015
MSIL	Manesar	November 2015
HMSI	Alwar (Rajasthan)	December 2015–February 2016
Tamil Nadu inc. Chennai Metro Area (CMA)		
Pricol Ltd	Coimbatore	July 2007
Hyundai Motor India Ltd (HMIL)	Sriperumbudur	May 2008
HMIL	Sriperumbudur	April and July 2009
Pricol Ltd	Coimbatore	September 2009
HMIL	Sriperumbudur	June 2010
MRF Tyres	Chennai	October 2010–June 2011
HMIL	Sriperumbudur	April and Dec 2011
Caparo Engineering India	Sriperumbudur	December 2011
Dunlop Tyres	Ambattur	February 2012
Ford	Maraimalai Nagar	March 2012
HMIL	Sriperumbudur	October 2012
Maharashtra inc. Pune district		
Mahindra	Nashik	May 2009–March 2010
Bosch Chassis Systems	Pune	July 2009
Bajaj Auto	Pune	June 2013
Mahindra	Nashik	March 2013
Force Motors	Pune	March 2015
Bajaj Auto	Pune	January 2017
Gujarat		
General Motors (GM) India	Halol	March–May 2011
Tata Motors	Sanand	February–March 2016
Tata Motors	Sanand	June 2017

Contd.

Firm	Location (region/ state)	Date
Karnataka inc. Bengaluru (Bangalore)		
Toyota Kirloskar	Bengaluru	April–June and December 2001
Toyota Kirloskar	Bengaluru	January–March 2002
Volvo India	Bengaluru	August 2010
Bosch India	Bengaluru	September 2011
Bosch India	Bengaluru	November 2013
Tata Marco Polo Motors	Dharwad	February–March 2016
Other locations		
Dunlop Tyres	Hooghly, West Bengal	October 2011
ASAL Auto Stampings	Pantnagar, Uttarakhand	June 2013
Bosch India	Jaipur, Rajasthan	March–April 2015

These conflicts portray a vision of Indian industry that the country's policy-makers and business-people would prefer to transcend. The need to invigorate the manufacturing industry remains a central concern of the State. Recently, the 'Make in India' initiative has become part of the central government's mantra (see Chapter 3). Automotive manufacturing is central to the logic of 'Make in India', with industry and central government policy-makers collaborating to set ambitious targets to increase auto production as a percentage of national income and employment. India is currently the world's sixth-largest auto producer and may well increase its global ranking in the near future.

The Make in India initiative flows from a longer-standing policy concern that, despite India's transformation into a relatively high-growth regional economic power since the 1990s, the country lacks the capacity to continue expanding its economy and its global influence without a significant expansion in manufacturing. The underlying policy assumption is that emerging economies with a strong, dynamic manufacturing sector can lay the basis for broader economic development, prosperity and a rise in living standards. The high level of conflict in Indian auto manufacturing is a problem for this vision as it undermines the global image, stability and, potentially, the investment climate for the industry.

The core aim of this book is to explain why Indian auto manufacturing has experienced such a high level of industrial, social and political conflict in recent years. In doing so, it will address some of the implications of the trajectory of India's economic development. The answer to this problem, the book will argue, lies in the intersection of social, political, economic and institutional forces at a regional level with economic and institutional forces at a global level. It shows that global forces have shaped the configuration of firms, institutions, workforces and social classes in ways that have generated and reproduced a high level of conflict.

The book also shows how different forms of conflict have shaped industrial development. These forms include commercial conflict between firms, industrial conflict between employers and workers, social conflict between groups of workers from different regions and different castes, institutional conflict involving labour market intermediaries and trade unions and political conflict between firms, workers and state institutions. The evidence presented in the book suggests that this process is likely to continue.

Indian auto manufacturing, and these various expressions of commercial, industrial, social and political conflict, have been shaped by the intersection of global production networks with 'actors' – firms and non-firm institutions – in key regions of the country. Regional actors, including State governments and domestic public and private sector companies, have succeeded in attracting significant FDI in domestic auto manufacturing. This has transformed the productive capacity of local industry through 'value capture'.

This process is represented by automotive assembly manufacturers – known in industry parlance as Original Equipment Manufacturers (OEMs) – and their larger 'Tier-1' suppliers. At this high-end of the industry, production is usually capital-intensive, design-oriented and technologically sophisticated. The production, appropriation and capture of value by this high-end of the supply chain is key to the developmental allure of auto manufacturing.

Conflict can be a major problem for operational stability and profitability. Within the global production networks that dominate auto manufacturing, this problem manifests itself in different ways depending upon the size of the firm, its product focus and product variety and its relationship to client firms 'upstream' and supplier and vendor firms 'downstream'. But, in some cases, conflict can also provide employers with a means of disciplining or controlling workers and regulating consent and dissent on the shop-floor.

For workers, conflict can undermine the socio-economic security of their households and families. However, just as employers can utilise conflict for their own ends, workers can collectively leverage conflict to pursue their interests. These interests vary, based on the different employment configurations in which they work. Besides 'regular' workers, these include temporary and casual workers, trainees, apprentices and workers whose employment is regulated by labour market intermediaries.

Conflict is also a problem for state institutions that want to promote the investment climate in manufacturing regions. While conflict has been an issue for economic management at a national level, it has particularly been an issue at the regional level where State governments have competed to attract domestic and foreign investment from OEMs.

One infamous example of this inter-regional competition concerns the Indian OEM Tata Motors and its investment in small-car production in Sanand, near the city of Ahmedabad in the western Indian State of Gujarat. Tata began producing a cheap small car, called the Nano, at its Sanand assembly plant in 2010. Four years earlier, the Nano had been earmarked for production at a new assembly plant in the town of Singur, over 2000 km to the east of Gujarat, in the State of West Bengal.

The West Bengal State Government, at the time the Communist-led Left Bloc, used land acquisition laws to forcibly acquire 1,000 acres of village land around Singur. This was strongly opposed by many local landowners, political activists, and political opponents of the Communists, especially by the Trinamool Congress Party which used the controversy to win the elections and form the government in the State five years later. In October 2008, Tata announced it was shifting the proposed plant to Sanand. According to various media reports, Narendra Modi, then Chief Minister of Gujarat, sent an SMS to Tata Group chairman Ratan Tata on the day he decided to quit West Bengal, with the simple message: '*Suswagatham*' (welcome).[5] The controversy over Tata's investment in Sanand is a high-profile example of how conflict can spread from the social interests of communities and the commercial interests of firms to the politics of the State.

In focusing on industrial conflict among workers and employers, this book argues that the high level and, occasionally, fierce character of conflict in auto manufacturing can be understood by exploring four inter-linked historical and spatial processes. First, conflict has been generated through the transformation of domestic manufacturing by foreign and domestic OEMs since the 1980s. These firms have increasingly operated through global production networks which have integrated with established regional social structures of accumulations – ensembles of social and political institutions which facilitate economic activity within regions – which rely upon various kinds of informal and precarious work. As part of this process, the imposition of global best-practice 'lean manufacturing' principles and techniques has transformed commercial relations between firms and work organisation and employment relations within firms, laying the foundations for industrial conflict.

Second, this process of global-regional integration has been shaped by two broad phases of state-led economic liberalisation. In the first phase of *restricted openness* from 1982 to 1991, a small number of first-mover foreign OEMs

---

[5] For critical accounts of land acquisition policy in West Bengal, see Le Mons Walker (2008), Sampat (2008) and Bishnu (2009).

and established domestic OEMs were allowed by the national government to transform regional supplier networks and work organisation by implementing lean manufacturing practices. In the second phase of *emergent neo-liberalism* after 1991, the liberalisation of financial markets, trade and investment, including FDI, transformed the segmentation and structure of market competition for vehicle manufacturing. This process led to commercial conflict between foreign and domestic OEMs engaged in joint venture projects and placed significant pressure on market leaders to restructure labour costs.

Third, first-mover OEMs, marshalled by Maruti Suzuki as the country's largest passenger car manufacturer, responded to gradual economic liberalisation in the 1990s by transforming labour standards and employment relations. OEMs and their strategic partners and key independent components suppliers imposed systems of 'contract labour' in key manufacturing regions. This process led to a major shift in employment configurations within these 'high-value' firms. In turn, reliance on contract workers and labour market intermediaries led to high levels of social and industrial conflict in the industry.

As the book explains, contract workers in India are generally employed on short-term contracts and managed by multiple, competing labour contractors. They represent an employment configuration based on precarious work and 'de facto informal work'. The evidence presented in this book casts doubt on claims that OEMs and major auto components manufacturers have followed a 'high road' path of labour standards and employment relations.

The fourth and final factor relates to conflict in the 'low value' end of OEMs' global production networks. Auto assembly manufacturing in OEMs' facilities and in large auto components manufacturing plants relies upon extensive networks of small and medium-sized enterprises which cluster throughout industrial regions. The rise of global production networks in auto-manufacturing has generated new types of commercial conflict between firms of different sizes operating in different 'tiers' of the industry.

This has encouraged the operation of regional casual labour systems which have reproduced conflict between workers and employers in low-end firms. As the book demonstrates, the types of employment configurations and manifestations of labour agency and social conflict, have a radically different character in these small enterprises compared to those documented in the high-value end of the industry.

This book focuses on work, livelihoods and conflict through the lens of inter-disciplinary economic sociology. This lens reflects its search for social-relational explanations for conflict. Analytically, the book's main focus is on commodified social relations linked to work. This includes employment relations between employers, managers and workers, social relations between people who work in different employment configurations, between workers, employers and labour market intermediaries, and between employers, workers, state institutions, residents and landowners in industrial towns and villages.

This sociological approach also draws upon political economy through its analysis of collaboration and distributional conflict between state institutions, private firms, labour market institutions and individual workers and jobseekers. It also draws upon economic geography through its focus on global production networks in auto manufacturing regions. An inter-disciplinary approach seems particularly fitting since the Global Production Network (GPN) tradition in economic and labour geography has economic sociological roots through Global Commodity Chains (GCC) and Global Value Chains (GVC) analysis. The book also draws upon the sociology of work and employment and its links to scholarship in employment/industrial relations.

The book's findings challenge the widely-held view that the emergence of the auto-manufacturing industry leads to 'high road' regional economic and social development 'through economic gains that make wage gains and improvements in social conditions feasible, as well as safeguarding workers' rights and providing adequate standards of social protection' (Pyke and Sengenberger, 1992: 13). Within employment relations literature, a further argument is that auto firms' demand for low-waste 'lean manufacturing' is complemented by workers employed with high employment security, training and skill development (MacDuffie, 1995). Part of this logic is that labour costs comprise a relatively low proportion of total operational costs in auto firms in comparison to firms in less capital-intensive sectors. Production based on sophisticated design, technology and robotics should therefore advance through investment in 'efficiency enhancement and innovation' rather than cutting labour costs.

The important recent study on auto manufacturing in BRIC (Brazil, Russia, India, China) economies by Jürgens and Krzywdzinski follows this logic. Despite their expectations that OEMs 'would exploit the scope for low-cost strategies offered, in some respects, by the BRICs' regulatory and social environments', the authors argue that these countries are potentially undertaking 'a broader process of economic upgrading' (Jürgens and Krzywdzinski, 2016: 317). Although they acknowledge the incidence of fixed-term employment and agency employment – known as temps/casual and contract labour in India, respectively – the investment of OEMs in training and employee development 'can be seen as foundation stones for a future high-road strategy in the BRICs' (Jürgens and Krzywdzinski, 2016: 316).

While it is beyond the remit of this book to discuss their comprehensive findings across all four BRIC countries, their study in India is especially focused on Volkswagen India's (VWI) assembly plant in the Chakan-Special Economiz Zone (C-SEZ) in Maharashtra, which was established in 2009. They argue that VWI built up a 'core workforce' by investing in the training and career development of poor but upwardly-mobile young (mostly male) workers. Since they were only able to enter the site in its early phase, only a tiny proportion of the workforce – just 20 out of about 2000 workers – had made the transition from temporary or traineeship positions to regular workers with open-ended contracts. For example, only these 20 workers were able to join a management-recognised trade union at the time of their research (Jürgens and Krzywdzinski, 2016: 293).

Despite the scope of their work, which also includes information about Japanese OEM Toyota and Indian OEM Mahindra and Mahindra, and their evidence of employer investment in training and employee development, these specific findings do not support generalisations about a 'high road' path in Indian auto-manufacturing as a whole. Jürgens and Krzywdzinski's work does not focus on workers' experiences or perspectives, and makes little mention of the role of labour market intermediaries in employment relations. Importantly, it does not discuss the *regional* character of auto-manufacturing and the implications of this for work. Their focus is on OEMs' operations rather than suppliers' operations, and hardly ever mentions the structure of the industry as a global production network.

In practice, auto manufacturers in India have made innovative and efficiency-enhancing investments *and* incorporated, reproduced and reshaped labour standards and employment relations that exploit relatively flexible, low-cost workforces. In making this point, the arguments in this book come closer to the conceptual arguments made in Zhang's (2015) work on Chinese auto workers.

Based on substantial fieldwork in six Chinese cities, Zhang argues that local auto factories underwent a transition to 'labour force dualism' during the 2000s, which she defines as 'a labour control mechanism' that deploys permanent and temporary workers 'side by side on production lines, having them perform similar or identical tasks but subjecting them to different treatment' (Zhang, 2015: 12).

Following Price (1995) and Silver (2003), Zhang argues that this model is akin to a Japanese-style 'lean and dual' model in which economic security is offered to a core of regular workers with a 'large buffer of periphery workers' who are denied these rights (Zhang, 2015: 40). Zhang's sample of foreign and domestic OEMs suggests that by 2011, the percentage of temps employed as production-line workers ranged from 33–60 per cent.

Very similar findings have been made in the case of India (Hammer, 2010; Bose and Pratap, 2012; Gopalakrishnan and Mirer, 2014; Barnes, Lal Das and Pratap, 2015; Monaco, 2015; Nowack, 2016; Monaco, 2017). However, most of this literature has not focused explanations for the trajectory of work organisation, labour standards and employment relations upon the interaction of global production networks and regional institutions.

This omission is problematic since the character of social relations *within* firms in auto manufacturing industries is strongly shaped by commercial relations *between* firms, as well as relations between firms, state institutions and civic institutions. While these factors have shaped labour relations within OEMs, on which most of the literature mentioned above has focused, they have also shaped labour relations within the networks of components manufacturers where most industry employment is concentrated.

Searching for a social-relational explanation for conflict in Indian auto manufacturing thus ought to *begin* with the transformation of regional industry by global production networks. This, in turn, can help to explain the incidence and character of conflict in its various forms. A GPN and GVC-based framework can help to address the relations between inter-firm conflict in global production networks and intra-firm conflict at different levels of each network.

The following section of this introductory chapter situates the book's research enquiry in the context of the GVC and GPN analytical traditions. It demonstrates where this study of Indian auto manufacturing is framed by these traditions, and where it departs in seeking explanations for conflict. This discussion begins by exploring the dominant focus in the GVC literature on governance types in different industries and its relevance for studies of social, industrial and political conflict.

Automotive manufacturing as a global value chain

The evolution of debates within the large academic literature on global value chains helps us to understand and frame the structure of the auto industry globally, and its emergence in India. A simple definition of a global value chain is the fragmentation and dispersal of a commodity supply chain across more than one country, with coordination by a lead firm. The vast majority of global trade is organised along these lines (UNCTAD, 2013).

However, despite the concern of the Global Value Chain (GVC) literature to unpack complex processes of production and distribution, there has been a surprising lack of focus on work and workers within the literature until quite recently (Starosta, 2010; Barrientos, Gereffi, and Rossi, 2011; Riisgaard and Hammer, 2011; Lakhani et al, 2013; Taylor et al, 2013). As this section attempts to demonstrate, the tradition's preoccupation with the parsimony of ideal types based on commercial and institutional governance between lead firms and suppliers can divert attention from the labour dynamics that enable value chains to function.

Since its emergence in the last quarter of a century, the GVC tradition has undergone several modifications. Originally framed as Global Commodity Chain (GCC) analysis, a core distinction was drawn between buyer-driven and producer-driven commodity chains (Gereffi and Korzeniewicz, 1994). The buyer-driven commodity chain described the role of lead firms exercising commercial power over groups of suppliers in foreign countries via control over retail markets through branding and marketing. As a rule, this type of chain was used to explain the operation of more labour-intensive global commodity chains like textiles, garments, agriculture and food production.

In contrast, the automotive industry is a key example of a producer-driven commodity chain, which is characterised by more capital-intensive, technology-intensive and higher entry-barrier operations in which lead firms exercise more direct control over suppliers in multiple countries. Other examples of this type include the aeronautical industry, ship-building, and some electronics and semi-conductor manufacturing.

At the beginning of the 2000s, the field underwent a notable shift from the language of the 'commodity chain' to that of the 'value chain'. This was described by some critics as a move away from the radical or Marxian roots of the field in World Systems Theory (Bair, 2009) and even as a 'strategic move to increase its appeal for donors from international development and philanthropic agencies' (Neilson, 2014: 42).

In the mid-2000s, Gereffi, Humphrey and Sturgeon (2005) offered a modification of this new GVC framework, by positing a more sophisticated, five-way typology in place of the old two-type buyer vs. producer driven model. These types primarily distinguish different forms of value chain governance. The key concept of governance in GVC analysis refers broadly to the way in which the production and distribution of a specific commodity – either a good or service – is organised and managed from initial conception to final consumption.

Gereffi, Humphrey and Sturgeon (2005) distinguished five governance types: market, modular, relational, captive and hierarchy. 'Markets' and 'hierarchies' were presented at either end of this spectrum as two comparatively pure forms of global value chain governance. Market-based governance represented the dispersal of production and distribution activities across multiple global suppliers, with lead firms relying on market transactions between these firms to guarantee production and arrival of the finished commodity. At the other end of the spectrum, hierarchy-based governance represented internalisation of production and distribution activities 'in house' by the lead firm.

In this typology, modular, relational and captive governance were presented as intermediate types that operate between these two pure forms of global value chain governance. Gereffi, Humphrey and Sturgeon (2005) suggested that some industries could undergo a transformation between governance types based upon changes to global market conditions, technology or market competition. They also argued that industries could move in different directions, switching between governance types or potentially exhibiting features of more than one type as market relations and technology developed.

'Fitting' the global auto industry into any one of these governance types has proved to be challenging. In part, this difficulty reflects the complexity of the automotive design, production and distribution process. Although the auto industry is often defined by the assembly of passenger cars, the industry as a whole encompasses a very wide range of activities. Other than cars, the industry includes materials, components and assembly manufacturing for two-wheeled vehicles (motorcycles and scooters), three-wheeled vehicles, trucks, buses, tractors and other commercial vehicles and equipment, as well as vehicles and equipment used in agriculture, construction and mining.

For each type of vehicle, there is a wide range of manufacturing processes, including the extraction and processing of raw materials like oil and steel, forging and casting of metal alloy, moulding and bonding of rubber, plastics and fabric production. These materials feed into the manufacturing of multiple parts and components used to assemble engines, transmissions, fuel and exhaust systems, vehicle chassis, brakes, ventilation systems, electronic systems, vehicle interiors, tyres and accessories.

Manufacturing design is linked to distinctive processes of product differentiation, branding and marketing that characterise vehicle consumption in different national markets. Production and consumption is also linked to financial derivatives and consumer finance markets. It relies upon public investment in roads, railways, ports, electricity and the supply of other essential utilities. Along with infrastructure provision, state institutions are usually required to provide sufficient vacant land to enable manufacturing on a scale that matches the sales and profit demands of large transnational OEMs.

In short, the emergence and presence of automotive manufacturing in a region has an expansive and socio-economically transformative character that few industries can match. The sophistication of vehicle manufacturing also represents a major logistical challenge for global OEMs which oversee global value chains connecting supplier-manufacturers located in various regions and countries. The functional role of firms within the automotive value chain is based upon their technical role; e.g., the type of product, component or material they process, and their relationship to other firms in the industry.

Inter-firm relations between OEMs and suppliers are usually 'tiered'. For example, Tier-1 firms primarily sell parts or components directly to OEMs. Tier-2 firms sell primarily to Tier-1 firms, Tier-3 sell primarily to Tier-2 firms, and so on. Tier-1 firms are often large transnational corporations in their own right. In several cases, OEMs have outsourced core manufacturing functions to recently-established Tier-1 firms who operate with them in global partnerships to pursue common strategic objectives.

Well-known examples include Delphi's relationship with General Motors (GM), Visteon's relationship with Ford or Denso's global partnership with Toyota. In some cases, these Tier-1 firms are part of the same parent company. This process of OEM spin-offs has become more significant in the global auto industry since the 1990s (Sturgeon et al, 2008).

While the place and function of firms in the automotive value chain is primarily defined by inter-firm relations, it is also expressed in the different sizes of the firms based on their market capitalisation, sales and production volumes, or employment levels. For instance, Tier-2 firms tend to range from large and sometimes transnational manufacturers that employ hundreds of workers, down to more localised, medium-sized enterprises that employ dozens of workers.

Tier-3 and Tier-4 firms usually range from medium-sized enterprises to micro-enterprises which employ a small number of waged workers, or rely upon the unpaid work of family members to operate. In India, some of these enterprises lie within the informal economy – known locally as the 'unorganised sector'. Many of these firms are unable to satisfy the demands of global value chain production or do not seek to enter them. Some Tier-3 and Tier-4 firms are represented by own-account operators who perform temporary, occasional or ad hoc services – known in India as 'job work' – for higher-tier enterprises.

The complexity and diversity of activities in auto manufacturing have led scholars in the GVC tradition to apply different governance types to auto-based global value chains. In using Gereffi, Humphrey and Sturgeon's (2005) five-way governance typology, some have framed the industry as a 'captive' value chain in which key suppliers are highly dependent upon OEMs for the coordination of their activities. In this view, governance operates as a 'quasi hierarchy' in which OEMs have the power to include or exclude suppliers (Pavlinek and Zenka, 2010).

For others, governance in auto value chains is primarily 'relational' in nature, characterised by close collaboration and interdependence between OEMs and Tier-1 suppliers rather than hierarchical domination of the latter by the former (Lakhani et al, 2013). This is a significant question for auto manufacturing because relational value chains are expected to correspond to a high level of employment quality and economic security for workers (Nathan, 2016). Others have argued that the industry 'oscillates' between relational and market-based governance (Sturgeon et al, 2008). In this argument, Japanese OEMs have played the key role in shifting from captive to relational governance.

Although *any* typological approach represents a snapshot of real commercial and social relations in time and space, the fact that leading scholars can attribute three out of the five widely-used GVC governance types to auto manufacturing raises questions about the explanatory power of this approach. There are at least four empirical problems in trying to 'fit' the auto industry into a single governance type.

First, some OEMs are also suppliers to other OEMs. In India, for example, there are some locally-owned OEMs in this category, such as Force Motors Limited, which assembles vans and agricultural vehicles, but also manufactures engines and axles for Mercedes and engines for BMW (see Chapter 2).

Second, many firms operate *inside and outside* global value chains. Many major auto manufacturers in India are locally-owned and oriented towards domestic markets. Some are focused on retail consumer and spare parts production known as the 'aftermarket', as well as upstream value chain production. The value chains in which some of these companies operate are predominantly or sometimes entirely located within India, i.e. within *regional* or *national* rather than *global* value chains. This issue is important for firms which attempt to enter or exit global value chain relations. This book explores this problem in detail for Tier-3 firms in the National Capital Region (NCR) (see Chapter 6).

Third, many firms that operate in the automotive value chain are *multi-industry* in character. To take one example, Bosch India, a wholly-owned subsidiary of German conglomerate Robert Bosch GmbH, manufactures components for various automotive OEMs in India, and manufactures components used in the construction industry, consumer electronics and engineering and design services. There are also several Indian firms which have a multi-industry role. One example is Premier Limited, an OEM which makes a relatively small number of final-assembled vehicles, but also makes machine tools and a range of components used by Indian Railways and wind mill manufacturers.

Fourth, it is common for auto suppliers to sell products to multiple OEMs and, conversely, for OEMs to switch between suppliers on a regular basis. This complexity gives the industry a *networked* character in which commercial relations between firms are neither linear nor fixed. While this reality is acknowledged in the GVC literature (Gereffi, Humphrey and Sturgeon, 2005; Sturgeon et al, 2008), the networked character of auto global value chains presents a challenge for any typological approach.

Whichever governance type we may choose, a related and over-arching problem is the ongoing assumption that the governance structure of auto manufacturing value chains, based on consumer and OEM demand for high quality products, strict design specifications, efficient technology and workforce skills, should lead to a 'high road' development path for workers (Lakhani et al, 2013). While there is some truth to this contention when applied in a Western historical context (Babson, 1986; Sugrue, 2010), this book demonstrates that this has not been the case in India.

In short, there are numerous exceptions to the rule that challenge a governance-based analytical framework. In contrast, some scholars have posed the GPN framework as a more refined, if complementary, theoretical approach to the categorisation of global value chain activities. If GVC analysis is about understanding the global reach and power of lead firms that exercise control over production and distribution across multiple countries, advocates of GPN analysis claim to draw more explicit links between global value chains and broader questions of regional economic development (Coe et al, 2004).

More recently, Coe and Yeung (2015) have attempted to move towards an updated version of GPN analysis – 'GPN 2.0' as they call it – to more explicitly theorise the dynamics of global production networks and regional development. They make the significant claim that GPN 2.0 can potentially explain 'uneven developmental outcomes' on a global level. They also suggest that the GPN 2.0 can better incorporate questions of labour control and labour agency through an emphasis on 'non-firm actors'.

Automotive manufacturing and global production networks

Coe and Yeung define a global production network as 'an organisational arrangement, comprising interconnected economic and non-economic actors, coordinated by a global lead firm and producing goods or services across multiple geographical locations for worldwide markets' (Coe and Yeung, 2015: 1–2). They argue that a global production network is best defined by a *single* lead firm. This is different from the implication in much of GVC analysis that a global production network or a global value chain is synonymous with an *industry*.

In this section, it is argued that 'GPN 2.0' offers a more streamlined way of exploring regional development and industrial conflict in Indian auto manufacturing than much of the governance-oriented GVC literature. This reflects its clearer focus on regions, on inter-industry as well as intra-industry firm-level dynamics and, above all, because of its incorporation of 'extra-firm actors'. At the same time, it will be argued that GPN 2.0 needs to be combined with a 'labour-centred' approach to regional development (Selwyn, 2016) in order to address the problem of conflict in the Indian auto industry.

Many of the problems mentioned above, encountered when generalising a single governance approach across a whole industry, can be addressed with this streamlined definition. GPN 2.0 emphasises the externalisation of activities to a single lead firm's strategic partners, single-industry or multi-industry specialised independent suppliers, generic product suppliers or key customers. This approach can incorporate OEMs who also act as suppliers in different global production networks, suppliers that play roles in multiple auto global production networks or auto firms that also engage in non-automotive business.

Like GVC analysis, the key actor in GPN 2.0 is the firm: 'Business firms are the basic building blocks of a global production network' (Coe and Yeung, 2015: 39).

While they start with, and to a significant extent focus upon, the drivers of firms' participation in global production networks, Coe and Yeung also stress the role of 'extra-firm actors'. These include state institutions, international organisations, trade unions, consumers and civil society organisations.

They define 'intermediaries' as a third group of actors which connect the activities of firm and extra-firm actors. These include financial intermediaries like banks, logistics firms, organisations which codify, standardise and enforce knowledge used at an industry or occupational level, and, finally, a range of other intermediaries such as management consultants, legal service providers, recruitment agencies and labour market intermediaries. As this book will explain, labour market intermediaries have grown to play a core, even indispensable, and often controversial role in the regulation of employment relations in the Indian auto industry.

Coe and Yeung offer four types of firm-level strategy within global production networks in place of the five governance types pioneered by Gereffi, Humphrey and Sturgeon (2005). These are: inter-firm coordination, inter-firm control, inter-firm partnerships, and extra-firm bargaining.

Inter-firm coordination occurs when a firm operating within a GPN undertakes horizontal integration of production or distribution activities by internalising them (Coe and Yeung, 2015: 134–35; Yeung and Coe: 2015: 44).

Inter-firm control occurs when a lead firm externalises activities to suppliers, but continues to exercise significant control over how these suppliers perform these activities.

Inter-firm partnerships occur when relations between firms are based on mutual cooperation. Finally, the idea of extra-firm bargaining suggests that the cooperative role of non-firm actors in the operation of GPNs cannot be taken for granted (Yeung and Coe, 2015: 50).

The authors suggest that the auto manufacturers will tend to pursue *either* an inter-firm control or inter-firm partnership approach, although all four strategies seem to be relevant at some level. They also suggest that the national origins of firms will influence the path that owners and managers choose. For example, American automotive OEMs are arguably more likely to pursue inter-firm control due to the need to carefully manage the activities of suppliers. This model is similar to the captive governance type described by Gereffi, Humphrey and Sturgeon (2005). In contrast, Japanese and South Korean OEMs will be more likely to pursue inter-firm partnerships by, for example, investing directly in the businesses of their partners and suppliers (see Chapter 2). Coe and Yeung suggest this strategy is somewhat similar to the relational and modular governance types described by Gereffi, Humphrey and Sturgeon (2005).

'GPN 2.0' offers three main advantages for the analysis offered in this book. First, its focus on the region – which Coe and Yeung frame as a 'sub-national territorial unit' – is critical for the analysis of Indian auto manufacturing due to its regionally uneven character. While production takes place in many different parts of the country, three core manufacturing regions have emerged to dominate the local industry: the National Capital Region (NCR) surrounding New Delhi, the Chennai Metropolitan Area (CMA) and the Chakan Special Economic Zone (C-SEZ) and neighbouring Pune District in the State of Maharashtra. The second advantage of GPN 2.0 for this book is its greater flexibility to explore inter-industry, as well as intra-industry dynamics. Third, its re-orientation towards multiple actors in global production networks fits well with this book's focus on workers and labour agency.

At the same time, there are two problems in applying GPN 2.0 which justify modification to strengthen the book's enquiry into social-relational explanations for conflict. First, in contrast to GPN 2.0's firm-centric approach, this book takes a 'labour-centred' approach to regional development. Second, the book frames regional development as a process constituted by forms of conflict and different distributional outcomes rather than as a general rise in material conditions.

To take the first question, the firm remains the analytical focus for GPN 2.0. All other social groups or institutions are framed from the perspective of the firms' interests, despite the important recognition of non-firm actors (Coe and Yeung, 2015: 151). While they have a strong theoretical claim for doing this, since the definition of a global production network is firm-dependent, Coe and Yeung do not delve far into the epistemological reasons for this focus: for example, why GPN analysis should not be framed from the perspective of state institutions or civil society organisations.

On the other hand, they have recognised that labour studies have been historically downplayed in GVC and GPN analysis. Some critics have been particularly scathing about this absence. Carswell and de Neve (2013: 62) even suggest that articles on governance or labour standards 'typically end with a paragraph on labour, usually concluding that labour employed at the tail end of the network needs further empirical research'. Radical critics argue that labour's historical absence in GVC studies can be explained by the tradition's origins in World System Analysis (Hopkins and Wallerstein, 1982), which framed capitalism as an economic system defined primarily by 'production for profit for world markets', rather than a system defined by capital-labour relations in sites of production (Newman, 2012; Selwyn, 2012: 210).

Despite this emphasis, the GVC lineage *has* incorporated intra-firm relations, including employment relations and conflicts over labour standards, to the extent that they are shaped and influenced by commercial inter-firm relations (Bair,

2009; Barrientos, Gereffi, and Rossi, 2011). The question remains, *how effectively* the GVC or GPN frameworks have made this incorporation. When workers have been discussed, they have often been treated as an 'object' rather than a 'subject' that shapes development by acting upon its own set of interests: 'little has been said about labour as an active constituent of the global economy, rather than the passive victim of restructuring processes' (Cumbers et al, 2008: 369).

For some critics, processes and outcomes of regional economic development are 'co-constituted' by workers and firms through relational conflict in sites of production (Selwyn, 2012). The question then becomes *how* and *in what form* workers are able to exercise agency over these processes. 'Labour agency' takes multiple forms, including individual and collective acts of 'reworking' and 'resilience' (Cumbers et al, 2008; Coe and Jordhus-Lier, 2011) and 'everyday' forms of resistance (Carswell and de Neve, 2013), including types of individual and social acts to which firms must adapt (de Haan, 1999). At the same time, labour agency is expressed in constrained socio-economic contexts. As Coe and Jordhus-Lier (2011) argue, workers' agency at a regional level is embedded in, and therefore constrained by, the structures of global production networks, state power and regulation, community politics and labour market intermediation.

While Selwyn (2012) also argues that workers' agency interacts with firms and state institutions to shape development, his *analytical entry point* is not the firm but, rather, the multiple social interests of people whose work is linked to global production networks. This means approaching commercial and social relations within global production networks from the vantage point of various 'classes of labour' which depend, in different ways, upon the exchange of labour power for money to survive (Bernstein, 2010). The research question then becomes how workers can derive associational power to leverage concessions from employers or state institutions from the structural power that corresponds to their location in different regions and different levels of global production networks (Wright, 2000; Silver, 2003; Selwyn, 2012), or from different 'tiers' as they are known in auto manufacturing.

In addition to the study of workers', firms', and state institutions' respective roles in automotive global production networks, this book also draws on the study of caste and gender as social structures and social relations. These factors are critical for explaining the regional operation of global production networks in India but cannot be reduced to work-based social interests. For example, caste plays a central role in regulating market activity and employment in India, but transcends workplace and social class divisions (Harriss-White, 2003; Basile, 2013). Its complexity also flows from its dual character as a formal feature of Indian society. For example, caste is formally recognised in the Indian constitution as well as an informal, ideational structure that shapes occupational and workplace divisions of labour, social relations in sites of production, and behavioural norms and expectations.

Gender too plays an important role in this analysis. While employment in the core occupations of auto manufacturing is predominantly male – in India as well as globally – women's work plays an increasingly important role in the industry. These jobs and occupations range from a minority of women employed in production-line manufacturing roles in OEMs and Tier-1 firms, to Tier-1 and Tier-2 factories in which women play a major shop-floor role, down to Tier-3 and Tier-4 factories and workshops where women perform a variety of functions. Apart from production-line jobs, roles in large manufacturing firms vary between ancillary jobs as office 'staff', cleaners and canteen workers. In small firms at the 'low value' end of the industry, women's roles vary between semi-skilled machine operators and ancillary roles such as sorters and 'helpers'.

The gendering of work in Indian auto manufacturing is, like other industries, strongly linked to regions. To take the example of garments manufacturing, Mezzadri has shown how the character of women's work is strongly shaped by regions, with southern States more likely to rely on women as factory or shop-floor workers and northern States more likely to incorporate women in 'value addition' through informal enterprises and home-based work (Mezzadri, 2016a; 2016b). Such regional impacts are broadly true for auto manufacturing, albeit with less reliance on a direct production-line role for women.

Following the above-mentioned scholars, this book adopts the concept of a *regional social structure of accumulation* to help frame the role of caste and gender in workplace and occupational divisions of labour, labour standards and employment relations. This concept comes from the work of radical political economists in the 1980s who linked it to 'long-wave' theories of economic crisis to explain the unravelling of the long post-war economic boom in the United States (Gordon, Weisskopf and Bowles, 1987; Kotz, 1987).

Their idea was that long periods of economic expansion and prosperity rely upon the interaction of social and political institutions unifying to form a 'social structure of accumulation'. These institutions are very broad in scope and range, for example, from the structure of the nuclear family to the regulation of labour and consumer markets. An advantage of this approach is its attempt to internalise various political, social, and cultural institutions in explaining the process of capital accumulation (Jessop, 1990).

In the context of Indian auto manufacturing, this concept helps to explain how the rise of global production networks in key manufacturing regions has adapted to established forms of social organisation which are largely based upon gendered and caste-based work roles in informal enterprises. As Mezzadri has put it, 'the informal economy and its regulatory mechanisms are increasingly incorporated into neo-liberal global production structures' (Mezzadri, 2008: 605).

The second problem with analysing work and employment within a GPN 2.0 framework relates to the definition of economic development as 'a process that results in the improvement of economic conditions within a particular territorial unit' (Coe and Yeung, 2015: 167). Selwyn (2016a: 1771) suggests that this understanding frames labour conflict as an impediment to development, with development understood as an 'outcome', rather than co-constitutive to development as a 'process'.

This criticism pre-supposes alternative theorisations of regional and national economic development which arguably make a more explicit claim of incorporating social and political conflict. For studies of development in India, examples include Saraswati's (2012) analysis of the Information Technology (IT) industry, which draws upon a class-based 'linkage-agency' approach (Fine, 1992; Fine and Rustomjee, 1996), and D'Costa's framing of India as a type of 'compressed capitalism' (D'Costa, 2014).

The modernisation of Indian auto manufacturing since the 1980s seems to fit with D'Costa's concept, since it has combined pre-existing regional social structures of accumulation – what he calls 'primitive accumulation' following Harvey (2003) – with 'advanced forms of accumulation such as innovation-led economic expansion in a global setting' (D'Costa, 2014: 319). This argument draws upon the classical Marxian theory of uneven and combined development (D'Costa, 2003; Trotsky, 1922; 1934; 1962), which is a novelty for India where most Marxist scholarship has framed economic development as national rather than global in origin (Bardhan, 1998; Bhaduri, 1983; Patnaik, 1990).[6]

The problem foreshadowed in Selwyn's criticism is that, despite GPN 2.0's analysis of competing, regional value-capture strategies among firms and extra-firm actors, the perspective lacks focus on the political economy question: value capture *for whom*? If development is understood as a conflict-based process, then an 'improvement of economic conditions' becomes a potential outcome for *some* people who live and work within a given region. This conflict can take a commercial form between firms, a political form between state institutions and non-state actors, an industrial or labour-process form between managers and workers, or other social forms involving labour market intermediaries, local

---

[6] Despite the revival of this theory among mostly UK-based scholars in the last decade (Dunn and Radice, 2006; Rosenberg, 2006; 2009; Callinicos and Rosenberg, 2008; Anievas and Nisancioglu, 2015), its focus has largely been on long-term historical processes of development rather than recent or contemporary ones. Although this book briefly explores the postcolonial history of industry policy in India in order to explain policy settings for auto manufacturing (see Chapter 3), a study of the longer-term historical antecedents of Indian capitalism in colonial oppression, agrarian production, state development and social class transformation is beyond its analytical remit.

landowners and civic institutions. In this book, development is framed by these different forms of conflict which take place between actors over the generation, capture, enhancement, retention or loss of value, as they interact within regions.

The role of precarious and informal work in auto manufacturing

This book offers four inter-linked areas of explanation for high levels of conflict in Indian auto manufacturing, as outlined above. These relate to the intersection of GPNs with regional social structures of accumulation based on precarious and informal work, together with phases of state-guided economic liberalisation and the transformation of employment relations in OEMs, Tier-1, and Tier-2 firms since the 1990s. These processes, the book will show, contradict claims about a 'high road' path of labour standard and employment relations.

This section foreshadows how these processes have led to the emergence of two regional 'labour control regimes' in the upper and lower tiers of the auto industry. Each regime relies upon different 'employment configurations' which reflect workers' different pathways through labour markets and different forms of social regulation. Each regime also reproduces specific types of precarious and informal work which shape the interests and agency of workers and different modes of conflict.

A useful starting point for this discussion of precarious and informal work is the apparently anomalous character of economic development in India. Despite the country's transition to high economic growth, India's development path is anomalous when compared with previous transitions in East Asia, Europe and North America. Put simply, India has not developed a comparably large manufacturing sector and has, instead, continued to be marked by a services-intensive economy.

While the proportion of people employed in agriculture has been falling for decades – by 2012, the proportion of people employed in the primary sector had dropped to 48.9 per cent (Government of India, 2013) – this has not led to a major rise in the manufacturing share of national income, which remained at about 16 per cent of national output from 1980 to 2002, where it roughly remains today. Over the same period, services increased from 37 to 49 per cent of national income (Singh, 2008: 235).

Consequently, many scholars argue that there has not been a transition to an 'industrial society' in India. Some characterise India as an economy based on small-scale or 'petty commodity production', concentrated in small towns and villages where people have struggled to sustain paid work as agriculture-based livelihoods have gradually declined (Basile, 2013). For Breman, India has developed as a 'post-agrarian' rather than an 'industrial' variety of capitalism:

[The] history of industrialisation suggests an evolution that finds its climax when the great majority of the working population has become factorised. This is the classic path of economic development which structured western society. However, the capitalist route followed in India during the second half of the twentieth century has clearly not been in accordance with this dominant model. The importance of agriculture has certainly decreased, but the labour expelled from it has not been absorbed by urban factories (Breman, 1999: 428).

This path of national development is reflected in the predominance of work via small-scale, petty commodity production across most Indian regions. Most people earn a living by working in small enterprises based in agriculture, trade, construction as well as small-scale manufacturing. Most of this work is concentrated in the 'unorganised sector', which officially includes all non-agricultural enterprises with fewer than 10 workers.[7] In India, this concept has often been used interchangeably with 'informal sector' or 'informal economy'.

By the early 2000s, over 93 per cent of work was measured by the International Labour Organisation (ILO) as informal in nature (ILO, 2002). Most of this occurred in the unorganised sector, but a growing proportion also occurred in firms in the organised sector. While informal work plays a similarly dominant role in work across regions of Asia, Africa, and Latin America (Portes and Hoffman, 2003; Carré and Heintz, 2010; Park and Cai, 2011), few countries can match the scale of informal work in India in absolute or proportional terms.

The concept of informal work intersects strongly with the concept of precarious or insecure work (Arnold and Bongiovi, 2013), although there has been considerable debate about the relative usefulness of the two concepts in high-income or low-income countries, or even whether scholars should abandon the former in favour of the latter (Standing, 2008: 364; Kalleberg and Hewison, 2013; Standing, 2016: 197). The accumulation of vast literatures on informal work over the last four decades has made the task of unifying and operationalising a working concept of informal work extremely challenging (Adam and Harris-White, 2007: 15; Williams and Lansky, 2013: 355).[8]

---

[7] Or fewer than 20 workers for firms without power.

[8] The concept of informality – and its various presentations as a 'sector', 'enterprise', 'economy', 'activity' or type of 'employment', 'work' or 'worker'– have historical antecedents in modernisation theory and its critics (Lewis, 1955; Geertz, 1963; Hart, 1973; ILO, 1972). Since the 1970s, a vast literature has splintered into competing definitions and positions, including neo-liberal rational choice theorists (De Soto, 1989; Maloney, 2004; Perry et al, 2007) and structuralist and radical critics (Castells and Portes, 1989). For overviews of the concept, see Chen (2006), Hill (2010), Maiti and Sen (2010), Williams and Lansky (2013) and Barnes (2015).

Despite these conceptual challenges, it is critical to recognise how the transformation and modernisation of auto manufacturing since the 1980s has intersected with regional social structures of accumulation in which most work is informal or precarious in nature. The majority of workers in key auto manufacturing regions are young men from inter-state villages, towns and cities who migrate on a semi-permanent or seasonal basis through formal and informal networks of labour market intermediation. Along with social and kinship ties to their places of origin, the agency of these workers is also shaped by the precarious, and often temporary, character of employment in auto firms. Relations between employers, landowners, 'local' workers and 'migrant' workers are also shaped by caste and regionalism. These factors form a critical part of the explanation for the incidence and the character of conflict in the industry.

However, the manifestations of informal and precarious work, and forms of social conflict and labour agency differ radically depending upon the tier of the industry. The modernisation of Indian auto manufacturing has reproduced at least two types of local or regional 'labour control regime' which correspond to these different tiers. Each of these regimes is predicated upon the employment of people in multiple 'employment configurations' based upon different forms of labour market intermediation, different modes of social and political regulation, and different degrees of (in)formality and (in)security.

In OEMs, Tier-1 firms and Tier-2 firms, this book will show that labour control is based on a 'contract labour' system in which employment of the largest group of production-line and shop-floor workers is regulated by multiple, often competing labour contractors. This argument is similar to Zhang's (2015) use of 'labour force dualism' in the Chinese context, although its extent in India is much greater. This regime is explained in detail in Chapters 4 and 5. While this argument draws particularly upon the author's fieldwork in the NCR, it can also be applied to other regions of auto manufacturing.

The second regional labour control regime occurs in Tier-3 and Tier-4 firms, many of which operate at the low 'value capture' end of global production networks. In this regime, the behaviour of the employer is shaped by twin forces: on the one hand, the cost pressures of operating within global production networks and, on the other hand, the circular migration of workers. Employers have adapted to these pressures by continuously churning – that is, shedding and hiring – groups of workers who move through and between manufacturing zones and 'colonies'. This has generated a radically different basis for employment relations and labour agency in these firms compared to larger, upstream client firms. This regime of labour control is outlined in detail in Chapter 6.

The concept of a regional or local labour control regime is adapted from Jonas (1996), who defined it as 'a historically contingent and territorially embedded set of mechanisms which co-ordinate the time-space reciprocities between production, work, consumption and labour reproduction within a local labour market' (Jonas, 1996: 325). This concept has important precursors in the work of Burawoy (1985; 1992). More recently, the concept has been adapted by, among others, Anner (2015) in the case of international garments production, and Pattenden (2016) in the case of rural-based labourers in the South Indian State of Karnataka.

As useful as this concept is, the forms of conflict and labour agency that shape regional development are not solely determined by the type of labour control regime. Within each regime are numerous constitutive types of work and employment. In this book, the concept of an *employment configuration* is used to describe types of work which have a specific relationship to labour markets and a specific mode of social regulation. This concept comes from Swider's (2015) analysis of Chinese construction workers.

Modifying Burawoy (1985) and Lee (2007), Swider defines an 'employment configuration' as a 'specific pathway into employment linked with a specific mechanism that regulates the employment relationship' (Swider, 2015: 8). While somewhat similar to Banaji's (2010) concept of a 'form of exploitation', which denotes a specific type of value extraction from work, the concept of 'employment configuration' has the advantage of making a more explicit link between the mode of social regulation used to extract value and the labour market through which individuals access work. For Swider, a pathway into employment is the process through which people find work. This involves forms of labour market regulation which are much broader than the regulation of employment relations. Furthermore, the mechanisms that regulate the employment relationship can be formal or informal in character.

In this book, 'informal' refers to work which is not recognised or regulated by state institutions or state-based regulatory mechanisms, or where these mechanisms are relaxed or systematically evaded by non-state actors. The strength of an approach based on 'employment configurations' is its recognition that all work is regulated *socially* even if it is not always regulated *formally* by state institutions.

The type of work that is excluded from formal regulation varies significantly by industry and by country. For example, India retains a formal distinction between agricultural activities, which are subject to fewer formal, work-based rules and lower tax collection, and non-agricultural activities. India also retains an enterprise-based distinction between the 'organised' and 'unorganised sectors'. Unlike high-income countries in which an 'activity-based' definition of informality is more common due to incentives to hide value-generating or value-shifting activities from states, a 'job-centred' definition of informality is more appropriate for India as a low-income country in which informal work is pervasive and typical (Williams and Lansky, 2013).

As a locus of 'job-centred' informality, most people who undertake informal work in India do so because of their circumstances rather than their informed choice. For informal work in which there is an employment relationship, employers can take advantage of the lack of formal recognition or, in other cases, systematically evade state-based regulations to lower enterprise costs, or enhance their control over value extraction in the labour process.

These practices are widespread in India and the failure of state institutions to recognise or protect workers is widely documented (Bardhan, 1998; Harris-White and Gooptu, 2000; Hensman, 2000; Harriss-White, 2003; Shyam Sundar, 2012a; Agarwala, 2013). While workers in firms in the unorganised sector undertake informal work by official definition, it is common for employers to rely on informal work in organised sector firms. Widespread methods include hiding, disguising or distorting firm accounts, employment musters or payroll data in order to avoid tax obligations, or protective social and labour legislation.

Formal or written employment contracts are a rarity in the informal economy. In addition, workers are commonly misreported as 'trainees', 'apprentices' or 'interns' to fraudulently lower costs even if these labels misrepresent the work undertaken, or mis-allocate workers to jobs that do not match their occupational experience or skills (Shyam Sundar, 2005; Hill, 2010). In many of these cases, workers themselves are undeclared and unregistered, as is the economic value generated through their work. Whether such cases occur through an employer's conscious strategy or simply through firm or industry-level custom and practice, they rarely involve employees' consent or even their knowledge.

A common method used to cut costs in firms in the organised sector is to hide the employment of workers from the Ministry of Labour and Employment in order to avoid payment of medical insurance and private pension contributions. In India, the main form of medical insurance is represented by the *Employees' State Insurance Corporation Act 1948* (ESI), which applies to all workers in firms in the organised sector who earn ₹21,000 (about US$325) or less per month.[9] Under ESI, employers must contribute 4.75 per cent of payroll costs and the employee must contribute 1.75 per cent of their wage to this scheme to fund workers who fall ill, develop long-term sickness or who are injured at work. The scheme also funds public hospitals.

Pensions are organised under the *Employees Provident Funds Act 1952* (PF), which is applicable to all companies with 20 or more workers. Workers are entitled to draw on a private pension from the official retirement age of 58. Other widespread methods of cutting costs in organised sector firms include ignoring statutory minimum wages or restrictions on paid working hours under the *Factories Act 1948*.

---

[9] All Rupee conversions to US dollars in this book use current exchange rates.

While what is now understood as informal work has always been widespread in India, it has expanded as a proportion of total employment in India since the 1970s. The reasons for this expansion are complex, but, in short, relate to changes in the agrarian economy, the character of the Indian state and regulatory framework, conflict between workers and employers and, more recently, the integration of Indian regions with the global economy (Barnes, 2015).

The agrarian economy is unable to provide sufficient income or livelihood for India's predominantly rural population, influencing waves of inter-state, regional migration between villages, towns and cities (Radhakrishna, 2009; Bernstein, 2010). This multi-caste workforce has fundamentally shaped firm preferences to employ poor women and men from rural areas in informal work (Breman, 1996; De Haan, 1999). High levels of industrial conflict, particularly in the 1970s and 80s, also strongly influenced the tendency of employers to rely on informal work (Van Wersch, 1992; Subramanian, 1997; Datt, 2003; Breman, 2004). India's national regulatory framework is also important in the context of the failure of a state-centric model of Import Substitution Industrialisation (ISI) from the 1950s to the 1990s, and the shift towards a neo-liberal framework for economic policy-making from 1991 onwards.[10]

Like other countries, some types of work and employment in India are more likely to be informal than others. These include self-employed, own-account workers as well as wage workers. A category which can blur the distinction between self-employment and wage work is the industrial out-worker or home-worker who works contractually under vendors or buyers from larger enterprises. These workers are especially likely to be women and far less likely to be recognised, formally or socially, as 'workers'. The same problem of recognition is true for women, and some men, employed as domestic workers in households.

Among wage workers, casual or temporary employment and day labouring is common in some sectors. Among these workers, the use of labour contractors – called by different names depending on the region – is common for casual labour placement, recruitment and workforce management (Breman, 1994; Roy, 2008; Picherit, 2012). Labour contractors themselves can operate on a formal or informal basis. Many workers employed on this basis can be characterised as 'bonded' workers if they are tied to an employer through physical coercion, late or irregular wage payments, debt caused by wage advances, or a combination of these practices (Barrientos et al, 2013).

Contract labour takes a specific form in the Indian auto industry. The operation of the regional contract labour system as a means of labour control is almost entirely

---

[10] This transition has been the subject of radically divergent interpretations, e.g., Das (2001), Chibber (2003), McCartney (2009).

concentrated within auto manufacturing firms in the organised sector. As will be outlined in Chapters 4 and 5, there is a long-standing formal system of labour regulation which is meant to control the employment of contract workers and protect them from employer abuse or exploitation. Most of these workers thus appear, at face value, to be formal workers – in theory, their work and employment arrangements are formally recognised, regulated and protected by the state.

In reality, the state does not protect contract workers from unscrupulous employer practices and does not even recognise that these workers are being employed in ongoing production-line roles. To categorise this group of workers who dominate operations in OEMs, Tier-1, and Tier-2 manufacturing firms, this book develops the concept of *de facto informal work*. Modifying Chang's (2009) idea of the 'in fact informal worker', this concept describes individuals whose work is formally-recognised, regulated and protected under the law but who, in practice, have little or no social agency to access institutions that can redress legal violations or provide compensation.

Chang applies this concept at a general level to include many international migrant workers who lack the knowledge, social networks, socio-cultural capital or the incentives to redress legal violations due to their status as non-citizens. He also includes many workers who are employed in export-processing zones or who find work via labour market intermediaries. In this book, 'de facto informal work' is contextualised in the contrast between the formal system of contract labour regulation and industry-wide practices. As will be shown, contract workers are commonly employed in ongoing production-line jobs on much lower wages than regular workers, with few enterprise-level benefits and no formal collective voice. In India's largest auto-producing regions, contract workers are practically – and sometimes violently – prevented from forming or joining trade unions.

Informal work (including 'de facto informal work') overlaps with the concept of precarious work. If the defining question for informal work is a lack of formal and social *recognition* by state institutions, then the corresponding question for precarious work is the lack of adequate formal or social *protection* to mitigate the imposition or transfer of market-based risks onto workers (Kalleberg and Hewison, 2013).

In practice, there is a strong relationship these two characteristics of work. For India, and many other low to middle-income countries, it is reasonable to conclude that the prevalence of informal work overlaps significantly with the absence or denial of social and economic security. However, it is clearer to define the concepts separately, since not all people who undertake informal work can be described as precarious or insecure and, in turn, not all people employed in formal jobs can be described as secure. As this book demonstrates, even a 'regular job' in auto manufacturing, with relatively high wages and relatively generous enterprise benefits, is no guarantee of *ongoing* socio-economic security.

Precarious work has been framed by the absence, denial or withdrawal of various forms of social and economic security which emerged in Western countries in the twentieth century (Vosko, 2010; Standing 2011). For Standing, 'industrial citizenship' in these countries was based on forms of 'labour-related security'. Despite legitimate criticisms that this framework downplays the historical normality of precarious work in colonial and ex-colonial regions (Scully, 2016), it can be applied to India due to the foundation of its economic planning and industrial relations framework in modernisation theory.

The assumption of many policymakers in colonial and postcolonial governments was that India could eventually transform into a 'modern' industrial society if the right economic policies were pursued. This assumption underpinned the drafting of an industrial relations system to regulate wages and employment in the organised sector, stemming from the first iteration of the *Factories Act* in 1911 and, later, the 1931 Royal Commission of Labour (Holmström, 1984: 53).

These principles were refined after independence and have largely remained unchanged since, despite some efforts by national and regional governments to consolidate and reform labour laws since 2014. For regular workers in organised firms – known legally as 'workmen' – working hours and employment conditions are meant to be regulated by the *Factories Act 1948*. Wage fixing is centralised through the *Trade Union Act 1926* and employment levels in the organised sector are regulated through the *Industrial Disputes Act 1947* (Shyam Sundar, 2005; Hill 2009).

Despite the dominant role of informal work across India, this regulatory core is based on the regular (normatively male) worker in a recognised employment relationship with social protection. The persistence of this normative standard means that Standing's concept of labour-related security is applicable and relevant in framing precarious work in India. Indeed, such regular work in firms in the organised sector expanded as a proportion of total employment in the 1950s and 1960s, and only began to decline proportionally and, in some periods absolutely, from the mid-1970s onwards (McCartney, 2009).

For Standing, labour-related security takes seven forms. These are: *labour market security* as sufficient income-earning opportunity; *employment security* as protection against arbitrary dismissal; *job security* as the opportunity to retain a niche in employment, to build a career and have upward mobility in income and status; *work security* as protection at work from accidents, illness or unsociable working hours; *skill reproduction* as opportunities to utilise existing skills or gain new skills; *income security* as stability of social income; and *representation security* as collective voice (Standing, 2011).[11]

---

[11] Standing goes a step further in describing precarious workers as a distinctive (albeit emerging)

This book shows that most work undertaken in Indian auto manufacturing can be classified into eight different employment configurations, each of which exhibit differing degrees of informality and socio-economic insecurity. These categories are: the contract worker; the casual worker; the undeclared worker; the trainee; the apprentice; the wage worker in Tier-3 enterprise or informal enterprise; the own-account worker, Tier-4 job-worker or industrial outworker; and the regular worker.

Following Swider's (2015) definition, each employment configuration represents a set of work activities with a specific pathway into employment via labour markets, and a specific mode of social regulation.[12] While some of the eight categories share pathways into employment – for example, contract workers, casual workers and trainees may, in practice, enter job application and recruitment processes in the same way in OEMs and Tier-1 firms – each one has a different mode of social or legal regulation which shapes the terms of employment. Also, while occupations are an important component of these categories, employment configurations transcend occupational groups – for example, product assemblers can be employed as contract workers, casual workers or regular workers.

Different pathways and modes of regulation mean that workers in each employment configuration have different work-based interests and forms of agency. This means that workers in each category stand to benefit from *particular* reforms to the formal and social regulation of labour markets and employment, although some of these reforms stand to benefit workers in multiple employment configurations. This book will show, for example, why contract workers would generally benefit if their primary employer, rather than their labour contractor, took direct responsibility for the regulation of their employment. In contrast, undeclared workers would benefit from formal access to medical insurance and pension schemes.

---

social class. More recently, he has clarified that the precariat is distinguished by distinctive relations of production, which he defines via the seven forms of labour-related security, as well as distinctive relations of distribution, expressed by increasing reliance on money wages rather than non-wage forms of social income, and distinctive relations with the State, expressed by demonisation or marginalisation by policymakers (Standing, 2014). However, the framing of this social class has been sharply criticised by labour scholars (Breman, 2013; Paret, 2016; Wright, 2016) and is not adopted here. Instead, precarious work is framed by an absence of desirable attributes rather than a unitary set of social class interests (Kalleberg, 2009; Campbell and Price, 2016).

[12] In her research on Chinese construction workers, Swider identifies three employment configurations (mediated via labour contractors; embedded via workers' social networks; and individualised via street labour markets). However, she also suggests there are different configurations based on different empirical cases.

The agency of workers in each employment configuration – in other words, their capacity to act to further their own interests or leverage concessions from firms or state institutions – is strongly shaped by the regional labour control regime in question. Figure 1.1 outlines the basic relationship between global production networks in auto manufacturing, the two regional labour control regimes and the eight employment configurations outlined above. At the level of regional labour control regimes, it shows that a regional *contract* labour system predominates in OEMs, Tier-1, and Tier-2 firms whereas a regional *casual* labour system predominates in Tier-3 and Tier-4 firms.

Fig. 1.1: Employment configurations, regional labour control regimes and global production networks in Indian auto manufacturing

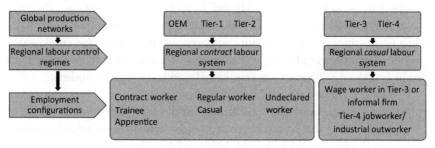

At the level of employment configurations, Figure 1.1 shows which categories are most common in each regime. Although some employment configurations are present across both regimes, they are more likely to appear in one or other labour control regime. For example, contract workers are employed in Tier-3 firms but are much less common in these firms than in higher-tier firms. Alternatively, undeclared workers are employed in both regimes, but are arguably more common in lower-tier firms.

In the regional contract labour system that operates in OEMs, Tier-1 firms and Tier-2 firms, workers' action is incentivised by the lack of employment security, income security and collective voice for contract and casual workers, despite these workers commonly undertaking similar tasks as regular workers. However, workers' action is constrained by the capacity of employers to encourage competition among labour contractors and by the ineffective formal regulation of the contract labour system by national and regional state institutions.

In the casual labour system that operates in Tier-3 and Tier-4 firms, workers' action is incentivised by abundant entry-level work in industrial zones and often by socio-cultural expectations about wage bonuses for religious festivals and holidays. However, it is constrained by seasonal labour migration and by the low-margin, low-wage working environments maintained by firms linked with the global production networks.

Each labour control regime relies on particular employment configurations more than others. This book's core argument is that the interaction between global production networks, regional regimes of labour control, and workers in different employment configurations has shaped the emergence of different forms of social, industrial and political conflict.

Looking ahead in the book

While this book draws upon several previous studies (Gulyani, 2001; Lal Das and George, 2006; Becker-Ritterspach, 2009; Awasthi, Pal and Yagnik, 2010; Hammer, 2010; Suresh, 2010; Bose and Pratap, 2012; Gopalakrishnan and Mirer, 2014), it offers one of the few book-length appreciations of work and employment relations in the Indian auto industry. For example, Gulyani (2001) offered an excellent study of regional clusters and historical development but did not discuss work or employment relations in any detail. Becker-Ritterspach (2009) discussed employment relations at Maruti Suzuki, Fiat, Skoda and Mercedes Benz but did not link this discussion to the structure of the industry via global production networks. Similarly, Jürgens and Krzywdzinski's (2016) recent analysis of VWI, Toyota and Mahindra, in the context of an international comparative study of auto manufacturing in BRIC countries, does not tie employment relations within auto firms to the commercial relations between them.

Despite their radically different conclusions to this book – Jürgens and Krzywdzinski argue that Indian auto manufacturing is on a 'high road' path of development – these scholars rightly argue that insufficient attention has been paid in emerging economies to work and employment patterns in capital and technology-intensive industry. In the case of informal and precarious work, most major studies in India have focused on informal enterprises based in agriculture, trade, home-based work or construction where work is generally labour-intensive (Breman, 1996; Hill, 2010; Agarwala, 2013).

The book will also explore the intersection of industrial development and informality in the *newer* industrial zones of India. While there are some excellent studies of informal work in Indian factory environments, these tend to focus on de-industrialised urban regions in which regular workers have been 'expelled' from organised sector factory production in traditional regional centres of industry (Van Wersch, 1992; Joshi, 1999; Breman, 2004). There has been far less research conducted on newer industrial zones, including the auto industry clusters examined in this book, where informal work is being drawn into contemporary forms of industrialisation.

The book proceeds by, first, outlining the emergence and transformation of the auto industry in India since the 1980s. Chapter 2 sets the scene for the book's analysis of work organisation, labour standards and employment relations by outlining the key OEMs operating in India today, their strategic partners and independent suppliers. This chapter also outlines the regions in which auto manufacturing has taken root and clustered global production network activity. This chapter will show how inter-firm relations have been shaped by the emergence of global production networks.

Chapter 3 focuses on the role of state institutions at a national and regional level. It shows how the liberalisation of manufacturing investment, domestic and foreign, at a national level and industrial subsidies at a regional level, encouraged OEMs to transplant their operations and global production networks in key regions. This process gradually transformed the structure of market segmentation and competition in vehicle manufacturing, with major implications for employment relations in recent decades.

Chapter 3 also summarises key industry and government texts on the role of manufacturing and the auto industry in economic development strategy. This chapter looks behind the rhetoric of the contemporary 'Make in India' strategy and provides analysis of the Automotive Mission Plans published jointly by the Government of India and the Society of Indian Automobile Manufacturers (SIAM), the peak body for OEMs in India.

Chapter 4 explores the implications of global production networks and economic liberalisation for work organisation, labour standards and employment relations in Indian auto manufacturing firms. The discussion focuses particularly upon the role of Maruti Suzuki in the 1980s and 1990s, and its impact upon work organisation throughout the company's production network in the NCR. The chapter shows how changes to domestic market conditions encouraged the dominant passenger car and two-wheeler manufacturing OEMs to transform their employment relations practices. Along with integrating global production networks with regional social structures of accumulation based upon informal and precarious work, this process also shifted practices towards contract labour systems in multiple regions.

Chapter 5 focuses on the operation of the regional contract labour system in the NCR. The analysis is based on field research undertaken over several years. Most data come from interviews with auto workers in all tiers of the regional auto industry, as well as employers, managers, employers' representatives, labour contractors, trade union officials, labour and civil society activists and state officials (see Appendix for full explanation of field research and interviews). The chapter shows how the contract labour system is linked to the industrialisation of town and village life in the NCR and how the result has been the reproduction of contract labour as a type of 'de facto informal work'.

Also based on extensive field research in the NCR, Chapter 6 focuses on the operation of a regional casual labour system as the preferred regime of employer control in Tier-3 and Tier-4 enterprises. This chapter will demonstrate how this system of control is shaped by inter-firm commercial relations within global production networks. It will also show how employers linked into global production networks have adapted to the dominant forms of labour agency and labour mobility in lower-tier firms.

Finally, Chapter 7 concludes the book by revisiting the challenge of recent modifications to GVC and GPN analysis in light of the book's empirical evidence. This chapter brings the concerns outlined in this introductory chapter to a full circle by summarising the employment configurations that frame workers' interests and agency in each labour control regime. Chapter 7 reiterates how each category is based upon different combinations of informal and precarious work and how forms of industrial, social and political conflict in the industry since the 1990s have both challenged and been constrained by these regimes. These findings raise questions about the trajectory of 'high value' manufacturing in modern India and widely-held assumptions about the socially-transformative, socially-reforming character of automotive industrialisation on a global level.

2

The Auto Industry in India Today

Motor vehicle manufacturing is a highly complex industry that encompasses the production and distribution of passenger cars, motorcycles and scooters, three-wheeler vehicles, tractors and other agricultural vehicles and equipment, as well as vehicles used in the construction and mining sectors. The branded manufacturers that assemble finished vehicles tend to represent firms at the head of vast global production networks, with varying levels of global sourcing of raw materials, components and industry services. These are the auto industry's global lead firms, known as Original Equipment Manufacturers (OEMs) in industry parlance. This book focuses on those firms engaged in the production of passenger cars and two-wheelers as well as some commercial vehicles and three-wheeler models.

The global production networks of these OEMs have largely been imposed and entrenched in key Indian manufacturing regions since the early 1980s, transforming commercial relations between foreign and local producers and work organisation within firms. The intersection between these global production networks and regional social structures of accumulation predicated upon low-wage, precarious and informal work helps to explain why Indian auto firms have not reproduced 'high road' labour standards and employment relations (Chapter 1).

This chapter sets the scene for this discussion by outlining the key OEMs and key regions of Indian auto manufacturing, including the configuration of key OEMs' global production networks. This chapter represents the 'who, what and where' of the book by providing context for the discussion of industrial, social and political conflict in the ensuing chapters. In doing so, it shows how the domestic industry has been transformed by global production networks in an era of economic openness and liberalisation.

The rapid growth of the auto industry is one of several indicators of India's social and economic transformation over the past three decades. In 2014–15, the auto industry had a gross turnover of US$58.9 billion (SIAM, 2016). Although this was below its peak of US$67.6 billion in 2012–13, India is currently the world's sixth largest producer of passenger cars and commercial vehicles (Table 2.1). Although well behind China's production volumes, it compares favourably with other major passenger car producers like Germany, the United States and South Korea. After China, India also had the second-fastest growing automotive output of the top 10 producers from 2000 to 2014, although its growth recently fell behind the major North American producing regions (Table 2.2).

Table 2.1: Top 10 countries for passenger cars and commercial vehicles
by production volume, 2014

Rank by total	Country	No. cars	No. commercial vehicles	Total	Percentage share, world total
1	China	19,928,505	3,803,095	23,731,600	26.4
2	USA	4,253,098	7,407,601	11,660,699	13.0
3	Japan	8,277,070	1,497,488	9,774,665	10.9
4	Germany	5,604,026	303,522	5,907,548	6.6
5	S. Korea	4,124,116	400,816	4,524,932	5.0
6	India	3,162,372	682,485	3,844,857	4.3
7	Mexico	1,915,709	1,449,597	3,365,306	3.8
8	Brazil	2,314,789	831,329	3,146,118	3.5
9	Spain	1,898,342	504,636	2,402,978	2.7
10	Canada	913,533	1,480,357	2,393,890	2.7
–	World	67,530,621	22,203,607	89,734,228	100.0

Source: OICA (2014).

Similarly, India also has enormous production volumes in two-wheelers, producing 18,829,786 motorcycles and scooters in 2015–16, making it the second-largest two-wheeler manufacturing country after China. Two-wheelers represented 78.6 per cent of all vehicles manufactured in India in 2015–16. India produced 933,950 three-wheelers in the same period (SIAM, 2016). These statistics compare highly favourably with other emerging auto-producing regions in Asia, such as Thailand, Indonesia and Malaysia (Doner and Wad, 2014).

The industry has also experienced a growing export profile. Table 2.3 indicates that total industry exports had increased to 3,641,212 units in 2015–16, representing an increase from 13 per cent of total vehicle production in 2010–11 to 15.2 per cent in 2015–16. For passenger cars, the proportion of exports in total volume increased from 14.9 to 19.2 per cent in this period, compared to commercial vehicles (from 9.7 to 13 per cent), three-wheelers (from 33.8 to 43.3 per cent) and two-wheelers (11.5 to 13.2 per cent). This reflects significant export growth in the context of recent global market turmoil.

Today, the majority of global OEMs, and most of their strategic partner Tier-1 suppliers, have established manufacturing operations in India. The presence of foreign manufacturers has also shifted domestic components manufacturing towards participation in global production networks. In this context, there remains an underlying concern with the capacity of India, like many other emerging

Table 2.2: Annual growth (%), production of passenger cars and commercial vehicles, 2000–14

Country	'00	'01	'02	'03	'04	'05	'06	'07	'08	'09	'10	'11	'12	'13	'14	Av. '00–14	Av. '10–14
China	13.1	12.8	40.8	35.2	17.8	9.1	25.9	22	4.7	48.3	32.4	0.8	4.6	14.8	7.3	19.3	12.0
USA	-1.7	-11	7.5	-1.3	-1.0	-0.4	-6.0	-4.5	-19	-34	35.4	11.5	19.3	7.1	5.4	0.4	15.7
Japan	2.5	-3.6	4.9	0.3	2.2	2.7	6.3	1.0	-0.2	-32	21.4	-13	18.4	-3.1	1.5	0.6	5.1
Ger.	-2.8	3.0	-3.9	0.7	1.1	3.4	1.1	6.8	-2.7	-14	13.4	6.9	-8.1	1.2	3.3	0.6	3.3
S.Korea	9.6	-5.4	6.8	1.0	9.2	6.6	3.8	6.4	-6.8	-8.2	21.6	9.0	-2.0	-0.9	0.1	3.4	5.6
India	-2.1	1.7	9.8	29.8	30.1	8.4	24.2	11.6	3.5	13.3	34.7	10.7	6.3	-6.6	-1.5	11.6	8.7
Mexico	24.9	-4.9	-2.0	-13	0.1	6.8	22.4	2.4	3.5	-28	50.0	14.4	12.0	1.8	10.2	6.7	17.7
Brazil	24.5	8.1	-1.4	2.0	26.8	9.2	3.3	14.8	8.0	-1.0	6.2	0.7	-0.2	9.1	-15	6.3	0.1
Spain	6.3	-6.0	0.2	6.1	-0.6	-8.6	0.9	4.0	-12	-15	10	-1.4	-17	9.3	11.1	-0.8	2.5
Canada	-3.2	-15	3.8	-2.9	6.2	-0.9	-4.3	0.3	-19	-28	38.8	3.2	15.4	-3.4	0.6	-0.6	10.9
World	3.8	-3.5	4.8	2.8	6.3	3.1	4.1	5.8	-3.7	-12	25.8	3.2	5.5	4.0	2.8	3.5	8.3

Source: OICA (2014)

Table 2.3: Automobile Export Trends, 2010–16

Category	2010–11	% total output	2011–12	%	2012–13	%	2013–14	%	2014–15	%	2015–16	%
Passenger Vehicles	444,326	14.9	508,783	16.2	559,414	17.3	596,142	17.3	621,341	19.3	653,889	19.2
Commercial Vehicles	74,043	9.7	92,258	9.9	80,027	9.6	77,050	9.6	86,939	12.4	101,689	13.0
Three Wheelers	269,968	33.8	361,753	41.1	303,088	36.1	353,392	36.1	407,600	43.0	404,441	43.3
Two Wheelers	1,531,619	11.5	1,975,111	12.8	1,956,378	12.4	2,084,000	12.4	2,457,466	13.3	2,481,193	13.2
Total	2,319,956	13.0	2,937,905	14.4	2,898,907	14.0	3,110,584	14.0	3,573,346	15.3	3,641,212	15.2

Source: SIAM (2016).

market economies, to nurture internationally-competitive domestic firms (Becker-Ritterspach, 2009; Irawati and Charles, 2010; Doner and Wad, 2014; Pavlinek, 2014; Natsuda Otsuka and and Thoburn, 2015).

While domestic suppliers in India tend to be smaller and less technology-intensive than many OEM global strategic partners, this situation is gradually changing. Of significant advantage to India, compared to many similar emerging economies, is the existence of powerful local business groups with manufacturing expertise. Most of these firms were established long before the liberalisation periods of the 1980s and 90s. One of the manifestations of this is India's role as a growing source, not only of manufacturing exports, but also of investment by Indian firms overseas, indicated by growth in outward-flowing Foreign Direct Investment (FDI) (Hattari and Rajan, 2010).

Like China, supply chain production and distribution in India has tended to 'cluster' around new and established manufacturing-assembly facilities. However, this clustering is more geographically concentrated than in China, partly because India's domestic automotive market is less developed, and also because of poorer quality transport infrastructure in many parts of the country.

Table 2.4 outlines the main regions of motor vehicle manufacturing in India and key OEMs based in each one. The dominant clusters in terms of vehicle production capacity, output, sales and employment are in the National Capital Region (NCR) surrounding New Delhi, the Chennai Metropolitan Area (CMA) in the state of Tamil Nadu, and in the Chakan Special Economic Zone (C-SEZ) near the city of Pune in the state of Maharashtra. These three regional clusters are represented graphically in Map 2.1.

The NCR is a special metropolitan area designated under the Constitution. As well as the National Capital Territory of Delhi, the NCR covers parts of the states of Haryana, Rajasthan and Uttar Pradesh. The NCR is one of the world's most populated urban regions with upwards of 46 million people living there according to the 2011 Indian Census. It is also the largest industrial centre in India today, with the industrial townships of Gurugram and Manesar on New Delhi's southern fringe, and Greater Noida to its east. These urban centres, particularly Gurugram and Manesar, are the bases for India's largest passenger car and two-wheeler manufacturers.

The CMA, which surrounds the administrative and industrial capital of the southeastern state of Tamil Nadu, represents the fourth largest urban region in India and is now the second largest hub of passenger car production in the country, as well as a major centre for automotive exports. The C-SEZ is centred on an industrial zone earmarked by the Government of Maharashtra that surrounds the town of Chakan, about 32km north of the city of Pune and about 140km east

Map 2.1: Main auto manufacturing regions of India

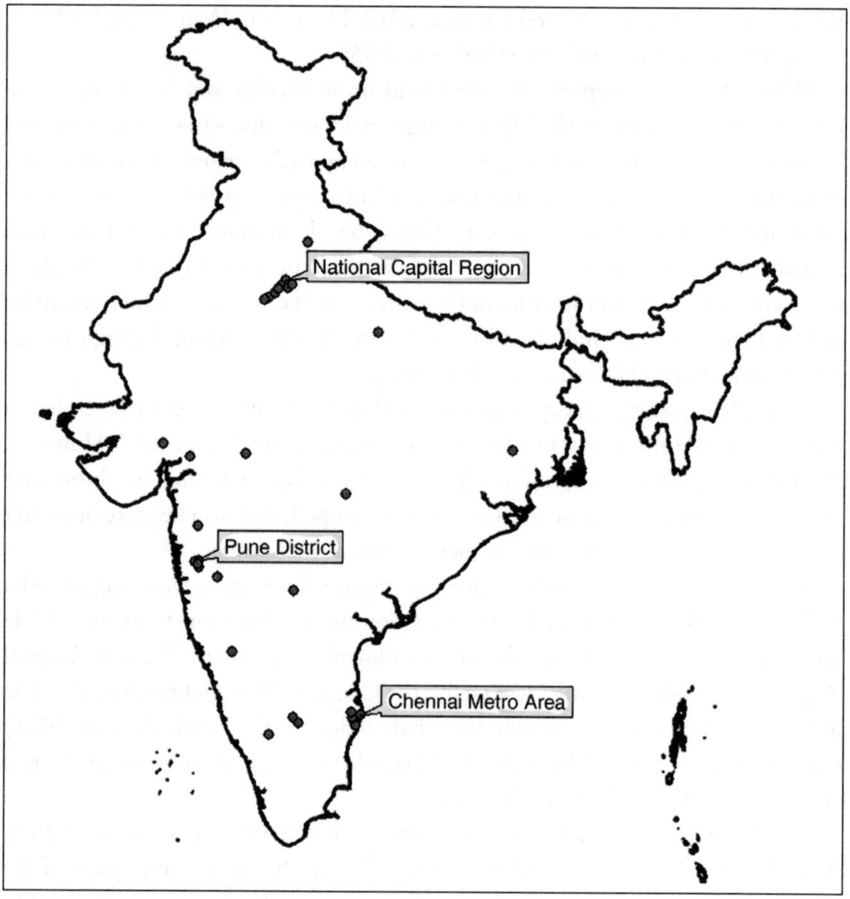

National Capital Region

Pune District

Chennai Metro Area

Source: Author's calculations.

of Mumbai, the state's administrative capital and India's financial and one-time industrial powerhouse. The leading status of the NCR, CMA and C-SEZ will be substantiated below as the chapter explores the key OEMs and global production networks that dominate motor vehicle manufacturing in each region.

There are two other regions with the potential to rival the leading pack. One is in the state of Gujarat, which represents a high-growth region where auto manufacturing is centred around two locations about 160 km apart: Sanand, near the state capital of Ahmedabad, and the town of Halol, 150 km west of the border that the state shares with Madhya Pradesh. Gujarat is the subject of much anticipated investment, although, as we shall see, it has also experienced recent problems of divestment from American OEM General Motors (GM).

Table 2.4: Main motor vehicle manufacturing regions in India and key OEMs in each region[1]

Region	Locations		OEMs
	Location	State	
National Capital Region (NCR)	Bawal	Haryana	Harley-Davidson
	Dharuhera		Hero MotoCorp
	Faridabad		Yamaha
	Gurugram		Hero MotoCorp, Maruti Suzuki
	Manesar		HMSI (Honda), Maruti Suzuki
	Neemrana	Rajasthan	Hero MotoCorp
	Tapukara		Honda
	G. Noida	U. Pradesh	Honda Cars
Chennai Metropolitan Area (CMA), *Tamil Nadu*	Chennai		Chrysler (Fiat), Daimler (buses), Force Motors
	Maraimalai Nagar		BMW, Ford
	Oragadam		BharatBenz (Daimler), Renault-Nissan, Royal Enfield (Eicher)
	Sripurumbudur		Hyundai
	Tirvullur		Mitsubishi/Hindustan Motors, Royal Enfield (Eicher)
Chakan Special Economic Zone (C-SEZ) and surrounding plants, *Maharashtra*	Baramati		Piaggio
	Chakan		Bajaj, Bajaj/KTM, Force Motors, Mahindra, Mercedes Benz, Volkswagen/Skoda
	Pimpri-Chinchwad		Jaguar/Land Rover, Premier Ltd
	TalegaonDabhade		General Motors/SAIC
	Ranjangaon		Fiat, Tata Motors
State of *Gujarat*[2]	Halol		General Motors[3], Hero MotoCorp
	Sanand		Ford, Tata Motors
	Vitthalapur		Honda

Contd.

[1] Table includes OEM passenger car, two-wheeler and some commercial vehicle manufacturing and assembly facilities. Supplier facilities and facilities that solely manufacture vehicles for agriculture, construction or mining have been excluded, as well as sites devoted entirely to research and development, design, testing, warehousing, training or sales.

[2] Maruti Suzuki began production at a new 700-acre facility in Hansalpur, 60 km west of Ahmedabad in 2017. Honda Cars also claims it has plans to commence manufacturing in Gujarat.

[3] GM's Halol factory closed in April 2017 with reports of plans by Chinese OEM, SAIC Motor, to commence vehicle manufacturing at the site by 2019.

Region	Locations		OEMs
	Location	State	
State of *Uttarakhand*	Haridwar		Hero MotoCorp, Mahindra
	Pantnagar		Bajaj, Tata Motors
Other states/locations			
Himachal Pradesh ˙	Nalagarh		TVS
Jharkhand	Jamshedpur		Tata Motors
Karnataka	Bengaluru (Bangalore)		Honda, Mahindra REVA, Scania, Toyota Kirloskar, Volvo
	Dharward		Tata Motors
	Mysore		TVS
Kerala	Thiruvananthapuram		Kerala Automobiles Ltd
Madhya Pradesh	Pithampur		Force Motors, Hindustan Motors, Tata Motors, Volvo/Eicher
Maharashtra (other than C-SEZ)	Alibag		Chinkara Motors
	Aurangabad		Audi, Bajaj, Skoda
	Bhandara		Mahindra
	Mumbai		Tata Motors
	Nashik		Mahindra
Tamil Nadu (other than CMR)	Hosur		TVS
Telangana	Zaheerabad		Mahindra
Uttar Pradesh (other than NCR)	Lucknow		Tata Motors

Source: Author's analysis of company reports/internet searches by July 2016; also adaptation of Barnes et al (2015); Gulyani (2001).

The second emerging region is in the northern state of Uttarakhand, centred around the city of Haridwar and the town of Pantnagar, approximately 100 km west of the India-Nepal border on the foothills of the Himalayas. Other than these locations, there are, as indicated in Table 2.4, several other regions where motor vehicle manufacturing plays a role in regional economies, including the fringes of the city of Bengaluru (Bangalore), the Tata Group's base in the city of Jamshedpur in eastern India and some nodes for global production networks in eastern and central Maharashtra. In addition to this, there is a major auto components cluster located around the city of Ludhiana in the state of Punjab.

As well as outlining the key regional clusters and global production networks that comprise India's auto industry, this chapter addresses some of the strengths and weaknesses of Global Value Chain (GVC) and Global Production Network

(GPN) analysis (see Chapter 1 for outline). This chapter will demonstrate that many of the network configurations and firm-level strategies developed via GPN 2.0 appear in India's auto industry and, furthermore, that some of these correspond with features of the main governance types developed in GVC analysis. As Coe and Yeung (2015) suggest, inter-firm partnership and inter-firm control are common strategies adopted in the auto industry.

The National Capital Region

The core of the NCR is the National Capital Territory of Delhi, a union territory with its own elected government under the Indian constitution. Large-scale industry in the NCT of Delhi has been historically compartmentalised in the south of the capital by urban planners, overlapping with the state of Haryana. More recently, during India's gradual economic liberalisation, large-scale industry has shifted to the eastern and southern fringe of the region, overlapping with Uttar Pradesh, Haryana and, most recently, the northeast corner of Rajasthan. Most significantly, the satellite cities of Gurugram and Manesar in Haryana–lying 30 km and 40 km southwest of New Delhi respectively–have emerged in the last quarter of a century as major centres for global production networks in the automotive industry as well as in ready-made export garments, call centres, global financial institutions and retail shopping malls.

In addition, the district of Faridabad, 30 km south of New Delhi and also in the state of Haryana, has been a major centre of manufacturing since the 1960s and is, today, the base for several OEMs and auto suppliers. Taken together, the districts of Faridabad and Gurugram (which includes the town of Manesar) accounted for about a third of all waged employment in the state of Haryana by the mid-2000s. By the late 2000s, the Government of Haryana claimed that half of India's cars, half of its motorcycles, a third of its fridges and a quarter of its tractors and bicycles were manufactured in the state (Government of Haryana, 2009). Along with the key OEMs' activities outlined below– Maruti Suzuki, Hero MotoCorp and Honda–Yamaha India operates a plant in Faridabad and Harley-Davidson assembles motorcycles by importing fully-manufactured sub-assembled components known as Complete Knockdowns (CKDs), from the US to its factory in Bawal, about 100 km south of Delhi.

Maruti Suzuki India Limited

Maruti Suzuki India Limited (MSIL) is India's largest passenger car-maker by production volume and market share, a position it has held for nearly 30 years. In 2014–15, MSIL held a 45 per cent share in the Indian passenger car market, representing an increase from 38.3 per cent in 2011–12. Based on an average for the five years from 2014–15, MSIL held a 42 per cent market share during this period (MSIL, 2015). While this is lower than previous phases of the company's development due to increasing competition in the domestic passenger car market – the company held a 63 per cent share in 1990–91 and 51 per cent by 2004–05 (Becker-Ritterspach, 2009: 94–95) – it is nevertheless the market leader by a considerable margin. A further sign of MSIL's importance on the global stage is that, having started operations in 1982 as a Public Sector Unit (PSU) with a 26 per cent equity share by Suzuki Motor Corporation (SMC), it has grown into a full subsidiary that, today, has a 56 per cent equity stake in its own parent company in Japan (MSIL, 2015: 36).

In 2014–15, MSIL sold 1.37 million vehicles domestically, of which nearly 90 per cent were passenger cars (MSIL, 2015). Until 2013, MSIL's success in the passenger car market was spearheaded by a high-selling small car model, the Maruti 800, which represented 43 per cent of MSIL's Indian car sales in the early 2000s (Becker-Ritterspach, 2009: 102). Another important feature of the firm's recent development is that it has increased its market share in a period of relatively volatile sales for car production in India. After hitting highs of 28 per cent annual growth in 2010–11, passenger car sales grew at an annual average of just one per cent for the following four years, with sales even falling by 6 per cent in 2013–14 (MSIL, 2015).

MSIL is also developing as a car exporter, with 121,713 units exported in 2014–15, almost entirely to the Middle East, Latin America or African countries. In the same year, MSIL spent ₹4292 *crore* (about US$668 million) on imported goods, of which over half was on raw materials and components. By comparison, the company spent nearly 13 times this amount (₹30473 *crore* or over US$4.7 billion) on domestically-sourced raw materials and components. The company claims that 86 per cent of supplier production by value is manufactured within 100 km of its main factories in Haryana (MSIL, 2015).

MSIL emerged as the pioneer of the Indian auto industry's modernisation in the 1980s and 90s. The decision by SMC and industrial policymakers in the Governments of India and Haryana to establish a joint venture was, in hindsight, the key historical moment in the transformation of the industry (see Chapter 3). MSIL operates two main facilities in India. The Gurugram assembly plant was established in 1982 and production commenced at the Manesar facility in 2007. By March 2015, the company claimed to employ 22,476 people at these two facilities, of which 57 per cent were regular workers (i.e., workers employed directly by the company on an ongoing or permanent basis), 38 per cent were temporary workers and five per cent were apprentices.

Among the regular workforce, 52 per cent were workers with higher technical qualifications (such as engineers and managers), 42 per cent were semi or less-skilled workers (known as 'associates' or technicians) and six per cent were trainees, including a mix of junior entry and graduate trainees. Of the regular workforce, three per cent were women (MSIL, 2015: 104). The temporary workforce is a mix of casual workers directly hired by the company and workers hired through labour contractors. There have been significant changes in MSIL's hiring practices for temporary workers since 2012, which are closely tied to a spate of serious industrial conflicts between management and workers (see Chapter 4).

By March 2014, MSIL claimed to have 326 key suppliers. Since establishing operations in Gurugram in 1982, MSIL has completely transformed commercial relations between manufacturing firms in the NCR and its influence has been reflected across the auto industry on a national level. A key part of MSIL's strategy has been co-investment in Tier-1 supply firms. This has taken the form of equity investment to form joint ventures with suppliers, or, in a few cases, full adoption of suppliers as subsidiary companies. By 2015, MSIL controlled seven subsidiary companies, mostly in insurance and sales, and held a controlling stake in six joint venture companies, including Mark Exhaust (with 44 per cent ownership), Bellsonica (30 per cent), Krishna Ishizaki (15 per cent), FMI Automotive Components (40 per cent), Inergy Automotive Systems (26 per cent) and Manesar Steel Processing India (12 per cent).

These represent firms in which MSIL uses its equity share and market power to exercise direct influence over operational management. Some of these firms are entirely Japanese in ownership structure, such as Bellsonica, while others like Mark Exhaust or Krishna Ishizaki, have a joint Indo-Japanese ownership and management structure. While MSIL exercises a controlling stake in these suppliers' operations, some also operate as independent suppliers to other OEMs. For example, Mark Exhaust manufactures door frames for MSIL and exhaust pipes for Honda Motorcycle and Scooter India (HMSI), which operates a vast facility near Manesar.

In addition to these joint ventures, in 2014–15, MSIL held equity shares in 12 'associate companies': Halla Visteon (39 per cent ownership), SKH Metals (49 per cent), Jay Bharat (29 per cent), Caparo Maruti (25 per cent), Machino Plastics (15 per cent), Bharat Seats (15 per cent), Krishna Maruti (16 per cent), Asahi India (11 per cent), Denso India (10 per cent), Nippon Thermostat (10 per cent), Sona Koyo Steering (7per cent) and Magneti Marelli Powertrain India (19 per cent). Some of these firms represent equity partnerships between MSIL and Indian family-owned companies, such as SKH Metals, Machino Plastics and Bharat Seats.

Some key MSIL suppliers are independent, locally-owned specialist suppliers with links to Indian family business groups. One example is JBM Industries, which is a Tier-1 supplier for several foreign OEMs such as Ford, Fiat, General Motors, Honda, JCB, Renault-Nissan, Toyota, Volvo and Volkswagen, as well as

MSIL and several domestic OEMs including Ashok Leyland, Bajaj Auto, Hero MotoCorp, Mahindra, TVS and Tata. It is part of the multi-industry JBM Group which operates in partnership with major multi-industry lead firms like Arcelor Mittal, Magnetto and Sumitomo (JBM Group, 2016; Khan, 2014).

In other cases, MSIL has formed partnerships with foreign companies. For example, MSIL has an equity stake in Asahi India's glass manufacturing facility, a Japanese multi-industry independent supplier. Similarly, MSIL operates in partnership with Caparo Maruti, which is co-operated by British transnational supplier of steel parts, Caparo Engineering. Caparo's 1994 entry into India was co-managed by MSIL and, from starting with one factory in Pithampur in the state of Madhya Pradesh, the firm has expanded to two Pithampur-based facilities (with 408 and 60 employees respectively by 2016) and sheet metal stamping factories in Gurugram (330 employees), Bawal in Haryana (302 employees), Greater Noida (236 employees), Jamshedpur (302 employees), Chennai (87 employees), and two factories each in the city of Pune (329 and 93 employees respectively) and Halol in the state of Gujarat (81 and 90 employees respectively) (Caparo Engineering, 2016).

Interestingly, MSIL has equity stakes in Tier-1 suppliers that represent strategic partnerships with *competing* OEM brands. For example, Halla Visteon, which manufactures air ventilation and air conditions systems, is a multi-industry supplier and US-South Korean joint venture with the Visteon Corporation, a key global strategic partner of Ford.

Similarly, Denso, another MSIL partner, is part of the Toyota Group. On a global level, 47 per cent of Denso's revenue in 2016 came from Toyota. Its close connection with Toyota's global operations means Denso is a large multinational corporation in its own right, with 146,000 employees globally. Yet this strategic partner of Toyota's has also become integrated into numerous rival global production networks as a supplier in the NCR, producing parts for Honda, Hero MotoCorp and Yamaha as well as MSIL and Toyota, from several manufacturing sites spread across the country (Denso, 2016).

Another similar case is MSIL's investment in Magneti Marelli, part of the Fiat Group of companies from Italy. Like Denso and Visteon, Magneti Marelli is an OEM strategic partner and a major multinational corporation in its own right. In India, it operates three facilities in Gurugram (an exhaust, engine and electronics factory), exhaust plants in Chennai and Ranjangaon (Maharashtra), and a shock absorber factory and an auto lighting plant in Pune. Other than its role as a major Fiat and MSIL supplier, Magneti Marelli operates joint ventures with some Indian companies, including an engine factory in Manesar and a plastic-moulding plant in Delhi (Magneti Marelli Motherson) and a suspension factory in Faridabad (Magneti Marelli Talbros Chassis Systems) (Magneti Marelli, 2016).

In other cases, MSIL suppliers were formed by joint ventures between a combination of foreign, private domestic and state capital. For example, Subros Limited, an air conditioning manufacturer with two plants in Greater Noida and one each in Manesar, Pune, Chennai and Sanand (Gujarat), was founded in 1985 as a joint venture with 40 per cent ownership by the Suri family, 13 per cent each from SMC and Denso and the remaining 34 per cent from the Government of India (Subros, 2016).

Hero MotoCorp

If Maruti Suzuki is India's dominant passenger car manufacturer, Hero MotoCorp is currently the market leader for two-wheelers. As mentioned above, motorcycles and scooters represent about four fifths of total production volume in the Indian auto industry. Hero MotoCorp is an Indian-owned company, part of the Hero Group operated and part-owned by the Munjal family. Following India's independence and partition, the Munjal family commenced bicycle manufacturing in the city of Ludhiana in the State of Punjab. Today the Group is an industrial-financial conglomerate with subsidiaries in call centres, renewable energy manufacturing, electronics, real estate and education, as well as auto manufacturing.

In the auto industry, Hero MotoCorp currently operates four manufacturing and assembly facilities: in Gurugram in the NCR, in the town of Dharuhera in Haryana 40 km to the southwest of Gurugram, in the town of Neemrana, also in the NCR across the border in the northeast corner of Rajasthan, and in Haridwar in the northern state of Uttarakhand. It also has a fifth site in Halol in Gujarat which was due to commence assembly production in 2016–17.

For the last 15 years, Hero has claimed to be the world's largest two-wheeler manufacturer by output volume (Hero MotoCorp, 2016), although this performance is closely linked to its former joint venture partner, Honda (see below). By 2014–15, Hero had a 40 per cent share of the two-wheeler market in India, although this had steadily fallen from 45 per cent in 2010–11, due primarily to competition from Honda (Baggonkar, 2015).

In 2014–15, Hero manufactured 6,631,826 units and, on average, has manufactured 6,118,150 units each year since 2010–11. Hero operates an overwhelmingly domestically-oriented business. In 2014–15, it exported just three per cent of its production volume, which is significantly less than the 13.2 per cent rate of exports for two-wheeler production as a whole in India in 2015–16 (Table 2.3 above). However, its exports are growing at a fast rate – 53 per cent by volume in the most recent financial year – and its products can be bought in a wide range of international markets, including several South Asian, Latin American, African and Middle Eastern countries.

In order to enhance market access in Latin America, Hero established an assembly plant in Colombia in 2014 and, in the same year, established its first plant in Bangladesh with a 55 per cent stake in a joint venture with the local Nitol Niloy Group. The company also operates assembly factories for imported Complete Knock-Down (CKD) kits in Uganda, Tanzania and Kenya (Hero MotoCorp, 2015).

Across all four of its currently-operating facilities, Hero claimed to employ 7,331 regular workers by 2015, with a further 16,412 temporary or casual workers, representing 69 per cent of its total workforce. Among its regular workforce, just 1.2 per cent were female. Hero claims to rely on 247 key supply companies, of which 80 per cent are based near its Gurugram and Haridwar plants (Hero MotoCorp, 2015).

The Hero Group commonly prefers to partner with suppliers in which it has a controlling equity stake or which fall into the Munjal family's network of companies. For example, one key supplier, Rockman Industries, emerged in the 1960s as a bicycle components maker and has diversified into a manufacturer of aluminium die-cast components with plants in Ludhiana, Haridwar, Chennai and Bawal and over 5000 employees nationally. As part of the Hero Group, Rockman supplies group companies, especially Hero MotoCorp, but also manufacturers parts for the aftermarket (Rockman, 2016).

Similarly, the Munjal family controls another key Tier-1 supplier, Satyam Auto Components. Established in 2001 as a motorcycle chassis manufacturer and sub-assembler for fuel tanks and brake systems, the company operates manufacturing plants in Manesar, Haridwar and Ludhiana (Satyam Auto Components, 2016). However, not all key suppliers to Hero MotoCorp are captive companies; their supply base includes several independent domestic and foreign suppliers, including partners with other OEMs such as Magneti Marelli.

Hero's brand and reputation as a major two-wheeler manufacturer is historically linked to a joint venture it operated with Japanese OEM Honda from 1984 until 2010. As a result of the joint venture, Hero Honda became the dominant two-wheeler manufacturer in India by the late 1980s. Honda's entry into India took advantage of Hero's existing national network of bicycle distributors and the knowledge of regional markets it had accumulated over many decades. Like MSIL's role in the passenger car market, this joint venture was a critical part of the Indian Governments' industrial policy and market segmentation strategy in the 1980s and 90s (see Chapter 3).

However, conflict between the Munjals and Honda was always an element of this partnership. Long before the split between the two companies in 2010, Honda had already established a wholly-owned subsidiary plant in Manesar in 1999–known as Honda Motorcycle and Scooter India (HMSI)–which gave Honda a strong base in the domestic two-wheeler market. But the 2010 split appeared to reflect different views about managing the company's supply chain. Whereas the Munjals preferred to deal with captive suppliers, especially those within the Hero Group of companies, Honda preferred to force competition among suppliers to adhere to strict price and quality controls.

Besides tensions regarding the competition with HMSI and control of companies within the supply chain, the Munjals were constrained from exporting Hero-branded vehicles to countries (other than Sri Lanka) under the terms of the joint venture agreement. These tensions underlie the 2010 split in which the Munjals purchased Honda's stake in the venture for approximately US$1 billion and offered Honda ongoing royalty payments for use of their products and technology (Doval, 2010).

Today, Hero MotoCorp's largest shareholder (41 per cent) is a group of foreign equity investors, in addition to a 35 per cent share owned by the Hero Group with a range of smaller investments from banks, insurance companies and a seven per cent stake from the Government of India (Hero MotoCorp, 2015: 96). This arrangement has thus far enabled the Hero Group to finance its expansion into domestic and international markets while continuing to maintain its control over local manufacturing operations.

Honda

As suggested above, Honda's penetration of Indian automotive markets is due, in a large part, to its 26-year joint venture role in Hero Honda. Honda has become the major competitor with its former joint venture partner, Hero MotoCorp, in the two-wheeler segment. Honda's two-wheeler company, Honda Motorcycle and Scooter (HMSI), has its major facility in Manesar, but now also operates a plant in Tapukara in the northeast corner of Rajasthan, about 40 km to the south, as well as factories in Vitthalapur, 90 km northeast of the city of Ahmedabad in the state of Gujarat, and in the Narasapura Industrial Area on the northwest corner of Bengaluru. HMSI's share of the national two-wheeler market has been steadily growing, especially at Hero MotoCorp's expense, from 13 per cent in 2010–11, when it split from Hero, to 27 per cent by 2014–15 (Baggonkar, 2015).

Honda is also a major passenger car manufacturer. It originally intended to operate as a major competitor in this market, but its early efforts were blocked by the Government of India as part of its market segmentation policy in the 1980s (see Chapter 3). Despite these initial restrictions, Honda Cars has succeeded in becoming a growing player in the passenger car market. It operates a passenger car assembly plant–originally known as Honda Siel – in Greater Noida in the NCR, as well as a car assembly factory, engine (powertrain) plant and press shop in Tapukara, adjacent to the HMSI plant. The Greater Noida plant was established as a 'greenfield' site in 1997, making Honda one of the first foreign OEMs to take advantage of FDI liberalisation reforms which allowed foreign firms to establish operations without seeking joint ventures with Indian-branded manufacturers. The 150-acre site in Greater Noida currently has an annual capacity of 120,000 cars and specialises in small cars and small SUVs. The Tapukara site was established in 2008 over 450 acres, and car assembly commenced in 2014 with the same capacity as the Greater Noida site (Honda Cars, 2016).

As a global OEM, Honda has several core suppliers that it relies on across multiple countries and regions. Several of these are also based in India, including Japanese Tier-1 suppliers like AGC Automotive, Nippon Seiki and Takata Automotive, major German multi-industry independent supplier like Thyssenkrupp and auto-focused suppliers like Mahle Behr, or American Tier-1 suppliers like BorgWarner. Gurugram-based AGC Automotive is part of the Asahi Group which manufactures glass parts and, in India, is partially influenced by MSIL's equity investment in local operations (see above) (AGC Automotive, 2016).

Nippon Seiki operates a wholly-owned subsidiary company, NS Instruments, with plants in Gurugram as well as Chennai and Chittoor in the state of Andhra Pradesh, and a joint venture – JNS Instruments in Gurugram – with the Indian-owned JP Minda Group (Nippon Seiki, 2016). Japanese supplier Takata Automotive manufactures textile fabrics for seatbelts, seats, airbags and other vehicle interior products from its three factories in Neemrana in Rajasthan as well as Chennai and Pune.

While Thyssenkrupp manufactures brake calipers for Honda, it also operates in India as a wholly German-owned manufacturer of engine components, bearings and undercarriage parts for multiple industries including steel, marine craft, elevators, aerospace and machine parts from its main facilities in the C-SEZ, in Nashik in the state of Maharashtra and in the city of Hyderabad (Thyssenkrupp India, 2016).

Honda also buys parts from Mahle Behr, a Tier-1 joint venture between the German conglomerate Mahle Behr GmbH and the Indian-owned Anand Group. From its the base in the C-SEZ, as well as in Sanand (Gujarat) and Chennai, this joint venture manufactures engine cooling and air conditioning systems, and also supplies numerous Indian and foreign-owned OEMs, including key Honda competitors in the passenger car market like MSIL, Renault-Nissan and Mahindra (Mahle Behr, 2016).

Thus, Honda's production network represents a wide range of global partners, many of which operate as multi-industry suppliers and some as specialist Tier-1 automotive components suppliers. Some key suppliers are also strategic partners with rival OEMs (Denso is another company that also supplies Honda), or independent suppliers for multiple OEMs. In addition, Honda's production network draws upon suppliers in relatively close proximity (within the NCR) and those based in other regional clusters like the C-SEZ or in the CMA. Many of these firms are foreign firms operating in joint ventures with Indian private firms.

Honda also relies on several Indian-only suppliers. Key examples include Rajhans Pressings which specialises in sheet metal parts for engines and other auto components from its two plants in Faridabad and its plant in the town of Pantnagar (Uttarakhand) (Rajhans Pressings, 2016). Some Indian-owned suppliers are also multi-industry in orientation, such as Suprajit Engineering which makes cables for manufactures in several industries from its main base in Bengaluru as well as Pune, Manesar, Pantnagar and Haridwar (Suprajit, 2016).

The Chennai Metropolitan Area

The Chennai Metropolitan Area (CMA) has emerged as a key region for auto manufacturing since the 1990s. The CMA has also emerged as the key regional competitor with the NCR in passenger car production. The CMA centres upon the capital of Tamil Nadu, Chennai, in the south of the India. Chennai is currently India's fourth most-populated urban region. Apart from Chennai itself, the CMA's key hubs for auto production are Sriperumbudur, a city 40 km to the southwest of the capital and a base for Hyundai's operations as well as a hub for global electronics producers like Taiwan's Foxconn, China's Lenovo and the US giant, Dell; the town of Maraimalai Nagar, 50 km southwest of Chennai, and base for Ford and BMW; the town of Oragadam, 55 km southwest of Chennai, and the base for Renault-Nissan's Indian operations as well as Bharat Benz (Daimler) and, on a smaller scale, Indian motorcycle manufacturer, Royal Enfield. Further afield from the auto belt connecting Oragadam, Maraimalai Nagar and Sriperumbudur is Tirvullur, a suburb of Chennai about 40 km northwest of the city centre, which is the base for Mitsubishi Motors' joint venture with Hindustan Motors and some auto components and construction equipment manufacturing.

By 2010, the CMA as a whole accounted for over 30 per cent of passenger car production in India (Gopalakrishnan and Mirer, 2014). Its emergence has mirrored economic liberalisation reforms in the 1990s which allowed an increased number of foreign OEMs to establish operation in India (see Chapter 3). In the CMA, the key turning point was the 1996 decision of the Government to allow the Hyundai Motor Company from South Korea to establish a fully Korean-owned subsidiary from a 'greenfield' site in Sriperumbudur, the first of its kind in India.

Hyundai Motor India Limited

From its establishment in 1996 and the commencement of manufacturing in 1998, Hyundai Motor India Ltd (HMIL) has emerged as a major passenger car manufacturer and a growing rival to MSIL's historical domination of the small car market. In 2014, HMIL sold about 613,000 cars, which represents Hyundai Motor Company's (HMC) third largest market at over 12 per cent of its total global car sales. By comparison, 38 per cent of HMC's global sales in 2014 were in South Korea and 23 per cent in China (HMC, 2015). In comparison with its key domestic competitor in India, MSIL sold over 1.23 million passenger cars in India in 2014–15 (see above), or approximately double HMIL's sales for 2014.

However, since the mid-2000s, HMIL has become the leading passenger car exporter in India. Its car exports peaked in 2009 at over 270,000 and it exported just under 202,000 cars in 2014 (HMC, 2016). By comparison, MSIL exported under 122,000 units in 2014–15. Along with its main manufacturing and assembly plant in Sriperumbudur, HMIL established a technical centre in the central Indian city of Hyderabad in 2008 run by a separate HMC subsidiary, Hyundai Motor India Engineering. This is one of five research and development sites operated by HMC globally, and it designs vehicles specialised for Indian markets, especially in the small car sector (HMC, 2015).

Like other OEMs discussed in this chapter, HMIL's global production network draws upon a wide range of supply companies. This includes strategic partners, captive suppliers and many South Korean Tier-1 independent suppliers, including some that manufacture for rival OEMs. Captive South Korean suppliers include seat manufacturer Dymos Lear, part of the Hyundai Group of companies, which operates a plant in Sriperumbudur and one in Tirvullur (Dymos Lear, 2016).

Another example is Dongsun Automotive, which manufacturers parts for Computer Numerical Control (CNC) machinery in Sengadu village outside Sriperumbudur (Dongsun Automotive, 2016); Hwashin Automotive, which manufactures multiple components from two local plants, employs 850 workers (including a small number of South Korean expatriate workers) and sells to HMIL and Renault-Nissan (Hwashin Automotive, 2016); Woojin Automotive, which manufactures parts for exhausts, chassis, suspension and steering systems, from its Sriperumbudur factory (Woojin Automotive, 2016); and Woory Automotive, a Chennai-based supplier of HMIL and Renault-Nissan (Woory Automotive, 2016).

HMIL also relies upon a large number of Indian-owned independent suppliers. These include the Tier-2 firm Jagdambay Forgings from Ludhiana, which has customers across multiple tiers of the industry and is also multi-industry in orientation, forging metal parts for tractors, construction scaffolding and metal gates as well as auto parts from its two plants (Jagdambay Forgings, 2016); Anand Enterprises, a Tier-2 manufacturer which sells cylinder lines, sleeves and blocks from its 260-employee warehouse, casting plant and machine shop in Rajkot, Gujarat (Anand Enterprise, 2016); and Ashutosh Rubber, another Tier-2 raw materials supplier, also from Rajkot, which sells rubber products used in HMIL's production process (Ashutosh Rubber, 2016).

Renault-Nissan

Renault-Nissan is a global equity partnership between Groupe Renault from France and Japanese OEM, Nissan. As part of this alliance, Renault has a 43 per cent equity share in Nissan globally. The alliance formed a fully foreign-owned joint venture in India in 2010, based at a manufacturing and assembly facility in Oragadam. In 2014–15, the alliance sold 53,848 units in India, representing a 1.7 per cent market share.

However, Renault-Nissan is highly ambitious about small car production in Indian markets (Groupe Renault, 2015: 22). As part of this vision, the alliance has established a joint design and engineering centre in the region and, after establishing a factory with a 480,000-strong annual volume capacity for multiple car models and employing around 15,000 workers, made a major foray into the small car market with the launch of the Renault Kwid in 2015.

The Kwid has been marketed as a direct competitor with MSIL and HMIL's dominant small car brands like the Maruti Alto 800 or the Hyundai Eon and has recently outsold small cars in the Mahindra, Honda and Tata range (Business Today, 2015; Khan, 2016). A further sign of Renault-Nissan's market expansion plans is the 250 acres allotted to its supplier park in Oragadam – enough to fit around 100 suppliers – on top of the 640 acres allotted for its vehicle assembly operations. By comparison, HMIL was originally allotted 526 acres in Sriperumbudur by the Government of Tamil Nadu in 1996 (Anand, 2008). Like its key competitor OEMs in the passenger car market, Renault-Nissan has established a sophisticated global production network that draws upon a wide range of different supply companies.

Due to its strategic location in the CMA, some of these suppliers are South Korean Tier-1 suppliers to HMIL, such as Dymos Lear, Hwashin or Woory Automotive (see above). Some are Tier-1 suppliers from other countries, like Pune-based Italian iron casting manufacturer ComauSpA – part of the Fiat Group – (Comau India, 2016), German engineering conglomerate, Bosch, Japanese textile fabric manufacturer and key Honda supplier, Takata Automotive, and American Tier-1 exhaust and emission systems manufacturer, Tenneco Automotive.

Most of these foreign Tier-1 firms represent large transnational manufacturers which supply to multiple OEMs in the auto industry. Tenneco, for example, supplies exhaust systems to MSIL, Tata, Mahindra, Ford, Volkswagen, TVS, Toyota and General Motors, as well as Renault Nissan (Tenneco Automotive,

2010). However, like its key OEM competitors, Renault-Nissan also draws upon a wide range of Indian-owned independent Tier-1 and Tier-2 suppliers in its supplier park in Oragadam and from other auto manufacturing regions.

Renault-Nissan claims that 98 per cent of parts used in the Renault Kwid are locally-manufactured. For instance, steering and engine parts are locally-manufactured by the Rane Group, an Indian conglomerate, electric power steering technology is provided by Mando Automotive India–a joint venture between India's Anand Group and South Korea's Mando, car-lights by Indian firm UNO Minda and, Lumax – an American-Japanese-Indian joint venture based in the NCR–provided gear parts and accessories (Mathur, 2016).

Ford India

Ford India Private Limited (FIPL) is a full subsidiary of the Ford Motor Company (FMC) based in Maraimalai Nagar. India remains a target market for FMC globally, but it lacks the power and influence of MSIL, HMIL, Honda or Indian firms like Tata and Mahindra in the passenger car market. In 2015, FIPL's market share in India was 2.1 per cent in comparison to its global passenger car share of 7.3 per cent, 4.5 per cent in China and 14.7 per cent in the US (FMC, 2015). FMC first entered India in a 50/50 joint venture with Mahindra in 1995, gradually increasing its equity share until the local operation became a full subsidiary of the global parent company.

Other than its plant in the CMA, Ford now operates a plant and oversees a supplier park in Sanand, near the city of Ahmedabad in Gujarat (see below). In the CMA, FIPL operates its facility as an assembly plant and engine manufacturer and oversees an adjacent supplier park which includes a variety of foreign and domestic Tier-1 suppliers including Visteon, JBM Auto, Mando India, Suprajit Engineering, Yapp Automotive Systems, Tata Johnson Controls and many others.

Visteon is part of the Ford Group of companies that was, until 2000, a division of FMC specialising in the manufacture of auto electronic parts and instruments. Today the company has about 11,000 employees globally and, in India, is based at the Ford India Supplier Park in Oragadam where it operates as Visteon Automotive Systems India (VASI) which specialises in auto electronic components production. From Oragadam, it also operates the Visteon Technical and Services Center (VTSC), a software development facility. Visteon also runs a technical centre with a showroom and design facility in Pune in the state of Maharashtra which employs nearly 400 software, electrical and mechanical engineers (Visteon, 2016).

FIPL also relies upon support from independent foreign suppliers like Mando India Limited, a South Korean automotive lighting manufacturer which supplies

HMIL and Renault-Nissan's assembly facilities in the CMA. Another key supplier, Johnson Controls, is an American components manufacturer which originally entered India as a joint venture with Tata Motors but, since 2013, has established a full-subsidiary business as an independent supplier. The firm now manufactures electronic parts and seating and interior parts, with 2,100 employees spread over 11 sites across India, including the CMA (Umbrajkar, 2013).

Thus, FIPL relies upon a wide range of Tier-1 suppliers. One key example is independent Indian Tier-1 company, JBM Auto System. Besides Ford, JBM is a major supplier to its key competitors, including MSIL, Renault-Nissan, Fiat, Toyota and General Motors. Similarly, FIPL purchases cables from the multi-industry and multi-region manufacturer, Suprajit Engineering (see above for JBM and Suprajit's activities in India).

Another major supplier is Yapp Automotive Systems, a Tier-1 Chinese manufacturer of fuel systems from Yangzhou, and global supplier to multiple OEMs including Japanese, American and European corporations, as well as major Chinese state-owned enterprises like SAIC Motor (see below). Yapp is majority-owned by a Chinese state-owned enterprise and claims to be the third largest fuel tank manufacturer by sales volume in the world. It has established a base in India from the city of Kanchipuram (Kanchi), 70 km southwest of Chennai and about 45 km west of the Ford facility in Oragadam (Yapp Automotive, 2016).

Other companies in the Chennai Metro Area

Other than the key passenger car brands manufacturing vehicles in the CMA – HMIL, Renault-Nissan and FIPL – there are numerous other OEMs that are either smaller players in the passenger car market or specialise in other sectors of auto industry production. The German OEM, Daimler, operates a subsidiary truck and bus manufacturing plant – branded as BharatBenz – in Oragadam. This plant manufactures engines and chassis for different models at one site, including mass-produced buses that use chassis made by the British manufacturer, Wrightbus, and a smaller number of Mercedes Benz-branded buses. BharatBenz also competes in the truck market, having sold about 14,000 trucks in India in 2015. Daimler operates research and development facilities in Bengaluru and Pune and, as outlined below, Daimler runs a luxury car plant in the C-SEZ in Maharashtra. Mercedes Benz Research and Development India in Bengaluru employs nearly 2,900 people, making it Daimler's largest R&D site outside Germany (Daimler, 2015).

Another Germany luxury brand, BMW, manufactures eight passenger car and SUV models from its plant in Chennai. In recent times, the company has sought to explicitly align its brand with the Modi Government's 'Make in India' programme by announcing plans to increase locally-manufactured content in car and SUV production from 20 per cent to 50 per cent (Subramaniam, 2015). In order to achieve this, BMW has partnered with seven locally-based suppliers; a mix of foreign Tier-1 suppliers as well as one local OEM and a joint venture supplier. The local OEM is Force Motors which, along with its Chennai plant, has facilities in Baramati (Maharashtra) and Pithampur (Madhya Pradesh).

Force Motors is both an OEM, which manufactures a relatively small number of vans and commercial vehicles – 36,700 units in total forecast by the company for 2015–16 – from its main facility in Pithampur, and a Tier-1 supplier, which manufactures engines and axles for Mercedes Benz in Baramati, and engines and gearboxes for BMW in Chennai (Chaudhary, 2016). While Force Motors sources 30 per cent of its raw material, components and spare parts from imports, it mainly relies upon a range of local manufacturers including Indian Tier-1 suppliers like Suprajit, Gabriel and Jaya Hind Industries, foreign Tier-1 suppliers like Mahle Behr, and machine tools supplied by Japanese OEM, Mitsubishi (Force Motors, 2015).

BMW's key foreign Tier-1 suppliers are American manufacturers, Tenneco Automotive (which provides exhaust pipes) and Lear India (seats), German firms Mahle Behr (heating, ventilation and air conditioning) and Draexlmaier India (door panels) and French firm Valeo India (also heating, ventilation and air conditioning), which also runs plants in Pune and Sanand where it manufactures engine and auto-electric parts (Chaudhary, 2016).

BMW's key joint venture and Tier-1 supplier, ZF Hero Chassis Systems, which manufactures axles for their Chennai operation, is a 50/50 partnership between the Hero Group and German transnational conglomerate, ZF. The joint venture has its headquarters in Delhi, with manufacturing plants in Talegaon Dabhade in the C-SEZ and Halol (Gujarat), and General Motors forming its main client base in India (ZF Hero, 2016). In addition to its global production network in passenger car production, BMW has also recently launched a TVS-manufactured, BMW-branded motorcycle for the local market (BMW, 2015).

Another well-known Indian OEM based in the CMA is Royal Enfield, which has plants at Tirvullur and Oragadam. Originally a famous British motorcycle brand, Royal Enfield was revived in the 1990s through a merger with Indian OEM, Eicher Motors Ltd, a truck and bus manufacturer. The company has succeeded in carving out a niche market and now dominates Eicher Motors' total sales. In 2014, Royal Enfield sold 302,592 motorcycles, of which two per cent were exported. Eicher Motors' total manufacturing base is also primarily located in the CMA where it employed a total of 1,259 full-time workers and sold 39,892 commercial vehicles in 2014. From here, Eicher's commercial vehicles base relies upon a mix of independent, foreign and local Tier-1 suppliers (Eicher Motors, 2014).

Eicher's Indian suppliers include Porwal Auto Components, Suprajit Engineering and Setco Automotive, which is a major clutch manufacturer for commercial vehicles and also supplies Tata Motors, Bharat Benz, Ashok Leyland, Mahindra and other firms from its two Indian plants (Halol, Gujarat and the city of Sitarganj in Uttarakhand), and one each in the UK and the US (Setco, 2016). Eicher also draws upon a range of foreign manufacturers, including the British firm Caparo Engineering, and American brake manufacturer Wabco India, which has emerged from a joint venture with the Indian OEM TVS, to become a major independent commercial vehicle supplier with over 3,200 employees spread across five Indian plants, including Pantnagar in Uttarakhand, Jaipur in Rajasthan, Jamshedpur in Jharkhand and, in the CMA, Chennai and Tiruvullur (Wabco, 2016). Eicher has also been part of a truck manufacturing joint venture with Volvo Trucks India – known as VE Commercial Vehicles – based in the town of Pithampur in the state of Madhya Pradesh (Eicher Motors, 2014; Volvo Group, 2015).

The Chakan Special Economic Zone and Pune district

The Chakan Special Economic Zone (C-SEZ) is an industrial area designated by the Government of Maharashtra via its development arm, the Maharashtra Industrial Development Corporation (MIDC). This SEZ is based around the town of Chakan which lies 32 km north of Pune, Maharashtra's most populated city after the capital, Mumbai. Within the C-SEZ are foreign OEMs – Skoda, Volkswagen and Mercedes Benz. In addition, the C-SEZ has major manufacturing facilities operated by Indian OEMs, including passenger car and commercial vehicle manufacturer Mahindra, two- and three-wheeler conglomerate Bajaj Auto, as well as a smaller site for Indian OEM and parts supplier, Force Motors.

In the Pimpri-Chinchwad area, Jaguar/Land Rover and Indian OEM, Premier Limited, each operate a factory. This area forms the northwestern part of the Pune metropolitan area that accounts for around half of the city's population. The town of Talegaon Dabhade, 35 km northwest of Pune, is the base for a General Motors (GM) factory co-run with SAIC Motor, a Chinese state-owned enterprise from Shanghai which operates as GM's key strategic partner in the Chinese market.

There are also several OEM facilities in the state that lie outside the immediate vicinity of the C-SEZ. For example, the regional city of Baramati lies about 100 km southeast of Pune and is the base for major Italian two-wheeler and commercial vehicle manufacturer, Piaggio. Finally, Indian OEM and industrial conglomerate, Tata Motors, and the Italian OEM Fiat, operate plants in the village of Ranjangaon, about 50 km northeast of Pune.

All of the various sites mentioned above fall within the District of Pune, one of 36 districts within the vast geographic expanse of Maharashtra, India's third largest state by area and second most populated, with over 120 million inhabitants. The C-SEZ and it surroundings are also the base for global production networks based in other industries, especially consumer electronics and white goods. As outlined towards the end of this chapter, Maharashtra has several cities and regions further afield that also provide a base for motor vehicle manufacturing. However, the bulk of production in this state lies within the C-SEZ and its surrounds.

Bajaj Auto and Piaggio

These two companies – the first, an Indian OEM and industrial conglomerate, and the second, an Italian OEM and global scooter brand – are discussed here together because of their competition in the two- and three-wheeler market. Piaggio's brand is often synonymous with the Vespa scooter, a global brand among two-wheeler consumers. Bajaj Auto is also a global brand in two-wheeler production, although perhaps better-known as a brand for three-wheeler passenger vehicles and auto rickshaws, as well as small trucks, frequently used to transport goods and people across the great urban centres and urban-rural corridors of South and Southeast Asia.

By March 2016, Bajaj Auto claimed to employ 9,347 people at four plants across India. Apart from its factory at Mahalunge Village, outside Chakan, the company also has factories in Pune, as well as the village of Waluj outside the city of Aurangabad, 235 km northeast of Pune, and in the town of Pantnagar in the northern Indian state of Uttarakhand. Of these, the Waluj facility has the largest capacity (capable of making over three million vehicles per year), followed by Pantnagar (1.8 million vehicles) and Chakan (1.2 million vehicles). In 2015–16, Bajaj Auto sold a total of 1,898,957 motorcycles in India and exported a further 1,459,295 motorcycles (Bajaj Auto, 2016).

In terms of domestic motorcycle sales, it remains well behind Hero MotoCorp and Honda (HMSI). In this context, the company has framed 'creative differentiation' of products as the 'the single most important factor that separates a market or segments leaders from others' (Bajaj Auto, 2016: 14). The company's key low-cost exports products are led by its Waluj facility, while its Chakan site focuses on 'high end' motorcycle brands.

In contrast to its domestic sales, Bajaj is India's leading motorcycle exporter, exporting 44 per cent of its total motorcycle production in 2015–16 – with an annual average share of 36 per cent in the eight years to 2015–16 – and claiming markets in a total of 78 countries. The company's largest export market is in Africa (43 per cent of total export sales in 2015–16), followed by South Asia and Middle East (31 per cent) and Latin America (20 per cent). Most of the company's exports come from its Waluj facility, which exported 72 per cent and 53 per cent of its total motorcycle and three-wheeler production volume respectively in 2015–16. By comparison, Hero MotoCorp exports about three per cent of its total two-wheeler production volume. In 2014–15, Bajaj exported nearly eight motorcycles for every Hero bike exported. It is also India's leading producer and exporter of three-wheeled vehicles. In 2015–16, Bajaj's three-wheeler sales of 942,533 represented a 57 per cent market share, including a 47 per cent share of domestic sales and a 69 per cent share of exports (Bajaj Auto, 2016).

The company maintains a seven-day inventory policy with suppliers, which it calls 'business partners'. These suppliers are offered training for personnel, as well as training in sales, maintenance and aftermarket production (Bajaj Auto, 2016). Importantly, Bajaj looked to implement its own version of lean production during the 2000s as economic liberalisation and market competition increased in Indian auto markets. From 2002 until 2010, it streamlined its supply base from about 800 to 185 key suppliers.

By 2010, just 15 companies supplied 75 per cent of components to its Pantnagar facility and 50 companies supplied all components to its Chakan facility (Seth, 2010). By 2016, Bajaj had nearly 200 key components and raw materials suppliers for all of its main assembly facilities. These include JBM – part of the multi-industry independent supplier, JBM Group (see above) – which supplies chassis frames, MRF and Dunlop for tyres, Minda for locks and ignitions, Endurance and Makino Auto for brakes and clutches, Varroc for plastic parts and Silco for wires and cables.

MRF (Madras Rubber Factory) Limited, is an Indian, family-owned, company which claims to be the largest tyre manufacturer in India. It operates factories in Chennai, Perambalur district and Arkonam in Tamil Nadu, Puducherry, Kottayam (in the state of Kerala), Medak (Andhra Pradesh) and in Goa (MRF, 2016). Minda is part of the Indian-owned JP Minda Group which is also a key supplier to Honda's motorcycles operations in northern India (see Honda section above).

Endurance Technologies is another large, Indian-owned, independent components manufacturer. With over 5000 employees, 18 plants across India and seven plants in Europe, it claims to be India's largest aluminium die-casting components manufacturer, although it also manufacturers cast iron and bonded plastic parts. Apart from the brakes and clutches it manufactures for Bajaj, Endurance makes aluminum die cast alloy wheels, engine, suspension and transmission parts. Its European operations mainly sell engine and transmission parts to passenger car OEMs. In India, half of its 18 plants are in the city and surrounds of Aurangabad, in the east of Maharashtra, as well as four plants in Pune, two in Pantnagar and one each in Manesar, Chennai and Sanand (Endurance Group, 2016).

However, Bajaj does not rely exclusively on Endurance for brake and clutch parts, also buying from another Indian-owned Tier-1 supplier, Makino Auto, to satisfy its operational needs in Pantnagar. Makino Auto is based in Haridwar, 200 km northeast of Bajaj's Pantnagar facility, as well as in two plants in Greater Noida and Sahibabad in the NCR (Makino Auto, 2016). Another key Bajaj supplier, the Varroc Group, is a major Indian-owned conglomerate which manufacturers and exports engine, chassis and electrical parts. It claims to have tripled its revenue in the 2000s as Bajaj expanded and implemented lean production supply chain relations, with Bajaj constituting about half of the company's revenue (Seth, 2010; Varroc Group, 2016).

While Italian OEM Piaggio competes with Bajaj in the two- and three-wheeler markets in India, it remains a much smaller manufacturer in terms of volume and sales. In 2014–15, Piaggio sold 212,600 units in the country. However, this represented 41 per cent of the company's total global sales, making India by far its largest country market. Piaggio regards India as its 'most important two-wheeler market' and the 'most important motorcycle market in Asia' (Piaggio Group, 2015: 24). The company's 2,761 India-based employees in 2015 represented 37 per cent of its total global employee base, just behind its employee base in Italy (48 per cent). Piaggio is present in India as a low-cost but relatively low-value operation. While its Indian operation's share of total group production volume and employment is very high, Piaggio's investment in R&D in India in the same period was just 10 per cent of its global investment in R&D.

Piaggio's investment in India is thus focused on high-volume, low-value markets in three- and four-wheeled light commercial vehicles, in which it competes primarily with Bajaj, and Vespa scooters which represent a portion of a national market dominated by Honda. All its Indian products are assembled from a single plant in Baramati, 100 km southeast of Pune. For three-wheelers, Piaggio compares more favourably with the market leader, Bajaj. In 2014–15, the company produced 514,000 three-wheeled vehicles. Together, Bajaj and Piaggio dominate the three-wheeler market in auto rickshaws and other light commercial vehicles (Piaggio Group, 2015).

Mahindra

Mahindra and Mahindra Limited – commonly known simply as Mahindra – is part of an Indian family-owned industrial, financial and business services conglomerate (the Mahindra Group) that includes an IT services company (Tech Mahindra) and Mahindra financial services, as well as agricultural vehicles and equipment and automotive manufacturing arms. Globally, the Mahindra Group has around 200,000 employees and claims a presence in 20 industries. Among several subsidiaries, Mahindra also owns and operates the former Korean-owned automotive OEM, SsangYong.

In the auto industry, Mahindra represents a major OEM in the Indian market, having previously partnered with Ford in a joint venture (see FIPL section above), and occupies significant positions in the commercial vehicles and passenger car markets. It claims to be the market leader in utility vehicles and small commercial vehicles, with a 38 and 51 per cent market share respectively in 2015–16. It also claims to be India's largest tractor manufacturer, with a 40 per cent market share, and exports to dozens of countries, including to the US via its local subsidiary, Mahindra USA (MUSA) (Mahindra, 2016).

Across its automotive and agricultural vehicle divisions, most of Mahindra's value is generated within India, with less than three per cent of its total costs comprised of imported raw materials or components in 2015. In addition, Mahindra's exports have been growing, exporting over 36,000 passenger cars and commercial vehicles and a further 11,545 tractors in 2015–16, mainly to African and other South Asian countries (Sri Lanka, Nepal, Bangladesh and Bhutan) as well as Latin America. Across both of these divisions, Mahindra employed nearly 39,300 workers by March 2016, or around 20 per cent of the Mahindra Group's total global employment. Forty-nine per cent of this (19,176 people) was comprised of 'temporary, contract or casual' workers. Three per cent of its regular workforce was female (Mahindra, 2016: 137).

Mahindra operates assembly factories in Chakan, as well as the regional cities of Bhandara and Nashik in the state of Maharashtra, where it has an engine plant at the hill station of Igatpuri; Haridwar in northern India, the town of Zaheerabad in Telangana state (about 100 km west of Hyderabad); and an electrical vehicle manufacturing facility (Mahindra REVA) in Bengaluru. Across its automotive and agricultural divisions, the company has over 800 suppliers, which are mainly clustered in supplier parks in Chakan and Zaheerabad (Mahindra, 2016). These facilities are strategically located, with the C-SEZ reachable from Zaheerabad in a single day's drive east-west along the Mumbai Highway via Pune. Nashik is a 200km drive north of Chakan, while Bhandara is a one-day drive north of the Zaheerabad plant and supplier park.

In 2014, the company announced plans to consolidate its supplier base from 800 down to 450 (Seth, 2014). Mahindra has a high number of Indian-owned Tier-1 suppliers like the multi-industry JBM Group and the Mungi Group, which supplies Mahindra from its bases in Chakan, Nashik and Zaheerabad. Mahindra also operates several joint ventures and partnerships with Tier-1 suppliers including Mahindra Sona and Mahindra Ugine Steel. In addition, the company buys from some foreign-owned subsidiaries like the NCR-based American-Japanese joint venture, Lumax Industries, and the American auto-electrical and seating manufacturer, Lear Automotive (Pawar, 2009; Seth, 2014).

Volkswagen India and Skoda Auto India

The Volkswagen Group's (VW-AG) foray into the Indian passenger car market was initially led by its Czech subsidiary company, Skoda – known in India as Skoda Auto India Private Limited (SAIPL). SAIPL's first Indian plant was established in 2000 in the city of Aurangabad in central Maharashtra, 230 km northeast of Chakan. This was followed in 2009, with the beginning of car production at Volkswagen India's (VWI) major plant in Chakan. In 2014–15, the VWI Chakan plant and the SAIPL Aurangabad plants manufactured 12,676 and 14,445 vehicles respectively.

For the sake of comparison, this total (27,121) is just two per cent of MSIL's sales volume over the same period. VW-AG's total sales volume in India is a fraction – just 0.74 per cent – of VW-AG's global sales. Overall, compared to India, the group sells 51 times more vehicles in China, where it is a pioneering and highly-successful foreign manufacturer (Volkswagen AG, 2016). VW-AG also has an indirect presence in truck manufacturing in India via the Swedish brand, Scania, which operates in the Narasapura Industrial Area, on the northwestern fringe of the Bengaluru (Bangalore) urban region. VW-AG is the majority shareholder in Scania and effectively controls the company's global operations (Scania, 2014).

VWI and SAIPL remain relatively small players in the Indian passenger car market due, in part, to their late-comer status. SAIPL's production volume in 2014–15 is very similar to its volume nearly a decade earlier, producing 12,599 vehicles in 2006 (when it employed just 378 workers). SAIPL has remained a 'bridgehead' investment by VW-AG since its foundation in 2000, with a focus on imported parts due to the lack of its own local supplier base in Aurangabad and a focus on low-cost production.

Today, the Aurangabad plant also manufactures VW and Audi-branded cars (Skoda, 2015). In 2015, over 11,000 Audi-branded luxury sedans were manufactured at this plant using fully-imported parts from Audi's plants in Germany, Slovakia, Hungary and Spain (Audi, 2015). The Aurangabad plant operates on a similar basis to Skoda's plants in Eastern European countries like Bosnia and Herzegovina, Poland, the Ukraine and Russia, but lacks the geographical proximity to fully benefit from Skoda's manufacturing base at Mladá Boleslav in the Czech Republic (Becker-Ritterspach, 2009: 214–19). SAIPL has a strong focus on assembling imported, fully-manufactured engine and transmission components with other parts. Kits for engines and transmissions are transported in trucks from Mladá Boleslav to the German port of Breman, then shipped to Mumbai and transported in trucks to Chakan via Pune. The whole process of CKD importation takes up to two months from plant to plant (Hogg,

2015). However, other components such as chassis, axles, wheels and interiors are locally-manufactured, with the VW claiming that 82 per cent of non-engine and transmission parts were manufactured in the region-up from 40 per cent in 2009 – and publicising an aim of 90 per cent (Mondal, 2015).

Like most other OEMs, SAIPL purchases from a mix of foreign and Indian suppliers. Foreign suppliers include German sheet metal and moulding company FIBRO which acts as a Tier-2 supplier, manufacturing press tools for Spanish auto components manufacturer, Gestamp, which presses the chassis for Skoda and other VW-branded models (Economic Times, 2011). Other suppliers include American industrial conglomerate, Honeywell, and the Italian-Spanish company, Sogefi India, which operates three joint ventures with Indian companies in Chakan as well as Bengaluru, and employs a total of 350 workers. These joint ventures manufacture a range of components, including suspension bars, air ventilation parts, fuel and oil filtration parts (Sogefi Group, 2016).

Finally, Gabriel India is a major independent supplier, part of the Indian family-owned Anand Group which claims a total of 16 manufacturing joint ventures, various associate companies and 14,000 employees spread across 61 locations in 11 Indian states. Of this, Gabriel claims 2,700 employees, and operates two plants in Chakan that service VWI's assembly plant, as well as one in the town of Ambad, 200 km to the southeast, and, in southern India, the towns of Malur in Karnataka and Hosur in Tamil Nadu. To the north, Gabriel operates plants in the village of Parwanoo in Himachal Pradesh, Khandsa village in Haryana, the city of Dewas in Madhya Pradesh and Sanand in Gujarat (Gabriel India, 2016).

General Motors and SAIC Motor

The General Motors Company (GM), the largest of America's 'Detroit Three' automotive OEMs ahead of Ford and Fiat Chrysler (FCA), has operated in India since 1995 in partnership with the Chinese state-owned enterprise, SAIC Motor, which was formerly known as the Shanghai Automotive Industry Corporation. In India, GM owns the majority of the local operation, with SAIC Motor owning a minority share in an assembly plant in the town of Talegaon Dabhade, 20 km west of Chakan. However, GM closed its second assembly plant in the town of Halol in Gujarat in April 2017.

By 2012, GM had amassed 722 components suppliers for its Indian operations, including 200 companies that supply for GM's global and local operations (Pandit, 2012). Among the company's key suppliers are a range of global manufacturers, such as BorgWarner (see Honda section above), domestic manufacturers like Sundram Fasteners and Suprajit, and global-local joint ventures like ZF Hero (see

BMW section above) and Mahle Behr (see Honda section). Sundram Fasteners is a subsidiary of the TVS Group, an Indian OEM with its headquarters in Chennai, and Tier-1 component suppliers, which manufactures metal parts, fasteners, radiator caps and other parts.

The role of SAIC Motor as a minority shareholder in GM's Indian operations is linked to its role as GM's strategic partner in China's auto assembly industry. This, in turn, reflects the peculiarities of industry policy and automotive industry development in China. Since allowing foreign OEMs to establish operations in the 1980s, the Chinese government has maintained a strict policy that forces foreign OEMs to participate in joint ventures with local State-Owned Enterprises (SOEs) in which they are limited to a 49 per cent equity share. The Shanghai-based SAIC Motor was one of the earliest SOEs to establish a joint venture in the auto industry in the 1980s (with Volkswagen). In 1997, SAIC Motor formed a new joint venture with GM (Gallagher, 2006; Chin, 2010).

Like Shanghai Volkswagen, Shanghai GM has gone on to become one of the most successful industry partnerships in China. This enabled GM to take advantage of SAIC Motor 's capital to expand its Indian operations. In 2012, SAIC Motor purchased a share of GM's assembly operation near Talegaon Dabhade in the C-SEZ. This has led to recent speculation that SAIC Motor, as well as privately-owned Chinese OEM Great Wall Motors, is considering their own independent investments in the C-SEZ. It has also led to reports that SAIC Moor might take-over management of GM's currently-closed plant in Gujarat (Hindustan Times, 2016).[4]

Fiat India

FCA India Automobiles Private Limited (Fiat India, or FI) is a full subsidiary of its Italian parent company, FCA SpA Italy, and operates a manufacturing assembly facility in Ranjangaon, approximately 50 km northeast of Pune. From this site, it manufactures small car models and employs around 2500 people. Through Fiat's global acquisition partner, Chrysler, which also operates a small facility in Chennai, FI is also licensed to distribute Jeep-branded vehicles in India. FI recently entered into a new joint venture with Tata to produce Tata-branded medium-sized cars, engines and gearboxes (Fiat, 2013). FI also has a presence in domestic commercial vehicle manufacturing via Fiat Group company, New Holland Fiat India Private Limited.

---

[4] Other Chinese OEMs reportedly considering new investments in India are BeiqiFoton and Changan Automobile in the C-SEZ and in the state of Andhra Pradesh, respectively (Thakkar, 2017b).

Fiat first entered India in 1996 through a joint venture with Indian OEM, Premier Limited, which gave the Italian subsidiary the local knowledge, ties and production platform to commence vehicle manufacturing. Interestingly, Fiat first established a licensing agreement with Premier in 1951, with Premier tasked to manufacture Fiat-badged cars (the Fiat 500 and 1100). This agreement expired in 1972 and Premier continued to use the same model designs and technology under its own brand (Becker-Ritterspach, 2009). Premier itself was, and remains, a very small OEM within the auto industry – with less than 600 production-line employees and producing fewer than 200 vehicles in 2014–15 – and is more focused on engineering and manufacturing tools, Computer Numerical Control (CNC) machinery and components used in railways and windmills (Premier Ltd, 2015).

Lacking the capacity to establish a greenfield site, Fiat initially used its 51 per cent stake in the joint venture to import Fiat Uno CKD kits for assembly at Premier's existing site at Kurla in the outskirts of Mumbai. This operation was later turned into a full subsidiary of Fiat and became part of Fiat's global strategy – the 'World Car project' formulated in the mid-1990s – in which 'mature' or older model designs were manufactured and sold in emerging markets, while state-of-the-art designs were reserved for European markets (Becker-Ritterspach, 2009). In 1997, Fiat established a new company, a full subsidiary of the Fiat Group called Fiat India Auto, and signed an agreement with the Government of Maharashtra to establish a greenfield site at Ranjangaon.

However, progress in this new venture was stalled as Fiat became preoccupied with gradually buying-out Premier's stake in its existing joint venture until it became a full subsidiary of Fiat in 2004. FI consistently struggled to manage the factory according to its parent company's World Car strategy. Based on Fiat's Cordoba plant in Argentina, this assumed the production of at least 400 vehicles per day. The Kurla site struggled to manufacture half of this volume which made it less economical for FI to establish an adjacent supplier park. While, by 2002, FI had around 120 suppliers in India, the vast majority were based hundreds, and even thousands, of kilometres away – in Pune (21 per cent of the total number of suppliers), the NCR (24 per cent), Chennai (9 per cent) and Bengaluru (6 per cent). Even though 36 per cent of suppliers were based in Mumbai, this was still over 100 km from the Kurla site (Becker-Ritterspach, 2009: 168).

Finally, in 2006, FI shifted its whole car production capacity from Kurla to Ranjangaon where it began a joint venture with Tata Motors, with 50 per cent ownership each in the new operation. From its base in Ranjangaon, Fiat currently purchases automotive components from a wide range of suppliers. The company has previously claimed that 90 per cent of the components used in its production line are domestically manufactured, although it also imports parts from China, Brazil, Poland and Turkey, as well as Italy. Among locally-produced components,

Fiat claims that half come from Indian-based global companies and 90 per cent are based within 100 km of the Ranjangaon plant (Kumar, 2014).

Key Fiat suppliers include captive Tier-1 suppliers like Magneti Marelli and Comau, foreign Tier-1 suppliers like Denso and Mahle Behr, foreign/domestic joint ventures such as Western Thomson and a large number of domestic Tier-1 suppliers. As a key part of the Fiat group of companies globally, Magneti Marelli is also a strategic partner of Fiat in India with manufacturing plants in Ranjangaon as well as Pune, Chennai and Gurugram (Magneti Marelli, 2016). Interestingly, while Magneti Marelli is a captive Tier-1 supplier for Fiat, it also acts in India as a major Tier-1 components supplier for MSIL's engine operations (Suzuki Powertrain) in the NCR (see MSIL section above).

The design, product and technological capacity of Fiat's strategic partners like Magneti Marelli means that rival OEMs like MSIL and Fiat are able to mutually benefit from these cross-networking arrangements: the Fiat Group benefits, if indirectly, from MSIL sales, profits and ongoing demand for Magneti Marelli products, while MSIL benefits from Fiat's product quality and capacity.

By utilising Magneti Marelli's capacity in this way, the Fiat Group has been able to invest in alternative auto markets. For example, Magneti Marelli established a joint venture with Hero MotoCorp in late 2012 to produce engine components for the Indian OEM's two-wheeler operations in the NCR, with Magneti Marelli holding a 40 per cent stake in the operation (Fiat, 2013: 76). Like Magneti Marelli, ComauSpA, which operates an iron casting plant in Pune, is both a captive Tier-1 supplier to Fiat and a major supplier to Renault-Nissan in the CMA.

In addition, there are a variety of Indian-owned Tier-1 suppliers that sell components to Fiat's Ranjangaon operation. Some of the suppliers are captive operations of Indian OEMs, such as tool-maker, ASAL Auto Stamping, 75 per cent of which is owned by the Tata Group. ASAL began as a PSU in the 1950s and today the Government of India has 25 per cent ownership of the company. It operates four plants across India, including at Chakan, Pune (in the Bhosari industrial area), Halol in Gujarat and Pantnagar in Uttarakhand. Other than Fiat and Tata Motors, ASAL Auto Stamping sells tools to GM, Piaggio and truck manufacturer Ashok Leyland (ASAL, 2016).

Fiat also purchases components from independent Indian Tier-1 suppliers, including the subsidiary of an Indian OEM, Eicher Engineering Components, and Rasandik Engineering Industries, which operates a manufacturing facility nearly 1000 km to the south of Fiat's assembly plant, in the city of Mysuru (Mysore) in southern Karnataka (Rasandik, 2016). Fiat also purchases components from Saket Metal Technocraft Private Limited which is linked to Magneti Marelli's operations in the Ballabhgarh industrial area of Faridabad in the NCR, where it operates three plants, as well as a plant in the city of Dharwad, about 450 km to the south of Ranjangaon (Saket MTC, 2016). Another independent, multi-industry

Indian Tier-1 supplier is OmrBagla Automotive Systems India, which transports aluminium alloy components from its plant in the city of Aurangabad, 180 km to the northeast (OmrBagla, 2016).

Mercedes Benz India

Mercedes Benz India (MBI) operates a CKD assembly factory in Chakan, which it established in 2009. Its parent company Daimler is also a major truck and bus manufacturer in the CMA and, with MBI, operates R&D facilities in the cities of Pune and Bengaluru (see above). MBI initially entered India in 1994 in a joint venture with truck manufacturer Tata Engineering and Locomotive Company Limited (TELCO). Daimler had established relations with Tata as early as 1954, when it began sharing technology for truck production. While technology-sharing ended in 1969, Daimler continued to hold a 10 per cent equity stake in Tata's truck manufacturing operations.

In the 1990s, MBI moved to establish itself as a leading luxury car manufacturer in India. Initially based in Pune, MBI followed a similar strategy to Daimler's approach in other emerging markets like Indonesia, Malaysia, Thailand, Vietnam, the Philippines and South Africa by relying upon CKD assembly production. Initially, the partnership with TELCO failed to live up to relatively modest volume expectations. By 2002, with a fully-installed capacity of only 20,000 vehicles, the site was producing only 1500 cars per annum with 320 workers. However, by this time, MBI had transformed the site into a full subsidiary of its parent company, and it swiftly moved to establish a dominant position in the luxury car segment by the mid-2000s (Becker-Ritterspach, 2009: 173–76).

Other regions and lead firms in India

Gujarat

The western Indian state of Gujarat has been a locus for economic and political change during the period of India's economic liberalisation. Gujarat represented one of India's higher-growth states during the 1990s and 2000s. Part of this process has been the rise of a new cluster for auto manufacturing since the 1990s, centred on Sanand, which lies adjacent to the state capital Ahmedabad, and the town of Halol, about 150 km to the southeast .

These two industrial regions represent sites which potentially enable Gujarat to become the fourth key automotive cluster in India and a potential rival to FDI, production volumes and exports in the NCR, CMA or C-SEZ in passenger car production. There are several reasons why this is possible. First, Gujarat is now home to five global OEMs, including Tata Motors and Ford (FIPL) in Sanand, Honda in Vithalapur, and GM and Hero MotoCorp in Halol. Hero's facility was due to begin production in 2016–17. FIPL's facility in Sanand includes an adjacent 150-acre supplier park, where 15 Tier-1 companies are based, including captive Tier-1 suppliers like Visteon, the Indo-Japanese joint venture Motherson Sumi and the Canadian manufacturer, Magna (Das, 2013). In addition, MSIL commenced passenger car production at a new 700-acre facility in Hansalpur, 60 km west of Ahmedabad, in 2017. Assuming these plans are fully implemented, Gujarat will soon become a base for six high-volume global OEMs, which is more than the existing clusters in the NCR and CMA. MSIL's future presence as the market leader in passenger car production may even enable Gujarat to outstrip the NCR as a car-producing region.

Despite this potential, there is considerable uncertainty about the future of GM's currently-closed plant in Halol. This has become a pressing issue for GM, given the difficulties it has experienced in expanding in the Indian passenger car market, with its share of local sales falling against the industry's dominant players like MSIL and HMIL (Kannan, 2016). A related problem has been regulatory change, with the Supreme Court of India recently restricting the use of diesel-fuelled passenger vehicles in the national capital, New Delhi, a decision that has also had an impact on Ford and Fiat's investment strategies (Business Insider, 2016).

GM's challenges led to the company announcing plans to close its Halol plant and its intention to centralise subsidiary operations to its Talegaon Dabhade plant in the C-SEZ. By 2016, the Halol plant employed about 900 regular workers and a further 300 contract workers across its 172-acre site with an annual capacity of 110,000 passenger cars. However, the Government of Gujarat pressured GM to delay plans to close from its original cessation date (June 2016) until March 2017 at the earliest (Hindu Business Line, 2015; Pathak and Rodricks, 2016).

Despite the closure of GM's Halol plant, the presence of major car manufacturers like Tata, MSIL, FIPL and, in the two-wheeler segment, Hero MotoCorp and Honda, is likely to ensure that Gujarat remains a major and growing cluster for auto manufacturing. In particular, Tata Motors' operation in Sanand is internationally famous for its production of the Nano small car. This has become an important manufacturing base for this bastion of Indian industry and engineering.

Tata Motors forms part of the Mumbai-based Tata Group, an Indian multinational industrial, financial and business services conglomerate which is predominately owned by members of the Tata family, one of the most famous and powerful business families in the country. The Tata family first emerged as a corporate power late in the nineteenth century as a textiles manufacturer. Its operations were central to the transformation of Mumbai into India's erstwhile industrial centre. Tata Motors was originally established by a family-run holding company as a locomotive manufacturer in 1945. In 1954, it was able to leverage its influence to establish a joint venture with Daimler Benz to manufacture trucks in India. In 1969, Tata began to manufacture and sell trucks and buses under its own brand, establishing itself as the dominant commercial vehicle manufacturer in the country in the 1970s and 80s (Ray and Ray, 2011).

Thus, the Tata Group was already a key player in Indian auto manufacturing, primarily in commercial vehicles such as trucks and buses, prior to the establishment of MSIL and Hero Honda as government-favoured joint ventures in the 1980s. In 1985, Tata was granted a license to manufacture passenger cars. In 1995, Tata Motors began to compete in the small car market with the launch of the Indica under Ratan Tata's leadership. The Indica went on to become the third best-selling small car in India.

However, Ratan Tata pushed to compete directly with the Maruti 800 (see MSIL section) by producing a much cheaper version that would be affordable to poorer sections of society who were focused on two-wheeler purchases and remained locked out of the passenger car market. According to Tata, there was a developmental as well as a commercial imperative for such a low-cost, 'people's car':

> The mandate has gone out to our people that we now really need to look seriously at the needs of the larger part of the Indian income pyramid, where most consumers can be found. But there is also a social or dreamy side to it. Today in India, you often see four people on a scooter: a man driving, his little kid in front, and his wife on the back holding a baby between them. It's a dangerous form of transportation, and it leads to accidents and hospitalisations and deaths. If we can make something available on four wheels–all-weather and safe–then I think we will have done something for that mass of young Indians (Ray and Ray, 2011).

From this vision emerged the Tata Nano – a small car marketed at Indian families. Dubbed the 'one lakh' car by the Press, the Nano cost around ₹100,000 or approximately half the price of a Maruti 800. In order to keep input costs down, Tata Motors engaged several independent suppliers in the design process as well as components manufacturing, including Lumax Industries for headlights and taillights, Sona Kayo Steering Systems for the steering column and Bosch India for the adaptation of a motorcycle starter motor for use in a small passenger car. The Nano used a two-cylinder engine rather than the four normally used in small cars. This produced the same horsepower as a mid-range motorcycle manufactured in the United States (Ray and Ray, 2011). This innovation and cost-cutting allowed Tata to launch the Nano in 2008 in the small car market.

While the Nano was rolling off the line from Tata's Sanand factory by early 2010, the car has not succeeded in denting MSIL's domination of the small car market or staving off the challenge from other key passenger car producers including HMIL and, more recently, Renault-Nissan. In 2014–15, only 16,901 units were sold, or the equivalent of one month's production at full capacity at the Sanand plant. By 2015, Tata was focused on marketing more expensive, upgraded Nano models – the CX and LX, and the basic Nano model was no longer featured on its website. Bo Nielsen and Wilhite (2015) have argued that the core problem was the failure of the car to tap into consumerist aspirations and middle-class distinctions of taste in the passenger car market. Put simply, the Nano's frugality and simplicity – crucial to keeping the vehicle's price low – gave the car's owners 'nothing to brag about' (Bo Nielsen and Wilhite, 2015: 381).

Despite this setback and the apparent failure of Ratan Tata's grand vision, Tata Motors remains a core part of the Tata Group, which also has multiple interests in steel production, energy, IT, telecommunications and software services, chemicals, consumer retail, food and beverage manufacturing and hospitality. Tata Motors remains a market leader in commercial vehicles production and, in this segment, primarily competes with another local conglomerate, Mahindra (see above). In 2015–16, Tata Motors sold 511,931 units (both commercial vehicles and passenger cars), 11 per cent of which was exported. Of its total domestic sales volume, 70 per cent was in the commercial vehicles market, with the remainder in passenger cars. If we include exports as well as domestic sales, commercial vehicles represented 7 per cent of Tata's production volume (Tata Motors, 2016).

The company's exports are overwhelmingly commercial vehicles, representing 93 per cent of total company exports in 2015–16, with major markets in South Asia (Sri Lanka, Bangladesh and Nepal) as well as the Middle East, Africa, Southeast Asia and Australia. Tata Motors is also a major military vehicle manufacturer for the Government of India. The company overwhelmingly relies on locally-manufactured components and raw materials, which represented 96 per cent of total purchases in 2015–16 (Tata Motors, 2016). In addition, the company has major overseas investments, especially via its acquisition of British auto brands, Jaguar and Land Rover, from Ford in 2008.

Under Tata's watch, Jaguar and Land Rover operate a plant in the Pimpri-Chinchwad area of Pune where it assembles CKD kits which have been imported from the subsidiary's export platform in England (Jaguar Land Rover, 2015). Daewoo, the South Korean OEM purchased by Tata Motors in 2011, sold 9,116 vehicles globally in 2015–16 (Tata Motors, 2016: 78). In China, Tata Motors operates in a joint venture with the state-owned OEM Chery Automobile. Tata Motors has manufacturing facilities in Bangladesh, Brazil, China, Senegal, South Africa, Thailand, Ukraine, and R&D facilities in Germany, Italy, Spain, Sweden, the United Arab Emirates and the United States. It also holds a 50 per cent share in Fiat's Indian operations.

Other than its car assembly plant in Sanand, Tata Motors operates two assembly manufacturing plants, plus the Jaguar Land Rover assembly in Pune District, plants in the city of Jamshedpur (Jharkhand), Pantnagar (Uttarakhand), the city of Dharwad (Karnataka), the town of Pithampur (Madhya Pradesh), and in the cities of Lucknow (Uttar Pradesh) and Mumbai, which serves as headquarters for the company's operations. Across these plants, the company employed 52,825 workers by March 2016. Of this, 50 per cent were employed on a 'temporary/contractual/casual basis' and three per cent of its regular workforce was female (Tata Motors, 2016: 191).

Tata Motors' supply policy favours Tier-1 suppliers which form joint ventures with the company. The Tata Group has generally used another subsidiary company – Tata AutoComp Systems Limited (TACO), in which Tata Motors has a 26 per cent investment – to establish joint ventures and co-investment schemes with foreign suppliers. Key examples of this include German brake manufacturer Knorr Bremse, or Japanese companies like Tata Yazaki Auto Comp Limited, a wire harness manufacturer, or Tata Toyo Radiators Limited.

Tata's aim in these cases is to use the joint ventures to tailor foreign expertise to its local product specifications, particularly in the commercial vehicles sector. Johnson Controls, the American seats and interior parts manufacturer, is an example of a company which originally entered India via a joint venture with TACO but, in 2013, split to form a full subsidiary business.

Tata Motors also relies on a range of foreign and Indian suppliers, including the Anand Group, the German conglomerates Bosch and Continental, Delphi – the American captive supplier to GM, and Denso – the Japanese captive supplier to the Toyota Group. Other independent suppliers include American brake manufacturer Wabco, and the Indian companies – Suprajit, Dali and Samir Engineering and Highco Engineers.

Many of these firms operate facilities in Tata 'vendor parks' in Sanand and Pantnagar, established by the company in recent years to facilitate lean production supply relations. Tata also purchases from some other OEMs, such as Indian firm TVS, and, from FIPL for Jaguar Land Rover's plant in Pune (Tata Motors, 2016: 148).

Uttarakhand

The second emerging region in Indian auto manufacturing is in the northern state of Uttarakhand, centred on the city of Haridwar and the town of Pantnagar, approximately 100 km west of the India-Nepal border on the edge of the Himalayas. Like the centres of automotive manufacturing in the state of Gujarat, production in Uttarakhand does not so much represent a *single* regional cluster of production, but two sub-clusters, with Pantnagar located over 200 km to the southeast of Haridwar, or about a five-hour drive along National Highway 34.

However, unlike Gujarat and the three large regional clusters of Indian auto manufacturing, which generally incorporate a mix of foreign and domestic firms, Uttarakhand's production centres are based entirely upon the global production networks of Indian-owned OEMs. The larger centre, Haridwar, provides a base for two Indian OEMs, Hero MotoCorp in the two-wheeler segment, and Mahindra in passenger car production. Pantnagar is the base for Bajaj two-wheeler manufacturing and Tata Motors' commercial vehicle production.

Due to the role of Indian OEMs, the supply chain in both urban regions tends also to be dominated by Indian-owned Tier-1 and Tier-2 manufacturers, including the strategic partners of these OEMs. Tata Motors oversees a 'vendor park' in Pantnagar, for example, which is one of the company's three main supplier clusters – the other two are based in Sanand to supply the Nano plant, and in Jamshedpur in the state of Jharkhand (see Tata Motors section above). Similarly, Hero MotoCorp's supplier park in Haridwar is rivalled only by its cluster at its first factory in Gurugram (see Hero MotoCorp section above).

Like Tata Motors, the Hero Group prefers to partner with suppliers in which it has a controlling or influential equity share, and which also enables the Group to draw suppliers into the Munjal family's network of companies. For example, the Munjals control key Tier-1 suppliers in Haridwar like Satyam Auto Components and Rockman Industries, although many of these suppliers also sell products to rival OEMs or to companies in other industries.

Other regions and producers

Apart from the three main auto manufacturing regions of India (the NCR, the CMA and the C-SEZ) and the emergence of smaller but fast-growing regional clusters in urban centres of Gujarat and Uttarakhand, auto-based global and regional production networks also occur in many other parts of the country. While a much smaller player in South Asia than in East Asia, leading Japanese OEM, Toyota has manufactured cars in India since the 1990s from its base in Bidadi village, on the southwestern fringe of the Bengaluru (Bangalore) urban region. Toyota entered India in 1997 with a ₹700 *crore* investment (nearly US$110 million) in a joint venture with Indian engineering conglomerate, the Kirloskar Group, to form Toyota Kirloskar Motors Limited (TKML). TKML began as a 50/50 joint venture between Toyota and the Kirloskar Group, but Toyota moved quickly to increase its equity share to 79 per cent in 2001 and finally to 99 per cent in 2003, effectively establishing TKML as a subsidiary of the Japanese global parent company.

TKML commenced manufacturing mid-sized and large passenger cars in 1999 and also began exporting gearboxes. The Bidadi site was based on one assembly plant with a 60,000-unit annual capacity, a supply factory, Toyota Auto Parts Limited (TKAPL), and a supplier park (Toyota Techno Park) which includes five Tier-1 supply companies, including Toyota Group strategic partner Denso, GM strategic partner Delphi, and Indo-Japanese joint venture Motherson Sumi. TKML's main assembly plant included a press shop, welding shop, chassis parts assembly, paint shop and final assembly, while TKAPL focused on the manufacture of axles and gearboxes (Lal Das and George, 2006).

TKML suppliers have formed an organisation – the Toyota Kirloskar Suppliers Association (TKSA) – which has over 50 members. These include numerous captive Tier-1 suppliers and Toyota Group companies like Denso, Toyota Boshoku, Toyota Tsusho and Aisin, as well as independent Japanese suppliers like Asahi Glass and other foreign independent suppliers like German multi-industry manufacturer Bosch, or American suppliers like Johnson Controls and Tenneco. TKSA members also include several Indo-Japanese joint ventures outside the Toyota Group such as JBM Ogihara and Motherson Sumi (TKSA, 2016). Many of these firms sell products directly to TKAPL as well as TKML. TKAPL itself has nearly 50 suppliers, including Motherson Sumi, Tenneco and Lumax, as well as Indian components manufacturers like Pricol (Mitra, 2013).

Another OEM with a base in Karnataka is the Indian firm TVS, which operates both as a two-wheeler and three-wheeler vehicle manufacturer, and as a Tier-1 supplier to larger OEMs such as Tata Motors. TVS exports motorcycles to Southeast Asian countries like Indonesia, where it sends CKD kit for local assembly, and to Colombia, and some African countries. TVS also operates import businesses in the United States, China, Singapore and the Netherlands, and manufactures some components for wind farms. By early 2016, TVS claimed over 5,200 regular employees at its three Indian manufacturing sites, as well its corporate headquarters in Chennai. TVS operates in the city of Mysuru, and operates a plant in the town of Hosur which, while just across the border in Tamil Nadu, is barely one hour's drive to the southeast of Bengaluru. TVS also operates a plant in the small town of Nalagarh in the northern state of Himachal Pradesh.

In 2015–16, TVS manufactured and sold around 2.57 million two-wheelers, including 359,000 exports, and exported a further 95,000 three-wheelers (TVS, 2016). TVS thus compares favourably with other two-wheeler manufacturers in India. While its 2015–16 sales result is much smaller than the industry leaders Honda and Hero MotoCorp, it is not far behind Bajaj's 2015–16 combined sales of

3.36 million motorcycles, and around 12 times larger than Piaggio's total Indian sales for the previous year.

Finally, it is perhaps fitting to conclude this section by mentioning a company that for decades defined passenger car production in India, but which has fallen upon difficult times recently. From its inception in 1958 until very recently, Hindustan Motors' Ambassador was widely regarded as *the* definitive Indian-manufactured passenger car. While the passenger car remained a rare luxury in India throughout this period, the Ambassador provided transport for an elite minority of business leaders, senior public bureaucrats and politicians.

As part of the CK Birla Group of companies, Hindustan Motors, along with Premier Limited (see above), was the dominant force in Indian car manufacturing until the arrival of MSIL in the early 1980s. The situation is radically different today. In 2014, Hindustan Motors suspended all production, including the Ambassador, at its Uttarpara plant in the north of Kolkata. Although Hindustan Motors claimed total sales of 2.6 million vehicles, including over 1.8 million passenger cars, and a further 382,000 light commercial vehicles in 2014–15, the company's Uttarpara plant had become a loss-making operation. The May 2014 suspension of production was followed by redundancies for around 1160 employees at Uttarpara, and the closure of its facility in Pithampur in Madhya Pradesh, although by March 2015, the company claimed it had retained over 1300 workers (Hindustan Motors, 2015).

More recently, a potential opportunity has emerged for the CK Birla Group to revitalise its local operations through an international partnership with the French OEM – Groupe PSA, which owns passenger car brands Peugeot, Citroën and DS, and had previously operated a joint venture with Premier (1994–97). In January 2017, Groupe PSA and Birla announced plans to commence two new joint ventures for passenger car assembly and engine manufacturing in Tamil Nadu (Raj, 2017).

Conclusion

This chapter has offered a broad outline of the key global production networks that characterise the local industry, their role within particular regional clusters and also provided keynote examples of the Tier-1 and Tier-2 suppliers on which OEMs rely in each network. Following Coe and Yeung's (2015) framework for global production network configurations, this chapter has outlined multiple examples of lead firm OEMs and their strategic partners, as well as single- and multi-industry independent suppliers.

Strategic partners of key OEMs operating in India include Visteon (which is linked to Ford's global operations), Denso (Toyota), Delphi (GM), Magneti

Marelli and Comau (Fiat), ASAL (Tata Motors), Mark Exhaust, Bellsonica and Krishna Ishizaki (Maruti Suzuki), Rockman Industries and Satyam Automotive (Hero MotoCorp). In addition, there are numerous independent suppliers which focus almost exclusively on components manufacturing for automotive OEMS, such as AGC Automotive (from Japan), Tenneco (from the US), Yapp Automotive (China) and, from India, firms such as Lumax and Endurance Technologies.

There are also numerous independent suppliers which operate as Tier-1 suppliers in multiple industries, such as Bosch and Thyssenkrupp (from Germany), Mahle Behr (a Indo-German joint venture), or Indian firms such as Jagdambay Forgings and Anand Enterprises. For many of these firms, auto manufacturing represents a fraction of their total sales and customer base. Some of these companies, such as Bosch and Thyssenkrupp, operate as lead firms in their own global production networks.

Among these various supply companies, it is sometimes difficult to distinguish between independent suppliers and 'generic suppliers' (Coe and Yeung, 2015) which mass produce standardised goods and services for multiple clients. While there are some Tier-1 firms, such as tyre manufacturers MRF or Dunlop, which fit into the latter category, many genuine generic suppliers operate as manufacturers below Tier-1 where there is a greater reliance on domestically-owned and operated firms.

Regional and market segmentation and competition in the industry have been such that it is common for OEMs to form partnerships with the strategic partners of *rival* OEMs. For example, MSIL has an equity stake (10 per cent) in Toyota's strategic partner Denso's Indian operations. This seems to operate partially because MSIL and Toyota operate in different segments of the passenger car market and also, perhaps, because their manufacturing bases are in different regions of the country.

The same is true for MSIL's sizeable equity share (19 per cent) in Fiat's strategic partner Magneti Marelli's Indian engine operations. In this case, the different actors are able to mutually benefit from cross-over partnership and equity arrangements despite the existence of rival OEMs formally competing in the passenger car market. Similarly, Honda is a major customer of Denso, and Hero MotoCorp is a major customer of MagnetiMarelli.

These cases represent the intersection of competing strategies of inter-firm partnership and control that cut across rival global production networks. But there are also several examples of OEMs that fit closely with the firm-level strategies outlined in GPN 2.0 (Chapter 1). MSIL, as the market leader in passenger car production, had clearly deployed a strategy of inter-firm partnership by establishing multiple controlling equity stakes in Tier-1 suppliers. This includes the six Tier-1 suppliers with which it currently has joint ventures, and 12 more Tier-1 'associate companies' in which it held controlling equity shares by 2014–15.

These commercial relations are akin to relational value chain governance given the close monitoring and hands-on managerial approach that MSIL takes to production throughout its supply chain. However, there is also an element of market-based value chain governance through MSIL's encouragement of price-competition among most of its 300-plus suppliers with whom it does not have equity-based relations. MSIL encourages Tier-1 suppliers to switch between generic product suppliers in lower-tiers of the industry, with significant implications for employment relations practices and labour standards in these firms (see Chapter 6). Like MSIL, Toyota (TKML) seems to follow inter-firm partnership through relations with several members of the Toyota Group, like Denso, Toyota Boshoku and Toyota Tsusho, while more generally adopting a relational governance approach to numerous independent Tier-1 suppliers.

One might expect other large Japanese OEMs to follow a similar network strategy, and rival OEMs with origins in different countries to perhaps follow an alternative strategy. However, the evidence suggests that country of origin is not a straight-forward guide for firm-level strategy in India. A bigger factor in explaining the configuration of global production networks in Indian auto manufacturing has been the *timing* of foreign OEMs' entry into regional markets. The following chapter shows that this timing has been shaped by two distinctive phases of state-guided liberalisation in auto manufacturing; one which lasted from 1982 to 1991, and one from 1991 until the present day.

The historical path of the auto industry's development, including the role of pioneering early-investors like MSIL and Honda in contrast to the strategies adopted by global OEMs which arrived later, is closely tied to the role of state institutions – both at a national and at a regional level – in attracting and managing the entry of foreign manufacturers and balancing this process with the gradual liberalisation of trade and investment rules. The order of OEM arrival in India, their regional embeddedness, and the impact upon their regional network strategy cannot be understood without placing the state at the heart of the story. It is to this story that the following chapter turns.

3

Auto Manufacturing and the Evolution of Industrial Policy

State institutions have played a critical role in the modernisation of automotive manufacturing in India and the emergence of new regional industrial zones. They have also played an important role in the evolution of conflict in the auto industry. The previous chapter showed how Indian auto manufacturing has been transformed by global production networks since the 1980s. This chapter turns to the role of the state in this process and its gradual impact on work organisation, labour standards, and employment relations.

At a regional level, key State governments in India have played a strong and consistent role in attracting, encouraging and shaping automotive-based investment from foreign and domestic lead firms known as Original Equipment Manufacturers (OEMs). This chapter shows how successive governments in the State of Haryana – a 45,000 square km territory overlapping with the National Capital Region (NCR) – played a leading role in this process, working with national governments to facilitate the rise of global production networks orchestrated by Japanese OEMs.

This chapter shows how, at a national level, this process of regional development was shaped through two phases: first, a period of 'restricted openness' from 1982 until 1991 and second, a longer period of 'emergent neo-liberalism' after 1991. The first period represents a bridgehead between India's postcolonial planning tradition, based on Import Substitution Industrialisation (ISI), to an era of neo-liberal policy-making after 1991.

In this first period, industrial policy was based upon gradual measures to extract the benefits from foreign investment, technology and 'lean manufacturing' while maintaining a series of restrictions on foreign capital via auto market segmentation, industrial licensing, joint ventures with Public Sector Units (PSUs) and private domestic, industrial conglomerates and targets for locally-manufactured components in global production networks. Despite these restrictions, the sheltering of domestic auto markets enabled pioneering foreign OEMs to impose much of their preferred models of work organisation, labour standards and employment relations via lean manufacturing.

In the second phase, the gradual liberalisation of financial markets, trade rules and restrictions on domestic and foreign investment from 1991 until the 2000s dramatically re-shaped auto market segmentation and competition. This had major implications for labour standards and employment relations in the operations of OEMs, their strategic partner firms, and key independent suppliers. As subsequent chapters show, regulatory changes shaped a series of events which eventually led to the imposition of regional contract labour systems across the industry in the 2000s and a sharp increase in industrial, social and political conflict.

Following from the empirical information in Chapter 2, this chapter first looks at the interaction of global production networks in auto manufacturing with regional institutions in the 1980s and 1990s. Modifying Coe and Yeung's (2015) approach, it argues that a type of 'first-mover coupling' took place between global production networks and regional institutions which enabled pioneering foreign OEMs from Japan – above all, Maruti Suzuki – to transform work organisation and employment relations in line with their corporate versions of lean manufacturing. The chapter then explores how the state both facilitated and transformed this process. This leads into the chapter's discussion of the two phases of national industry policy before and after 1991.

First-mover coupling in auto manufacturing

As outlined in Chapter 1, the ultimate ambition of Global Production Network (GPN) analysis is to explain uneven development. 'Unevenness' refers to inequalities between regions in terms of 'value capture'. Regional development is a process shaped by institutions and 'actors' pursuing different value-capture strategies. This includes firms already part of an established global production network looking to incorporate institutions located within a particular region (i.e., firms looking at a region from the 'outside-in'), or firms and state institutions based in a region looking to insert themselves into a particular global production network (i.e. from the 'inside-out'). Participation of a given firm in a 'reasonably stable transactional' form signifies 'strategic coupling' between that firm, its home region, and a given global production network (Coe and Yeung, 2015: 171).

Coe and Yeung (2015: 184) propose three modes of strategic coupling: 'indigenous innovation', 'functional coupling' and 'structural coupling'. Indigenous innovation occurs when regional actors successfully pursue a stable and enduring 'inside-out' strategy by drawing global production network into their orbit. 'Functional coupling' occurs when regional actors are able to meet the needs of global production networks, resulting in international partnerships. Such partnerships can result either from inside-out or from outside-in strategies.

Finally, 'structural coupling' occurs when external actors, pursuing an outside-in strategy, take the initiative to incorporate regional actors and regional assets into a global production network. Structural coupling can, in theory, lead to problems of dependency for regional actors where local value capture is much lower, or occurs on much less-favourable terms that the other two models of strategic coupling. Examples include export-processing zones in parts of Mexico or Thailand – or Special Economic Zones as they are officially known in India – which commonly specialise in low-cost, labour-intensive manufacturing.

However, Coe and Yeung caution that 'a theory of strategic coupling can never fully encompass the range of economic development impacts that are associated with such couplings' (Coe and Yeung, 2015: 190). This is due to the diversity of likely coupling outcomes in the real world, variations within regions – for example, between those who benefit and those who might not benefit from strategic coupling – and the reality that politics, and thus policy-making, is primarily national, not regional, in its focus.[1] Such analytical flexibility means that we can modify and add to their typology in this spirit of empirical openness.

While acknowledging this typology, the findings from this book suggest that a fourth model is needed to capture the coupling process in the context of auto manufacturing in Indian regions. Specifically, the chapter proposes a model of *first-mover coupling*. While this model can be regarded as a variant of structural coupling, because first-mover advantages have primarily been accrued through the 'outside-in' initiative of OEMs looking for new market opportunities, it overlaps with functional coupling as well, since the stability and durability of the transactional form between OEMs, domestic suppliers and state institutions is relatively high compared to late-entrant foreign OEMs and auto supply companies.

This model thus adds the critical factor of time – specifically, the timing or sequencing of the entry of a firm into regional sites of production and consumption, as outlined below. This modified framework can also incorporate some distinctive characteristics of India's national political economy, especially the existence of established domestic OEMs such as Tata Motors and Mahindra and Mahindra (herein Mahindra) which had a multi-regional and multi-network presence prior to the entry of global production networks in auto manufacturing in the 1980s.

However, the capacity of select *foreign* OEMs to entrench their respective global production networks and their preferred network strategies is linked to the timing of their entry into regional markets as well as the mode of their entry and the operational regulations imposed on new entrants by state institutions. Timing is critical to explaining the extent to which lead firms have been able to implement their preferred network strategies and models of work organisation.

---

[1] Selwyn (2016a) has also suggested that coupling in the real-world is less consciously 'strategic' on the part of firms and regional actors and more contingent or path-dependent than Coe and Yeung imply.

The timing of OEM entry into Indian regions has had a bigger impact on firm-level strategies within GPNs than their national origin. Based on the analysis of firms in Chapter 2, there is a relatively weak link between an OEM's country of origin and the strategy they pursue among networked suppliers in Indian regions. Although global production network theory predicts that Japanese OEMs are more likely to pursue 'inter-firm partnerships' through horizontal integration and direct equity investment in their Tier-1 suppliers, this has not been the uniform approach among Japanese OEMs in India.

For example, MSIL, the largest passenger car manufacturer in India, has pursued a strategy of inter-firm partnership, but its home-country rival, Honda, has pursued a strategy of 'inter-firm control'. MSIL's strategy flows from its equity positions in a range of Tier-1 firms, including six Tier-1 suppliers with which it had joint ventures and a further 12 Tier-1 'associate companies' in which it held controlling equity shares by 2015. These investments have given MSIL managers significant operational as well as financial control over its supplier base.

In contrast, Honda, which is a market leader for two-wheeler production as well as car production, has followed a strategy that is closer to inter-firm control. In this strategy, the company retains the same strict demands for design and product quality as rivals like MSIL without pursuing the same equity investment approach in its supply base. Honda draws upon a wide range of Japanese Tier-1 suppliers like AGC Automotive, Nippon Seiki and Takata Automotive, as well as major German suppliers like Thyssenkrupp, or American suppliers like BorgWarner, but lacks the same degree of equity investment as MSIL in its key components and service providers.

Another contrast to Honda's strategy is the one adopted by its main rival in the two-wheeler market – Hero MotoCorp. This Indian OEM has followed an MSIL-like strategy of inter-firm partnership via the Hero Group's preference for strategic partnerships with firms in which it has a controlling or influential equity stake. Unlike MSIL, however, this tends to follow the economic interests of the Hero Group's family ownership structure, with key strategic partnerships formed with companies in which the Munjal family has significant interests, such as Tier-1 suppliers, Rockman Industries, and Satyam Automotive.

This outcome – in which a Japanese OEM pursues a strategy of inter-firm control while its main domestic rival pursues an inter-firm partnership approach – is tied to these firms' previous relationship as long-term joint venture partners. One of the key issues that led to the cessation of the 26-year Hero Honda joint venture (1984–2010) was the difference over their respective attitudes towards value chain governance. Honda appeared to favour market-based, competitive tendering for contracts among suppliers, and Hero favoured companies in which the Munjal family held, or could more easily establish, shareholding interests (see Chapter 2).

Another major Indian OEM that has pursued a version of inter-firm partnership is Tata Motors, which has pursued equity stakes in Tier-1 suppliers via the Tata Group's joint venture investment arm, Tata AutoComp Systems Limited (TACO).

If we look more generally at the strategies of key OEMs in Indian auto manufacturing, we find a similar pattern in which different firm-level strategies transcend country origins. Hyundai (HMIL), which is MSIL's main rival in the passenger car market and the dominant OEM in the Chennai Metropolitan Area (CMA), has also adopted a version of inter-firm partnership. Its key suppliers include Hyundai Group members like Dymos Lear, as well as a wider range of South Korean Tier-1 suppliers in which HMIL is able to directly influence operations – like Dongsun, Hwashin, Woojin, and Woory Automotive.

Several of these firms supply components to rival OEM, Renault-Nissan, which is also based in the CMA. Renault-Nissan's late-comer status, compared to HMIL, means that it relies upon several of these HMIL strategic partners, as well as those of other rival OEMs like Comau (from the Fiat Group), and a range of independent foreign and domestic suppliers.

Overall then, the diversity in firm-level strategies adopted in automotive global production network cannot be solely explained by country origins of OEMs. Among Japanese OEMs, some adopt inter-firm partnership (MSIL and Toyota), whereas others adopt inter-firm control (Honda). Among Indian OEMs, some have similarly adopted a version of inter-firm partnership (Hero MotoCorp, Tata Motors). For other foreign OEMs like Renault-Nissan neither of these firm-level strategies seems to capture firm-level approaches.

A bigger influence on firm-level strategy relates to the different market positions occupied by OEMs which begin from the timing of their entry into Indian auto markets. As the pioneer of modern passenger car production in India in the 1980s, MSIL was able to successfully pursue its parent company's strategy of choice more closely than its late-comer rivals. While MSIL began as a PSU with a Japanese private equity stake, the Suzuki Motor Corporation was able to gradually increase its equity stake until the operation became a full subsidiary of the parent company.

Similarly, HMIL's role as the first 100 per cent foreign-owned greenfield automotive assembly operation in India in 1996, its dominant role in the south of the country, and the use of its base in the CMA as an export platform has enabled the company to pursue its parent company's preferred strategy. Late-arriving foreign lead firms have been largely forced to fit into the pre-established networks of these pioneering OEMs. Chapter 4 explains how MSIL and HMIL's pioneering efforts enabled these firms to transform supply chain relations and work organisation through lean manufacturing.

Although these firms led the way in modernising Indian auto manufacturing, their efforts were also strongly influenced by the role of state institutional actors looking 'inside out' at the transformative potential of foreign OEMs' global production networks. The role of state institutions was critical both at a national and regional level.

At the regional level, a model of state institutional support for foreign OEMs was pioneered by the Government of Haryana in the 1980s and 1990s in collaboration with the Government of India. MSIL acquired 330 acres of industrial land from the Government of Haryana in Gurugram Sector 18 following the failure of domestic prototype vehicle manufacturing in the 1970s. Through its public infrastructure investment arm – the Haryana State Industrial and Infrastructure Development Corporation (HSIIDC) – the State government provided MSIL with additional land at below-market rates and channeled investment into major road, electricity and telecommunications infrastructure in the vicinity of its assembly operations (Government of Haryana 2006). In 1996, the HSIIDC orchestrated the sale of 250 acres of land in Manesar for the company at below-market rates to establish a specialist supplier park. In 2007, this site was transformed into Maruti's second assembly facility and an engine ('power-train') manufacturing plant.

Besides facilitating MSIL's capacity to reshape local production networks through the implementation of lean manufacturing practices (Becker-Ritterspach, 2007; Gulyani, 2001), these policies helped to transform Gurugram from a rural district centred on a small administrative town into a major financial and industrial city in a single generation (Debroy and Bhandari, 2009). HSIIDC channeled investment into transport infrastructure to connect the Gurugram site in Sector 18 to the township of Old Gurgaon and the city of New Delhi via National Highway 48 (Government of Haryana, 2006). The State-run HSIIDC aimed to 're-establish industry as a key driver of economic growth… To generate employment and entrepreneurial opportunities across all sectors of the economy [and to] develop economic hubs through infrastructural initiatives' (Government of Haryana, 2005: 2).

Later, these policies were successfully emulated by State governments in Tamil Nadu, Maharashtra, Gujarat and others. For example, the greenfield operations of Ford and Hyundai in the CMA were boosted by tax exemptions, public infrastructure investment and hundreds of acres of subsidised land offered by the Government of Tamil Nadu (Gulyani, 2001: 133–35). The primary aim of the Government of Tamil Nadu's Automobile and Auto Components Policy, written in 2014, was to 'make Chennai one of the top five centres in the world in the auto and components industry' and to 'double the exports of auto and components from Tamil Nadu by 2016' (Gopalakrishnan and Mirer, 2014).

In Bengaluru, the Government of Karnataka granted major concessions to Toyota Kirloskar on entry tax, pollution controls, land acquisition and investment subsidies for power and water supply (Lal Das and George, 2006: 279). In the

Haridwar auto manufacturing cluster in northern India, which is a major base for Hero MotoCorp, and Mahindra's global production networks, the Government of Uttarakhand established a Special Economic Zone (SEZ) with large exemptions on excise and income tax for local manufacturers, attracting over 850 companies, and employment for around 70,000 people in consumer goods, capital equipment, and auto manufacturing (*Economic Times*, 2012).

The model of regional state support for auto manufacturing in Haryana and other states was influenced by a similar approach developed to support software and IT-enabled Services (ITES) industries, particularly in Bengaluru by the Government of Karnataka. The IT industry's emergence as a world-leader in software services by the 2000s was underpinned by support from governments, including tax cuts and subsidised power for export-oriented firms and foreign investors based in SEZs (Pinglé 1999; Upadhya and Vasavi 2006; D'Costa, 2009; Barnes, 2012). In cities like Bengaluru, Hyderabad and New Delhi, the emergence of a powerful software industry built upon existing technical and workforce foundations in manufacturing for military institutions and other state institutions via PSUs in electronics, telecommunications and aeronautics (D'Costa, 2009; Dutta and De, 2009).

In Haryana, IT and ITES were initially linked to the demands of the State government, organised through the State-owned Haryana State Electronics Development Corporation (HARTRON), established in 1983. The absence of a 'municipal corporation' in Gurugram until 2008 meant that HARTRON was able to negotiate directly with private firms and investors without having to involve local government institutions (Debroy and Bhandari, 2009). In these circumstances, state-guided infrastructure investment contributed to Gurugram's emergence as a base for Foreign Direct Investment (FDI) in the services sector as well as in auto manufacturing (Government of Haryana, 2007).

The first significant offshore services operation in Gurugram was GE Capital's 1996 investment which, in 2005, was transformed into an independent company called Genpact. Gurugram also became the base for several other foreign transnational corporations in IT, electronics and telecommunications such as IBM, Siemens and Alcatel, as well as large locally-owned ITES and business services firms like Tata Consultancy Services (TCS), Wipro, HCL and Daksh. Several global IT and financial services providers, including Microsoft, American Express, Dell, Citibank, Deutsche Bank and Hewlett Packard, also off-shored call centre work to the NCR, including Gurugram as well as Okhla in South Delhi and Greater Noida in Uttar Pradesh.

Besides gaining from a similar model of public infrastructure investment to IT and ITES, auto manufacturing benefitted from the model of land acquisition used to support these companies and attract FDI. State governments in the NCR, like many State governments across the country, had established SEZs as duty free zones and havens from income, sales and service taxes.

Manesar in Gurugram District is a prime example of this process of land acquisition for commercial development. Manesar is centred on auto manufacturing. The major assembly factorues of MSIL and HMSI are located in its vicinity. Commercial and residential construction commenced in Manesar in the 1990s as an 'Industrial Model Township' (IMT) which would include 'campuses for large industries, ICT parks, industrial plots, flatted factories, residential colonies, labour housing, commercial and institutional areas, entertainment zones, educational and health care facilities' (Government of Haryana, 2005: 4). Construction projects in IMT Manesar were overseen directly by the HSIIDC.

In the 2000s, the Government of Haryana framed IMT Manesar as a model for other proposed IMTs across Haryana, using SEZ policy to accelerate this process. By 2006, it had requested that 26 industrial sites be similarly given SEZ status by the Government of India, following the passing of the national *SEZ Act 2005* (Government of Haryana, 2006). By mid-2008, Haryana held 38 out of India's 462 SEZs, over eight per cent of the national total (Banerjee-Guha, 2008). This is despite having less than 1.5 per cent of India's total land area and only about two per cent of the country's total population.

This rounded approach to commercial development has meant that, besides lead firms establishing global production networks in multiple industries and sectors, Gurugram has also become a centre for real estate development and retail consumerism for middle-to-high income residents. A testament to this process is the corridor of glitzy shopping malls, high rise office-blocks and towering apartments that line either side of the Mehrauli-Gurgaon Road as it passes through the district's residential and commercial heartland in Gurugram Blocks A, H and M.

Regional development has been driven by the first-mover coupling of pioneering OEMs' global production networks with regional assets marshalled by State governments. However, this process of global-regional integration has also been profoundly shaped by a state-driven process at the *national* level. These phases, and the implications for labour standards and employment relations within auto manufacturing firms, are outlined in the following section.

Restricted openness, 1982–1991

Leading manufacturers from Europe and the United States have invested in Indian regions for decades, but the political and institutional environment for OEMs in the auto industry was comparatively unfavourable and occasionally hostile prior to the 1980s. From the early 1950s until the mid-1980s, Indian governments pursued a model of development based on Import Substitution Industrialisation (ISI) which included a central role for Public Sector Units (PSUs) and restrictions on the activities of private industrial capital in the organised sector. India's first Five Year Plan (1951–56) introduced a system of industrial licensing which reserved strategically-designated sectors of the economy for PSUs, while allowing privately-owned conglomerates to operate only in approved areas of industry and commerce.

The Second Five Year Plan (1956–61) initially outlined a scaled-up level of public investment in industry led by PSUs. This ambitious plan was underpinned by hopes for industrial modernisation which fed into state regulation of work and labour markets. These ideas emerged from the colonial period (Holmström, 1984) and were then absorbed by the Indian National Congress (INC) policymakers in the newly-independent central state apparatus in New Delhi. Combining assumptions that India could modernise by nurturing the organised sector, and Gandhian views on the need to nurture small-scale agriculture and village industry, agriculture and the non-agricultural unorganised sector were exempted from many of these economic planning laws.

In this model, investment activities in the organised sector were tightly regulated and restricted by the industrial licensing system. Pilloried by opponents as a 'license permit raj', this system created few incentives for private sector industrialists to seek improvements in productivity through large-scale investment in labour-saving technology (Clark and Wolcott, 2003; Felipe, Lavinā and Fan, 2008). Even those economic historians who praise the state's role during the 1950s and early 1960s have argued that there was a 'general lack of investment in technological upgrading and plant maintenance' in key industries (McCartney, 2009: 138).

The Second Five Year Plan was ultimately derailed by a foreign currency shortage. Following political instability exacerbated by war with Pakistan in 1965, and food grain shortages in 1965/66, further restrictions on industrial capital were imposed by governments led by Prime Minister Indira Gandhi. For example, the *Monopolies and Restrictive Trade Practices Act (MRTPA) 1969* restricted the size and diversity of industrial firms, and placed limits on their product volumes, product ranges and product varieties. This was followed by the *Foreign Exchange Regulation Act (FERA) 1973*, which restricted the access of firms to foreign technology, capital and investment. The *FERA* restricted foreign equity in Indian companies to 40 per cent. During this period, the Government also tightened restrictions on employment levels through the *Industrial Disputes Act (IDA) 1947* which required large-scale employers to seek state permission before shutting down workplaces or retrenching workers.

Despite the restrictions on their investment activities and operations, India's most powerful industrial firms had been able to retain significant economic power by the time of the Emergency (1975–77). By 1976, the 20 largest businesses in India controlled about two-thirds of total productive capacity in the private sector (Bardhan, 1998: 43). Having cooperated with industrial licensing and import substitution in the 1950s and early 60s (Kidron, 1965; Chibber, 2003; Kudaisya, 2009a), these conglomerates retained the power to evade many of the state restrictions imposed on their operations in the late 1960s and 1970s.

For example, industrialists segmented their workforces into permanently employed 'regular workers' – known as 'workmen' under the *Factories Act 1948* – and casual or temporary employees. Another popular category was workers hired by labour contractors, known in India as 'contract workers'. Many firms were able to easily avoid legal obligations such as minimum wage laws or hire-and-fire restrictions in the *IDA* by relying increasingly on the employment of contract workers, or subcontracting work to smaller units which fell outside the regulatory scope of the organised sector (Harris-White and Gooptu, 2000; Hensman, 2000; Singh and Sapra, 2007).

In many sectors of manufacturing, industrialists expanded the practice of outsourcing or sub-contracting in-house production to networks of smaller firms, 'colonies' of workshops and home-based workers. While sub-contracting was a feature of industrial organisation throughout the twentieth century – for example, via the *badli* (substitute) system in Mumbai's textile mills in the early 1900s – it had generally been used to supplement factory production during cycles of excess demand. From the mid-1970s onward, sub-contracting became a growing and permanent feature of large-scale industry in India's urban regions.

The expansion of these employment practices coincided with growing openness in India's economic policy-making framework in the early 1980s, followed by a gradual process of economic liberalisation. Although some scholars emphasise the role of neo-liberal reforms of 1991 in transforming India's economy (Joshi and Little, 1994; Ahluwalia, 2002), India's transition towards a high-growth economy began in the early-to-mid 1980s. After some export incentives were introduced in the early 1980s, Rajiv Gandhi's Indian National Congress (INC) government undertook a 'pro-business' re-orientation based on a series of measures to liberalise trade and investment (Subramanian and Rodrik, 2008).

These measures were particularly beneficial for export-oriented firms. The 1985 national budget allowed 50 per cent of export profits to be deducted from company tax bills. This was raised to 100 per cent in 1988. Exporters were also given access to cheaper credit. In 1986, exporters were allowed to buy imported capital goods duty-free. In addition, Rajiv Gandhi's government began to loosen some licensing restrictions by allowing firms in 32 industries to invest in new products without obtaining a license. From 1983, licensed firms in 28 industries were allowed to diversify production within existing facilities, known as 'broad banding'.

Broad banding was applied to the auto manufacturing industry in 1985. For example, car manufacturers were allowed to start manufacturing commercial vehicles such as trucks and buses and vice versa (Becker-Ritterspach, 2009: 88–89). The Tata Group, as a leading industrial conglomerate, was now able to take advantage of its role as the market leader in domestic commercial vehicles manufacturing via Tata Engineering and Locomotive Company Limited (TELCO) to establish a new subsidiary in passenger car production, which later became Tata Motors. In addition, restrictions under the *MRTPA* were loosened for firms in 27 industries, enabling them to increase their market capitalisation. The liberalisation of domestic price and investment rules also created a space for foreign lead firms to begin investing (or reinvesting) in Indian regional markets.

The spread of investment liberalisation across multiple industries from 1985 to 1991 was, to a significant extent, pre-empted by MSIL's relationship with the Government of India. In 1982, the Suzuki Motor Corporation (SMC) agreed to purchase a 26 per cent share of the PSU, Maruti Udyog Limited (MUL). This deal gave the SMC significant operational control over MUL's dormant assembly site in Gurugram and, over time, had a profound impact on the design of Indian industrial policy.

MUL had emerged from the failure of a 'people's car' project led by Sanjay Gandhi – youngest son of then-Prime Minister Indira Gandhi – in the early 1970s. Sanjay Gandhi oversaw the establishment of 'Maruti Limited' as a privately-owned enterprise which was licensed to produce a low-cost passenger car through import substitution. The venture was given 330 acres of land in Gurugram Sector 18, a range of investment subsidies by the Government of Haryana, and tax exemptions from the Government of India. A combination of political instability, ineffective management and lack of technical know-how meant that the site failed to move beyond prototype development. Production activities had ended at the site by 1977.

In 1981, Maruti Limited was nationalised by the Government of India and the holding renamed Maruti Udyog Ltd (MUL). In the context of emerging interest in passenger car manufacturing from foreign OEMs, industrial policymakers in the national government saw an opportunity to resurrect and modernise domestic passenger car manufacturing by reviving the dormant MUL venture.

In doing so, these policy-makers concluded that industrial revival was only viable with foreign investment, technology, and operational expertise. Within an ISI-based policy framework, policy-makers were prepared to allow a limited financial and operational stake in MUL by a foreign OEM, provided the company remain a majority state-owned PSU. The government finally settled on SMC due to its higher equity share offer than rival OEMs, and its promise to transfer the lean manufacturing management technique and culture associated with Japanese OEMs (Becker-Ritterspach, 2009: 100).

For the SMC, India represented an opportunity to experiment with an export platform in a relatively untapped market for global OEMs. Although the company minimised corporate risk with a minority shareholding, the decision was nevertheless bold, given the luxury status of passenger cars in India at the time. It was also bold because of the uncertainty regarding the future direction of FDI in India in the context of an ongoing ISI policy framework and the aftermath of major political instability in the late 1970s.

The SMC's decision also reflected its status within the global hierarchy of automotive OEMs. Unstable economic conditions in North America and Europe in the early 1980s worsened the position of second-tier producers like SMC, who found themselves squeezed out of Western passenger car markets by dominant American, European, and rival Japanese small car producers like Toyota, Honda and Mazda (Becker-Ritterspach, 2007).

Unfavorable conditions in the key markets of Western Europe, North America and Japan pushed SMC into the adoption of an internationalisation strategy which focused on nascent and emerging markets for passenger cars. In 1976, SMC established a passenger car assembly site in Indonesia and, in 1982, the firm commenced assembly operations in Pakistan, as well as signing its Memorandum of Understanding (MOU) with the Government of India for the MUL operation. SMC followed up these decisions with the establishment of new assembly sites in New Zealand, Colombia and Egypt (1984–87). In the 1990s, SMC established wholly-owned assembly operations in South Korea, China and Vietnam (Becker-Ritterspach, 2009). SMC's strategy in these emerging markets was to mass-produce small, low-cost passenger cars for upwardly-mobile and aspirational middle-income and high-income consumers (D'Costa, 1995). For national industrial policymakers in India, SMC provided an opportunity for the Government to reinvigorate domestic auto manufacturing.

There are important historical reasons why Indian governments, at both the centre and the state level, became enthusiastic about the emergence of the automotive industry. Auto manufacturing helped to play a historically transformative role in the West and in Japan. In the US and in Western Europe, the auto industry became a setter of standards in quality manufacturing, technology, wages and employment relations (Babson, 1986; Sugrue, 2005).

In Japan, a new model of production and work organisation was developed by Toyota, initially in the 1950s and 60s. Later known as the Toyota Production System (TPS), this method radically modified the structure and operation of auto manufacturing by cutting costs and aiming to eliminate waste in assembly line production (Womack, Jones and Roos, 1990; MacDuffie, 1995). The TPS had implications for commercial relations between firms and for relations between workers and managers on the factory floor. Inside assembly factories, the TPS encouraged a 'flatter' hierarchy by devolving product quality monitoring to teams of workers on the shop-floor. Outside factories, costs and waste could be reduced by outsourcing many core functions of the manufacturing process to a range of supply companies. In hindsight, much of the underlying idea behind of the concept of a *production network* or *value chain* was embedded in the TPS approach.

The tiered character of commercial relations between automotive OEMs and their suppliers was accelerated by the advance of Japanese FDI and Japanese manufacturing techniques in Western markets between the 1960s and the 1980s. By the mid-1980s, the TPS had been generalised into a management philosophy of 'lean production' or 'lean manufacturing' (Womack, Jones and Roos, 1990; Sako, 1992). Today, most OEMs with a trans-national presence have adopted and modified their own version of lean production – even if implemented under a different name – with knock-on effects on work organisation and commercial relations within complex global production networks.

Auto-based global production networks commonly incorporate hundreds of businesses, ranging from large multi-national corporations with thousands of employees to locally-owned and locally-based small-to-medium sized factories and workshops. In every region where auto manufacturing has a presence, foreign and domestic OEMs and Tier-1 suppliers have, to differing degrees, attempted to 'hybridise' their own versions of lean production with policies, institutions, and commercial and social practices at a local level.

The potential for auto manufacturing to play a socially transformative role through the impact of foreign investment, foreign technology and lean manufacturing helps to explain the enthusiasm that successive Indian governments, both at the centre and the state levels, have expressed for the industry. At the same time, a series of restrictions on foreign firms were maintained during the key phase of Japanese FDI in the 1980s: hence the phrase 'restricted openness' which is used here to describe the period from 1982, when MSIL entered India, to 1991, when the country embarked upon a more radical phase of economic liberalisation. In hindsight, this period marked a transitional phase that transformed, but also continued to be framed and influenced by, ISI.

Restrictions on firms' operations took three main forms: market and industry segmentation through industrial licensing, joint ventures as the preferred mode of entry and operational regulation, and local content measures in production networks. For market segmentation, MSIL's role in passenger car manufacturing was sheltered by the Government of India in this period. Rival foreign OEMs were prevented from entering India's auto manufacturing market until the early 1990s, giving MSIL more than a decade to establish a dominant position as the market leader in passenger car production. Other OEMs which were considered for the MUL revitalisation project in Gurugram included Honda and Peugeot. After being overlooked for the MUL project, Honda's attempt to establish a majority private-owned joint venture in passenger car manufacturing with Tata (via TELCO) was blocked by the Government.

However, Honda was able to benefit in other ways through the Government's policy of restricted openness. In 1984, the Government allowed Honda to establish a new joint venture with the Hero Group in motorcycle and scooter manufacturing from a site in Gurugram. The Hero Group was operated by the Munjal family which had transformed its family business into a multi-industry conglomerate over the previous four decades, originally from its base in Ludhiana in the State of Punjab. The new venture – Hero Honda – combined Honda's expertise in lean manufacturing and supply chain management in two-wheeler production with the Hero Group's network of bicycle manufacturing and distribution outlets across India.

In the 1980s, the Government of India thus pursued a strategy of segmenting the auto industry between MSIL in passenger car manufacturing, Hero Honda in two-wheeler manufacturing, and Tata in commercial vehicle manufacturing. However, some smaller producers were allowed to occupy niche market positions in these segments. In each case, the designated lead OEM was sheltered from market competition through industrial licensing. This sheltering was done to such an extent that, when FDI was required for industrial modernisation, it was orchestrated through a joint venture policy

From 1982, when the agreement between the SMC and the Government of India was finalised to revive the MUL operation, until the late 1990s, all foreign OEM involvement in auto assembly operations had to be run through joint ventures with domestic manufacturing firms. Local partners could be privately-owned or PSUs.

Another policy approach was the use of 'Phased Manufacturing Programs' (PMPs) to encourage local content manufacturing in the supply chains of OEMs. In part, this policy was designed to prevent OEMs from using Indian regions purely as low-cost labour platforms based on importing fully-manufactured components like engines and transmissions for final assembly which, depending on the stage of production, were known as Complete Knockdowns (CKDs) or Incomplete Knockdowns (IKDs). It was also designed with the intent to increase foreign investment in Tier-1 and Tier-2 suppliers in key manufacturing regions.

From 1982 to 1991, MSIL was required to follow a PMP which aimed for a target of 95 per cent local content production for manufacturing inputs. This presented a major challenge for a new operation in an untested market for foreign OEMs. However, this policy encouraged the SMC to pursue a Japanese-style inter-firm partnership strategy in two senses: first, by encouraging key Tier-1

Japanese suppliers to establish operations close to the Gurugram assembly site and, second, by directly investing in the operations of key Tier-1 and Tier-2 firms. By the early 90s, most of MSIL's key components suppliers were based within 80 km of the Gurugram assembly site (Gulyani, 2001).

The restrictions and targets imposed on MSIL were counter-weighted with a range of incentives and subsidies to encourage an expanded role for the SMC in the region. While the firm was restricted under the *FERA* from owning more than 40 per cent of any Indian company for the first three years of the MUL operation, this restriction was loosened from 1985 onwards. Some restrictions on product levels and ranges under the *MRTPA* were also lifted by Rajiv Gandhi's government, which also implemented cuts to import duties to benefit auto manufacturing. These changes to the *FERA*, the *MRTPA* and import duties were implemented specifically to benefit the MUL operation, although they eventually had far-reaching benefits for the auto manufacturing sector as a whole.

Emergent neo-liberalism, post-1991

The economic liberalisation measures of the 1980s were sharply accelerated by neo-liberal economic reforms in 1991 under the INC-led government of Prime Minister and Industry Minister, Narasimha Rao and his Finance Minister (and later Prime Minister) Manmohan Singh. Introduced in response to a short-term balance-of-payments and foreign currency crisis in mid-1991, reforms included substantial measures to liberalise banking and finance, privatisation and government divestment from PSUs, and abolition of the industrial licensing system. FDI was welcomed on a large-scale across multiple, rather than selective, sections of the industry for the first time.

While these events represented some continuity with the economic openness of the 1980s, they also represent a historical rupture which marked the end of ISI as a guiding framework for economic policy (Sengupta, 2008). The 1991 events marked the beginning of a transition to neo-liberalism as the dominant economic policy-making paradigm, represented by the treatment of the international economic order as a benign or beneficial force, by a systematic preference for private ownership over state ownership, and by the gradual removal of barriers to the activities and investment choices of large, privately-owned foreign and domestic firms.

The shift towards neo-liberal policy-making after 1991 had a major impact on the auto industry. By 1993, the last vestiges of industrial licensing were abolished for auto manufacturers. Automatic approval was granted to foreign manufacturers to invest up to 51 per cent of equity ownership in local operations (Becker-Ritterspach, 2009: 89). The 1991–93 policy changes were followed by a range of foreign OEMs deciding to invest in joint venture assembly operations in different regions of India. In 1994, the Government of India approved a new joint venture between Daimler-Chrysler and TELCO. Daimler had held a 10 per cent stake in TELCO's truck manufacturing arm for the previous 25 years and leveraged this to expand truck manufacturing in the CMA and a small luxury passenger car assembly plant (Mercedes Benz India) in the C-SEZ, near the city of Pune.

In 1995, Honda entered a joint venture with Indian firm Siel Limited, to establish a small car factory on a 150-acre site in the city of Greater Noida on the eastern fringe of New Delhi. The same year, Ford entered a joint venture with Mahindra. In 1996, Fiat entered a joint venture with Indian OEM Premier Limited, which had manufactured Fiat-branded cars in India from 1951 to 1972. In 1997, Toyota entered a joint venture with the Kirloskar Group, an Indian engineering and manufacturing conglomerate, to establish Toyota Kirloskar Motors Limited (TKML) in Bengaluru. In 1999, General Motors (GM) entered a joint venture with Hindustan Motors.

However, the joint venture policy was transformed in the context of the new policies of the 1990s. After the 1991 reforms jettisoned underlying assumptions of ISI in industrial policy, the joint venture structure was gradually reduced to an entry scheme for foreign OEMs. This allowed global companies to make relatively low-risk, experimental forays into Indian regional markets while benefiting from the institutional knowledge and political connections of Indian joint venture partners. If an operation persisted beyond this initial phase, the foreign partner commonly sought to lift its initial equity share by lobbying regional state institutions and attempting to exert greater control over local operations.

Table 3.1 summarises the key foreign OEMs operating in Indian auto manufacturing, the year of their most recent entry into Indian markets and the mode of entry and firm structure. Of the 18 firms listed in the table, six entered India after 1995 as fully-owned foreign operations. Eight began as joint ventures with Indian private or state interests and subsequently transformed into fully-owned foreign operations. Thus, the nature of joint venture policy gradually shifted from a framework for carefully-managing foreign investment in production, management, and technology to an entry scheme that enabled foreign OEMs to limit and manage investment risk.

By the 2000s, most of these joint ventures had expired either through conflict or mutual agreement between foreign OEMs and domestic partners or, alternatively, persisted in name only. For example, Honda transformed Honda Siel into Honda Cars Limited as a full subsidiary in 2010 and, along with expanding production at the Greater Noida site, opened up a new assembly factory in Alwar District in Rajasthan in 2008. Ford gradually increased its equity in the Ford-Mahindra operation in the CMA from its initial 50 per cent share until the operation became a full subsidiary of the Ford Motor Company.

Table 3.1: Mode of entry for key foreign OEMs in Indian auto manufacturing

Firm	Year of entry	Mode of entry	Current mode of regulation
Maruti Suzuki	1982	PSU joint venture	Joint venture subsidiary of Suzuki Motor Corporation (Japan)
Hero MotoCorp	1984	Joint venture with Honda Motor Company (Japan)	Private equity partnership operated by Hero Group (India)
Honda Motorcycle and Scooter India	1984	Joint venture with Hero Group (India)	Fully-owned subsidiary of Honda Motor Company (Japan)
Yamaha India	1985	Joint venture	Fully-owned subsidiary of Yamaha Motor Company (Japan)
General Motors	1994	Joint venture with Hindustan Motors (India)	Fully-owned subsidiary of General Motors (US)
Daimler	1994	Joint venture with Tata Group (India)	Fully-owned subsidiary of Daimler AG (Germany)
Ford	1995	Joint venture with Mahindra (India)	Fully-owned subsidiary of Ford Motor Company (US)
Hyundai	1996	Fully-owned subsidiary of Hyundai Motor Company (South Korea)	Fully-owned subsidiary of Hyundai Motor Company (South Korea)
Fiat	1996	Joint venture with Premier Ltd (India)	Joint venture with Tata Motors (India)
Toyota Kirloskar	1997	Joint venture with Kirloskar Group (India)	Joint venture subsidiary of Toyota Motor Company (Japan)
Honda Cars	1997	Joint venture with Siel Ltd (India)	Fully-owned subsidiary of Honda Motor Company (Japan)
Piaggio	1998	Joint venture with Greaves Cotton Ltd (India)	Fully-owned subsidiary of Piaggio (Italy)
Skoda	2000	Fully-owned subsidiary of Volkswagen Group (Germany)	Fully-owned subsidiary of Volkswagen Group (Germany)
BMW	2006	Fully-owned subsidiary of BMW (Germany)	Fully-owned subsidiary of BMW (Germany)
Volkswagen	2009	Fully-owned subsidiary of Volkswagen Group (Germany)	Fully-owned subsidiary of Volkswagen Group (Germany)

Contd.

Making Cars in the New India

Firm	Year of entry	Mode of entry	Current mode of regulation
Mercedes Benz	2009	Fully-owned subsidiary of Daimler AG (Germany)	Fully-owned subsidiary of Daimler AG (Germany)
Harley Davidson	2009	Fully-owned subsidiary of Harley Davidson (US)	Fully-owned subsidiary of Harley Davidson (US)
Renault-Nissan	2010	Joint venture between Groupe Renault (France) and Nissan (Japan)	Joint venture between Groupe Renault (France) and Nissan (Japan)

Source: Authors' analysis of company reports/internet searches

Fiat's initial 51 per cent investment in the Fiat-Premier operation in Kurla, near Mumbai, was expanded gradually due to the difficulty the company had in implementing its global lean manufacturing strategy, known as the 'World Car Project'. In 2004, the Kurla site became a full subsidiary of Fiat. In the case of Toyota Kirloskar, Toyota gradually increased its equity investment from 50 per cent to 79 per cent in 2001 and to 99 per cent in 2003. Although the operation is now effectively run as a subsidiary of Toyota, the Kirloskar Group remains a small minority shareholder in the Bengaluru operation.

A turning point in the erosion of joint ventures as a mode of operational regulation was the Government of India and the Government of Tamil Nadu's approval for Hyundai to establish a 100 per cent foreign-owned operation at a greenfield site near Chennai in 1996. After commencing assembly production in 1998, Hyundai Motor India Ltd (HMIL) grew into a rival of MSIL's dominance in domestic passenger car sales. The Hyundai decision was the first in a series of case-by-case interventions which laid the basis for a further shift in industrial policy in 2000, when the national government allowed automatic approval for 100 per cent foreign ownership in auto assembly operations (Narayanan and Vashisht, 2008).

Prior to 2000, several foreign OEMs with existing investments in joint venture operations took advantage of the Hyundai precedent and established fully-owned subsidiary companies. They used the new operations to hedge their investments in joint ventures, either by using them as leverage to increase their equity share and operational control in joint ventures, or by using them as a strategic fallback position to enable the OEM to reorient production in the event that the joint venture failed or expired.

In the case of Ford, the global parent firm – the Ford Motor Company – was eventually able to win control over its joint venture with Mahindra in Maraimalai Nagar, southwest of Chennai. This gave Ford the impetus to establish a new plant in Sanand, Gujarat, which was established as a fully-owned foreign operation. In the case of Hero Honda, the foreign partner established a second, fully-owned subsidiary as a strategic counterweight to joint venture operations with the Indian partner.

Conditions of trade and investment liberalisation in the 1990s exacerbated tensions between Honda and the Hero Group, with Honda forced to adopt an inter-control strategy within HMSI's production network. In contrast, the Hero Group persisted with an inter-firm partnership strategy based on the Munjal family's equity interests (see above). These tensions culminated in the end of the joint venture in 2010, with Honda withdrawing its investment to pursue an independent strategy in two-wheelers via HMSI and in passenger cars via Honda Cars which had split from Honda Siel during the same year.

Honda strategically preempted this split by establishing a wholly-owned HMSI assembly plant in Manesar in 1999 with a focus on scooter manufacturing, but also as a potential rival to products manufactured at Hero Honda's Gurugram and Dharuhera facilities. Following Honda's departure, the Munjal family renamed their venture Hero MotoCorp and replaced most of Honda's share with a range of foreign equity investments. This arrangement enabled the family to maintain operational control in India from a minority shareholding position (35 per cent by 2015).

By the 2010s, the joint venture policy had atrophied to the point that the vast majority of passenger vehicle and two-wheeler operations in India were wholly-owned subsidiaries of large global car-makers. These operations were mainly foreign-owned or, in other cases, owned by large Indian family conglomerates like Tata, Mahindra or Hero. The joint venture, while still operating in formal equity terms of major OEMs like MSIL or Toyota Kirloskar, was no longer the primary mode of operational regulation for foreign OEMs.

Although the joint venture model was reshaped in the 1990s and 2000s, this long period of emergent neo-liberalism also involved elements of continuity with the period of restricted openness in the 1980s. One element is the continued willingness of the national government to covet auto manufacturers with state subsidies, while encouraging lead firms to source locally-manufactured inputs. The most recent manifestation of this has been Narendra Modi's 'Make in India' initiative.

Announced in 2014, 'Make in India' is intended to attract new and expansive FDI in manufacturing with an underlying assumption that emerging economies with a strong, dynamic manufacturing sector can lay the basis for broader economic development, prosperity and a rise in living standards (GoI, 2016; 2016a). Auto manufacturing lies at the core of this plan, with an ambition to transform India into 'the primary global automobile manufacturer' (GoI, 2016).

These aspirations borrow heavily from economic goals established through the collaboration between the Society of Indian Automobile Manufacturers (SIAM) and the Ministry of Heavy Industries under the previous INC-led Government (2004–14). These led to the publishing of the first *Automotive Mission Plan 2006–2016 (AMP-1)* in 2006, which outlined ambitions to increase auto manufacturing as a proportion of Gross Domestic Product (GDP) and aggregate employment.

The Department of Heavy Industry, which has historically overseen auto industry policy development on a national level, strongly emphasised the *under-development* of local auto markets as a pitch to local and foreign investors: 'At present, India has amongst the lowest vehicle densities globally at 11 cars per thousand persons and 32 two-wheelers per thousand persons' (GoI, 2010: 34). By comparison, in 2010, South Korea and Brazil had 219 and 96 cars per 1000 persons, respectively (GoI, 2010: 40). This point has been echoed by several global OEMs. Renault-Nissan used this as a core reason to risk major investments in India's small car market, despite this market's current domination by rival OEMs like MSIL and HMIL: 'At 1.4 billion, the Indian population will overtake the Chinese population in 2022. With a car ownership rate of 15 vehicles per 1,000 inhabitants, some seven times less than China and 35 times less than Europe, the potential of the Indian market is spectacular' (Groupe Renault, 2015: 22).

In this global context, *AMP-1* was highly ambitious. It aimed to transform India into 'the destination of choice in the world for design and manufacture of automobiles and auto components' (GoI, 2006). *AMP-1* aimed to increase total industry output to US$145 billion or a forecast 10 per cent of GDP, and to increase 'direct and indirect' industry employment to 25 million by 2016. If successful, this target would have represented a near-doubling of the industry's contribution to GDP, which stood at 5.2 per cent in 2005.

Ultimately, India fell short of this target. Gross industry turnover peaked at US$67.6 billion in 2012/13 and, by 2014/15, was US$58.9 billion (SIAM, 2016). Perhaps reflecting the limitation of such ambitious target-making, the Modi Government has outlined an aspiration to eventually achieve total auto industry output of US$100 billion, which is substantially lower than the original target earmarked in *AMP-1* (GoI, 2016a).

The mixed outcomes of *AMP-1* fed into the drafting of a new *Automotive Mission Plan 2016–2026 (AMP-2).*[2] *AMP-2* noted the shortfall in industry turnover and claimed that *AMP-1*'s employment target was 'incremental'. However, *AMP-2* continues *AMP-1*'s highly ambitious emphasis on future output, employment and export growth with an aim 'to propel the Indian automotive industry to be the engine of the "Make in India" program' (SIAM/GoI, 2015: 3) through 'Vision 3/12/65'.

---

[2] *AMP-2* was announced with a 'curtain raiser' document launched in September 2015 (SIAM/GoI, 2015) with plans for full publication in 2016. At the time of writing, the full document had not been made publicly available.

'Vision 3/12/65' is shorthand for a target to transform India into one of the top three global sites for auto engineering, manufacturing and exports, to achieve an output target equivalent to 12 per cent of GDP, and an 'incremental' employment target of 65 million by 2026. This forecasting relies on an output expansion of 3.5–4 times of the levels of 2015, and assumes an annual average GDP growth of 5.8–7.5 per cent.

To achieve this, the *AMP-2* draft recommends a similar range of industrial subsidies as *AMP-1*, including the 'rationalisation' of all customs and duties for imported raw materials, components and sub-assembled parts, tax exemptions and other subsidies for Research and Development (R&D), design, engineering and testing, expanded government subsidies for auto supplier parks via infrastructure investment, and support for Make in India's general – albeit somewhat rhetorical – push for erasing the existing and residual 'red tape' in government regulation.

AMP-2 also contains several new policy ideas, including encouragement for the Government of India's FAME policy (Faster Adoption and Manufacturing of Hybrid & Electric Vehicles) to prepare for the likely mass marketing of electrical vehicles by the 2020s. This follows initiatives by several global OEMs in auto manufacturing to accelerate research in electrical vehicles. This has led to the establishment of a consortium by MSIL, Mahindra (which had already invested in electrical vehicle manufacturer Reva), Ford and Tata Motors to develop supplier capabilities for electric vehicle manufacturing across the country (Raj, 2016).

Another new idea is the establishment of an 'Auto Sector Skill Development Council' as a new national agency for skill development in the industry, with the capacity to establish 'independent testing and certifying agency for automotive industry skills' (SIAM/GoI, 2015: 9). In part, this recommendation is linked to the role auto manufacturing can play in creating employment for a 'large number of semi-skilled and low-skilled workers' (SIAM/GoI, 2005: 3). *AMP-2* also defines the auto industry more broadly than *AMP-1*. Other than vehicle assembly and components manufacturing, its focus includes automotive R&D, engineering, design, testing, sales and distribution.

Despite these differences, *AMP-2* continues the state's focus on industrial subsidies to attract FDI. A further element of continuity in industrial policy is land acquisition. As outlined above, this has been instrumental to industrial policy at a regional level. At a national level, the practice of land acquisition has long been shaped by colonial-era legislation – the *Land Acquisition Act 1894* – which provided for compulsory public acquisition of agrarian land with clauses for 'market value' compensation for landowners, farmers and forest-dwellers. Along with acquisition for mining, energy and public utility projects, the acquisition of land for export-oriented manufacturing and services has gradually grown in economic and political significance since the mid-1960s.

The importance of land acquisition for economic development projects led to the passing of the *Special Economic Zone (SEZ) Act 2005*, as well as the more recent revision of colonial-era rules for landowner and tenancy compensation represented by the *Right to Fair Compensation and Transparency in Land Acquisition, Rehabilitation and Resettlement Act (Land Acquisition Act) 2013*. According to the Ministry of Commerce and Industry, 19 SEZs were in operation prior to the passing of the *SEZ Act 2005*. Since 2005, a further 421 SEZs have been formally approved, 33 given 'in-principle' approval, and a further 345 'notified' to the Government of India or relevant State governments.

Of the formally approved SEZs, 59 per cent are related to the IT industry via software production and maintenance, ITES, electronics manufacturing or telecommunications equipment manufacturing. However, many other SEZs have been established for foreign and domestic investment in industrial, commercial, and residential construction, and shopping complexes (Banerjee-Guha 2008; Levien, 2012; Menon and Nigam 2007). The Government of India has claimed that these SEZs had cumulatively generated over ₹423,189 crore (over US$65 billion) of investment and directly generated over 1.7 million jobs by March 2017 (GoI, 2017).

SEZs can range from relatively small areas – as small as 10 ha – to vast peri-urbanised spaces of up to 5000 ha. SEZs are generally established as 'Public Private Partnerships' (PPPs) between state institutions which act as landed asset brokers, property developers and private and public institutional investors who act as financial rentiers, and firms investing and operating within SEZs who act as private tenants (Levien, 2011; 2012). The interaction between these institutional and class interests has generated new regional market-based speculation over asset prices. This process has generated major inequalities over value capture between rentiers, who have arguably captured the largest value share, and affected landowners and farmers. Landowners' share of rent has varied between those who have profited greatly and those who have been increasingly forced to survive by undertaking informal and precarious work in the non-agrarian economy.

The degree to which landholders and ex-tenants have benefited from land acquisition depends upon a range of factors, including spatial proximity to proposed development sites, ownership scale and caste relations. In turn, re-investment by beneficiary landholders has influenced the formation of new inequalities at the village level through a concentration of land ownership in cultivation. As outlined in Chapter 5, the dispossession of agrarian land for industrial re-purposing in Gurugram District has generated new conflict over value capture between social strata which reflect differences in caste and region-of-origin. This village-level conflict has strongly influenced industrial conflict within auto manufacturing firms.

Although industrial subsidies and land acquisition represent elements of continuity in industrial policy since the 1980s, there is a further area of economic policy-making which has barely changed throughout this period: the 'industrial relations' system used to regulate labour standards and employment relations in manufacturing firms in the organised sector. As outlined above, planning has been based on the distinction between the organised and unorganised sector, on the history of ISI, on the restrictions imposed on large industrial firms especially during the 1960s and 70s, and on the capacity of industrialists to evade these restrictions after periods of economic and political instability in the 1970s and 1980s.

In this context, it is highly significant that India has retained the core of the labour law framework it inherited in the 1940s and 1950s. The economic liberalisation process that transformed rules for trade, investment and finance in the 1980s and 1990s did *not* include changes to labour laws, which have barely changed since Independence. This relative stasis has persisted despite ongoing demands from businesses, international financial institutions, and economists for labour market 'de-regulation'. In this context, reform of labour laws has become one of the catch-cries of Narendra Modi's government, which was elected in 2014.

In India, there are many labour laws that were designed primarily to regulate employment relations in PSUs and firms in the organised sector. Many of the regulations in these laws are relaxed for firms in the unorganised sector. Key examples include the *Factories Act 1948*, the *Trade Union Act 1926* (TUA), which centralises wage fixing in the hands of the State, and the *IDA* which is supposed to regulate the employment levels in the organised sector. There is also the *Contract Labour (Abolition and Regulation) Act 1970* (*CLARA*), which was intended to restrict the employment of 'contract workers' and regulate their employment conditions. In addition, there are dozens of other national and state-level laws (Shyam Sundar, 2005; Hill, 2009).

The idea of 'work' as a focus for regulation historically centred on the 'workman' employed in the organised sector firm as described in the *Factories Act 1948*. This law regulates the working conditions and working hours of regular workers. The 'workman' reflected the (usually male) blue-collar manufacturing worker employed in an ongoing job in a medium-to-large establishment with a clearly-identifiable employment relationship and a legally-enforceable employment contract.

At the time of writing, the *IDA* requires firms in most States of India with 100 or more employees to seek state permission to lay-off workers or close facilities. Section 25B of the *IDA* stipulates that workers employed for 240 days or more are entitled to compensation if they lose their jobs. Many employers argue that these restrictions necessitate a 'contract labour system' due to the unwarranted costs of hiring and firing regular workers (Shyam Sundar, 2012a).

In most States, the *CLARA* currently applies to firms and labour contractors with 20 or more workers. It outlaws the employment of contract labour in 'core' business activities or for more than 240 continuous days. The *CLARA* also requires that contract workers' wages be equal to that of 'workmen' (regular workers) if they perform similar work. Perhaps its most debated clause is Section 10(1), which enables governments to prohibit contract labour if their work is found to be 'core', ongoing or better-suited to workmen (Shyam Sundar, 2012a).

However, due to the prevalence of informal work in most sectors of the economy, several trade unions and labour-based Non-Government Organisations (NGOs) have focused on establishing new forms of regulation among workers employed outside formal employment relations. Key examples of this include the regulation of work in construction, *bidi* (hand-made cigarette) making, street vending and domestic work.

In the construction industry, the *Building and Other Construction Workers' Welfare Cess Act 1996* legislated the establishment of a Construction Workers Welfare Fund and Board. This oversees a tax (cess) on construction firms in the organised sector which is meant to be spent on entitlements for registered workers, including death and accident insurance, maternity leave, education scholarships for workers' children, and funding for marriages. A similar policy has been implemented for *bidi* workers via the *Bidi Workers Welfare Cess Act 1976* (Agarwala, 2013: 51–52; Barnes, 2015: 166–67). Benefits for workers' children have intersected with enforcement of the *Right to Education Act 2009*, which stipulates free and compulsory, education for children below 14 years of age.

For street vendors, the *Street Vendors (Protection of Livelihood and Regulation of Street Vending) Act 2014* was passed in order to protect self-employed workers who routinely face harassment, eviction or corruption in order to obtain permits to operate in public areas (Austen Soofi, 2012). For domestic workers, labour activism has focused on national-level adoption of the International Labour Organisation's (ILO) Convention on Domestic Workers which, although passed by the ILO in 2013 as a framework to regulate working hours, minimum wage entitlements, and workers' freedom of movement, has yet to be adopted in India.

Several labour organisations have also focused on implementation of the *Unorganised Workers' Social Security Act 2008*, which, as the name suggests, is meant to provide social security for informal workers (Sengupta, 2008). In other cases, organisations have focused on protecting workers' rights under the *Mahatma Gandhi National Rural Employment Guarantee Act 2005* (*NREGA*) which has provided limited manual work at sub-minimum wages for rural households (Lerche et al , 2012). Besides reducing the scope and impact of the *NREGA*, the Modi government has also recently proposed to collapse all existing social security provisions into a single labour code (Gopalakrishnan, 2017). This reform would, if implemented, collapse 15 separate laws into a single labour law.

Debates about informal workers' social security have largely bypassed debates over reforming traditional labour laws which tend to focus on the small minority of regular workers employed in organised sector firms. Despite the dominant reality of informal work, much of the popular debate has focused on the business case for reforms to these traditional laws. While partially addressing the flexibility requirements of firms in the organised sector, these reforms do little to address the interests and rights of the majority who rely on informal work for their livelihood and survival. This debate has also often tended to ignore the reality that core labour laws such as the *CLARA*, and multiple minimum wage laws, are routinely ignored by employers (Lerche, 2012; Government of India, 2009; Rani and Belser, 2012).

More recently, the Modi Government has responded positively to business demands even though it must negotiate changes through the Rajya Sabha (national Upper House of Parliament). Modi has expressed sympathy for reforms enacted by State governments led by his Bharatiya Janata Party (BJP). For example, the Government of Rajasthan has lifted the threshold for the *Factories Act* from firms with 10 or more workers to firms with 20 or more workers.[3] It has also lifted the threshold for firms regulated by the *CLARA* from 20 workers to 40 workers. The Government of Maharashtra recently lifted this threshold from 20 to 50 workers (Kadokari, 2017). The Government of Andhra Pradesh has allowed contract workers to be employed continuously in 'non-core' business activities and in a limited number of 'core' activities.

The Governments of Rajasthan, Haryana and Madhya Pradesh have also lifted the threshold under the *IDA* for employers seeking permission to sack workers, or close factories from 100 or more employees to 300 or more employees. In addition, no party to a dispute (for example, a retrenched worker) will be able to officially challenge an employer's decision under the *IDA* for three years after implementation.

The Modi government has also proposed changes to the *Minimum Wage Act* and the *Apprenticeship Act*, which would allow inter-state migrant workers to be hired as apprentices, set their wages as a 'stipend' of 70–90 per cent of the minimum wage (with no medical insurance payable), and enable State governments to pay half this stipend for one year for 'small' enterprises.

In April 2015, the Modi government introduced a new bill in the Lok Sabha (Lower House), the *Labour Code on Industrial Relations Bill 2015*, which aimed to consolidate three central labour laws – the *IDA*, the *TUA* and the *Industrial Employment (Standing Orders) Act 1946* – into one simplified law. While this bill had not been passed into law at the time of writing, it would follow the Government

---

[3] For firms without power, the threshold has changed from firms with 20 or more workers to firms with 40 or more workers.

of Rajasthan's lead in lifting the threshold for State permission to lay-off workers or close establishments with 100 to 300 employees.

Although the new law would increase minimum compensation for retrenched workers[4], it would give the national government the power to unilaterally exempt any firm from the code's provisions. In addition, the code would extend the *IDA*'s restrictions on strike action. Currently, PSU employees must give an advance notice of two weeks for any strike. The proposed change would extend this restriction to all workers and impose fines of ₹20,000–50,000 (c. US$300–780), and potential imprisonment for 'illegal' strike action. The definition of a 'strike' has also been widened in the bill to include unexplained leave by at least half of the workers in an establishment (Gopalakrishnan and Shyam Sundar, 2015).

Modi's reform agenda is popular among many business leaders, including many employers in the auto industry. Industry leaders in auto manufacturing have joined other employers in demanding that the *CLARA* allow contract labour in core business activities, and an end to hire-and-fire restrictions in the *IDA*, although it is noteworthy that the Modi government is, thus far, proposing to modify but not abolish these restrictions. Some employers argue that auto components manufacturing is particularly vulnerable to the restrictions in the *IDA* because labour costs are proportionally higher in supply firms than in OEMs (Narayanan and Vashisht, 2008: 24). These claims continue to be advanced despite long-term evidence of industrialists' capacity to evade the many labour law provisions supposed to protect workers' rights.

Conclusion

To understand the roots of commercial, industrial, social and political conflict in Indian auto manufacturing, and the changes to labour standards and employment relations that underlie them, we must first understand the interaction between global production networks and state institutions. This chapter has argued that pioneering foreign OEMs like Maruti Suzuki (MSIL) and Hero Honda were largely able to implement their preferred approaches to supply chain relations and work organisation through a process of first-mover coupling. This means their operations were sheltered by the Government of India through auto market segmentation and industrial subsidies.

First-mover coupling also means that the stability and influence of these early global production networks is generally higher than that of late-arriving OEMs. Such OEMs have been forced to adapt their commercial operations to

---

[4] Compensation would be increased from the equivalent of 15 days' wages for each completed year of service to 45 days' wages.

the established global production networks of rival foreign and domestic OEMs. Throughout this process, state subsidies have played a key role in attracting and supporting investment by OEMs at a regional level. The Government of Haryana played a pioneering role with its industrial and urban development policies in Gurugram. These policies have been emulated by state governments across the country.

The process of first-mover coupling occurred through two phases of national industrial policy. A period of restricted openness was pursued from 1982, when the SMC agreed on terms with the Government of India to revitalise and modernise auto manufacturing at the Maruti Gurugram site, until 1991. Openness was characterised by policy-makers' realisation that foreign investment, technology and managerial expertise was necessary to modernise domestic auto manufacturing. However, this openness was shaped by an underlying policy assumption of ISI which meant that FDI was controlled through residual industrial licensing, market segmentation between passenger car, two-wheeler and commercial vehicle manufacturing, joint ventures as a mode of operational regulation, and by local content targets in components manufacturing.

The second phase of emergent neo-liberalism in industry policy was ushered in by the neo-liberal reforms of mid-1991. These reforms jettisoned residual ISI in economic policymaking. The 1991 events heralded the beginning of a process in which auto manufacturing was gradually opened to unrestricted FDI. In line with this, the joint venture was transformed from a mode of operational regulation into a mode of entry for foreign OEMs. Marked by the success of Hyundai's operations in southern India, the mid-1990s signalled a shift towards assembly operations which were fully owned and operated by foreign OEMs.

In an increasing number of cases, foreign OEMs established fully-owned greenfield sites for manufacturing. In other cases, foreign OEMs already engaged in joint ventures with domestic industrial firms have established separate greenfield projects to mitigate risk in joint venture operations to leverage equity against joint venture partners, or to establish a way to circumvent and eventually jettison joint venture restrictions.

The implications of these two phases of industry policy were profound for labour standards and employment relations in the auto industry. The next chapter explains how, during the first phase of restricted openness, foreign OEMs engaged in first-mover coupling were able to implement their preferred model of work organisation and employment relations. MSIL's Gurugram site was the pioneer of this process, with Japanese managers able to adapt principles of lean manufacturing to work organisation on the shop-floor in the 1980s and 1990s.

For the second phase of emergent neo-liberalism, Chapter 4 will show that the transformation of market segmentation and competition incentivised OEMs and their key suppliers to change their employment relations practices. MSIL was again the pioneer in this process. In the late 1990s, MSIL began to restructure labour standards for its regular workforce and, after a period of industrial conflict in the early 2000s, began to systematically replace its regular workforce with contract workers and casual workers on lower wages. MSIL's experiment with a contract labour system was later generalised at a regional and a national level.

At a regional level, this approach was adopted by key rivals, especially by Hero Honda, and by Tier-1 and Tier-2 components manufacturers, including several strategic partners to MSIL and the Hero Group. At a national level, these practices were emulated by OEMs and key suppliers in other auto manufacturing regions, especially in the south where Hyundai's operations were underpinned by a regional contract labour system in the CMA.

These changes were part of a broader process of industrial development which transformed town and village life in auto manufacturing regions. Key examples include the peri-urban areas of Gurugram in Haryana and Greater Noida in Uttar Pradesh; in the satellite city of Sriperumbudur and towns of Maraimalai Nagar and Oragadam on the outskirts of Chennai; in the Pimpri-Chinchwad area of Pune and the village of Chakan in central Maharashtra; and in peri-urban sub-regions in several other parts of the country. As outlined in the following chapters, social and political conflict was central to this process of regional industrialisation.

4

The Transformation of Labour Relations

The previous chapter outlined the mutually constitutive role of global Original Equipment Manufacturers (OEMs) and state institutions in the modernisation of Indian auto manufacturing and the industrial transformation of regional economies. Through a process of 'first-mover coupling', a minority of foreign and domestic OEMs were able to reap positional advantages by undertaking pioneering investments in the 1980s and 1990s. During this period, India was emerging from an Import Substitution Industrialisation (ISI)-based economic policy framework to a neo-liberal economic policy framework through a gradual process of trade, investment and financial liberalisation.

Firms like Maruti Suzuki India Limited (MSIL) – or Maruti Udyog Limited (MUL) as it was known until the 2000s, Honda and Hero MotoCorp – which operated as the Hero Honda joint venture from 1984–2010, Tata Motors and Hyundai Motor India Limited (HMIL) played critical roles in modernising local industry by establishing their global production networks in key regions. These firms were rewarded with dominant shares in their respective vehicle markets and, for MSIL, Hero, and HMIL, with the capacity to pursue the preferred firm-level and network strategies of their global parent companies.

Along with the capacity to reshape commercial relations with networks of components manufacturers and vendors on a regional level, these pioneering firms were also in a position to strongly influence practices of employment relations and norms in Indian manufacturing. One of the key features of labour standards and employment relations in Indian auto manufacturing is its transformation in the hands of these firms and their key suppliers via tension and conflict with state institutions, key competitors and employees.

Yet the liberalisation of trade and investment in domestic auto manufacturing has also reflexively challenged the capacity of these pioneering firms to shape employment relations as they originally intended. As this chapter will demonstrate, this led to dramatic changes in the social regulation of employment relations which began in the early 2000s, and have continued to reverberate over the last 15 years. While there is evidence that labour standards in smaller components supply firms – in Tier-3 and Tier-4 firms – have long been predicated upon employment in various forms of precarious and informal work (see Chapter 6), labour standards in OEMs, Tier-1, and Tier-2 firms have been reshaped by the systematic preference of employers for workers employed on lower wages and short-term contracts in entry-level production-line jobs. This preference has shaped the emergence and reproduction of high levels of industrial conflict.

Some of these conflicts have been brutal. As outlined in the beginning of this book, the worst cases have led to the deaths of company employees, such as the case of Italian gearbox manufacturer, Graziano Trasmissioni, in Greater Noida in September 2008, Indian components manufacturer, Pricol Limited, in Coimbatore, Tamil Nadu, in September 2009 and, most recently, the death of a Human Resources (HR) manager at MSIL's Manesar facility, in July 2012.

The fact that the conflict at MSIL in July 2012 had such a devastating outcome for employees – including the retrenchment of thousands of workers and the eventual imprisonment of dozens of workers on serious criminal charges – is particularly important, given the central role that MSIL played in the modernisation of Indian auto manufacturing and the transformation of the NCR into one of the world's largest auto manufacturing zones.

As this chapter documents, MSIL radically shifted the focus of its employment relations practices from the 1990s to the 2000s. The company pushed to reduce the enterprise benefits given to its unionised, regular workforce. When workers' resistance led to major industrial conflict, the company used this opportunity to systematically replace retrenched workers with new recruits hired by labour contractors and casual workers who were paid much lower basic wages and were given fewer enterprise benefits.

This marked a radical break with MSIL's previous practice of relying on generous wages and enterprise benefits in order to win workers' consent to the company's version of 'lean manufacturing'. Through MSIL's dominant role in the NCR and in the passenger car market at a national level, these practices strongly influenced Tier-1 and Tier-2 components suppliers, including MSIL's strategic partners and joint venture firms, and several key competitors in auto assembly manufacturing.

MSIL's initial efforts to restructure workers' wages in the late 1990s – which precipitated its first major industrial conflict and the eventual shift in its recruitment and employment relations framework – came in response to rising market competition as new foreign OEMs entered Indian regions to produce cars for the country's growing strata of middle and high-income households. This change in competitive conditions was, in turn, shaped by the radical liberalisation of financial rules in 1991, ongoing trade liberalisation and, above all, by the gradual liberalisation of investment and FDI rules. These changes erased the last vestiges of ISI and paved the way for fully-owned and operated subsidiaries of global OEMs to supplant joint ventures as the primary mode of operational regulation (Chapter 3).

In this context, MSIL became a pioneer in the auto industry in a dual sense: first, in the 1980s, as the moderniser of passenger car manufacturing under the managed protection of national and regional state institutions, and second, in the 2000s, as the national instigator in the transformation of labour standards and employment relations. Its practices were emulated in the early 2000s via the greenfield operations of HMIL in the CMA and by Toyota Kirloskar's operation in Bengaluru

This chapter begins to trace this narrative by exploring MSIL's role in the transformation of employment relations in the NCR. This is framed in two sections that follow from the discussion of institutional change and industrial policy in Chapter 3: for the period of restricted openness from 1982 to 1991, and for the period of emergent neo-liberalism after 1991. Second, this chapter explores the role of global OEMs, including HMIL, in the CMA before moving into a discussion of employment relations trends in other regions of India, including the C-SEZ, Pune District, Gujarat, Uttarakhand and Toyota Kirloskar's operations in Bengaluru.

Employment relations at Maruti Suzuki under 'restricted openness', 1982–91

In the 1980s, the Suzuki Motor Corporation's (SMC) operational control over Maruti Udyog Limited (MUL) – which later developed into MSIL – led to the implementation of a form of lean manufacturing. Lean manufacturing or lean production became a world-famous system of intra-firm work organisation and inter-firm commercial organisation which was based upon the Toyota Production System (TPS), pioneered in Japan after World War Two. Three decades after Toyota began generalising its distinctive approach across its emerging international operations, the core features of the TPS were generalised through research by the International Motor Vehicle Program at the Massachusetts Institute of Technology (MIT) (Womack, Jones and Roos, 1990).

Broadly speaking, lean production conveyed the idea of radical waste reduction in distribution and production by reducing costs associated with transportation, storage, production velocity and product defects, by making output more responsive to real-time customer demand and by constantly exploring ways to reduce the time required for each step of the distribution and production process while maximising product quality and value. For inter-firm commercial relations, this approach meant outsourcing multiple steps in the manufacturing process to a network of materials and components suppliers who would compete to provide the quality and price demanded by OEMs. In auto manufacturing, the notion of a commodity chain, value chain or production network is thus closely linked to the concept of lean production.

For intra-firm work organisation, lean production meant devolving responsibility for production speed by constantly and collectively exploring methods of work re-organisation to reduce the time needed for each cycle of production and distribution between points in the manufacturing process, and by devolving product inspection and quality control to the shop-floor rather than to separate corporate entities or divisions. By the 1980s, most global OEMs had adopted one or another version of lean production although, depending upon the firm, it came under a variety of labels.

In the ensuing two decades, versions of lean production spread across the Global South, including India, via the extension of global production networks in auto manufacturing. The spread and variegation of lean production across emerging markets in Asia coincided with the shift towards Human Resource Management (HRM) as an over-arching framework for recruitment, employee development, and employment relations in the 1980s and 1990s. With this shift came the idea that employment relations should be framed functionally in order to optimise organisational performance, rather than be framed structurally to represent the different interests of people at work.

Auto manufacturing has long been associated with 'high road' labour standards in Western countries (Babson, 1986; Sugrue, 2010). The demand of global vehicle manufacturers for high quality products, strict design specifications, efficient technology and workforce skills, should, in a normative sense, lead to work organisation, labour standards and employment relations based upon relatively high wages, long-term or open-ended employment contracts, stable career paths, social protection and enterprise-based benefits, as well as social protection through collective bargaining and trade union representation (Lakhani, Kuruvilla and Avgar, 2013).

Within the HRM literature, there has been a widespread view that the spread of lean production frameworks across the world's leading OEMs should extend but, at the same time, modify these assumptions. On the one hand, lean manufacturing and HRM's twin demand for organisational 'high performance' should also encompass high employment security, training and skill development. But, these demands should also lead to the re-organisation of work into small groups and shop-floor teams with responsibility for key operational decisions (MacDuffie, 1995). Wages, while still relatively high, should be differentiated on the basis of performance, although the basis on which to measure performance – whether based on an individual, an occupation or some other collective basis – varies strongly between OEMs from different countries (Jürgens and Krzywdzinski, 2016).

The SMC, although a much smaller player in world passenger car manufacturing than Toyota, had adopted lean production long ago, and sought to introduce this framework to operations at the revamped Gurugram site in the mid-1980s (Monaco, 2017). As outlined in Chapter 3, MUL's early attempt to establish car manufacturing in Gurugram was strongly shaped by FDI restrictions and conditions imposed under the Government of India's ISI-based framework, which included high tariffs on imported components and a Phased Manufacturing Program (PMP), which forced SMC to aim for a majority of local content in its supply chain. In addition, poor quality infrastructure in road transport in the NCR forced MUL to establish its supply base as close to the Gurugram site as possible (Gulyani, 2001).

While encouraging some Japanese Tier-1 components manufacturers to establish operations in Gurugram District was one way of gradually building operational capacity at its assembly plant, the need to accelerate production plans forced MUL to enter into multiple equity partnerships and joint ventures with Indian Tier-1 and Tier-2 suppliers. This role was important because Indian manufacturers had little experience of the 'just-in-time' supply responsiveness and relational value chain governance demanded under SMC's lean manufacturing model.

Direct Japanese investment, combined with operational and logistical oversight, provided the quickest means of establishing SMC's global production network in the NCR. In return, MSIL offered direct technical assistance to select Tier-1 suppliers via management personnel and offers of long-term contracts to key strategic partners.

SMC also attempted to implement lean production at the workplace-level. Local management, which was run jointly by Japanese and Indian managers, copied a template for local production from SMC headquarters in Japan. This was facilitated gradually by an influx of Japanese managers, technicians and supervisors. A large number of Indian employees were also given time to experience work and training in SMC's Kosai Assembly Plant in Japan. By March 2003, the company claimed that 41 per cent of its permanently-employed or 'regular' workforce (which numbered 4,590 at the time) had been trained in Japan on at least one occasion (Becker-Ritterspach, 2009: 122).

Deploying this template for work organisation proved to be challenging. Until the 2000s, MSIL was still a Public Sector Unit (PSU), albeit with substantive SMC operational oversight, and inherited several employment relations practices endemic to Indian PSUs. Indian manufacturing firms in the organised sector, especially industrial PSUs, were generally managed in a hierarchical and patriarchal manner. Firms were culturally framed like an extended family, with the factory manager treated as a 'father' and senior managers and supervisors treated like 'older sons' or 'older brothers' (Becker-Ritterspach, 2009: 77–78).

In this context, work designations represented status signifiers, and deference to hierarchy was the norm. Caste divisions were reflected in work-life and educational opportunities and occupational choices. There was a particularly strong division in the industry between white-collar office-based work and blue-collar manual work, and an aversion against interaction with workers from these backgrounds (Ramaswamy, 1996; Sharma, 1997; D'Costa, 2005). These traditions were challenged by introducing lean production norms like teamwork and job rotation.

These behavioural expectations and norms were reflected in auto manufacturing through the reproduction of differences between white and blue-collar work and, in particular, the aversion of managers to engage in manual work or mingle with workers on the shop-floor. Even by the 2000s, MSIL maintained a steep hierarchical structure based on 19 separate designations for operators, supervisors and managers from junior to the executive level in line with standard PSU practices (Becker-Ritterspach, 2009: 109).

However, over time, Japanese managers were successfully able to introduce teamwork principles. Teams were given the autonomy to stop the production-line in order to maintain a zero-defects policy, and workers were encouraged to participate in activities of 'continuous improvement' (*kaizen*) through quality circles and employee suggestion schemes (Becker-Ritterspach, 2007; Ishigami, 2004). Maruti's job rotation policy also encouraged 'visible egalitarianism' via common uniforms, shared toilets, and shared canteens (Becker-Ritterspach, 2009: 117–120).

R.C. Bhargava, the former CEO and (at the time of writing) Chairman of MSIL, explained the challenges of implementing these Japanese work traditions among Indian managers and workers:

> In Indian conditions, we initially did face problems introducing the Japanese management ethos in [MSIL]. There was, especially among managers, a certain amount of reluctance and hesitation about wearing a uniform and eating in the same canteen, sitting in the open offices, and all that. It required the top management to spend time with these managers and convince them that this was the only way to do things. It worked after some time. And as we went along, our managers realised that the concept not only produced results but also that it was not a bad thing to wear a uniform and eat in a common canteen with the workers... People got used to it and realised that it did not adversely affect them (cited in Becker-Ritterspach, 2009: 119–20).

In order to implement these changes to work organisation and workplace social relations, MUL increased the proportion that wage allowances and bonuses played in total remuneration. This practice decreased the income tax obligations of workers, offered regular workers a range of enterprise-based benefits, and linked wage bonuses to attendance, workplace productivity, participation in workplace suggestion schemes, and implementation. Other than helping to soften the impact of changes to work organisation, these policies also helped to encourage worker participation in *kaizen* initiatives like suggestion schemes and quality circles (Becker-Ritterspach, 2009: 123).

Thus, the implementation of lean manufacturing principles at a workplace level led to the co-implementation of high wage, secure, long-term employment contracts boosted with a range of incentives as a trade-off against forms of workplace organisation which contradicted managerial and social norms of industry. Importantly, this compact was implemented in the context of restricted openness in industry policy. For MUL, this meant protection from competition in the passenger car market via the Government of India's policy of auto industry segmentation and managed openness towards manufacturing FDI.

Employment relations at Maruti Suzuki under 'emergent neo-liberalism'

The process through which Maruti management gradually unraveled this compact began in the late 1990s. By the mid-2000s, MSIL had shifted from a policy of recruiting and employing most of its workers on open-ended contracts with high income, job, skill reproduction, and employment security towards a policy of recruiting all new production-line workers via multiple labour contractors employed on short-term contracts. These 'contract workers' were paid much lower wages. Through MSIL's financial and operational influence over key Tier-1 and Tier-2 suppliers, this practice was emulated by components manufacturers across the NCR – a finding established in detail in Chapters 5 and 6 based on the author's empirical research.

This process was not simply the result of unilateral profit-seeking by MSIL management, but occurred through the changing structure of market competition, changes to the regulation of private investment in auto manufacturing and, importantly, the reaction and collective resistance of the company's workers. The Government of India continued to pursue investment liberalisation policies after the economic reforms of 1991, including the abolition of industrial licensing restrictions and PMP-based targets for local content in auto components manufacturing.

These changes included allowing majority-owned foreign joint ventures in auto assembly manufacturing in 1993 and, following Hyundai's Memorandum of Understanding (MOU) with the Governments of India and the Government of Tamil Nadu in 1996, allowing foreign OEMs to commence passenger car assembly at fully-foreign owned greenfield sites. A case-by-case approach to foreign ownership and control from 1996 to 2000 was followed, in 2000, with automatic approval for all foreign-run ventures in auto assembly manufacturing.

During this period of gradual liberalisation from 1993 to 2000, nine foreign OEMs commenced new operations in India, either as joint ventures or as fully foreign-owned operations, including six OEMs with investments in the passenger car segment. While MSIL retained its position as the market leader in passenger car production and sales throughout this period, its role was challenged by market competitors for the first time. Combined with economic instability across Asia in the 1997/98, these new institutional and market conditions meant that MSIL's profitability fell for the first time since commencing operations in the early 1980s.

In 1998, MSIL management responded by proposing changes to the structure of employees' pay and conditions. The management proposed to lower bonuses and incentive payments for productivity as well as enterprise pension contributions of workers. They also made it more difficult for workers to access promotions within the company. Following these changes, the union which represented shop-floor regular workers, the Maruti Udyog Employees Union (MUEU), began to complain that the workers' share of the income was falling, even as the Gurugram plant continued to aggressively expand output (Becker-Ritterspach, 2007).

These tensions led to an MUEU-led strike in September 2000, which was met with a management lockout with the aim of forcing the union to accept its changes. By January 2001, the MUEU campaign had been defeated. Besides firing many striking workers, the company established a new union, the Maruti Udyog Kamgar Union (MUKU), which remains an active representative for regular workers to this day at the Gurugram plant. The MUEU was later de-registered by the Government of Haryana for alleged financial irregularities. The company also used a Voluntary Retirement Scheme (VRS) to reduce the size of its regular workforce from 5,770 in 2001 to 3,334 in March 2004 (Becker-Ritterspach, 2007: 40), a decline of 42 per cent over a three-year period. By 2004, the firm employed fewer regular workers than it had in the mid-1980s.

However, expanding production meant that MSIL would require more workers. From 2004 onwards, the company implemented a policy in which the vast majority of new workers were recruited through labour contractors. From 2004 to 2007, hundreds of workers were employed in this way. These workers were paid a gross wage around a quarter of regular workers' wages.

By 2007, the Gurugram factory employed around 1,800 regular workers and about 4,000 workers hired through at least 20 different labour contractors (FMS, 2011; Bose and Pratap, 2012). Using labour contractors represented a significant cost advantage for MSIL as most of these workers were denied entitlements previously offered to regular workers, such as productivity and holiday bonuses, and a range of allowances including attendance, dearness, rental, child education, transport, and uniform cleaning.

MSIL implemented a similar policy at its new Manesar assembly facility, 17 km southwest of Gurugram, which commenced production on the site of MSIL's old supplier park in 2007. The Manesar site grew into three plants which, by 2011, collectively employed about 1,000 regular workers, 800 trainees, 400 apprentices, and 1,200 contract workers. Regular workers at this time earned a basic wage of ₹13,000 per month and could earn a gross wage of ₹17,000 per month (about US$200–265).[1] In comparison, workers hired by contractors earned a basic wage of about ₹6,500 (about US$100), trainees were paid ₹8,000–10,000 (US$125–55), and apprentices ₹3,000–4,200 (US$45–65).

Interestingly, the regular workers' wage at the Manesar plants was much lower than workers at the Gurugram plant who could earn ₹30,000–40,000 (US$465–625). The Manesar plants were based on a range of new passenger car models. Although, like the Gurugram plant, it produced the popular Alto 800 small car, the Manesar plants' production network was otherwise separate from the components used in the Gurugram plant.

Production at Manesar was also segmented between the facility's three plants, each with different levels of labour intensity and robotic technology. In Plant A, engines were fixed into chassis, doors and front shields manually attached or welded by workers on an assembly line. In this plant, around a quarter of the workers were regular and over half were employed as contract workers by 2011. In Plant B, there was a higher level of automation on the assembly line with most welding tasks undertaken with robotic machinery. Here, nearly three quarters of the workers were contract and only 10 per cent were regular workers. In the most recently-established, most advanced Plant C, a greater proportion of the workers were regular. The capacity of managers to move workers between these different plants proved important for the company during the 2011/12 industrial conflict (see below).

As a rule, management at the Manesar facility used a system of probation. Most workers were hired as apprentices from Industrial Training Institutes (ITIs)[2] via labour contractors and then, if successful, offered work as temporary workers on

---

[1] In this book, all wage rates refer to monthly amounts unless otherwise specified. A 'basic wage' generally refers to monthly wages for an eight-hour day spread over a six-day week. A 'gross wage' is the basic monthly wage plus overtime payments (usually for up to an additional four hours per day) and any bonuses for productivity, holidays or festivals, and allowances such as attendance, dearness, rental, child education, transport and uniform cleaning. These bonuses and allowances are commonly specified in three-year or four-year collective wage agreements and generally only cover regular workers.

[2] ITIs are government-run institutions that provide technical and vocational training across India.

6–7 months contracts which were arranged between their labour contractor and the MSIL management. A minority of these contract workers were promoted as trainees, and a further minority of these trainees were given the opportunity to become regular workers on open-ended contracts.

MSIL thus maintained a pathway into regular employment for a small minority of recruits, but maintained the rest of its production-line workforce on a series of short-term or rotating employment contracts overseen by labour contractors (Three retrenched regular workers, MSIL [Manesar plant], interview with author, Old Gurgaon, March 2013). This practice divided the workforce into a shrinking core of regular workers employed on relatively high wages and relatively generous employment benefits, and a large majority of contract workers who were paid much lower wages and enjoyed far fewer employment benefits.

While MSIL was able to manage employment relations at its Gurugram plant in the decade post-2001 without a resumption of strikes or open industrial conflicts, tensions among the younger workforce at the three Manesar plants simmered over the treatment of workers and perceptions that workers in different employment configurations were being employed in similar production-line roles despite large disparities in wages and conditions. These tensions led to demands to eradicate these disparities and to convert the roles of many non-regular workers into regular or ongoing employment, that is, to 'regularise' the employment of workers.

These tensions crystallised into a campaign to form a trade union for all workers at the facility, known as the Maruti Suzuki Workers Union (MSWU). Management's refusal to recognise the MSWU led to the first conflict at the Manesar facility between April and June 2011. Eleven workers advocating for the registration of MSWU were fired by the company, leading to a sit-down strike involving most of the 3,500 workers at the site. Many of these workers occupied the front portion of the facility and blocked the entrance.

The workers behind the formation of the MSWU were supported by several major trade union confederations, officially known as Central Trade Union Organisations (CTUOs) in India, including the Communist-affiliated All-India Trade Union Congress (AITUC) and Centre of Indian Trade Unions (CITU), the Congress-affiliated Indian National Trade Union Congress (INTUC), and the left-wing nationalist Hind Mazdoor Sabha (HMS). The largest CTUOs in the region mobilised several thousand manufacturing workers in front of the factory gate in support of the unionisation drive and began to advise and consult with unionists inside, with AITUC playing the leading role. However, by mid-June, the Government of Haryana had declared the strike illegal.

The June strike ended with a stalemate: the 11 workers who had been fired were reinstated but the management docked the workers' pay for the strike – 26 days for regular workers and 13 days for casual and contract workers – and maintained its refusal to recognise the MSWU. According to some reports, the 13-day strike cost the company the equivalent of 12,600 cars and ₹420 *crore* (about US$63 million) in sales income (*Deccan Herald*, 18 June 2011).

Conflict re-emerged in late August 2011 after the management, having conducted its own investigations into the June troubles, insisted that workers involved in the occupation sign 'good conduct bonds' (Figure 4.1). These written agreements, formulated under the terms of Indian labour law – the *Industrial Employment (Standing Orders) Act 1946* – specified the terms under which the company would dismiss workers in future (Three retrenched regular workers, MSIL [Manesar plant], interview with author, Old Gurgaon, March 2013).

Fig. 4.1: The text of the Good Conduct Bond issued to striking MSIL workers, Manesar, June 2011

In Terms of Clause 25(3) of the Certified Standing Orders I, [*worker's name*], son of [*father's or parents' name*], do hereby execute and sign this good conduct bond voluntarily in my own volition in accordance with Clause 25(3) of the Certified Standing Orders. I undertake that upon joining my duties I shall give normal production in disciplined manner and that I shall not resort to go slow, intermittent stoppage of work, stay-in strike, work to rule, sabotage or otherwise indulge in any activity, which would hamper the normal production in the factory.

I am aware that resorting to go slow, intermittent stoppage of work, stay-in strike, or indulging in any other activity having adverse effect on the normal production constitutes a major misconduct under the Certified Standing Orders and the punishment provided for committing such acts of misconducts includes dismissal from service without notice, under clause 30 of the Certified Standing Orders.

I, therefore, do hereby agree that if, upon joining my duties, I am found indulging in any activity such as go slow, intermittent stoppage of work, stay-in strike, work to rule, sabotage or any other activity having the effect of hampering normal production, I shall be liable to be dismissed from service as provided under the Certified Standing Orders.

I agree that if on joining duty I am found indulging in go-slow, intermittent stoppage of work, stay-in strike, work to rule, sabotage or otherwise indulge in any activity which would hamper the normal production in the factory, I will be liable to be dismissed from service without notice, as provided under the certified standing orders.

   i. Apply or obtain leave on a false pretext
  ii. Lack of proper personal appearance, sanitation and cleanliness including proper grooming
 iii. Conduct in private life prejudicial to the reputation of the company
 iv. Remaining in a toilet for a substantially long period of time
  v. Habitual neglect of cleanliness

Date
Signature of the workman

In response to the issue of these good conduct bonds, MSWU leaders instigated a walk-out which was followed by a management lockout. During the lockout, management shifted about 900 workers from Plant A into Plant B in order to continue production. After one month, regular workers returned to work. After this, many workers signed the good conduct bonds, partly upon advice from CTUOs who hoped negotiations over union recognition would resume. However, about 1,200 contract and casual workers were dismissed from Plant A and, after the workers who had participated in the strike complained of victimisation, the site was re-occupied by workers on 7 October, 2011. After 12 days, this second occupation came to an end, partly because 30 workers who had filed to register the MSWU with the Department of Labour in Chandigarh, the administrative capital of Haryana, and whose employment had been suspended by the company, agreed to resign in exchange for termination payments which ranged from ₹16 *lakh* to ₹0.4 *crore* (about US$25,000–65,000).

This was a contradictory outcome for workers. A new (but still unofficial) union leadership emerged and the management gradually moved towards a position in which it would recognise the MSWU as long as the union remained independent from CTUO affiliation. The management also offered one-off pay increase for most workers. Contract workers and apprentices received a 30 per cent pay hike, including access to allowances for attendance, medicine, transport and clothing for ITI-qualified workers. Regular workers also received a raise. By November 2013, regular workers earned ₹32,000–36,000, representing a 146 per cent increase in basic pay and a 112 per cent increase in gross pay from June 2011 levels.

On the other hand, the management remained resolute that non-regular workers could not be part of any collective wage agreement negotiated with the MSWU, despite an offer from the new MSWU leadership to suspend wage increases for 12 months in order to include non-regular workers in the agreement. At the same time, the management kept around 100 police officers stationed at the site round the clock until December 2011.

Meanwhile, at Suzuki Castings and Powertrain, MSIL's diesel engine plant located nearby, around 50 police remained at the site until December 2011, where they camped in tents adjacent to the factory. By June 2012, there were still 15 police officers staying at the site. Here, the union leadership had not accepted offers to resign and a 'go-slow' had continued until as late as November 2011.

Although the MSWU was finally recognised by MSIL in March 2012, open conflict was soon reignited. In April and May 2012, 70 workers were sacked in various departments of the Manesar site for allegedly using fake certificates to claim technical qualifications. ITI-qualified workers were entitled, under MSIL's new wage regime, to higher gross wages and more enterprise benefits than unqualified workers. Some workers regarded these sackings as an unnecessary provocation. In addition, management, while offering limited pathways into regular employment for a small minority who were able to pass a series of tests, reiterated to workers that it would not regularise the work of most employees.

Then, on 18 July 2012, a Dalit worker was involved in an argument with his supervisor. Although the worker claimed that the supervisor addressed him using discriminatory casteist language, his employment was suspended.[3] That evening, a violent altercation took place between workers, supervisors, and managers in which dozens were injured. A fire broke out which culminated in the death of the HR manager Awanish Kumar Dev.

This conflict also proved to be devastating for the majority of workers at the Manesar facility. Production was closed for several weeks, 600 police officers were brought in to guard the site, and the Government of Haryana banned the assembly of five or more people within a 2-km radius of Manesar under a 'Section 144 order' under the *Criminal Procedure Code 1973*. This crackdown was supported by the local *Zila Parishad*, the main organisation for all block councils and village councils in the 1250 square km district of Gurugram, and, remarkably, even by the MUKU – the regular workers' union at MSIL's Gurugram plant. Despite the state crackdown on protest, around 7,000 workers marched in support of sacked workers in Gurugram in mid-August 2012.

About 1500 contract workers – the overwhelming majority of contract workers at the site – were retrenched, along with 546 regular workers. Around 148 workers were arrested and imprisoned in Bhondsi jail in Gurugram where, over four years later, 31 former-MSIL employees were convicted with a range of serious criminal offences. Of this group, 13 were given life sentences for murder (Sethi, 2017).

After August 2012, MSIL made significant changes to its employment relations practices in the aftermath of this violent dispute. Other than major rises in wage rates (see above), the company announced a shift towards the direct recruitment of 'company casuals' or 'company temps' rather than recruitment through labour contractors. Under this new system, company representatives met recruits at the factory gate or at ITI campuses, undertook background checks, orientation and basic training, and hired individuals directly. Casuals were employed on short-term contracts of up to seven months, while some apprentices had the opportunity to convert to a two-year traineeship after one year.

By March 2014, the company claimed a combined workforce of 12,500 regular workers, 6,500 temp workers (mostly 'company temps' but also a minority of contract workers) and 1,100 apprentices at its two sites in Gurugram and Manesar

---

[3] Dalits are members of castes historically known as 'untouchables' and regarded by many higher castes as outside the Varna system of the Hindu religion. Dalits remain socio-economically and culturally disadvantaged in India today.

(Mukherjee, 2014; Raj, 2016a). Company casuals were paid ₹11,000–14,000, itself representing a 29–65 per cent increase on top of the 30 per cent rise for contract workers and apprentices awarded in early 2012, while the remaining minority of contract workers was paid a comparatively lower wage of ₹5,500–6,000 (GWN, 2014). More recent reports suggest that 3,500 company temps were employed at MSIL's Manesar facility, compared to 1,600 regular workers, as well as a further 1,700 company temps at the Gurugram plant (Yadav, 2015).

MSIL's company reports do not distinguish between the total number of contract workers and company temps, reporting figures for both as one group. By March 2016, MSIL reported 13,259 regular workers, 10,626 contract workers or company temps and 1,276 apprentices. This represents a rise of 6 per cent, 62 per cent and 16 per cent for each category respectively from 2013 to 2016 (Raj, 2016a). Thus, MSIL's desire to employ most workers on short-term contracts remained strong despite its shift away from a reliance on services provided by labour contractors.

This rapid expansion in recruitment has occurred as MSIL has continued to maintain its domination of passenger car sales in India. By 2014/15, MSIL had a 52 per cent share of the national passenger car market, compared to its nearest competitors HMIL with 16 per cent and Honda Cars with seven per cent (Thakkar, 2015). In the same financial year, MSIL's market capitalisation outgrew the value of Tata Motors to make it India's most valued auto manufacturing company (Shyam, 2015).

MSIL also appears to have continued its earlier policy of offering relatively generous pay hikes to its regular workforce via union-negotiated collective wage agreements which exclude the majority of workers. A new deal finalised in September 2015 between MSIL and three unions – the MUKU at Gurugram, the MSWU at Manesar, and the Maruti Suzuki Powertrain Employees Union (MSPEU) at the company's diesel engine plant – promised an average raise of 38 per cent over three years backdated from April 2015 with half of this increase provided in the first 12 months. A further enterprise benefit was a promised ₹2,000 monthly salary top-ups over seven years for workers who elected to purchase a Maruti vehicle rather than use the company's bus service to commute to work (Khan, 2015).

Around 300–600 company temps responded to their exclusion from the wage agreement by protesting in front the Manesar site and organising a workplace meeting with around 100 participants (*Economic Times*, 2015; FMS, 2015). Following this, MSIL reported that it had increased the wage of company temps by an average of 10 per cent at its Manesar and Gurugram facilities to ₹15,000–16,000 (*Economic Times*, 2015a).

The collective wage agreement at MSIL also spurred unions at the NCR's two other major OEMs – Hero MotoCorp and HMSI – to bargain for a similar wage increase. According to union leaders at these plants, by October 2015, 69 per cent of HMSI's 5,800 production-line and shop-floor maintenance workers in Manesar were contract workers. At Hero's Gurugram plant, 56 per cent of the company's 6,250 workers were contract and a further 24 per cent were casuals. At Hero's Dharuhera plant, 40 km to the south, the equivalent figures for the company's 3,300 workers were 36 per cent and 3 per cent (Saleem, 2015).

Employment relations in the Chennai Metropolitan Area

The CMA is India's second-largest auto manufacturing zone and leading automotive export zone. Like the NCR, leading auto manufacturers in the CMA have also pursued techniques of recruitment and employment relations which rely on precarious-employed workers and which utilise the services of competing labour contractors. The key OEMs in the CMA are Hyundai Motor India Limited (HMIL), Ford India, Renault-Nissan, and a range of smaller, multi-network or niche market manufacturers like BMW, BharatBenz, Force Motors and Eicher Motors.

In terms of industrial action, the State of Tamil Nadu has been a region of contrasts. On the one hand, there are some firms which have been untouched by industrial conflict. One example is the TVS Group subsidiary, Sundram Fasteners, an Indian Tier-1 manufacturer of metal parts, fasteners and radiator caps, which has boasted of its strike-free history for many years (Madhavan, 2011; Sundram Fasteners, 2017).

In sharp contrast, the city of Coimbatore, nearly 500 km southwest of Chennai, was the base for one of the worst examples of violence in India's industrial history in September 2009 at components manufacturer Pricol Ltd. Pricol workers formed two plant-level unions in the late 2000s which were affiliated to the Communist All-India Central Council of Trade Unions (AICCTU). Pricol refused to recognise the union and targeted union activists with a series of dismissals and cuts to wage allowances (Suresh, 2010).

In 2009, Pricol workers engaged in a 15-day hunger strike, calling on the Government of Tamil Nadu to enforce an order by the Department of Labour for Pricol to cease employing contract workers in production-line work (Industriall, 2016). After the company sacked over 40 workers for stopping production at the plant, a group of workers were allegedly involved in a violent altercation in which the company's vice-president of HR was killed (Allirajani, 2009). In early 2016, eight ex-Pricol workers were convicted of murder and given double life sentences in prison.

While such violent conflict is atypical, some major disputes have occurred in the last decade at HMIL and Ford. HMIL manufactures and exports cars from its two assembly plants at Irangattukottai in Sriperumbudur Taluk, about 40 km southwest of Chennai's city centre. These plants were established as a greenfield site under a MOU with the Government of Tamil Nadu in 1996 and commenced production in 1998.

By 2014, the two plants had an annual production capacity of 630,000 units and manufactured around 2000 cars per day. The Ford plant in Maraimalai Nagar, 10 km southwest of HMIL's plants, had a smaller capacity of 200,000 cars and 340,000 engines, while the Renault-Nissan plant had a capacity of 400,000 units (Gopalakrishnan and Mirer, 2014: 23–24).

Ford signed a new collective wage agreement with unions in 2015 (FMC, 2015). The employment relations framework of Renault-Nissan fell under the influence of a Global Framework Agreement signed with European unions (Groupe Renault, 2015: 94).

However, according to Gopalkrishnan and Mirer's (2014) major study of work and employment conditions in the CMA, temporary and contract work has been normalised across the region.

Their study was based on over 300 interviews with workers from HMIL, Ford, Renault-Nissan and multiple components manufacturers. By March 2013, they found that 65 per cent of HMIL's 16,674 employees were contract workers earning ₹5,300–10,000, 12 per cent were regular workers earning ₹33,000–49,000 per month, 10 per cent trainees or probationers earning ₹9,200–11,500 and 14 per cent apprentices earning ₹8,000–9,000. Of Renault-Nissan's 6,529 workers, 25 per cent were regular workers earning ₹22,000 or more, 31 per cent were trainees earning ₹6,000–10,000, and 43 per cent were contract workers hired by 13 different labour contractors and earning around ₹8,000.

At Ford, the percentage of contract workers was much lower and had declined from 2012 to 2014. Of Ford's 5,041 workers in 2012, 26 per cent were regular workers, 42 per cent were trainees, 12 per cent were apprentices and 20 per cent were contract workers. In 2014, Ford's total workforce had increased by four per cent to 5,221 but, at that time, 58 per cent of this total was regular workers earning ₹36,800–52,250, just 3 per cent were trainees, 27 per cent were apprentices earning a 'stipend' of ₹7,900–9,900, and 13 per cent were contract workers earning ₹7,000–8,500. The number of regular workers had increased by 129 per cent over this period and the number of contract workers had decreased by 35 per cent (Gopalakrishnan and Mirer, 2014: 27–32).

This suggests that Ford was bucking a regional trend towards workforce contractualisation. It is important to also note that Gopalakrishnan and Mirer's (2014) data on contract workers includes ancillary workers such as IT workers, canteen, security and cleaning workers, as well as manufacturing and shop-floor maintenance workers. Since the main regulatory and political problem with contract labour in India concerns 'core' manufacturing workers (see Chapter 3), this suggests that their data on contractualisation is somewhat exaggerated.

Nevertheless, the central role that contract work plays in CMA auto manufacturing employment relations is clear (George, 2014). Data on major components manufacturers was also gathered by these authors to support this view.

The complete data collected from six firms in 2012 and 2014 shows that, of the total number of regular, trainee and contract workers, the average proportion of contract workers was 63 per cent. This closely resembled the data collected from the NCR (see Chapter 5). The percentage ranged from a low of 23 per cent to a high of 83 per cent (Gopalakrishnan and Mirer, 2014: 28).

Like the NCR, there were major income disparities between these categories of workers. Contract workers in supply firms were earning between ₹3,380–9,360 and trainees were earning between ₹3,500–8,500. Compared to this, regular workers were earning a minimum of ₹9,200 and a maximum gross wage of ₹27,000 per month.

Also like the NCR, the authors suggest that labour rights were being violated by the non-implementation of clauses in the *Contract Labour (Abolition and Regulation) Act 1970 (CLARA)* as well as a regional law – the *Tamil Nadu Industrial Establishments (Conferment of Permanent Status to Workmen) Act 1981* – which requires workers to be regularised on completion of 480 days of continuous work.

Finally, also similar to the NCR is the high proportion of migrant workers who comprised the factory workforces in these firms. Some of these workers were *intra*-state migrants from other parts of Tamil Nadu as well as migrants from other states like Bihar, Odisha, Assam and West Bengal, and some international migrants from Nepal. The latter group of inter-state and international migrants were more likely to be employed as contract workers. Unlike the NCR, there was a high proportion of female workers in the supply chain, although most workers in assembly manufacturers were male (Gopalakrishnan and Mirer, 2014: 26).

Like the NCR, trade unionism was largely absent among contract workers, although a minority of contract workers at HMIL employed via TVS Logistics – part of the Indian-owned TVS Group – was represented by an INTUC-affiliated union. At Renault-Nissan, no union was found to operate inside the plant for any workers. At HMIL, regular workers were represented, albeit through competition between three separate unions – the CITU-affiliated Hyundai Motor India Employees Union (HMIEU), the management-supported United Union of Hyundai Employees (UUHE) and the Hyundai Motor India Anna Thozhilalar Sangam (HMIATS), which is affiliated to a pro-Dalit political party in Tamil Nadu – the Aathi Thamizhar Peravai (ATP).

Although there was previously a workers' committee at the site meant to represent workers' interests, the HMIEU was initially established by a group of regular workers in 2007. The HMIEU was repressed by the HMIL management, which refused to recognise or bargain with it. Initially, the union president and secretary were fired and over 100 union supporters suspended.

An HMIEU-led workers' protest at the plant was suppressed by the police, with several arrests in May 2008. In April 2009, the HMIEU presented a charter of demands to HMIL. After management refused again to bargain with the union, the workers went on strike to demand union recognition, reinstatement of disciplined workers, and an end to the ban on workers' protests at the site.

Following an HMIL decision to form a settlement on wages and conditions through the workers' committee (thus bypassing the HMIEU), and its suspension of four more workers, workers went on strike again in July 2009. This five-day strike ended after the management agreed to reinstate 20 dismissed workers, although this left out a further 67 workers who were still fighting for reinstatement.

In June 2010, the HMIEU led a sit-in strike demanding the reinstatement of these workers and management recognition. Although this strike led to the arrest of around 250 workers, HMIL eventually agreed to a process of review involving the Government of Tamil Nadu. This led to the reinstatement of 35 workers but HMIL maintained its refusal to bargain with the HMIEU and, during this period, encouraged the establishment the UUHE as a counterweight force at the site.

The UUHE was formally registered by the Government of Tamil Nadu in 2011, and immediately afforded representative status by management. In December 2011, the HMIATS was formed and, during the following year, joined the HMIEU in opposing management-UUHE negotiations. Nevertheless, in October 2012, HMIL finalised a three-year collective wage agreement with the UUHE. This was met with a fifth strike led by the HMIEU, who demanded a secret ballot of all workers to determine the basis for union recognition and the reinstatement of 27 dismissed workers. Although the HMIEU accepted the terms of the collective wage agreement in return for the reinstatement for 20 workers during government-managed conciliation in November 2012, the management refused again to recognize the HMIEU.

At Ford, regular workers established a CITU-associated union, the Ford India Employees Union (FIEU), in May 2010. Like the HMIEU, the FIEU struggled to achieve recognition from the management, which similarly preferred to negotiate with a workers committee. In March 2012, FIEU members went on strike over the dismissal of nine workers who were punished for allegedly submitting fake medical bills for company assistance.

Although the strike lasted only two days, seven FIEU members were suspended by Ford, including the core leadership of the union's executive committee.

Interestingly, an appeal to the United Auto Workers (UAW) union, which represents Ford workers in the United States, led to the reinstatement of these workers in May 2013. In March 2015, five years after the FIEU was established, Ford finally recognised the union and established a new collective wage agreement (*Business Standard*, 2015; FMC, 2015).

However, it is not only in OEMs and Tier-1 firms where workers have had to endure conditions of precarious work and denial of income security, employment security, and representation security. Suresh's (2010) 2006–07 study estimated that there were around 90,000 workers employed in Tamil Nadu's auto manufacturing industry at the time, including in components manufacturing, of which half were employed in around 8,000 'small and tiny' units which were dependent on sub-contracted work from higher-tier firms. In these firms, informal work was the norm. Similar findings are true of Tier-3 and Tier-4 firms in the NCR (see Chapter 6).

One important conflict at Caparo Engineering India (established in 2007), part of a major British steel parts manufacturer, occurred in December 2011 in Sriperumbudur. Although the firm's aluminium die-casting and forging operations are located near HMIL's plants, it is a major Tier-2 supplier to Renault-Nissan and Ford. Following a strike led by the workers' CITU-affiliated union, the dispute ended with the company agreeing to increase monthly wages by 42 per cent to ₹10,200 and to regularise the work of 22 per cent of the company's 500 trainees at the site, with a promise to create pathways into regular work for other employees at the firm's stamping and foundry sites (*The Hindu*, 2011).

This approach of offering employment and income security concessions to a minority of unionised workers was reflected in the conflict resolution practices of several Tier-1 and Tier-2 firms in the NCR in 2011/12, which also coincided with the peak of the MSIL dispute in Manesar (see Chapter 5).

Employment relations in other industrial regions

While industrial conflict, regional systems of contract labour and precarious work have been hallmarks of employment relations in OEMs, Tier-1, and Tier-2 firms in the NCR and the CMA, there is also evidence of these questions arising in other industrial zones. Interestingly, Maharashtra's auto industry core, centred on the Chakan Special Economic Zone (C-SEZ), appears not to have suffered from the same level of industrial conflict and militancy compared to the NCR or CMA in recent years. The C-SEZ is a base for Skoda, Volkswagen (VW), Mercedes Benz, Mahindra, Bajaj, and Force Motors; and the Pimpri-Chinchwad area of Pune is the base for Jaguar/Land Rover's assembly factory. In addition, General Motors (GM) and Tata Motors operate assembly plants near these sites.

Although there are many vehicle manufacturing operations in Maharashtra, they tend to operate on a smaller scale, or have been introduced more recently than in the NCR or CMA. For instance, Skoda's assembly plant began with a small operation in central Maharashtra in 2000 and VW's larger facility only commenced production in 2009 and, by 2010–11, employed around 3,800 workers (Jürgens and Krzywdzinski, 2016: 17).

However, there is some evidence of industrial conflict at more established facilities. For example, Mahindra, which operates assembly factories at three sites in Maharashtra (Chakan, Bhandara and Nashik) suffered from strike action at its Nashik plant in 2013. Mahindra claimed that 94 per cent of its regular workers were unionised by 2016 (Mahindra, 2016: 137). The 2013 strike in Nashik, which had around 2,922 regular workers at the time, was called to demand an increase in the wages of 36 per cent of the workforce, who were paid ₹12,000 a month, to a higher salary range of ₹24,000–25,000. After a group of workers was sacked during the strike, the management agreed to reinstate workers in return for an end to the conflict (Pawar, 2013). An earlier strike at the Nashik plant led to losses of around ₹150 *crore* (US$23 million) for at least seven Mahindra suppliers in the State (Pawar, 2009).

Another example is the Tata Motors assembly plant in Pune District, where members of the Tata Motors Employees Union (TMEU) campaigned in 2015 and 2016 for a collective wage agreement covering the plant's approximately 5,000 production-line workers. At the same time, workers at Tata's nearby foundry and Tata subsidiary – TAL Manufacturing Solutions – were also pushing for the company to finalise collective wage agreements with the TMEU (Thakkar, 2016).

At Bajaj Auto's Akurdi motorcycle assembly plant, members of the Vishwa Kalyan Kamgar Sanghatana union, which had about 1,000 members combined at Bajaj's Pune and Chakan plants, initiated a hunger strike in January 2017 against alleged management harassment of union activists (*Economic Times*, 2017). An earlier example of strike action – this time at a foreign joint venture OEM – occurred in 2002 at the Kurla plant of Fiat-Premier Ltd, on the outskirts of Mumbai, which employed around 2,000 workers.

The background to this strike was that Fiat had been struggling to implement its version of lean manufacturing – the UTE concept as part of its World Car strategy – in partnership with the Indian management. Like the TPS, UTE-based work organisation involved flattening operational management into teams, and higher levels of worker involvement in decision-making. From its inception in 1996 to the 2002 strike, Fiat had significant difficulty implementing the UTE concept among the Premier-based Indian workforce, where the Indian industrial tradition of steep organisational hierarchies and hostile shop-floor/supervisor relations were the norm.

When Fiat took over operations at Premier's Kurla plant, management had to immediately deal with a six-month strike, a lockout, and the formation of a new union – the Kamgar Ekta Premier Sanghatana (KEPS). After this initial instability, Fiat tried to facilitate change in 1998 by using a VRS to lay-off around 1,500 workers and hiring 600 new ITI-graduates in their place (Becker-Ritterspach, 2009: 163–64).

However, in other new foreign-operated OEM operations, foreign managers were able to implement changes to work organisation and employment relations without provoking open industrial conflict. Achieving this outcome often meant hybridising foreign best-practice work organisation and management techniques with local workplace norms, customs and practices. At Mercedes Benz India's (MBI) small Complete Knockdown kit (CKD) assembly factory in Chakan, which was established in 2009, the company allowed Indian HR managers to found an internal company union at the outset to prevent CTUOs or other external bodies from campaigning for unionisation.

Furthermore, MBI adapted worker supervision according to Indian patriarchal, collectivist, and family-oriented customs. For example, in the early 2000s, MBI implemented 10 family-based 'principles'. These included the following principles: 'Coaching by the "family father" to the "family members" is a must'; 'In the "family", the "father" is always there. In his absence, the "eldest son" takes care' of the family; 'Supervisor works like a "father" of a "family"' (Becker-Ritterspach, 2009: 198).

Other than the above-mentioned firms, little has been documented of labour standards, work organisation and employment relations among the OEMs of the C-SEZ and Pune district. Perhaps the most comprehensive studies have been Becker-Ritterspach's (2009) study of Skoda and Mercedes Benz's operations, and Jürgens and Krzywdzinski's (2016) more recent international comparative study which included VWI and Mahindra's local operations. Like findings from the NCR and CMA, Jürgens and Krzywdzinski (2016: 58–59) emphasise the young migratory character of the workforce in the region, based primarily on young men from regional villages and towns who rent small rooms in industrial areas and aspire for upward social mobility through skilled, regular work.

However, Jürgens and Krzywdzinski (2016) suggest that this region has not suffered the scale of labour protests as other manufacturing regions in the country. They argue that VWI was, at the time of their research in 2010–11, focusing on building a 'core workforce' of regular workers since it had only commenced production in 2009. The company's plan was that all new recruits would be hired as temps on six-month contracts. Some could then become trainees for two consecutive 12-month contracts under a 'Trainee Development Scheme' sponsored by the Government of Maharashtra, followed by a further six month probationary period (Jürgens and Krzywdzinski, 2016: 100). By 2011, a union had emerged at the plant which had succeeded in establishing collective bargaining and seniority-based pay. However, only 20 workers out of 2,000 at the plant were regular workers by 2010. At the time, only these 20 workers were unionised (Jürgens and Krzywdzinski, 2016: 293–95).

Further afield, Italian OEM Piaggio has released some information about its employment relations practices in the State. Piaggio's two-wheeler assembly operations are based in the small city of Baramati, which lies about 100 km south of Pune. By March 2015, the 2,761 workers at the plant represented 37 per cent of the Piaggio Group's global manufacturing workforce, which was second only to the 48 per cent of the global workforce based in Italy. Of these India-based workers, around 36 per cent were on 'fixed term contracts' which compares to a global average in the company of 20 per cent, with such contracts virtually non-existent in the company's Italian operations. In addition, Piaggio recognised a union at its Baramati plant, having negotiated a four-year collective wage agreement in July 2013 (Piaggio Group, 2015).

Although based in a smaller manufacturing zone than the C-SEZ and Pune district, the operations of Toyota Kirloskar Motor Limited (TKML), from its base in Bidadi village on the southwestern edge of Bengaluru, has arguably been a more significant area of industrial conflict in auto manufacturing. Lal Das and George's (2006) brief study of industrial action at TKML in 2001/02 is useful, as this conflict occurred in the aftermath of the major changes at MSIL in Gurugram.

Like MSIL, TKML took the opportunity of this conflict to increase the proportion of contract workers in its operations. The proportion of contract workers was increased to 17 per cent of the approximately 1,800 production-line and shop-floor employees following this conflict. These workers were paid 40–50 per cent of regular workers' wages by July 2005. At Toyota Kirloskar Auto Parts Limited (TKAPL), the adjacent site which manufactured transmissions, axles, and other key components, the proportion of contract workers stood at around 18 per cent of the plant's 500 workers at the time.

The Toyota Kirloskar Motors Employees Union (TKMEU) was established for regular workers in July 2001 at TKML. By 2005, the TKMEU claimed a membership of 1,380 workers or around 87 per cent of regular workers ('workmen') eligible to join under the *Trade Union Act 1926* and *Factories Act 1948*. At TKAPL, a plant-level union had 98 per cent coverage of eligible workers although there was no CTUO involvement or affiliation.

Industrial unrest emerged at TKML when the company offered a 10 per cent rise in wages in response to long-term union demands for salary increases. In April 2001, workers boycotted lunch in protest of this offer and further protests led to disciplinary action against union leaders and the suspension of three workers. In order to combat the union, TKML pushed to form a workers' committee called a Team Member Association (TMA), which was formed with 15 elected members. However, management tried to restrict the TMA to matters of workers' welfare and safety and refused to discuss workers' demands or to engage in collective bargaining. This refusal, and the suspension of a fourth worker, led to a 12-day strike.

The workers' union was finally registered in July 2001. Although the union was able to reduce the trainee period for new recruits from three to two years, the company moved ahead with the termination of suspended workers against the union's protests. As a test case, the union agitated against a December 2001 decision by TKML to retrench a worker who had completed two years of his traineeship.

A strike was organised in January 2002 and, in response, two union office-bearers were dismissed. Workers counteracted with a 52-day strike to demand their reinstatement. In March 2002, the Government of Karnataka intervened to declare the TKML operation an essential 'public utility service'. This enabled the government to ban any industrial action at the site. This act of legal repression forced the workers back to work and marked an end to the union's campaign (Lal Das and George, 2006: 295–96).

There are also some records of industrial conflicts in recent years in Gujarat's auto manufacturing zones. At GM's assembly plant in the town of Halol, 50 km west of the Gujarat-Madhya Pradesh state border, workers went on strike for 51 days from March to May 2011 to improve health and safety rules, and achieve union recognition. After filing a complaint that around 450 workers had received spinal injuries through overwork, 14 workers were suspended by the GM management. The workers' union – the INTUC-affiliated Gujarat Kamdar Mandal (GKM) – also sought to win wage parity for workers on short-term contracts who undertook production-line work like regular workers.

In March 2011, the company closed down the company canteen. When workers walked out of the factory for lunch, they were locked out by management. This led to a wildcat strike by around 600 workers which lasted until May 2011. While the dispute led to a conciliation organised through the Government of Gujarat and, although GM agreed to offer concessions on workloads and wages, the company maintained its refusal to recognise or bargain with the GKM (Industriall, 2011).

More recently, workers' struggles have focused on GM's plans to close the Halol assembly plant and focus its Indian operations on its Talegaon Dabhade assembly plant in the C-SEZ, nearly 600 km to the south. By 2016, the Halol plant employed around 1,100 regular workers and 500 contract workers although, under pressure from the GKM, management recently increased the number of regular workers by 27 per cent and reduced the number of contract workers by

38 per cent. Like many other plants, there was large wage inequality between workers in these different employment configurations, with contract workers paid around 28 per cent of the regular workers' basic salary based on an hourly wage rate (Mehta, 2016).

Another recent case in Gujarat – in the municipality of Sanand in Ahmedabad District – concerns Tata Motors' Nano assembly plant, previously famed for manufacturing the 'one lakh car' (see Chapter 2). As of March 2016, Tata Motors claimed that the Sanand Nano plant, along with its Dharwad plant in Karnataka, was the only of its seven India-based assembly plants which did not have a workers' union or a collectively-negotiated wage agreement (Tata Motors, 2016: 191).

By 2017, workers at both the Sanand and Dharwad sites had been campaigning for collective wage agreements, with around 450 Nano workers boycotting food at the factory in June 2017 (*Times of India*, 2017). This occurred after Tata agreed to recognise a New Trade Union Initiative (NTUI)-linked plant union, the Bharatiya Kamdar Ekta Sangh (BKES), in March 2016, following an agreement to negotiate over the reinstatement of 26 workers suspended for alleged misconduct. These workers were part of a unionisation campaign run earlier in the year, which included a 19-day strike by BKES supporters (Ajay, 2016; *First Post*, 2016).

There have also been reports of industrial conflicts in other emerging auto manufacturing zones. In Pantnagar, the Himalayan foothill town in the State of Uttarakhand, which provides a base for a Bajaj Motors two-wheeler assembly plant and a Tata Motors assembly plant, a major confrontation at Tier-1 Tata supplier, ASAL Auto Stampings, led to a town-wide protest movement and political crackdown by the Government of Uttarakhand in 2013. For the first half of 2013, ASAL workers campaigned against their employers' practice of maintaining workers on a long-term traineeship basis. After the formation of a union, ASAL management suspended five workers and initiated a company lockout. Town-wide protests by workers and their supporters led to the District Administration enforcing a Section-144 order to ban protests in the area and prevent solidarity protest action with the ASAL workers (Shriya, 2013).

Trajectories of socio-political conflict in the National Capital Region

The next chapter moves into the book's empirical investigation into labour standards and work in the Tier-1 and Tier-2 auto components manufacturers of the NCR. First, it is worth revisiting some of the more recent manifestations of industrial and socio-political conflict in the region. Through the pioneering efforts of MSIL, labour standards and employment relations were completely transformed in the NCR in the 2000s, particularly across Gurugram District, as managers imposed a regional contract labour system and systematically removed multiple forms of labour-related security.

In March 2015, Hero MotoCorp claimed to employ 23,746 workers across its four Indian plants (Gurugram, Dharuhera and Neemrana in the NCR, and Haridwar in Uttarakhand), of which 69 per cent were hired on a 'temporary/ contractual/casual basis'. The company also recognised branches of the Hero MotoCorp Workers Union (HMWU) which represented regular workers at the Gurugram and Dharuhera assembly plants (Hero MotoCorp, 2015: 124).

By 2009, Honda HMSI in Manesar employed 1,872 regular workers and another 2,500 workers were hired through labour contractors (GWN, 2009). HMSI has largely been unwilling to recognise unions and, like Hero Motorcorp, has initiated lockouts in response to unionisation drives, leading to a major protest movement in mid-2005 (Ahn, 2007). In addition, there have been major strikes involving contract workers at Hero Honda in April-May 2008, and at automotive components firms such as Shivam Autotech, Rico Auto and Sunbeam Auto in September-October 2009 (GWN, 2007; 2009; Srivastava and Handique, 2009).

Sunbeam Auto, a components manufacturer and part of the Hero Group of Industries, employed about 650 regular workers, 2,500 casual workers, and around 600 trainees at its Gurugram plant in 2009 (GWN, 2009). Rico Auto employed 1,275 permanent workers and 1,675 contract workers (Handique, 2009). Campaigns for ongoing employment and union recognition have occurred at many other firms in the region during the 2000s (Ahn, 2007; Srivastava and Handique, 2009).

Industrialists have systematically divided and restructured their workforces to gain cost advantages, commonly surrounding a shrinking core of regular workers with a larger group of casual workers, trainees and workers hired by multiple labour contractors. This has become a common practice in this region. Government data suggests that 46.6 per cent of all workers in manufacturing firms in Haryana's organised sector were hired by labour contractors in 2010/11, which is significantly higher than the national average of 33.9 per cent.[4]

The industrial action at Hero Honda in 2008 presents a useful illustration of the problems generated by these practices. By this time, Hero Honda's Dharuhera plant manufactured about 16,000 motorcycles every day. The plant employed around 1,400 regular workers, 1,500 casual workers and 3,500 workers hired through five different labour contractors. Most of the production-line workers were casuals and contract workers, while some regular workers were employed as supervisors on the shop-floor.

---

[4] Author's calculations are based on data from the Government of India (2011a; 2013a).

Depending on their employment grade, regular workers earned a gross wage of ₹30,000–40,000 per month. In contrast, casual workers earned ₹5,000–6,000, and contract workers earned ₹2,800–4,800. Some contract workers had been employed by the company for 15 years. Inequality between regular and non-regular workers extended into other facets of factory life, such as working hours and canteen access. Regular workers worked 8 hour shifts over a 24-hour production cycle while, casual and contract workers were often required to work for up to 16 hours at a time, with overtime paid at the normal hourly rate. Regular workers received a ₹50 voucher for meals every day against ₹5 for casual and contract workers (Five regular workers, Hero MotoCorp [Gurugram], interview with author, Old Gurgaon, March 2013).

In April 2008, workers demanded employment security through ongoing work with the company, income security through pay hikes and the right to join the regular workers' union at the plant. However, a request by a group of casual and contract workers to join the plant union was refused by the union leadership. In May, a larger group of casual and contract workers working on the same shift (the A-shift) at the plant went on strike after they were prevented from participating in a 'cultural programme' which had been arranged for regular workers and their families. On the same day, casual and contract workers on the B-shift joined the strike, halting production for two days. Regular workers continued to work during this strike.

In response, Hero management promised a small group of workers that they would receive a pay increase and enterprise benefits in the future, enabling production to recommence. The plant union made a vague promise to accept casual and contract workers as members at some point in the future. However, these workers were not allowed to participate in the executive elections of the union later that month. After organising several meetings at the site in May and June, workers filed to register a new union, the Hero Honda Mazdoor Sangathan (HHMS) in late June, with the Department of Labour in Chandigarh. In early July, the HHMS notified managers that they would commence recruiting members to the unions and claimed to sign-up around 1,200 of the 5,000 casual and contract workers employed at the plant.

In early October, the plant management initiated a lockout and prevented all shift workers from entering the factory. After two days, regular workers were allowed inside. After a group of casual and contract workers staged a sit-in in front of the factory, management agreed to future negotiations and allowed a select group of casual and contract workers to return to work. However, 60 workers were suspended, and most of the 1,200 workers who had signed up to the HHMS were left without work. By 2009, the management had hired 700–800 new workers. Until July 2009, 600 of the retrenched workers continued to return to the plant to organise protests. However, most of them eventually found new jobs or returned to their families' villages and cities.

This story is not universal. The occupations and strikes at MSIL in 2011/12 united large numbers of regular and contract workers. There are other examples of this unity, such as a 2006 campaign at Manesar auto parts supplier – Shivam Autotech – in which regular and contract workers occupied their plant for five days, successfully achieving a wage increase (GWN, 2007). Another example is Napino Auto in Manesar, which supplies auto and electronic parts for Hero Honda and Maruti Suzuki. Workers here organised a joint campaign for improved conditions and equal pay for contract workers (Handique, 2009).

One of the most significant and recent examples of solidarity between regular workers, contract workers and casual workers – and, unusually for the NCR, between male and female workers – occurred at Asti Electronics India, a Tier-1 automotive and electronic components manufacturer based in Sector 7, IMT Manesar, in December 2014. A subsidiary of Asti Corporation from Japan, this company manufactures wire harnesses, switches, controllers and other electronic parts for various OEMs and Tier-1 suppliers in the NCR.

By mid-2014, the Asti plant employed 150 regular workers and 310 contract workers. In February 2014, regular and contract workers went on a one-day strike together, demanding ongoing employment and higher wages for contract workers and a collective wage agreement for all workers at the plant. A notable feature of the plant is the high proportion of female workers, representing around 250 workers or over 80 per cent of all contract workers employed at the site.

After the successful registration of a plant union in November 2014, the management terminated the employment of all contract workers. Retrenched workers commenced a sit-in protest at the factory gate and organised a protest in IMT Manesar which received support from unionists at MSIL and several Tier-1 firms, including some workers who had been suspended under similar circumstances at Indian-Japanese Tier-1 joint venture, Munjal Kiriu.

Having failed to win re-employment, seven Asti workers started a hunger strike in November 2014. Another large demonstration was organised at the factory with contingents of unionised regular workers from MSIL and at least six Tier-1 firms. In December, regular workers who were still working inside the plant openly supported the contract workers by participating in a one-day hunger strike and working in the factory with black bands wrapped around their heads as a form of protest against the management.

Following an alleged assault by a labour contractor against the secretary of the plant union in December, regular workers went on strike and forced the management into a half-day negotiation with the union. The management agreed to re-employ those contract workers who had commenced work prior to 2011, which comprised about 15 per cent of all workers retrenched in November 2014. Regular workers returned to work the following day. Thus, after an 11-month dispute, income and representation security had been significantly improved for regular workers but not for most contract workers. In addition, employment security had not been achieved for contract workers, although a minority of retrenched contract workers succeeded in winning their jobs back.

Another recent dispute, albeit much larger than the Asti case, occurred at HMSI's recently-established Tapukara assembly plant in Alwar District, Rajasthan, about 40 km south of its main Manesar assembly plant. By early 2016, around 84 per cent of the Tapukara plant's 3,500–3,600 production-line and shop-floor maintenance workforce were contract workers, compared to 13 per cent regular workers. The remaining 3 per cent was a mix of trainees and casual workers.. All shop-floor workers were required to have ITI-certificates. Most of the workers came from the local district or migrated from districts in Uttar Pradesh (UP), Madhya Pradesh or Maharashtra.

Workers reported that training was conducted on the job and workers were allowed to undertake full production-line tasks after 10–15 days. However, it took eight years in total to be eligible to complete the transition from a contract worker to a regular worker. After three years as a contract workers, some would be offered the opportunity to sit for a test. A minority of these workers would be made company casuals for a two-year period and, subject to satisfactory progress, as a trainee for a further three years. Even after this, contract workers could be regular workers after a three-year 'training period', which meant receiving a monthly 'stipend' which was lower than a fully-qualified regular worker. After this, workers could be converted to a full, regular contract after a final six-month period of probation (Dinhata, 2016).

A union was formed at the Tapukara plant by 227 workers in August 2015 and presented a charter of demands to management in December 2015. Following this, around 800 contract workers were retrenched in January and February 2016. In mid-February, around 2,000 workers at the plant, including contract workers and regular workers, undertook a wildcat strike and walkout, which was called in light of reports of a physical assault on a contract worker in the paint shop.

During these protests, there were violent clashes with the local police, around 44 workers were jailed, and the company reportedly brought in newly-recruited contract workers from the State of Odisha to maintain production. Despite this conflict, workers' demands for reinstatement of sacked workers and regularisation of contract workers were not met. A further 140 workers were retrenched. Like the MSIL campaign in Manesar in 2011–12, this conflict involved a high level of unity between contract workers and regular workers (Dinhata, 2016). However, the outcome was largely negative for the workers who lost their jobs.

Conclusion

This chapter has tried to move towards an overarching explanation for the high incidence of industrial disputes in India's auto manufacturing sector. Its starting point lies in the analysis of the practices of recruitment and employment relations of pioneering OEMs in the passenger car and two-wheeler markets, especially, MSIL, HMIL, Hero MotoCorp and HMSI.

These firms are pioneers in two senses: they are early entrants in the Indian auto industry, with the capacity to establish and configure their global production networks as closely as possible to global company preferences, and to entrench their particular corporate versions of lean manufacturing. Second, they are pioneers in the transformation of manufacturing work organisation, labour standards and employment relations. The historical process of this transformation suggests there is a link between these practices, the role of each OEM in their respective markets, heightened market competition and national and regional state facilitation of trade and investment liberalisation.

In the case of MSIL, Japanese management had significant scope to mould work organisation and employment relations with some constraints, given the operation's early guise as a PSU. In the case of Hero Honda, commercial and employment relations were heavily shaped by the Hero Group's preferences, leading to Honda's adaptation to rival OEM network practices in the NCR following the Japanese firm's split with Hero and the formation of two rival two-wheeler manufacturers – HMSI and Hero MotoCorp – in 2010. For HMIL, on the other hand, South Korean management's capacity to shape work organisation and employment relations flowed from its pioneer status as the first wholly foreign-owned greenfield operation in the auto industry and its emergence as the leading car manufacturer in South India.

The MSIL case demonstrates how the process of intra-firm work re-organisation was initially achieved. While MSIL's early guise as a PSU forced Japanese managers to retain a hierarchical management and formal supervisory structure, success was achieved in the late 1980s and 90s in implementing team-based shop-floor work organisation and supervision as well as employee participation in lean manufacturing schemes like 'quality circles' and employee suggestion schemes.

A key to MSIL's early success was the provision of jobs for qualified workers. These jobs had high levels of income and employment security, underpinned by union-negotiated collective wage agreements and basic monthly salaries boosted by generous bonuses, allowances and a range of enterprise-based benefits. In return for active participation in SMC's lean manufacturing approach, these standards represented a lean employment relations compact that contributed stability and, thus, helped facilitate the company's rapid emergence as India's leading car manufacturer.

This compact unravelled rapidly in the early 2000s through the impact of economic liberalisation policies implemented at a regional and national level, and through changes in the structure of market competition. Feedback from state institutions and market forces forced MSIL to reflexively transform its labour standards and employment relations framework and, in doing so, influence the character of employment relations across the industry as a whole.

Under conditions of heightened market competition, as well as global and regional economic instability in the late 1990s, MSIL experienced a period of declining profitability. One of the main reactions of the company to these changing conditions was to attempt to restructure the terms of its employment relations compact. This precipitated a series of events which have led to an industry characterised by a high level of industrial disputes, including several highly-charged confrontations.

MSIL's changes were resisted by workers at its Gurugram assembly plant, leading to a strike and lockout that ended with the defeat and displacement of their union. In place of the old compact, MSIL now pursued a strategy of employment relations which reserved this treatment for a minority of regular workers, including some lower-level managerial and supervisory workers. MSIL replaced the core of its production-line and shop-floor maintenance workforce with cohorts of temporary workers whose orientation and employment was managed by multiple, often competing labour contractors. These contract workers commonly undertook similar work to the old, core regular workforce although they were paid a fraction of their wages.

This employment relations strategy was eventually normalised throughout the industry. In the NCR, it was emulated by HMSI and Hero MotoCorp in motorcycle and scooter manufacturing. In the CMA, it was copied by HMIL and, more recently, by Renault-Nissan in the small-to-medium passenger car market. While this strategy is not universal, the practice of employing workers through labour contractors has been used by virtually every OEM in the industry to some degree, including in regional auto manufacturing clusters in Gujarat and Uttarakhand, in the urban region of Bengaluru and in the industrial zones of Chakan and Pune District Maharashtra.

While the C-SEZ and Pune District have experienced fewer industrial disputes than the larger auto manufacturing zones in the NCR and CMA, there is no question that contract work has become a dominant and, in some regions, pervasive aspect of recruitment and employment relations in auto manufacturing. This shift has occurred to the detriment of the socio-economic security of workers.

In the aftermath of the most damaging industrial conflict to date at MSIL's Manesar site in 2011/12, further revisions were made to the strategy of employment relations. In this most recent strategy, employers have regularised a slightly larger core of workers, and unilaterally implemented improvements in wages and employment conditions for workers in all employment configurations, while maintaining a version of the contract labour system in practice.

At MSIL's facilities in Manesar and Gurugram, this has meant the marginalisation of labour contractors and the proliferation of company temps whose work and employment is regulated directly by the company – albeit under similar short-term employment contracts – rather than by labour market intermediaries. However, the persistence of employment insecurity has led to renewed conflicts, such as the protest by company temps at MSIL in Manesar in September 2015.

In Tier-1 components manufacturers and in rival OEMs, the contract labour system has persisted in a more transparent fashion. Again, some differences remain. In the CMA, HMIL has maintained its reliance on contract workers and continued to refuse recognition of the HMIEU despite its decade-long effort to unionise the site. More recently, the 2015/16 HMSI dispute at its Tapukara plant in the NCR has demonstrated great similarity with the MSIL case, with violent conflict and repression from the company and regional state institutions implemented in response to solidarity between contract, casual and regular workers.

In Tier-1 and Tier-2 firms, the contract labour system has also persisted, although company practices have been strongly shaped by the character of conflict in key OEMs like MSIL and its rivals. The Asti Electronics dispute in Manesar in December 2014 provides an important recent example of this. The following chapter, based on the author's empirical research in Gurugram District in the NCR, provides a detailed outline of the transformation of labour standards and employment relations in Tier-1 and Tier 2 firms.. It will demonstrate that the contract labour system has persisted, but employment relations have also been shaken and reshaped by recent industrial conflicts. Importantly, these conflicts have also been shaped by the social interaction of workers at the 'industrial village' level as well as at the level of the workplace.

5

Auto Workers in India's National
Capital Region

The previous chapter focused on the transformation of work organisation and employment relations in India's automotive industry on a national scale. It also summarised existing literature on work and employment in the Indian auto industry. This chapter moves towards an explanation for the high levels of conflict documented in the auto industry by focusing on employment relations in the largest auto manufacturing region in India, the National Capital Region (NCR).

Despite considerable inter-regional competition since the 1990s, and the potential for rival regions like the Chennai Metropolitan Area (CMA) or regional clusters in Gujarat to challenge and eventually overtake the NCR, this region remains India's leading auto manufacturing region in sales, production volume, and by virtue of the leading role of its passenger car and two-wheeler manufacturers. Global production networks led by Maruti Suzuki India Limited (MSIL) in the passenger car market and Honda Motorcycle and Scooter Limited (HMSI) and Hero MotoCorp (Hero) in the two-wheeler markets dominate the auto industry. These networks have transformed the workplace and industrial landscape of communities across the NCR. This is especially true to the south of New Delhi in the semi-rural hinterland of Haryana.

As outlined in Chapter 4, MSIL's role in the industry epitomises the transformation of work organisation and employment relations under conditions of economic liberalisation. Its practice of systematically replacing most of its regular (or permanently-employed) shop-floor workforce with low-wage migrant workers hired through multiple labour contractors has been emulated by rival OEMs, by OEMs in other market segments, and by Tier-1 and Tier-2 auto supply manufacturers.

This argument is substantiated by focusing on the analysis of primary data drawn from several years of the author's field research in the NCR. Dozens of interviews with workers, including regular workers, casual and contract workers, as well as employers, managers, labour contractors, trade unionists, and local villagers and landowners were conducted over several months in late 2011, mid-2012 and mid-2013.

This enabled the author to assemble a database of firms and suppliers, including their employment relations practices and wage levels, as well as numerous other elements of work and life established through ethnographic research (see Appendix for full details of field research, data sources and interview participants). Access to these participants was gained in a number of ways. In some cases, it was possible to meet workers by approaching trade unions in Delhi or Gurugram, or labour movement activists in Faridabad, on the southern fringe of the national capital. Many more informal chats and social gatherings occurred in public areas, *dhabas* (roadside eateries) or in workers' homes.

However, most of the workers met in this way were regular workers. As a rule, trade unions do not represent contract workers, who form the overwhelming majority of workers in the regional auto industry. It was possible to meet *some* contract workers through contacts of regular workers and trade union members. Similarly, it was possible to meet some employers in Tier-1 and Tier-2 enterprises by approaching their peak representative organisation in Delhi – the Automotive Components Manufacturers Association of India (ACMA) – or through contacts with trade unions that had established plant-level collective wage agreements and were influential enough to provide access to senior managers, plant managers or company executives.

The key limitation of this approach was the lack of access it provided to contract and casual workers or to employers and self-employed workers in smaller, Tier-3 and Tier-4 firms in the auto industry. Approaching these participants on a larger scale required a range of more creative methods. These included spending days walking between the side streets that run off the Old Delhi-Gurgaon Highway between Udyog Vihar Phase 1, on the Delhi-Haryana border and Sector 18 in Gurugram where MSIL's first car manufacturing plant stands.

Every morning and evening, hundreds of thousands of workers walk and cycle through these streets between their modest homes in multi-story buildings or urban villages and their workplaces. Other than auto manufacturing workers marching through this area, there were garments manufacturing workers, electronics manufacturing workers, and the smartly-dressed employees of call centres, banks and IT companies.

Hundreds of discussions took place between the author and the workers. Some interactions were brief, lasting only five minutes, while others were longer discussions of half an hour or more. These commonly took place at tea stalls on street corners or, during hotter months, at street vendors' stalls selling juice.

Other methods played an important part too. In IMT Manesar, to the south, most workers live in semi-rural villages which clustered near the enormous manufacturing facilities of MSIL and HMSI. From across an expanse of dusty dirt roads and former wheat fields that lie between IMT Manesar and villages to its immediate south, these factories appear as enormous walled constructions that dominate the northern skyline, with barbed-wire on top of high walls lined with watch-towers. Thousands of workers live in these villages in rooms rented from local landowners.

The author spent many weeks in three of these villages – Kharkari, Binola and, within Manesar itself, Aliyar – and was able to visit several Tier-1 and Tier-2 auto manufacturing plants located in these areas. Managers, trade union leaders, regular workers, contract workers and self-employed workers engaged in long conversations about work and life in these industrial villages, inside workers' homes, in common areas, tea stalls and, occasionally, in factory offices where unions had a strong presence.

The author also spent several months walking through the alleys of Faridabad's industrial colonies, residential streets and visiting workers' families in slum communities. Many days were spent walking or driving between the *basti* (slum) at Mujesar, where hours of discussions were held in workers' homes, and the dusty hustle of Bata Chowk along Mathura Road, which links New Delhi with Faridabad. Similarly, the author spent days walking through Sanjay Colony and Shiv Colony in Sector-23 of Faridabad where hundreds of Tier-3 and Tier-4 firms are clustered. Many of these firms are now listed on local websites and some listed under the *Punjab Shops and Commercial Establishments Act 1958*[1] which was designed, historically, to regulate trading practices and working conditions in small establishments, including small-scale manufacturers.

Ultimately, the only practical way to establish contact with workers and employers in Tier-3 and Tier-4 firms – at least for outsiders with no local or social connections – is to physically visit these industrial colonies and approach establishments directly. The lanes and alleys along these industrial colonies contain myriad workshops and small factories, which visitors can easily enter. Many Tier-3 proprietors were happy to talk about their operations.

This books has constantly referred to the fact that the level of industrial conflict and hostility in the Indian auto industry has been very high. For a large part of the field research, the region was overshadowed by the severity of the dispute at MSIL's plant in Manesar. As outlined below, the legal, institutional and employment relations framework is such that many employers and labour market intermediaries are involved in unscrupulous or even illegal exchanges.

Violations of core labour laws are *the norm*. In this context, no senior managers or executives from the major regional OEMs – MSIL, HMSI, Hero and others – were prepared to speak to the author. However, things were different among employers and managers in several manufacturing supply companies, in which

---

[1] Until 1966, Haryana was part of the state of Punjab. The two states continue to share the same political and administrative capital, the city of Chandigarh, which is located about 250 km north of New Delhi.

the author was able to conduct several interviews and hold many more informal conversations.

The author's outsider status was somewhat advantageous when attempting to meet labour contractors, a group of often-shadowy figures who play an indispensable role in recruitment and employment relations practices in regional auto manufacturing. Despite several useful studies of labour relations in the sector (see Chapter 4), direct interaction with labour contractors has rarely been documented. Perhaps reflecting this difficulty, no worker, employer or trade union leader was able or prepared to connect the author with a labour contractor. As this chapter will clarify, much of the role undertaken by labour contractors is connected to illegal collusions with employers. Consequently, it was not possible to talk to a large number of labour contractors.

In the end, contact could be made with 90 labour contracting enterprises via post, and over 40 enterprises were approached physically in their offices, most of which are located in Old Gurgaon. Here they offer a range of labour market services in security, hospitality, domestic work, cleaning, garments, the public sector, agriculture and auto manufacturing. Most labour contractors refused to speak about their work. However, eight were prepared to hold discussions and, of these, four agreed to participate in formal interviews to document their activities, functions and relations with workers and employers in the auto industry.

Finally, gender was also a pressing issue in the author's field research. Only six of the 106 workers formally interviewed in this study were female, less than 6 per cent of the total, even though many more informal discussions were held with women. Of these six interviewees, five were casual workers in Tier-3 firms in Faridabad, with one employed as a contract worker in a local Tier-1 firm. No female employers, managers, or labour contractors were encountered. In part, this reflects the male-dominated character of paid work in the auto manufacturing industry – globally and in India. It specifically draws attention to the low rates of female labour participation in northern Indian States like Haryana. It also partially reflects the *hidden* character of much of women's work in India, in which substantial paid and unpaid work is undertaken by women in the informal economy (Mazumdar, 2007; Sudarshan and Bhattacharya, 2009; Hill, 2010).

Despite these challenges and limitations, the field research gleaned valuable information and insights into work and life in the regional auto industry. This chapter focuses on work organisation and employment relations practices in OEMs, Tier-1, and Tier-2 firms in the NCR. These practices are quite different in Tier-3 and Tier-4 firms, which will be discussed in detail in Chapter 6.

In this chapter, all firms are counted as part of the 'organised sector' as they each employ 10 or more workers. They are, thus, subject to core labour laws and social protections, including the *Factories Act 1948* which regulates working hours and conditions for regular workers in firms in the organised sector; medical insurance through the *Employees' State Insurance Corporation Act 1948*, or an employment-based pension scheme through the *Employees Provident Funds Act 1952.*

Other than offering analysis of work and labour conditions at MSIL, HMSI and Hero, this chapter will also focus on the range of auto components manufacturers that supply these OEMs, including their strategic partners, specialized independent suppliers, and suppliers of mass-produced, generic products. It will explore the relationship between supplier types, their country of origin, employment size, hiring of labour contractors, wage levels. and employment relations practices. In the NCR, supplier firms are mostly either Indian or Japanese-owned.

Most significantly, and perhaps most controversially, the chapter will argue that the majority of workers in these higher-tier auto firms, including OEMs, are employed in circumstances of *precarious and informal work*. This work is precarious because most of it is undertaken with an absence or lack of labour-related security and social protection. This work is also predominantly 'de facto informal', it will be argued, because multiple labour laws, which were designed to protect workers and restrict exploitative work-based practices, are widely ignored or easily evaded by employers.

This is reflected in the operation of a *regional contract labour system* as a regime of labour control that has enabled OEMs and manufacturing suppliers to keep wage costs as low as possible, to offload many additional costs of recruiting, supervising and monitoring workers, and to systematically thwart efforts by trade unions to establish collective bargaining for the mass of workers in the industry. The chapter will outline the functions of the regional contract labour system, the services provided by labour contractors, the types of individual who become labour contractors, and the evolution of their role within global production network over time. The regional contract labour system means that the 'principal employer' – in this case, the auto manufacturing firm – is effectively able to eschew responsibility over many employment conditions. The chapter will show that most of these workers are hired as ongoing production-line workers, in violation of the *Contract Labour (Abolition and Regulation) Act 1970.*

Furthermore, the role of labour contractors acting as intermediaries between capital and workers also intersects with the intermediary role of local landowners and trade unions. The relationships between land ownership, labour market intermediation and circular and seasonal migratory patterns of labour will be contextualised by exploring work and life patterns in three industrial villages that cluster near MSIL and HMSI's giant factories in IMT Manesar. These relationships, the chapter argues, are closely tied to the industrial and political practices of trade unions.

The roots of the contract labour system in the NCR lie in the transformation of market segmentation and competition during the period of emergent neo-liberalism after 1991 (see Chapters 3 and 4). However, they also lie in the more general integration of OEMs' global production networks with regional social structures of accumulation that rely on precarious and informal work. These structures are shaped by caste-based, inter-regional relations at the village level. This chapter thus begins by placing the labour practices of auto manufacturing firms in the context of the changing economic life in towns and villages in the southern fringe of the NCR.

The Industrialisation of Town and Village-life in Haryana

As outlined in Chapter 3, the political economy of regional industrialisation has been underpinned by relations between state institutions, municipal corporations and local landowners. The National Capital Region is an administrative area overseen by the National Capital Region Planning Board (NCRPB), which was tasked by the Ministry of Urban Development to outline a vision for the expansion and consolidation of space in India's most-populated urban region. The NCRPB is also tasked with planning for the development of transport, energy and, water infrastructure to connect the region's industrial and employment corridors.

The NCR is comprised of the National Capital Territory of Delhi (NCT), a union territory under the Indian Constitution with its own elected government, thirteen districts of the State of Haryana, seven districts of the State of Uttar Pradesh and two districts in the northeast of Rajasthan. Within the NCR, most manufacturing activities have emerged in the districts of Faridabad and Gurugram, although there is also substantial manufacturing activity in Okhla in South Delhi, Greater Noida to the east of New Delhi in Uttar Pradesh, the town of Dharuhera in Rewari district in southern Haryana and, more recently, in Alwar district in Rajasthan. The location of OEMs' main manufacturing facilities in the NCR, and key fieldwork sites for the research in this book, are represented graphically in Map 5.1.

This geographical configuration of industry stems from the historical structure of manufacturing in Delhi. The role of industry in postcolonial Delhi was shaped by mass migration, particularly from the northwest, following the partition of India in 1947 (Datta, 1986; Guha, 2007). The proportion of inter-regional migrants living in New Delhi rose from around 50 per cent in 1951 to 80 per cent in 1991 (Mazumdar, 2007: 314). The preference of urban planners to retain the city as a political and administrative centre, with a focus on state administration and civil services rather than large-scale manufacturing meant that many post-partition migrants were forced to find employment in small-scale industry and the unorganised sector. This included many who had previously worked in white-collar and middle-class occupations.

Map 5.1: Key auto manufacturing and fieldwork sites in the National Capital Region (NCR) of India

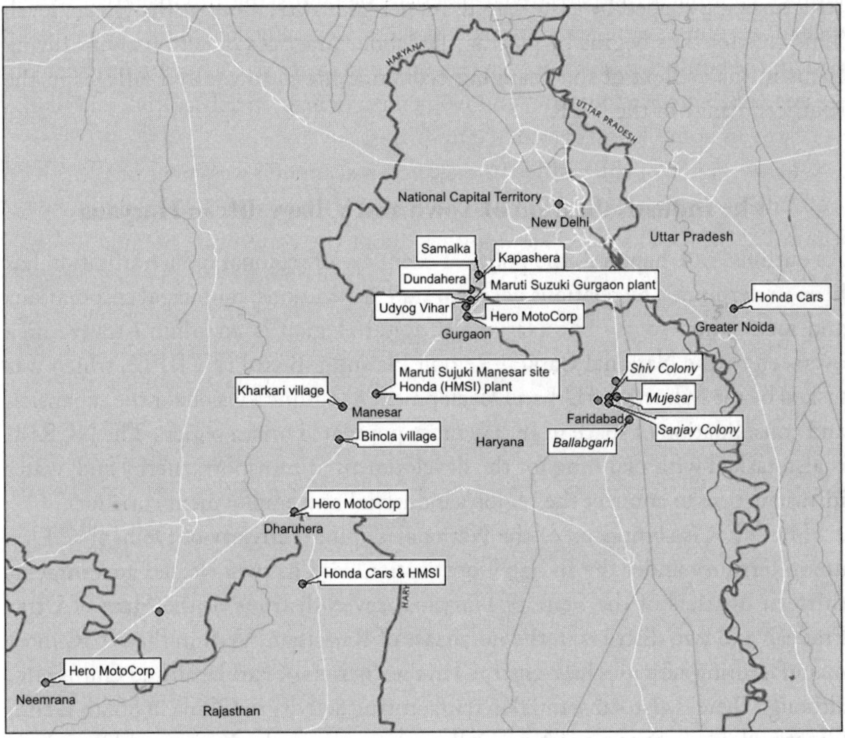

Source: Author's calculations

By the 1960s, urban planners in the Delhi Development Authority (DDA) encouraged the formation of new industrial estates to satisfy this demand for work. One of the most important examples was the Okhla Industrial Estate which was established to provide work for first and second generation refugees in South Delhi. Some of Okhla's small-scale employers were able to become major manufacturers and established larger-scale factory production to the south of the city in steel, pharmaceuticals, refrigerators and textiles manufacturing (Datta, 1986). Maintaining its opposition to large-scale and heavy industries near the city centre, the DDA encouraged these producers to shift manufacturing further to the south, across the NCT border into the Faridabad district of neighbouring Haryana. By the 1970s, Faridabad was a major centre for large-scale factory production and unorganised sector manufacturing. This transformation took place long before the commencement of economic liberalisation reforms in the 1980s.

Most of the growing paid work in areas like Okhla and Faridabad was occupied by male migrant workers. The shift of migrating rural families to the New Delhi urban region exacerbated the domination of paid work by men in the region. Many families continued the patriarchal practices of family life in villages in which women, as spouses or relatives of male workers, were expected to focus on unpaid work in the family home. However, female labour force participation has been on the rise, albeit from a low base, and women participate in substantial paid work, especially in home-based informal enterprises.

One of the major difficulties in making an accurate assessment of the direct contribution of women to commodity production is the culturally-embedded notion of familial duty and related assumptions about the conceptual boundaries that separate 'duty' from 'work', especially when women do not 'consider their unpaid assistance in family run shops or businesses as work' (Sudarshan and Bhattacharya, 2009: 62). At the same time, there has been growing female participation in factory work in the NCR, especially in garments manufacturing, but also in some lower-tier auto manufacturing enterprises.

Another process that has influenced the concentration of work for both women and men in informal enterprises across the NCR is the clearance of slum communities. Since the early 1990s, the Government of the NCT has initiated slum clearances based upon notions of 'public interest', such as the construction of new public amenities, environmental protection, or preparations for major events like the 2010 Commonwealth Games.

By the late 1990s, over a quarter of Delhi's population lived in slum communities (*jhuggi basti*) on high-value land earmarked for redevelopment by city authorities. Key decisions by the Supreme Court of India in 1996, 2000, and 2001 led to the cumulative displacement of up to three million people from enterprises in the unorganised sector which relied on these slum communities. Many of them were forced to relocate to peri-urban centres of the NCR (Menon and Nigam, 2007; Dupont, 2008). A well-publicised case of displacement in 2004 involved the forced eviction of around 90,000 people in the 'Yamuna Pushta', a slum community along the banks of the Yamuna River. Many of these people worked in informal enterprises in Old Delhi or the east of the city as traders, waste collectors, or as construction workers (Padhi, 2007).

Slum clearance initiatives have shifted work in informal enterprises further to the edges of the NCT or, across state borders, into industrial areas like Faridabad or Gurugram where abundant paid factory work has emerged. For home-based workers in Delhi, the resettlement of slum colonies has also moved workers further to the urban periphery.

Through this process, Faridabad's role as an industrial centre has been transformed since the 1970s. While it remains a major base for small-scale industry, including thousands of informal enterprises and hundreds of Tier-2, Tier-3 and Tier-4 manufacturers in the auto industry, several major global manufacturers have also established large factories in Faridabad since the 1980s. These include garments exporters, manufacturers of household electronics, consumer durables, and automotive OEMs like Yamaha and, in tractors and agricultural equipment, Escorts.

Gurugram has also been transformed, from a semi-rural town and a base for MSIL and its predecessor companies in the 1970s and 1980s (see Chapter 3), into the NCR's main area of large-scale industry, including global production networks in auto manufacturing as well as export garments, electronics, household consumer goods, bicycles, banks, Business Process Outsourcing (BPO) call centres, retail shopping malls and high-rise residential and office construction. This industrial development also spread to Manesar. By the late 2000s, half of all income tax collected and about a third of all paid work in Haryana was represented by the two districts of Faridabad and Gurugram, despite together representing less than 12 per cent of the State's population (Debroy and Bhandari, 2009; Barnes, 2015).

Land acquisition has been a critical element in the establishment of automotive global production networks in the region as sufficient space is required – usually hundreds of acres per site – for OEMs to construct manufacturing plants and to allocate space for key suppliers and strategic partners. As suggested above, the core of auto manufacturing in the NCR has been historically segmented between the district of Faridabad, which was reserved by urban planners as a base for small-scale industry as manufacturing gradually spilled over from Delhi's southern fringe; and Gurugram, which was originally set aside for the development of car manufacturing in the 1970s and 1980s and, more recently, has provided the base for several OEMs and global Tier-1 firms.

Regional industrialisation in the district of Gurugram, has centred upon MSIL's first factory in Sector-18, the industrial corridor in Udyog Vihar, Hero MotoCorp's base in Sector-33, and IMT Manesar. Most of these facilities have been built upon former agricultural land. To this day, several are surrounded by villages where cultivation, cattle rearing and dairy production remain important sources of economic and cultural activity to local communities. Village land is generally held in small plots of five acres or less, and land ownership tends to be held by a mix of caste groups. In some villages, like Khandsa which lies between Gurugram and IMT Manesar, land ownership is dominated by high castes such as Rajputs. Other villages have been turned over to municipal authorities for industrial development and turned into small townships, such as Kapas Hera, Samalka and Dundahera along the Delhi-Haryana border which house thousands of migrants who work in Udyog Vihar.

In villages further to the south, and into Haryana's rural hinterland, land ownership tends to be dominated by middle-ranking castes from the Jat and Yadav communities. The caste status of these numerically dominant sections of the Haryanvi population is a controversial political issue in India. Until recently, only the Yadav community was regarded by the Governments of India and the Government of Haryana as an Other Backward Class (OBC) — an official category for disadvantaged castes in India – and, thus, eligible for reservation in jobs in the public sector and educational institutions. Recently, activists from the Jat community have led major public protests in different towns across Haryana to demand inclusion in OBC lists and reservations in government jobs (Rao, 2016; Tiwari, 2016).

Other than dominant land-owning groups like Jats and Yadavs, there is also a significant population of Scheduled Castes, including Dalits, in the State. However, in the villages that surround the giant factories of IMT Manesar, Yadav and Jat communities tend to dominate local politics. Many, though not all, village landowners have profited significantly by organising through village representative organisations in order to bargain with state development authorities over compensation prices for industrial development.

Many have also benefited by offering rental accommodation to migrant workers who have flooded into the region for manufacturing work, or to labour contractors who use them as temporary shelter for newly-arrived migrants. In some villages, this accommodation is based in permanent buildings. In others, rooms are available in semi-*pukka* buildings and others are converted from agrarian use, such as cowsheds or grain stores.[2] In villages where auto manufacturing suppliers have taken root in recent years, the village population has usually become majority-migrant.

As with the *panchayat* system of village self-governance that operates across most regions of India, each of these villages has an elected *gram panchayat* (village assembly or council) which group together to form a *panchayat samiti* (block assembly or council) and, finally, the *zila parishad/panchayat* (district council or

---

[2] *Pukka* buildings are permanent constructions made from stone or brick while *kachcha* buildings are short-lived structures made from less durable materials like wooden frames or bamboo. Semi-*pukka* refers to a building that uses a combination of materials, such as a brick-walled edifice with a temporary roof or an additional room constructed with wood or bamboo.

assembly). For example, the District of Gurugram has a *zila parishad* which works with the Government of Haryana to oversee rural development, including the organisation of local transport and school education. The District is comprised of four 'blocks', each with a *panchayat samiti*, which oversees several dozen individual *gram panchayats*.

In Gurugram District, there were 32 *gram panchayats* by 2016 (District of Gurugram, 2016), including in villages like Kharkari and Binola, which clustered on the southwestern fringe of IMT Manesar. Kharkari is a village with about 1,000 inhabitants that lies adjacent to HMSI and MSIL's immense factories at IMT Manesar. Most landowners have small plots of 4–5 acres where wheat and pulses are grown. Many own water buffaloes, which, by early 2013, cost around ₹70,000–80,000 each (about US$1,000–1,250) on the open market. Families commonly produce their own dairy products including milk, buttermilk, butter and *dahi*. On most plots, landowning families – mostly Yadavs – live in multi-room brick houses. Male occupants in these households tend to work in a variety of relatively well-paid jobs, including public sector jobs as civil servants or police officers – often in inter-state regions – as well as regular, supervisory, and lower-level managerial workers in local auto manufacturing firms.

Female occupants are generally expected to work in the home and are responsible for household agrarian work. However, much of the harvesting and manual agricultural labour is undertaken by Dalit workers mainly from Rajasthan which is about one hour's drive to the southwest. By 2013, these workers lived with their families on the western fringe of the village in a makeshift camp comprised of *kachcha* dwellings made of wooden struts, plywood floors and tarpaulin and plastic sheets for shelter. Despite the temporary appearance of this site, it had been there since the early 1990s to provide agrarian labour, as village residents were increasingly drawn into industrial jobs in the area. As one local landowner, a retired police officer who had returned to his family farm (4.5 acres) after a career in Madhya Pradesh, explained: 'These workers move in and out between here and their villages in Rajasthan. They come here to look for work during harvesting and they can live in the *basti*' (Local landowner A, Kharkari Village, interview with author, 17 April 2013).

Although there was no large scale industry within Kharkari itself, several landowners had profited from the establishment of HMSI's vast scooter factory 15 years earlier and, in 2007, the conversion of MSIL's Manesar supplier park into its second passenger car assembly plant. By 2013, the market price for land per acre in this village was around ₹1.5–2 *crore* (US$230,000–315,000). As the retired police officer explained:

We were well compensated when Honda came here. We negotiated with the Haryana Development Authority[3] which runs all local projects. Because of this, I could build extra rooms in my family's house. This [house] has been here for 100 years. We could afford to send my [two] sons to a local [privately-run] school which costs ₹1 lakh each year [about US$1,500–1,600 for annual admission].

So we could afford these things. But the Haryana development authority wants to do more. Now they want to develop a local [shopping mall]. The villages [in this area] will accept this if the price per acre is enough and [if] the government promises to build local amenities. We need a new school, a new hospital, and a new bus service. And the roads are very bad too (Local landowner A, Kharkari Village, interview with author, 17 April 2013).

Indeed, all the roads within Kharkari were unsealed dirt roads and severely damaged by erosion and flooding. The village of Binola, 15 minutes' drive to the south of Kharkari, was similarly lacking in sealed roads in 2013. In contrast to Kharkari, several Tier-1 and Tier-2 automotive manufacturers, as well as Tier-3 and Tier-4 firms, and electronic component manufacturers, had clustered within the village in the past two decades alongside the small-to-medium plots held by local Jat and Yadav landowners. Many sons of landowning families in Kharkari and Binola are full-time workers in these manufacturing firms:

My eldest son works for [Firm 1O[4]] in Binola. He operates machines. He started there when the company began [in the area in 2009] (Local landowner C, Kharkari Village, interview with author, 7 April 2013).

My son works for [Firm 1R in Binola]… We have four acres of land here. We have some buffaloes and grow some seeds. We rent out some rooms for workers for ₹1400 [per room per month]. We also own some land in Hisar [a small city in central Haryana, 180 km to the northwest] (Local landowner A, Binola Village, interview with author, 16 April 2013)

Binola is larger than Kharkari, with 5,000–6,000 inhabitants. However, out of this, only about 10 per cent are Haryanvi families which own land in the area and have inter-generational roots in the village. Since the mid-1990s, and especially since the early 2000s, the village's population has swollen as workers have moved into the area in search of work. By 2013, 90 per cent of the village population was migrants from inter-state regions. About a third of the village population was

---

[3] The Haryana State Industrial and Infrastructure Development Corporation (HSIIDC) – see Chapter 3 for details.

[4] See Table 5.1 below for details of firms and firm codes used in this study.

households with a married couple who had migrated from inter-state regions. A tiny minority – less than five per cent – were women, both married and unmarried, who had migrated alone for production line work. However, the majority – over half the village population – were young, unmarried male workers who had migrated alone, or with relatives or friends. Most of these workers were brought in by representatives of labour contractors to work in Tier-1 firms, although some also worked in Tier-2 and Tier-3 firms or, in a few cases, had established themselves as self-employed maintenance technicians or own-account workers in Tier-3 or Tier-4 firms.

Most of these workers were from an OBC background with ties to marginal and small-scale cultivation in inter-state regions. Some of them were Dalits. Most of these migrant workers rented rooms from local Jat and Yadav landowners. By early 2013, a single room with no bathroom and no kitchen cost ₹1,400–1,500 per month (about US$21–23). These rooms were usually shared by two or three workers, or by families with children.

Some separate quarters with their own bathroom and kitchen cost were available for ₹3,000–4,000, but this was widely considered unaffordable, especially given that most workers expected to earn wages of ₹5,000–8,000 per month (about US$75–120), and many remitted a significant portion of their income to their families in towns and villages in the inter-state region (Interview with author, 3 contract workers, Firm 1O, 23 March; 1 regular worker, Firm 1T, 24 March; Regular worker (plant union president), Firm 1R, 6 April; Local landowner A, 16 April; 2 local landowners, 16 April; 3 regular workers, Firm 1Q, 17 April 2013).

In Aliyar Village, which lies within IMT Manesar and is about two kilometres north of the MSIL plant, the process of industrial development is more advanced given the looming presence of MSIL and HMSI. Since 2001, most of the village land has been forcibly acquired for industrial development by the HSIIDC. Landowners were initially offered around ₹3.5 lakh (nearly US$5,500) per acre for their land but they sued the Government of Haryana for higher compensation on the basis of claims that private housing developers paid the government 100–200 times more per acre than this.

Ultimately, some landowners were able to achieve a price 10 times higher per acre than the initial offer. This allowed some landowners – the ones forced to sell by the HSIIDC – to reinvest in land to the south, buy new motor vehicles or, like in Kharkari and Binola, to send their sons to expensive private schools. Other villagers began to rent out rooms to migrant workers. By late 2012, like Binola, Aliyar was comprised of about 500 Haryanvi residents and about 10,000 mostly migrant workers. Small rooms in multi-story buildings were given in rent for ₹2,500–3,000 per month – 50–80 per cent higher than in Binola – although some larger rooms in high-rise apartments were available for around double this price (Two workers, Aliyar Village, IMT Manesar, interview with author, 16 November 2012; two local landowners, Aliyar Village, IMT Manesar, interview with author, 17 November 2012).

Automotive manufacturers in the National Capital Region

As outlined in Chapter 2, the NCR is the base for several lead firms – OEMs – that oversee global production networks in the region. The key firms are MSIL, the country's largest passenger car manufacturer, based in Sector-18 Gurugram and in IMT Manesar; Hero MotoCorp in Sector-33 Gurugram and, 40 km to the southwest, the town of Dharuhera and the town of Neemrana in northeast Rajasthan; Honda Motorcycle and Scooter India (HMSI) in IMT Manesar; and Honda Cars in Greater Noida and, in northeast Rajasthan, Tapukara. In addition, there are smaller OEM assembly facilities run by Yamaha India in Faridabad and Harley Davidson in Bawal, Haryana, 100 km south of New Delhi.

This section begins by focusing on the operation of the three largest producers in the region: MSIL, HMSI and Hero. Data comes from interviews with 12 workers in OEMs, representing 11 per cent of the total sample of workers in this study. Of these 12 workers, three were employed at HMSI and were interviewed at a *dhaba* in IMT Manesar in December 2011; five were employed at Hero in Gurugram and were interviewed at a union office in Old Gurgaon in March 2013; three were retrenched MSIL workers who had lost their jobs during the industrial conflict in Manesar in July 2012 and interviewed in Old Gurgaon in March 2013; and, finally, one was a product quality inspector who moved between lower-tier suppliers in Faridabad on behalf of his company. All of these workers were – or, in the case of the ex-MSIL workers, had been – regular or permanently employed by their company. Several informal discussions were also held with OEM contract workers in Manesar and Gurugram in 2011, 2012, and 2013.

Hero MotoCorp dominates two-wheeler production in India alongside HMSI. Besides Gurugram, Dharuhera and Neemrana in the NCR, Hero operates facilities in the State of Uttarakhand and, at the time of writing, was due to commence production in Gujarat. The interview of the five Hero MotoCorp workers took place at the Gurugram office of the Hind Mazdoor Sabha (HMS), which is one of the two main trade union federations, along with the All-India Trade Union Congress (AITUC), that represent members in the NCR auto industry. They were employed at Hero's vast plant in Sector-33 of Gurugram which was supplied by over 800 components manufacturers and employed around 6,000 people in manufacturing by early 2013. According to these workers, around 80 per cent of employees were contract workers (Five regular workers, Hero MotoCorp, Gurugram, interview with author, 13 March 2013).[5]

Interviews conducted with HMSI workers in Manesar 15 months earlier found that there were about 6,300 manufacturing workers at their vast assembly plant, of which about 4,500 employees, about 71 per cent, were contract workers. In addition, the company employed about 400 workers in transport and logistics, about 500 workers as cleaners, about 200 as canteen workers, 300 contract-hired security guards, 400 truck drivers and about 120 contract-hired workers to drive company-provided buses to transport workers to and from the site. Apart from the truck drivers, all of these ancillary services workers were hired through labour contractors.

At HMSI, the wage difference between contract and regular workers working in production line roles on the shop floor was vast. Skilled regular workers with an engineering degree could earn over ₹29,000 per month, and some in supervisory roles could earn up to ₹45,000.[6] These wages were based on a combination of seniority-based wages stipulated through union-negotiated collective wage agreements, as well as overtime, bonuses and allowances.

In contrast, contract workers were paid a basic wage of ₹5,750–6,600, although some could earn close to ₹8,000 through overtime. The lowest wage of ₹5,750 was technically a sub-minimum wage as it was comprised of a ₹4,700 basic wage – about six per cent lower than the Haryana minimum wage at the time – with the addition of a ₹1,050 housing allowance and an optional ₹850 production bonus which was paid if production targets were met on the shop-floor.

In addition, the full wage of ₹6,600 was further reduced by ₹108 for medical insurance (ESI) and over ₹500 for employee pension contributions (PF) (Interview, three regular workers, HMSI, IMT Manesar, 7 December 2011).

Given the context of the industrial conflict at MSIL's Manesar plant in 2011–12, the information gathered from regular workers who lost their jobs at the site is significant. By July 2012, just prior to the mass retrenchments undertaken by MSIL management, the Manesar site had 2,950 shop-floor workers.

Having only commenced car assembly operations in 2007, the workforce was younger on average than workers in the Gurugram plant, and the plant had a high proportion of trainee workers and apprentices who were employed as production-line workers. Of the total manufacturing workforce, 29 per cent were regular workers who, by early 2012, were able to join a management-recognised union,

---

[5] For comparison, the company's own data suggests that 69 per cent of its total employees base are 'temporary or casual' across all four of its currently operating plants (see Chapter 2).

[6] Unless otherwise stated, all wage data in this book refers to monthly figures.

just like regular workers at the Gurugram plant and MSIL's nearby engine plant (Suzuki Castings and Powertrain). A further 27 per cent were contract workers, 10 per cent were apprentices and 34 per cent were trainees (Three retrenched regular workers, MSIL (Manesar plant), Old Gurugram, interview with author, March 2013).

While these hiring and employment relations practices are well-established for the largest OEMs in the region, there has been comparatively little research on conditions and practices in the auto components manufacturers that operate within global production networks of these lead firms. The practice of hiring most workers through multiple labour contractors is echoed in the practices of Tier-1 and Tier-2 components suppliers throughout the NCR. The most extensive data on firms and workers in this study comes from Tier-1 and Tier-2 suppliers.

In total, 47 workers in Tier-1 firms were interviewed, that is, 44 per cent of the total number of workers interviewed in this study. Of this, 13 were contract workers and the remainder (34) regular workers. For Tier-2 firms, 14 workers were interviewed, of which 12 were contract workers. In addition, it was possible to interview four Tier-1 employers (two plant managers, one senior manager and a senior company executive) and two Tier-2 employers (a senior executive and a plant manager), as well as a representative from the regional branch of the Automotive Components Manufacturers Association (ACMA) in New Delhi.

These interviews enabled a data set of firm types, employment numbers, contract labour practices and wage levels to be established. Table 5.1 shows the full listing of 20 Tier-1 firms and five Tier-2 firms for which significant data could be gathered. The firms have been coded to protect the identity and privacy of interview participants. In many cases, participants, including workers and managers, were risking their employment or disciplinary action by revealing company information for the study, or speaking openly about the company's policies and practices.

Most of these firms were Indian-owned and operated, demonstrating the importance of domestic firms to auto-oriented global production networks, even in a region in which Japanese OEMs play a dominant role. Seventeen of the 25 firms listed in Table 5.1 are Indian-owned, including all of the Tier-2 firms. Three were Japanese, one British and a further three were joint ventures between either Japanese, Indian or British firms. All but one firm (Firm 1B in Greater Noida) were located in the State of Haryana, where most of the field research was conducted. The firms manufactured a wide variety of components, including metal components, raw materials, sheet metal fabrication, cable and wire harnesses, brakes, chassis and exhaust parts, as well as plastic parts and more complex assembled components like air conditioning and ventilation units, vehicle transmissions and engines for both passenger cars and two-wheelers.

Table 5.1: Tier-1 and Tier-2 Auto Manufacturing Suppliers, National Capital Region[7]

Tier	Firm Code	Origin	Location	Products	Supplier Type	No. of workers	No. of LCs	CWs in total workers (%)	A. Wage (CW) ₹'000	B. Wage (RW) ₹'000	A/B (%)
					(December 2011)						
1	A	India/Japan	Gurugram	Wiring, cables	SISS	2000	X	X	3.8	10	38
	B	Japan	Noida	AC, ventilation, engine parts	SP	4000	X	X	15–20	38	40–53
	C	Japan	Manesar	Fuel pumps, MPFI systems	SP	550	X	X	8–18	27	30–67
	D	India	Gurugram	Die-casting	SISS	5000	2	X	4.5–10	40	11–25
	E	India	Gurugram	Die-casting	SP	3750	X	67	3.5	X	X
	F	India	Manesar	Plastic parts	GSS	335	3	90	X	X	X
	G	India	Manesar	Sprockets, welded parts	SISM	1250	5	80	X	X	X
					(November 2012)						
1	H	Britain	Manesar	Fuel pipes	SISS	550	X	55	X	X	X

Contd.

[7] Firms are presented in order of date of interview. See appendix for full list of interviews with codes. Supplier type = SP (strategic partner), SISS (specialised independent supplier – single industry), SISM (specialised independent supplier – multi-industry), GSS (generic supplier – single industry). LC = labour contractor, RW = regular worker, CW = contract worker, X = missing value

Tier	Firm Code	Origin	Location	Products	Supplier Type	No. of workers	No. of LCs	CWs in total workers (%)	A. Wage (CW) ₹'000	B. Wage (RW) ₹'000	A/B (%)
	I	India	Manesar	Press parts, axles	SISM	1050	X	67	X	X	X
	J	India	Manesar	Plastic fuel tanks	GSS	90	X	90	X	X	X
	K	Japan	Manesar	Cables harnesses	SISM	600	3	83	5.8–7	X	X
	L	India	Faridabad	Air cond. Units	SISS	1010	4	94	X	X	X
					(March–April 2013)						
1	M	India	Manesar	Plastic moulding	SISM	500	4	80	5–7	X	X
	N	India	Gurugram	Engine, gear parts	SP	1350	8	78	5.2	10	52
	O	Japan/ Britain/India	Binola	Door frames, exhausts	SP	1100	7	82	8–12	8–25	100–48
	P	Japan/ Britain/India	Gurugram	Sheet metal, interiors	SP	610	5	98	5	20	25
	Q	India	Binola	Sheet metal, tubes	SISM	670	8	41	8–10	18–20	44–50
	R	India	Binola	Bike parts	SP	1200	7	50	5.4	8	68
	S	India	Binola	Engine parts	SP	700	X	50	8	12	67

Contd.

Tier	Firm Code	Origin	Location	Products	Supplier Type	No. of workers	No. of LCs	CWs in total workers (%)	A. Wage (CW) ₹'000	B. Wage (RW) ₹'000	A/B (%)
	T	India	Binola	Gears, engine parts	SP	1200	X	52	5.3	10	53
T-1 Av.	(n=20)						6 (n=11)	72 (n=16)	6.5–8.6 (n=14)	18–20 (n=11)	48–50 (n=11)
(March–April 2013)											
2	A	India	Udyog Vihar, Gurugram	Brakes	SISS	200	X	70	5–7	7–12	71–58
	B	India	Faridabad	Engine parts	SISM	500	1	90	5.7–6	25	23–24
	C	India	Udyog Vihar, Gurugram	Steel forging	GSM	600	4	60	5.7	X	X
	D	India	Manesar	Electric parts	GSS	600	3	33	4.5	X	X
	E	India	Faridabad	Sheet metal	GSS	385	5	91	4.6–4.8	X	X
T-2 Av.	(n=5)						3 (n=4)	69 (n=5)	5.1–5.6 (n=5)	16–19 (n=2)	47–41 (n=2)
Av. (all)	(n=25)						5 (n=15)	71 (n=21)	6.1–7.8 (n=19)	17.7–19.9 (n=13)	48–49 (n=13)

The firms also represented a variety of different supplier types, defined by their strategic function within global production network. Of the 25 firms, nine were strategic partners with OEMs – for example, firms which operated through equity investments from an OEM, or who formed part of the same global parent company or business group as an OEM, or which operated through a global partnership arrangement. Five were specialised independent suppliers which focused on auto manufacturing, while six were specialised independent suppliers that also manufactured goods for clients in non-automotive industries. Four companies were generic suppliers of relatively simple, low-cost, mass-produced components, such as sheet metal parts or plastic parts, although each of these four firms only produced for clients in the auto industry.

For Tier-1 firms, the average number of manufacturing and production-line workers employed per firm was 1,376, ranging from a plastic fuel tank manufacturer in Manesar with just 90 employees up to a die-cast manufacturer in Gurugram with nearly 5,000 employees. For Tier-2 firms, the average was 457, ranging from 385 to 600 employees. Most firms made extensive use of labour contractors for their recruitment and employee management. Of the 15 firms for which reliable data was provided, an average of five labour contractors was used by the employer, ranging from one Tier-2 firm in Faridabad that used a single labour contractor to two Tier-1 firms that each used eight labour contractors.

Of the 21 firms for which reliable data was provided on number of contract and regular shop-floor workers, the average proportion of contract labour in total manufacturing and production-line employment[8] was 71 per cent, ranging from an electric parts manufacturer in Manesar which employed 33 per cent of its workers through labour contractors, to a sheet metal fabricator and interior parts manufacturer where 98 per cent of workers were hired through five different labour contractors. At this plant (Firm 1P), only 12 out of 610 manufacturing workers were regular workers.

Furthermore, there was a significant gap between the wages of regular workers and contract workers. While this sometimes reflected different occupational positions or a minority of long-serving or highly-credentialled regular workers taking supervisory or lower-level management roles, most regular workers appeared to undertake similar production-line work to contract workers. In part, these differences also reflected access by a significant number of regular workers to wage bonuses and allowances negotiated by unions in (usually three-year) collective

---

[8] Production-line or assembly-line employment does not include white-collar office jobs, plant, senior and executive management, skilled workers engaged in design and product testing and ancillary workers such as hospitality, transport workers and cleaners. However, it does include a minority of craft workers employed in shop-floor maintenance roles.

wage agreements. This was also an issue for many trainees and apprentices who were effectively used as production-line workers.

Wage levels in Table 5.1 are all monthly figures and also distinguish between basic pay and gross pay, which includes any possible overtime payment, bonuses, and allowance paid to workers. Taking these differences into account, the dataset shows that the average ratio of contract workers' wages to regular workers' wages was 48 per cent for basic pay and 49 per cent for gross pay in the 13 firms for which full wage data could be gathered. Across 13 firms, regular workers' wages averaged ₹17,700 for basic pay and ₹19,900 for gross pay (about US$270–315). Across 19 firms (where more comprehensive wage data could be gathered for contract workers), wages of contract workers averaged from ₹6,100 for basic pay up to ₹7,800 for gross pay (about US$95–125). Furthermore, the data shows that seven firms paid some workers basic wages that fell below the Haryana minimum wage for unskilled labourers in Haryana at the time (₹5,330 or US$80–85).[9]

A further important feature of this dataset is that only two of the firms listed in Table 5.1 employed a significant number and proportion of women. At Firm 1A, a strategic independent supplier based in Gurugram, about 55 per cent of the 2000-strong workforce was female in December 2011. Most workers at this site were paid sub-minimum wages (₹3,800) and contracts were re-issued after six months to prevent ongoing employment. At Firm 1K, a strategic independent supplier of cables and wire harnesses for clients in several industries, 67 per cent of the firm's 600 workers were women, who could earn ₹5,800 or up to ₹7,000 with an ITI certificate.

Overall, most firms made extensive use of the services of labour contractors, hired most of their workers through multiple labour contractors and maintained a large gap between the wages and employment conditions of regular workers and contract workers. These findings provide a strong indication of employment relations practices in the NCR auto industry even if they are not statistically representative. It is also possible to use this data to explore some of the impacts of different supplier types and the different national origins of different firms on wages, employment conditions and employment relations.

First, the data suggests that Japanese auto suppliers tend to pay higher wages than Indian auto suppliers. For *contract workers* in the 13 Indian Tier-1 and Tier-2 firms for which we have full wage data, wages range between an average of ₹5,400

---

[9] This calculation is based on the minimum daily wage of ₹205 per day assuming a 26-day month, since most people worked six days per week. In contrast, the minimum daily wage for skilled manufacturing labourers at the time was ₹230 per day or ₹5,980 per month. By September 2015, the minimum wage for unskilled labourers had increased to ₹7,600, around 43 per cent higher than at the time of this field research.

for basic wages to ₹6,300 for gross wages. In contrast, the equivalent average wage for Japanese-owned Tier-1 and Tier-2 firms was ₹9,600–15,000 (n = 3). For joint-venture manufacturing suppliers, which involved a combination of Japanese, Indian or British capital, wages ranged from ₹5,600 to ₹6,900 (n = 3). Similarly, for *regular workers*, Indian suppliers' wages ranged from ₹16,300–17,100 (n = 8) compared to two Japanese firms that averaged ₹32,500. Even if we focus only on Tier-1 firms – since all Tier-2 firms in Table 5.1 are Indian-owned – Japanese firms maintained higher average wages. For instance, Tier-1 Indian-owned firms (n = 8) pay an average of ₹5,600–6,800 for contract workers and ₹12,300–12,500 for regular workers, which is lower than wages in Japanese companies mentioned in this study.

However, there is no major difference in national origin between firms' practices in terms of the number of labour contractors they hire or the number of workers they hired through these intermediaries. The 17 Indian Tier-1 and Tier-2 suppliers for which there is full data on contract labour practices, have, on an average, 70 per cent of their workers hired by labour contractors. One Japanese firm for which there is similar data hired 83 per cent of its workers as contract workers, and for two joint-venture firms, the average was 90 per cent. While these figures are higher than Indian firms, they merely reflect the prevailing practice across all Tier-1 and Tier-2 firms in the region, as well as OEMs, to hire the vast majority of their employees as contract workers.

Furthermore, while Japanese firms tend to pay higher wages for both regular and contract workers, they seem to maintain a larger ratio between the *gross wages* of these two employment categories. Although the ratio between contract workers' wages and regular workers' wages in Japanese firms is 35 per cent, it is 60 per cent if we measure gross wages, including all overtime, bonuses and allowance, the lion's share of which is generally reserved for regular workers. This is higher than the 49 per cent ratio for total wages across all firms in the sample.

Second, if we look at wage and employment relations data by supplier type, it shows that strategic partners tend to pay higher wages than specialised independent suppliers. Generic suppliers, especially those focused entirely on the auto industry, tend to pay the lowest wages. For *contract workers*, strategic partners – all of which in this sample are partners with a single OEM in the region – paid workers an average of ₹7,000–9,200 (n = 9). In contrast, specialised independent suppliers focused on auto industry paid an average of ₹4,400–6,900 and generic suppliers paid sub-minimum average wages of ₹4,600–4,700 (n = 2).

However, this was not the case for *regular workers' wages*, with specialised independent suppliers tending to pay slightly higher average wages than strategic partners. Furthermore, there is very little difference between the use of labour contractors or the proportion of contract workers hired in total employment between firms with different network supplier characteristics. For example, generic suppliers (both single and multi-industry) hired an average of 73 per cent of their employees as contract workers. This was higher than OEM strategic partners (68 per cent; n = 7) but comparable to strategic independent suppliers (74 per cent; n = 9) and, also, broadly comparable to the overall average for all firms in the sample (71 per cent).

OEM strategic partners are more likely to be Japanese, given the practice of Japanese OEMs pursuing an 'inter-firm partnership' strategy by buying controlling equity shares in their key suppliers (see Chapter 2). This data shows that both Japanese firms and OEM strategic partners are more likely to pay higher wages than Indian firms or Indo-Japanese joint-venture firms. However, there is no significant difference in the hiring practices of Japanese and Indian firms in relation to the contract labour system and, if anything, the data suggests that Japanese firms maintain a higher level of income inequality in total wages between regular and contract workers than Indian firms, although both are high. The implications of these across-the-board practices have been profound for the mass of workers on whom the regional auto industry has relied upon for its rapid expansion.

A regional contract labour system

In the sample of firms listed in Table 5.1, all firms are part of the organised sector by virtue of their employment numbers, and thus subject to the *Factories Act 1948* and other relevant labour laws and social protections like the *Employees' State Insurance Corporation Act 1948* (ESI) or the *Employees Provident Funds Act 1952* (PF).

In addition, all but one (Firm 1J with 90 employees) are subject to the hire-and-fire restrictions in the *Industrial Disputes Act 1947* which means they must seek the permission of the state to retrench workers and close or scale-down operations. Similarly, the *Contract Labour (Abolition and Regulation) Act 1970 (CLARA)*[10] applies to all firms listed in Table 5.1.

Despite this coverage, the systematic and collective evasion of state regulations is rampant. For example, 7 of the 25 firms listed in Table 5.1 pay at least some of their production-line workers sub-minimum wages, including two (Firms 1A and 1E) that paid contract workers a maximum or gross wage lower than ₹4,000. The majority of these workers are systematically denied labour-related security. In order to understand this problem and its impact on industrial and political conflict, we first need to examine the strategically important role of labour contractors in regional auto manufacturing more closely.

---

[10] See Chapter 3 for recent proposed changes to these laws at a national and a state level.

The evidence presented above is consistent with earlier claims about the recruitment of workers in the auto industry of the NCR (Becker-Ritterspach, 2007; Bose and Pratap, 2012): that the overwhelming majority are hired through the services of multiple labour contractors. The data above demonstrates that more than 7 in every 10 production-line and manufacturing shop-floor workers are hired by contractors. On average, Tier-1 and Tier-2 firms hire five labour contractors.

A neo-classical economic view sees labour contractors as efficiency-enhancing intermediaries that assist firms and workers operating in 'imperfect' labour markets. Labour economists often treat this pathway as a 'stepping stone' to higher paid work for the young or less qualified (Autor, 2009). More critical scholars emphasise the exploitative role played by labour contractors or their potential to coerce workers and restrict their freedom of movement by locking them into debt obligations through wage advances (Barrientos, 2013). This remains a significant issue in India today in industries such as *bidi* (hand-made cigarette) making, agriculture, and construction (Breman, 2007; Roy, 2008; Government of India, 2009).

While there has been significant debate about whether these workers should, in general, be regarded as 'bonded' or 'unfree' (Brass, 1999; Lerche, 2007, 2011; Banaji, 2010; Barrientos, Gereffi and Rossi, 2013; Barnes et al, 2015), the disadvantages encountered by workers hired through labour contractors and their representatives in the NCR auto industry are more generally related to questions of low wages and other denials of labour-related security.

In the Indian auto industry, contractors perform many different functions for workers and employers, as well as providing services in numerous industries other than auto supply, like security, domestic work, transport, hospitality and construction. There are some large labour contractors who supply thousands of workers to the large OEMs and Tier-1 firms. However, all four of the labour contractors interviewed for this study ran modest operations from offices in Old Gurgaon. Based on interviews with labour contractors, employers and trade unionists, we can identify four different types of labour contractor.

First, there are Human Resources (HR) professionals who have become labour contractors after a career in management. For example, Labour Contractor LCA established his firm in 2003 after retiring from a career in HR and recruitment. In 2013, his company offered various services to automotive employers, including casual labour supply and skilled labour placement. His company charged a fee equivalent to 15 days' salary to employers and sent representatives of the company to wait at factory entrances to meet new recruits.

Second, some labour contractors are entrepreneurial professionals with a university education. For example, Labour Contractor LCB was an MBA graduate who started his business in 2001. By 2013, he employed nine people and had over

50 clients, including auto OEMs, Tier-1, and Tier-2 firms. A typical time-frame for workers' contracts was three to six months. Occasionally, his clients demanded casual labour supply of up to 50 workers at short notice and he paid agents who hailed from villages and towns in Bihar or UP and could mobilise groups of young workers. However, most of his clients organised their own recruitment and required him to focus on payroll management, payment of contributions for ESI and PF, counselling, and some performance management.

Third, there are individuals who have influence or links in local communities via family, clan or caste groups (Roy, 2008). This includes a range of people, such as retired public servants or individuals from political families, whose business or social networks put them in a position to influence groups of workers. For example, LCC was from a prominent political family and started his firm in 2000 as a partnership. He mainly provided placement for workers from ITIs to large OEMs and Tier-1 firms.

Finally, there are some ex-shop-floor workers who have been able to break into labour contracting through experience and connections accumulated after long careers in the industry, often after becoming supervisors or lower-level managers. For example, LCD was an ex-worker who provided placement services as a side business to a parts supply operation for sugar mills. He started offering placement services in 2011 and amassed 50 clients in auto components manufacturing as well as sugar mills and power plants in Haryana, charging a commission of 8.33 per cent of wages for placements.

Labour contractors offer a variety of services, depending on the type of service provider, their expertise, business networks and the size of their enterprise. First, labour contractors offer placement services by matching individuals to firms. This function is used particularly find a placement for more-skilled workers or managers who have arrived in the NCR with few social contacts or local knowledge. Second, labour contractors offer recruitment services by sourcing or managing new recruits on request from an employer. In the auto industry, many less-skilled or casual workers approach employers directly and are directed to labour contractors to receive initial training, as well as arrangements for their wage payments and other entitlements.

There are a variety of ways in which these workers encounter labour contractors in the recruitment process. Many travel directly to the factory gate where they meet labour contractors' representatives. However, in many cases, an employer or manager approaches a trusted or long-term employee, who then passes on a request through family and social networks for relatives, friends, or contacts to migrate for job opportunities. When new workers arrive, they are met by a labour contractor. In other cases, an employer or labour contractor asks a representative or agent in a regional area to supply workers. As explained by a plant manager at a plastic moulding factory:

Contractors have small, small agents who are the local expert in their region to collect the workers and bring [them] to Delhi and the surrounding area... They are small, small people. What contractors do is when these agents go back to their home, it gets activated. They get a pool of workers from these regions (Plant manager, Firm 1M, interview with author, 7 April 2013).

Labour contractors also send representatives to meet potential recruits at ITI campuses. In other cases, labour contractors send a representative directly, either a factory worker or the employee of a labour contractor, to bring potential recruits. These representatives are generally given money to pay for a return train ticket and food for one or two days. Workers are sometimes also recruited from 'labour chowks', a town or village square or street corner where workers gather looking for daily casual work. This type of recruitment is normal for casual labour hired in agriculture or the construction industry. Employers try to avoid this in auto manufacturing as workers commonly lack the skills or experience needed to commence work immediately, and labour contractors also charge additional fees for supplying these workers at short notice. Labour chowks are, instead, an option used in 'crisis situations' when temporary workers are urgently required (Plant manager, Firm 1M, interview with author, 7 April 2013).

In general, labour contractors hired by OEMs, Tier-1, and Tier-2 firms run a background or police check on new recruits. They commonly offer orientation for new workers, involving one or two days of unpaid training in which recruits are given information about company rules on appearance, punctuality, operations, and some safety guidelines. Finally, there are several HR roles performed by labour contractors, including payroll management and payment of workers' monthly wages, and maintaining records of workers' attendance, punctuality, physical appearance and dress-code. In this role, labour contractors often liaise with managers about the performance issues of individual workers.

For these various services, labour contractors typically charge a commission of 5–8 per cent of workers' wages for the duration of a 'contract'. Each contract specifies the number of workers and the length of time provided, although there is rarely a formal or written agreement between a labour contractor and a principal employer.

There are several advantages that labour contractors offer for employers in OEMs, Tier-1, and Tier-2 auto manufacturing firms. First, they enhance the flexibility of hiring-and-firing decisions. According to one Tier-1 plant manager:

The reason for this is that the consistency of demand is not there from the management' perspective. Management wants flexibility to have a 'bring in and bring out' situation. So [if] demand isn't there, we can pull people out easily and if demand is there we can take them in easily on the job (Plant manager, Firm 1M, interview with author, 7 April 2013).

According to a senior executive at a steel forging plant in Udyog Vihar Phase 1 (Gurugram), multiple labour contractors were necessary to manage his company's workforce: 'There is high labour turnover because of the large number of workers who leave Gurugram to return to their villages for festivals, weddings and farming' (Vice-President, Firm 2C, interview with author, 11 April 2013).

Second, large employers were able to use relations with labour contractors and officials of the Department of Labour in order to avoid restrictions on employing contract workers in core business functions under the *Contract Labour (Abolition and Regulation) Act 1970 (CLARA)*. One manager insisted that most firms paid bribes to government officials: '100 per cent of industry is paying bribes'. A labour inspector drove to his plant every weekend to collect a cash payment: 'Every government department is not an open kind of thing... We have to pay approximately ₹2–3 lakh [about US$ 3,000–4,700] per annum to this or that departments [in bribes], so we keep on paying' (Plant manager, Firm 1M, interview with author, 7 April 2013).

Labour contractors are incentivised to cooperate with this behavior because of high levels of competition among intermediaries for contracts with major firms. One labour contractor frankly explained that employers commonly avoided the restrictions in the *CLARA* by changing workers' job titles prior to the end of the 240-day limit to contract employment stipulated under the law. This was rarely checked by labour inspectors and, if the contractor took any worker's concern to firm owners or managers, the 'company would terminate my services' (Labour Contractor LCA, interview with author, 25 April 2013).

Third, labour contractors could help to undermine unionisation efforts. While seven Tier-1 firms (Firms 1B, 1C, 1N, 1O, 1P, 1Q and 1R) and one Tier-2 firm (2B) in Table 5.1 had plant-level unions, all members were regular workers. No example of contract workers joining or forming trade unions in the region was found. Some of these existing unions were aligned with national-level trade union confederations – known in India as Central Trade Union Organisations (CTUOs). For example, Firms 1O and 1P were linked to the Communist-aligned All-India Trade Union Congress, and Firms 1N and 1R were linked to the leftwing nationalist-aligned Hind Mazdoor Sabha (HMS).

Even in these cases, the wages, employment conditions and working conditions of contract workers were excluded from union-negotiated collective wage agreements. An extreme case was Firm 1P, a British-Indian-Japanese auto components manufacturing joint-venture, where a union represented the plant's

12 regular workers in effect, as shop-floor supervisors and low-level managers, but did not represent over 600 workers who were hired through five different labour contractors. Regular workers here explained that no attempt to represent or organise the contract workers had been made (Four regular workers, Firm 1P, interview with author, 11 March 2013).

The implications of this highly-restrictive institutional environment for unions are explored below. These observations suggest that restrictive and protective provisions in the *CLARA* have long-been systematically evaded in the NCR auto industry. A regional contract labour system operates in which the majority of workers in Tier-1 and Tier-2 firms are hired by multiple labour contractors. Most of these firms employ contract workers as ongoing, assembly- or production-line workers or as shop-floor craft workers – in other words, as 'core' workers.

Informal and precarious work in the auto industry

Based on the analysis of the regional contract labour system in the NCR, and following Chang (2009) – (see Chapter 1) – it can be argued that the majority of workers are 'de facto informal workers'. These workers may be formal by virtue of their entitlement to the full-range of legal restrictions on employer flexibility and social protections under Indian industrial planning and labour laws, but are denied access to these measures *in practice*.

This informal work also overlaps with precarious work, which is here defined by the denial of most forms of labour-related security. Precarious work incorporates a range of workers in different employment configurations in addition to contract labour. In OEMs, Tier-1, and Tier-2 firms, the diverse range of employment types include trainees who must work as production-line or shop-floor workers for a proscribed period of time before becoming eligible for conversion to an ongoing position, and apprentices who also work as full-time production-line workers.

In Firm 1E, a strategic partner to an OEM, several of the firm's 600 trainees – comprising 16 per cent of its total production-line workforce – had over 10 years' of experience working at the site. At Firm 1C, by December 2011, an OEM strategic partner in Manesar, all new recruits had to work for one year as a trainee on ₹4,500 followed by a further year of probation. Of these workers about half were taken on as regular workers (Two regular workers, Firm 1C, interview with author, 3 December 2011).

The precarity of this workforce is reflected in the systematic denial of most forms of labour-related security. First, most workers lack basic employment security, which refers to protection against arbitrary or unfair dismissal. While all paid work in OEMs, Tier-1 firms and Tier-2 firms is formally subject to the hire-and-fire restrictions in the *Industrial Disputes Act 1947*, employers have been successfully able to deploy a variety of ways of letting go workers when required, including the use of Voluntary Retirement Schemes (VRS) or victimisation of unionisation supporters and lockouts as a precursor to mass involuntary retrenchments (Plant union president, Firm 1N, interview with author, 13 March 2013; Plant union president, Firm 1O, interview with author, 22 March, 2013; Anil Kumar, Gurugram secretary, AITUC, interview with author, 6 March 2013; Jaspal Singh, Gurugram secretary, HMS, interview with author, 13 March 2013).

Second, workers lack basic job security, or opportunities for upward social mobility through career progression. Contract workers are commonly denied ongoing employment through use of the contract labour system. As has been argued already, it is common for workers to have their employment terminated at the end of a contract term prior to the 240 day limit in the *Contract Labour Act*. This can have a profound impact on the job security of workers. A 26-year old worker employed as a contract worker in a Tier-2 engine parts manufacturer in Mujesar, Faridabad explained his experience:

> I work for an automotive company with four plants in the local area... On average, each factory has 300–400 workers. Mostly, they are making auto parts for major producers like Maruti Suzuki. My factory has 500 workers, including 40–50 permanent workers. These are older workers who have been there for at least 20 years. They are paid ₹25,000 [about US$390]. The rest of the workers are hired through contractors. We are paid ₹5,700–6,000 [about US$85–95]...
>
> There is a union at the company although it is only for permanent workers. I am not interested in the union. If I have a problem at work, I talk to the permanent workers and they try to fix the problem. [Contract] workers are employed on a six-month contract. We work in one of the company's four plants for six months then our contract expires and we are given a break for a few weeks.
>
> To renew our employment, we are sent to another of the four plants. There is a rotation policy. I have been working for the company for the last four years. After each six month period, I go to the contractor for more work and get moved to another plant (Contract worker, Firm 2B, interview with author, 15 April 2013).

In some firms, there is a limited pathway into regular work, which can create opportunities for some casual and contract workers to step onto the regular workers' career path. The plant manager at a Tier-1 manufacturer in Binola Village explained the pathway at his firm:

> To become a regular worker, contract workers must pass certain tests. They must have at least 85 per cent attendance and demonstrate their qualifications by doing a questionnaire...

This is about managing workers who come in from outside [the region]. Permanency provides incentive for workers to stay... The most a [regular] worker can make, with overtime, is ₹25,000 (Plant manager, Firm 1O, interview with author, 6 April 2013).

However, for the majority of workers who remain in the contract labour system, there is little access to company promotion, and wages do not rise with negotiated increments due to their exclusion from collective wage agreements.

Third, there is some evidence that workers lack basic 'work security', which refers to protection from hazardous working conditions, including the threat of injury or illness, and from excessive or unsociable working hours. Although comprehensive evidence on the extent of work-related injuries is not available, the *Factories Act 1948* entrenches basic restrictions on working hours, including that a regular day of work should be nine hours long, and that 'no adult worker shall be required or allowed to work in a factory for more than 48 hours in any week' (Section 51); that workers engaged in more than nine hours work per day, or more than 48 hours in a week, shall be paid double-time wages for each additional hour (Section 59).

Based on interviews with workers and managers, an industry standard in the NCR auto industry is an eight-hour day and, depending upon the firm and the tier, up to four additional hours of overtime. Most workers work for six days a week, which is consistent with the *Act*'s requirement for a minimum of one day off work per week. However, all of the workers interviewed were paid the normal 'ordinary rate' for overtime hours in violation of the *Factories Act*.

Fourth, the lack of income security for most workers is reflected in the large cost differentials between regular and contract workers' wages. One of the main ways in which this wage income inequality is maintained is by excluding contract workers from collective wage agreements, which give regular workers access to a wide range of bonuses and allowances. Finally, the operation of the regional contract labour system means that most workers have been systematically denied representation security, which refers to the representation of workers' voice through collective bargaining and union representation. In India, unions have historically been organised into federal bodies, or CTUOs, which are usually linked to political parties with different ideologies, political programmess or patrons.

In the auto industry, most of the largest CTUOs have a presence, including the Indian National Congress-aligned Indian National Trade Union Congress (INTUC), two unions linked with the two largest Communist Parties – the Centre of Indian Trade Unions (CITU) and the All-India Trade Union Congress (AITUC) – the leftwing nationalist-aligned Hind Mazdoor Sabha (HMS) and, from rightwing nationalism, the ruling Bharatiya Janata Party (BJP)-aligned Bharatiya Mazdoor Sangh (BMS). In addition, affiliates to the New Trade Union

Initiative, a politically-independent federation with links to informal workers' organisations, have some engagement with auto workers.

There are also numerous independent or enterprise-level unions in the auto industry. Some of these maintain informal relations with the CTUOs who provide occasional advice and consultancy. In the NCR, the two most influential CTUOs are AITUC and HMS. By 2013, these CTUOs had collective wage agreements in-place in about 20 plants each in the NCR. However, the operation of the regional contract labour system, and the practical means it gives to employers to divide workers and circumvent unionisation campaigns, means that the effectiveness of these unions has been limited in practice.

The majority of workers have no *practical* entitlement to these protections. Although entitled to labour-related security under Indian labour and industrial planning laws, they are systematically barred access to these entitlements through a combination of employer hostility and flexible employment practices, the regional contract labour system, and a remarkably ineffective system of implementation and enforcement of labour regulations. The majority of workers are, in every practical sense, precariously-employed informal workers.

The recent history of workers' collective action in the NCR suggests that, while the structural power of workers can be considerable, a combination of political and institutional factors have prevented this from translating into greater associational power through a strengthening of trade unions or other labour organisations. In practice, the ability of employers to outsource recruitment and HR services to labour contractors has prevented contract workers from joining or forming trade unions in the NCR. While unionists acknowledged this problem, there was limited evidence of efforts to organise contract workers.

This problem partially reflects trade unions' historical reliance upon state institutions to fix wages, employment conditions and working conditions, or to arbitrate disputes with employers, often undermining their ability to independently bargain for workers' interests (Shyam Sundar, 2005; Hill, 2009). This includes key CTUOs in the auto industry like AITUC, HMS or CITU, despite evidence of a significant increase in CTUO membership nationally and attempts to organise informal workers (Menon, 2012; Shyam Sundar, 2012a). In some regions, like the city of Hospet in central Karnataka or the town of Nabha in western Punjab, unionists have successfully appealed to Global Union Federations (GUFs) to intervene in local disputes by lobbying global parent companies to curb the employment of contract workers (Shyam Sundar, 2012b).

But these agreements have been exceptional in India and, in Haryana, auto industry unions have not achieved similar victories. In practice, unions have mostly adapted to the restrictive institutional environment by pragmatically focusing on the protection of regular workers' labour-related security in individual enterprises.

In this context, it is significant that the MSIL dispute in Manesar in 2011/12 involved a high level of collaboration between regular, casual and contract workers and, despite the level of company and state repression that followed, MSIL eventually responded with major increases in wage levels for all categories of work and the introduction of directly-hired 'company casuals' (see Chapter 4).

These changes have had an impact on employment relations practices in Tier-1 and some Tier-2 suppliers. One common response has been for employers to allow a plant-level union to register – often on the condition that it remain independent from any CTUO – to negotiate a collective agreement with higher wages for regular workers and 'regularise' the employment of a minority of contract workers as a gesture of reform. During and after the MSIL dispute in Manesar, this occurred at three firms listed in Table 5.1.

The management at Firm 1O recognised a new union in March 2012, some two years after an initial registration attempt was made by contract workers, and regularised the employment of 247 workers, about 22 per cent of the factory workforce. Prior to this decree, *all* employees at the firm had been contract workers. Similarly, at Firm 1N in Gurugram, regular workers were given a ₹7,000 monthly increase over three years in March 2012 and 43 contract workers were regularised.

However, it is far from the case that the regional contract labour system is atrophying, despite the changes in MSIL's employment relations practices in the NCR. By mid-2013 – about nine months after the end of the MSIL dispute – the vast majority of workers in Tier-1 and Tier-2 firms continued to be hired, and have their work monitored and regulated, by labour contractors. The examples in which a minority of workers achieved permanency and union recognition did not address the wider problems of representation security for contract workers.

Contract workers sometimes have a relationship with union members, but this is limited. For example, at Firm 1N, contract workers could approach the plant union for assistance but could not pay fees and the union constitution prevented them from joining. At Firm 1O, the union president claimed that contract workers were 'informally represented', although they did not contribute financially, could not join, vote in union meetings, or stand as office-bearers (Plant union president, Firm 1O, interview with author, 22 March 2013; Three contract workers, Firm 1O, interview with author, 22 March 2013). The logic of CTUO leaders continues to reflect a position in which unions should attempt to organise contract workers *only after* formal registration and a collective wage agreement had been achieved for regular workers (AD Nagpal, National Secretary, HMS, interview with author, 8 March 2013; DL Sachdev, national secretary, AITUC, interview with author, 9 March 2013).

A further contributing factor to the weakness of unions concerns the material interests of local landowning families and their intersection with the politics of local trade union affiliates. As outlined in this chapter, several semi-rural and semi-industrial villages near IMT Manesar are populated by a mix of traditional Haryanvi landowners and migrant workers from inter-state regions. In these villages, some local landowners from Jat and Yadav communities act as intermediaries in land asset markets between regional state institutions, industrialists participating in global production networks, and labour contractors, who commonly sublet rooms to migrant contract workers for short periods of time.

Some of these landowning families play an additional intermediating role between migrant workers and industrial capital as plant-level trade union functionaries. For example, at both Firms 1O and 1Q in Binola Village, plant-level union offices were run by regular workers who came from local landowning families – in the former case, from a local Yadav family in Kharkari Village and, in the latter case, from a local Jat family in Binola. These families rented numerous rooms to migrant contract workers from inter-state regions, thus benefitting materially from the circulatory migration of workers through these villages and, indirectly, from the regional contract labour system that helped to facilitate it.

Regular workers in different companies in Binola have had several unionisation campaigns since 2007, with four Tier-1 auto firms succeeding in eventually registering plant-level unions with assistance from the AITUC and HMS. However, the contract labour system has persisted in these factories, providing the majority of recruits from the States of Bihar, UP or Uttarakhand.

Conclusion

This chapter has outlined the problems of deteriorating labour standards and employment relations in the auto industry of the NCR, India's largest auto manufacturing region. It has explained how processes of circular and seasonal labour migration in the region have intersected with its gradual industrialisation. Small- and large-scale industry spilled across the New Delhi border into Haryana between the 1960s and 1980s. This process accelerated in Gurugram district during India's economic liberalisation, leading to the emergence of enormous industrial zones, dotted with semi-industrial and semi-rural villages. These include the urban villages clustered between the Delhi-Haryana border and the industrial estates of Udyog Vihar, to the mixed-use villages that surround IMT Manesar along the Delhi-Jaipur Expressway.

Through this process of regional industrialisation, village and town life in and around the industrial centres of Haryana has been completely transformed. Today, social relations in local villages are shaped by commercial relations between groups of local landowners from middle-ranking castes, families engaged in cultivation, and a large mass of precariously-employed migrant workers from inter-state regions. In these industrial centres, a mix of foreign (mainly Japanese) and domestic firms have emerged with manufacturing roots across the fringes of the NCR.

Most of these firms use multiple labour contractors and the vast majority of employees – over seven in every 10 by 2013 – are contract workers. In implementing and entrenching this regional contract labour system, significant wage income inequality has been generated between regular and contract workers. While Japanese firms and OEM strategic partners tend to pay higher wages than domestic firms, virtually *all* firms make extensive use of a regional contract labour system and satisfy most of their recruitment and personnel management needs through this process.

This chapter has also outlined the different types and functions of labour contractors in the NCR and how they interact between workers and employers. The regional contract labour system plays a critical role in the denial of labour-related security to workers. Perhaps controversially, the chapter has framed the majority of these workers as 'de facto informal workers' – workers who are ostensibly entitled to labour-related security and social protection but who are, in all practical terms, denied access to these entitlement through a combination of industrial, social and institutional practices. These factors have combined to generate highly unfavourable conditions for trade unions, despite the structural power that workers possess when organising and acting collectively within the networked structure of regional auto manufacturing.

The potential and impact of trade unions has also been limited by the role of the dominant local landowning families in mediating the binary interactions of land and industry, regular worker and contract worker and the local and the inter-regional. Thus far, this discussion has not included the role of employers, workers and intermediaries in the heartland of small-scale industry in Faridabad district. This township district and expansive industrial area provides the base for most Tier-3 and Tier-4 auto production in the NCR. As we shall see in the following chapter, work organisation and employment relations are quite different at this 'low value' end of automotive global production networks. Here, the organisation of inter-firm, commercial relations through global production networks arguably has an even more profound impact on workers and the potential for development of associational power.

6

Work and Life at the Bottom of the Auto Supply Chain

This chapter focuses on the social organisation and social relations of work in small automotive manufacturing enterprises in India's National Capital Region (NCR). These enterprises are a mix of Tier-3 and Tier-4 firms. Tier-3 firms primarily manufacture automotive products for Tier-2 firms, although many produce for enterprises in different tiers of auto-based global production networks, including direct sales to the lead firm Original Equipment Manufacturers (OEMs) that dominate them. Tier-3 firms are generally much smaller than Tier-2 and Tier-1 firms when measured by production volume, sales, or number of employees.

This chapter will demonstrate that the participation of Tier-3 firms within global production networks in the NCR is usually based upon aggressive market price competition as well as strict oversight of product quality by OEMs and Tier-1 firms. These inter-firm, commercial relations have major implications for the capacity of these smaller firms to lock themselves into global production networks, and for the organisation of work and employment relations within them.

Some of the enterprises discussed in this chapter are informal enterprises by virtue of their small number of employees. In India, firms are informal enterprises if they employ fewer than 10 workers on a regular basis, or fewer than 20 if they lack electrical power. These firms form part of the 'unorganised sector' (see Chapter 1). Many state regulations and labour laws do not apply to firms in the unorganised sector, such as the *Factories Act 1948* which regulates working hours and conditions for regular workers in firms with 10 or more workers (the organised sector), medical insurance through the *Employees' State Insurance Corporation Act 1948* or an employment-based pension scheme through the *Employees Provident Funds Act 1952*.

However, many regulations, such as minimum wage laws at a national and state level, are meant to apply to all workers in firms in both organised and unorganised sectors. In the auto industry, some Tier-3 firms operate within the organised sector while others operate within the unorganised sector. In contrast, Tier-4 firms generally represent unorganised sector enterprises. Tier-4 firms tend to be own-account operations that function with a single, self-employed producer working with unpaid helpers from their family or with a small number of temporary wage workers.

This chapter will demonstrate the operation of a regional *casual* labour system as a regime of labour control in Tier-3 and Tier-4 firms in the NCR, in contrast to the regional *contract* labour system that operates in higher-tier firms. Within this regional casual labour system, most work conducted in Tier-3 firms is precarious and informal in nature. The idea of informal work used here concerns relations between employers, workers and state regulations while precarious work refers to the absence of most forms of labour-related security.

Like the previous chapter, these findings are based upon field research conducted in the NCR from late 2011 until mid-2013. Of the 106 workers interviewed for this book, 33 (or 31 per cent of the total) were workers employed by Tier-3 firms. In addition, 11 Tier-3 employers were interviewed, of whom six were owners or proprietors, three were managers and two were skilled workers in supervisory roles. Four Tier-4 owners – all own-account workers – were also interviewed (see Appendix for full list of interviews).

This chapter outlines the basic characteristics of the 10 Tier-3 and 4 Tier-4 firms represented by these workers and employers, including their location in the NCR, their product range, the type of supplier, the number of workers employed, and the wages and working conditions of skilled and unskilled workers. This chapter also introduces the concept of the 'captive generic supplier' as a type of small business that is completely reliant upon income from manufacturing in one or two global production networks via the production and sale of relatively simple low-cost components to higher-tier manufacturers.

This chapter will outline the interesting dynamic that occurs when some small firms move between captive participation in global production networks and retail or aftermarket production outside these networks. The commercial relations between Tier-3 and Tier-4 firms and high-tier manufacturers typically vacillate between versions of relational value chain governance and market-based governance. The chapter then explores the mobilisation and recruitment of workers in these firms and, despite the employment of many workers in Tier-3 firms within the regulatory framework of the organised sector, the absence of most forms of labour-related security among them. As the chapter explains, the precarious existence for many workers is sharpened by their status as inter-regional economic migrants and temporary residents in the industrial areas of the NCR.

Industrial colonies of the National Capital Region

If Gurugram and Manesar provide the core of the NCR's large-scale manufacturing global production networks, Faridabad remains the base for the largest concentration of employment in small-scale industry. For the auto industry, this means that Faridabad is the base for most Tier-3 and Tier-4 firms. These are clustered in several sub-district (*tehsil*) towns and industrial 'colonies'. These colonies are areas reserved by state and local authorities for small-scale industry and workshops. Faridabad also hosts several Tier-1 and Tier-2 auto manufacturing firms which engage in the manufacturing of various components, indicators, electrical and gear parts, rubber products and polymers, bonded metal and rubber parts, as well as metal forging, casting and pressing. However, there are many other small Tier-3 and Tier-4 manufacturers in this district. The main industrial colonies and fieldwork sites for Tier-3 and Tier-4 firms are mapped out in Figure 5.1 (see Chapter 5).

Many of these are smaller firms registered under the *Punjab Shops and Commercial Establishments Act 1958* which was designed, historically, to regulate trading practices and working conditions in small establishments, including small-scale manufacturers. Approximately half of the auto manufacturing firms listed under the *Act* are based in Sanjay Colony in Sector-23, Faridabad, where hundreds of workshops and small factories cluster in single-story brick buildings that line long, narrow streets adjacent to residential areas. Several of these streets are designated as an 'industrial complex' where predominantly Tier-3 and Tier-4 auto firms engage in manufacturing automotive, machine and electrical components, machine tools, springs, metal part casting and some mechanical and electrical engineering services.

Workers can be found resting throughout the day in tea-stalls and *dhabas* at the end of these streets during breaks from manual work in Tier-3 and 4 auto firms, or after their shift has ended. At any given moment, dozens of temporary and makeshift signs advertising paid work for jobseekers are scrawled along these lanes. These jobs usually advertise posts for 'helper' or 'operator' on iron gates, roller shutters and wooden doors of workshops and factories.

Most of the field research for this chapter was conducted in these 'industrial complexes' such as Friends Industrial Complex, Welcome Industrial Complex and Suraj Industrial Complex. At Friends Industrial Complex, there are about 50 auto manufacturing workshops, at Welcome Industrial Complex about 30 workshops and at Suraj Industrial Complex about 35 workshops, where workers variously engage in machine operating such as drills, grinders, cutters or lathes, unskilled manual tasks like sorting and counting basic components, cleaning or running errands and some metal forging and casting. While most workers in these enterprises are men, many employ significant numbers of women. Most of the women in these workshops are employed as less-skilled 'helpers', but some also work as semi-skilled machine operators.

Many other auto manufacturing enterprises cluster in brick and semi-*pukka* tenements in Shiv Colony in Sector-22, a short drive to the north of Sanjay Colony. By mid-2013, Shiv Colony lay next to a large fish market and slum community where many low-caste workers lived in *kachcha* dwellings made from scrap wood, corrugated iron and plastic sheets. A kilometre to the west of Sanjay Colony lies the Sarurpur Industrial Area where several industrial complexes and small factories lie in the middle of large vacant scrubland located adjacent to farming land.

Many other small auto manufacturers are located a kilometre to the east of Sanjay Colony in the town of Ballabgarh through which runs Mathura Road (National Highway 19), the main road that links Faridabad with New Delhi to the north and Haryana's rural heartland to the south. Many of these firms supply parts used by OEMs that operate facilities along Mathura Road, such as Japanese two-wheeler manufacturer India Yamaha Motor, British construction and agricultural vehicle manufacturer JCB India, which operates a large backhoe loader assembly factory and Indian tractor and agricultural equipment manufacturer Escorts. Escort's manufacturing facility is located in Mujesar, where dozens of manufacturing workshops are dotted beside a slum community which runs along an artificial canal. Many of these supply firms also manufacture parts that are processed by Tier-1 and 2 firms and sold to MSIL's plants in Gurugram and Manesar.

As outlined in Chapter 5, auto manufacturing in Gurugram centres upon two main areas: first, MSIL's first car assembly facility in Sector-18, Gurugram, which dominates a large industrial area between the Delhi-Jaipur Expressway (National Highway 48) and Old Delhi-Gurgaon Road, about 2 km to the west. In addition, Hero MotoCorp operates a major factory in Sector-33, Gurugram. The second main area is centred around IMT Manesar, with Honda Motorcycle and Scooter India (HMSI) along the Delhi-Jaipur Expressway, and MSIL's second facility 3 km to the west. Hundreds of manufacturing supply companies cluster in industrial areas centred around these two areas.

To the immediate east of Sector-18, Gurugram is Udyog Vihar, an industrial estate that runs in five 'phases' from the Delhi-Haryana border in the north to the Delhi-Jaipur Expressway in the south. Hundreds of thousands of workers walk, drive, and bicycle through this area each day to work in export garments factories as well as dozens of auto manufacturing suppliers. High-caste workers with better educational qualifications work in IT, call centres, and telecommunication offices in the area. To the south of Udyog Vihar are numerous high-rise offices, residential buildings and gated communities which are generally affordable only to the families of higher-paid workers, managers, white-collar professionals and expatriate workers. To the north is the Delhi-Haryana border, where several 'urban villages' cluster, including Samalka and Kapas Hera on the Delhi side and, on the border itself, Dundahera. Like earlier studies (Bose and Pratap, 2012), the research presented in this book finds that auto manufacturing predominantly relies on workers who have migrated from inter-state regions of India like Rajasthan to the southwest, Uttarakhand to the north, Odisha (Orissa) and Jharkhand to the east and, above all, from the towns and villages in the east of Uttar Pradesh and Bihar.

In these rural areas, hundreds of factory workers live in large tenements in which it is common for three or four workers to share a single room. By 2011, these rooms typically cost around ₹1000 a month (about US$15) in rent but, as they were often window-less and the air was stale due to lack of ventilation, many workers would spend evenings socialising and sleeping on the rooftop during the scorching summer months.

Surrounding MSIL and HMSI's vast industrial sites at IMT Manesar are numerous villages, including the workers' village of Aliyar to the immediate north of MSIL's facility. In villages like Kharkara and Binola, approximately 10 km to the south of Manesar, agriculture still provides livelihoods for numerous families. These villages house a mix of local (Haryanvi) residents and migrant workers as well as numerous Tier-1 and Tier-2 auto manufacturing firms. The roads connecting these village industrial sites to the Delhi-Jaipur Expressway are typically in poor condition, usually unpaved, and susceptible to flooding during the monsoon season.

The population in these industrial villages has increasingly been divided between a core of dominant land-owners with local roots and a much larger mass of migrant workers from inter-state regions, on whom the region's automotive global production networks rely.

Tier-3 and Tier-4 auto manufacturers in the National Capital Region

This chapter is mainly comprised of evidence from extensive fieldwork in the NCR conducted over several months in 2011, 2012, and 2013 (see outline in Chapter 5 and details of interviews in Appendix). For the ten Tier-3 firms in this study, complete data collected on the type of supplier, its location, main products, number of workers employed and the wages of skilled and unskilled workers, are included in Table 6.1. Note that the data for the four Tier-4 firms studied for this research are outlined in the text but not tabulated. As with other workers and employers who participated in the research and have been mentioned in this book, names of companies have also been coded, and individuals have not been named to protect their employment and livelihood.

All of the Tier-3 firms in Table 6.1 are Indian-owned and operated, which suggests that OEMs, Tier-1, and Tier-2 firms, which are more likely to reflect a mix of foreign and domestic companies, rely considerably upon small Indian enterprises to operate in this region. Nine of these firms are located in Faridabad and are listed in chronological order of interview dates.

Table 6.1: Tier-3 auto manufacturing suppliers, National Capital Region[1]

Firm code	Location	Products	Supplier type	No. of workers	A. Wages (unskilled labourer) ₹'000	B. Wages (skilled craft worker) ₹'000	Ratio A/B (%)
3A	Friends Industrial Complex, Faridabad	sheet metal fabrication, spare parts	SISS	60	5.7–7	X	see below[2]
3B	Sururpur, Faridabad	brake shoes, indicators	GSS	12	5.5	10	55
3C	Shiv Colony, Faridabad	engine parts	SISS	40	4.8	10	48
3D	Mujesar, Faridabad	electroplating	CGS	10	5–7.5	X	X
3E	Shiv Colony, Faridabad	spare parts	CGS	15	4–5	4–5	100
3F	Sanjay Colony, Faridabad	spare parts	SISS	60	5.3–9	5.3–9	100
3G	IMT Manesar	fan blades, spare parts	CGS	15	6.7	6.7	100
3H	Welcome Industrial Complex, Faridabad	spare parts	SISS	30	4.5	4.5	100
3I	Welcome Industrial Complex, Faridabad	engine parts, axle parts	CGS	40	4	8	50

Contd.

---

[1] All firms in this sample are Indian-owned. All interviews were conducted in March–April 2013. Firms are presented in order of date of interview. See appendix for full list of interviews with codes. Supplier type = SISS (specialised independent supplier – single industry), SISM (specialised independent supplier – multi-industry), GSS (generic supplier – single industry), CGS (captive generic supplier). X = missing value.

[2] For Firm 3A, 77 per cent of workers were hired by labour contractors and there was no difference between regular and contract workers' basic wages. This is the only Tier-3 firm found that relied on contract workers.

Firm code	Location	Products	Supplier type	No. of workers	A. Wages (unskilled labourer) ₹'000	B. Wages (skilled craft worker) ₹'000	Ratio A/B (%)
3J	Welcome Industrial Complex, Faridabad	engine parts, pulleys	SISM	7	8–10	8–10	100
Average (*n* = 10)				29	5.4–6.4	7.1–7.9 (*n* = 8)	82 (*n* = 8)

Although there are many Tier-3 firms located in Gurugram, Faridabad has a relatively greater concentration of economic activity in small-scale industry. Of these nine firms, four were located in Sanjay Colony (Sector 23), two in Shiv Colony (Sector 22) and one each in the Sururpur Industrial Area, Mujesar and Old Faridabad. Of the five firms in Sanjay Colony, three were located in the same street (Welcome Industrial Complex), and one in another street nearby (Friends Industrial Complex). Most information used to construct this dataset came from interviews with workers and employers who were approached directly in these industrial areas. Dozens more were approached and, while not granting formal interviews, spoke in detail about their work, livelihood and communities.

Of these 10 firms, five manufacture spare parts purchased by Tier-2 firms, such as metal pins and shift levers used in starter motors, as well as spark plug sockets, fuel tank caps, ball joints and springs (Firms 3E, 3F and 3H and Firm 3A produce small discs, and Firm 3G produces springs as well as ventilation fan blades). Three firms (3C, 3I and 3J) manufacture parts used in engine production such as gaskets, O-rings and small pulleys.

The other two firms manufacture brake shoes and indicators by bonding plastic and rubber polymers (Firm 3B) and electroplating metal parts (3D). Some of these firms specialise in more than one product. Other than Firm 3D, Firm 3A is a fabrication shop which cuts sheet metal parts used in chassis components as well as small discs used in engines. This also means that some firms also manufacture products for direct sale to higher-tier firms. For example, Firm 3I manufactures axle parts for an NCR-based OEM as well as engine parts sold to its main client, a Tier-2 firm in Faridabad.

Firm 3J is multi-industry in orientation, producing pistons used in the manufacturing of elevators and scissor-lifts as well as small pulleys sold to a Tier-2 client for engine manufacturing. The other firms are mainly a mix of specialised independent suppliers focused entirely on manufacturing products for the auto industry (3A, 3C, 3F and 3H) and *captive generic suppliers* (3D, 3E, 3G and 3I). The concept of captive generic suppliers refers to firms that produce relatively simple components that are processed by higher-tier manufacturers but who also operate a business model in which the entire existence of the firm depends upon the demand for these components by these clients.

For example, Firm 3D electroplates nickel onto metal parts which are sold to a vendor for processing in a Tier-2 firm in Faridabad and a Tier-1 firm in Gurugram, where they are used in components for a single OEM in the NCR. Firm 3E only produces gaskets, albeit with more than one basic design, which are used in engine components assembled by a single Tier-2 firm in Faridabad. Firm 3G in IMT Manesar manufactures fan blades and springs used in engine components for two main clients, both Tier-2 manufacturers in Manesar. Finally, Firm 3I is completely reliant on demand from its main Tier-2 client for engine parts. While it also manufactures ball-joints used for wheel axles directly for an OEM, these are irregular orders for which it occasionally hires temporary workers on piece-rate wages. According to its owner, this firm would not survive as a perennial Tier-3 firm without demand from its main Tier-2 client.

In contrast, specialised independent suppliers have some capacity to switch products or clients. For example, while Firm 3A's sheet metal products are sold to Tier-2 clients, it is not reliant on a single customer firm and has some capacity to switch clients depending on the volume of order and prices. A further category in this sample is the single-industry generic supplier, represented by Firm 3B. While 3B only produced products for the auto market, it was not part of any global production network and, at the time of field research, produced brake shoes, bonded metal and rubber indicators *solely* for the retail consumer market (known as the aftermarket).

This firm is classified as Tier-3 in here because it previously had a contract to produce bonded rubber parts for a Tier-2 auto manufacturer. However, it was unable to satisfy the customer's quality or quantity demands and subsequently lost the contract. The owner of this operation is a young man in his mid-20s from a local Yadav family which owns some agricultural land as well as two other manufacturing businesses in the area. He explained his preference to establish new contracts with higher-tier firms rather than rely on the aftermarket: 'I would make lower profits if I was in the supply chain in the short term but this would improve in the long term because demand would be continuous. So the company earnings would be continuous too' (Owner, Firm 3B, interview with author, 8 April 2013).

The firms in Table 6.1 each tend to have modest employment numbers. On an average, a total of 29 people worked in these firms, ranging from a low of seven workers up to 60 workers. In terms of formal rules, most of these firms fell under the *Factories Act 1948* in terms of regulations and restrictions on working conditions and working hours. In two of these firms (3C and 3I), owner-managers had posted this summary information about this law on the wall inside their small factories so workers were free to read it (although, in one case, the notice was written in English, a language few employees would be able to read or understand fluently). Only one of these firms was formally part of the unorganised sector (Firm 3J with just seven employees). However, all these firms were well below the threshold of the *Industrial Disputes Act 1947*, which meant they were all relatively free to hire or retrench workers without needing to seek permission from authorities.

In contrast to Tier-3 firms, the four Tier-4 firms in this study were all part of the unorganised sector or were informal enterprises. Firm 4L was represented by a single owner-operator who had a cutting machine and did 'job work' for Tier-3 firms in Sanjay Colony. These were generally one-off orders often made by clients who were struggling to meet a deadline or who had temporarily lost in-house capacity. If he received a tight deadline, this owner would ask for unpaid help from his family members.

The other three Tier-4 enterprises were run by an owner who occasionally employed wage workers to help meet large orders or tight deadlines. Firm 4K was managed by an owner in his late 30s who was a former skilled operator for a Tier-1 auto manufacturer in Binola village, near IMT Manesar. He regularly employed four or five casual workers. Firm 4M had an owner-operator with just one paid worker employed on a regular basis, and 4N had two paid employees (see Appendix for full list of interviews with Tier-4 proprietors).

For most Tier-3 firms, it was possible to get accurate data on wages and some working conditions from employers or workers. This data distinguishes 'skilled' workers from 'unskilled' workers. In reality, the notion of which activities require skill and which do not is highly complex. As a concept, skill can include formal qualifications and accredited training, such as Industrial Training Institute (ITI) certificates, diplomas, or college engineering degrees, as well as accredited on-the-job training, the occupational profile and experience of a worker, their school education level, and tacit skills developed through experience and acculturation at work.

The auto industry as a whole is comprised of a mix of occupations. Workers in shop-floor roles tend to be divided between craft workers, who take skilled and semi-skilled roles, and production workers, who take semi-skilled and less-skilled roles such as product assembly, process and machine operating for metal parts, rubber, plastic and textiles, and manual labouring such as packers and sorters. In this final category falls many assembly or production line tasks which can require skills that physically fit or able-bodied individuals can acquire in a matter of weeks or days, as well as many ancillary tasks such as cleaning or sorting.

In this chapter, the distinction between 'skilled' and 'unskilled' has been simplified based upon direct observations of work in Tier-3 and Tier-4 firms, and discussion with interview participants. Skilled work here refers to craft work and semi-skilled work such as machine operating, including Computer Numerical Control (CNC), cutting, drilling or shaping with lathes and the physical processing of parts and components. Unskilled work generally refers to the role of the *helper*: the worker who is tasked with counting, sorting and checking products, or with ancillary tasks such as cleaning, running errands, or bringing meals, tea, and drinks.

In most Tier-3 and Tier-4 firms, employers drew a distinction in terms of wage levels between these groups of 'skilled' and 'unskilled' workers. Furthermore, like in Chapter 5, a distinction is made between the *basic wage*, which is meant to reflect minimum wage laws and wage categories by occupation, and the *gross wage* which is the addition of paid over-time hours but, also, any cash bonuses paid to workers.

On an average, the basic wage of unskilled Tier-3 workers was ₹5,400 per month or just slightly above the minimum wage for unskilled labourers in Haryana which at the time was ₹5,330 (about US$80–85). The average gross wage was ₹6,400 per month, 19 per cent higher than the basic wage. Thus, less-skilled workers relied on overtime and bonus payments for nearly a sixth of their wage income. Basic wages ranged from a low of ₹4,000 – well below the Haryana minimum wage at that time – up to a high of ₹8,000. Five of the Tier-3 firms in the study – exactly half the total sample – paid basic wages that were below the minimum wage. Like some workers earning sub-minimum wages in Tier-1 and Tier-2 firms, some workers in Tier-3 firms were not aware that any law was being broken, or wrongly believed that their total wage included bonuses or 'gifts' from their employer to supplement their 'basic salary'.

Furthermore, some firms did not pay above a basic daily or monthly wage. For example, at Firm 3B, all helpers received a flat wage of ₹5,500 per month, while helpers at Firm 3C received ₹4,800, and at 3I just ₹4,000. Thus, some workers were paid below the minimum wage even if they worked extra hours. At Firm 3H, 30 workers, including drill operators, helpers and cleaners each earned a base salary of ₹4,500, including the three female workers at the factory. The owner stressed that workers were provided with lodging – directly above the shop-floor – and other amenities which justified this low wage:

Workers are provided with accommodation upstairs. Rent and electricity [costs are] taken from their monthly wage. We have some rooms upstairs. Workers must be available for job work when it comes. If we are very busy, we sometimes wake up workers at night and require them to work (Owner, Firm 3H, interview with author, 18 April 2013).

On an average, the skilled workers' basic wage was ₹7,100 per month (about US$110), 32 per cent higher than the unskilled workers' equivalent. The average gross wage was ₹7,900, 23 per cent higher than the unskilled workers' equivalent. On an average, the unskilled workers' wages were 82 per cent of skilled workers' wages in these Tier-3 firms. As suggested above, however, there were some firms – two in this sample (Firm 3H and 3E) – that did not differentiate pay between different occupations or work and paid all workers sub-minimum wages regardless of their skills or abilities.

While this is a small (and not a random or statistically representative) sample of Tier-3 firms, findings from this research nevertheless indicate that there is no clear or straightforward relationship between the type of supplier, employment numbers and wage levels. For example, independent suppliers tended to employ more workers – the average number of workers in the four independent suppliers was 39 compared to 18 in the five generic suppliers – but there was no clear relationship to wage levels. Wages in the sample's four independent suppliers ranged from a low of ₹4,500 per month to a high of ₹10,000, while the range of the five generic suppliers was ₹4,000 to ₹10,000.

A striking feature of the work in Tier-3 and Tier-4 firms is the general absence of labour contractors. As outlined in Chapters 4 and 5, work organisation and employment relations in the auto industry nationally has been completely transformed by the implementation of regional contract labour systems, a process pioneered by MSIL following major industrial conflict at its Gurugram facility in the early 2000s. In Chapter 5, it was demonstrated that automotive global production networks in the NCR have relied completely upon a regional contract labour system. Yet one does not find an operating contract labour system in most of the Tier-3 and 4 firms in these global production networks.

In the sample in Table 6.1, only Firm 3A, a specialised independent supplier in Faridabad, relied on labour contractors to regulate employment at its small factory. Of its total workforce of 60 employees, 45 were contract workers (75 per cent). Most firms at this tier of the industry cannot afford to pay labour contractors' fees – generally up to eight per cent of a workers' total wage for the duration of a 'contract' – and thus, only turn to their services when faced with exceptional or one-off circumstances, just as they turn to Tier-4 enterprises for job work when they need additional help to complete an order or production cycle. Apart from Firm 3A, all firms encountered in this study preferred to hire through workers' social or kinship networks, or by placing an advertisement in front of their premises – hence the numerous scrawls of 'helper' or 'operator' in the side alleys of Faridabad's industrial colonies.

Value Chain Governance

Commercial relations between firms in different tiers of global production networks, like those that comprise the auto manufacturing industry, have major implications for employment relations within these firms. This is especially so in the lower-level tiers where the constraints on employer choices and maneuverability are arguably the greatest. This means that the modes of governance that frame these relations are very important. In Chapter 1, the concepts used to frame governance come from both the Global Value Chain (GVC) and Global Production Network (GPN) traditions. We find some interesting observations when applying and testing these concepts in the context of contemporary auto manufacturing in India's NCR.

For Coe and Yeung (2015), firms in the auto industry tend to pursue network strategies based either on inter-firm control or inter-firm partnership. In the former case, one firm plays a dominant role in controlling the operations of another through global production networks relations. In the latter case, such firms collaborate through, for example, co-investment and equity shares. In the context of the auto industry, these concepts are somewhat similar to the idea of relational governance developed in the GVC tradition (Gereffi, Humphrey and Sturgeon, 2005), despite Coe and Yeung's warnings against generalising any one type of governance relations to an entire industry. The concept of relational governance is consistent with the complexities required by auto manufacturing suppliers to conform to OEMs' design specifications and standards of product quality.

The concept of relational governance is able to describe commercial relations between Tier-3 and Tier-4 firms and their higher-tier clients in the NCR. In most of the Tier-3 firms included in this study, it was normal for inspectors or representatives from higher-tier firms to frequently visit to meet with owners or managers, and to directly inspect finished products. At Firm 3A, the company's main Tier-2 client in Faridabad sent an inspector to their factory three or four times a year. In other cases, inspections were more frequent. In case of 3E, its main Tier-2 client, also in Faridabad, sent an inspector once or twice a month to inspect different designs of the company's engine gaskets. At 3J, a Tier-2 inspector visited the owner's workshop three or four times a year.

At 3G, the company's two main Tier-2 clients, which had adjacent factories in IMT Manesar, each sent inspectors on a weekly basis to monitor product quality. In this case, inspection was combined with purchasing, with the inspector also acting as a vendor. This streamlining of roles was made possible by the very close proximity – i.e., 5–10 minutes' drive – between Firm 3G and its main clients. At Firm 3I, managers expected visits from inspectors once or twice per month. One visit came from a Tier-2 inspector who checked the firm's engine parts and the other was a direct visit from an NCR-based OEM representative who checked its axle parts.

The example of Firm 3G demonstrates that, in some cases, inspections of product quality in Tier-3 firms were made *directly by OEMs or Tier-1 firms* even though most of company's products were sold for processing to Tier-2 firms. Similarly, Firm 3I received monthly visits from a local OEM representative as well as a Tier-1 client, even though most of its products were sold to a single Tier-2 firm in Faridabad: The OEM 'has 50 vendors and [the inspector] is always here to check on what we are doing. He is here to check and look around once or twice a month' (Owner, Firm 3I, interview with author, 18 April 2013).

At Firm 3C, the representative of an NCR-based OEM visited the factory in Shiv Colony, Faridabad twice a week to check product quality: 'I come here for a brief visit twice a week. I move between many of my company's vendors every day [in Faridabad]. My job is to ensure that the products are of good quality and to have discussions with vendors if there is any problem' (Product Quality Inspector, Firm X, interview with author, 9 April 2013).[3]

It is possible that there is some relationship between the type of supplier and the importance or frequency of these inspections. For example, while captive generic suppliers like Firm 3E, 3G and 3I variously received visits on a weekly or monthly basis, specialised independent suppliers (Firms 3A and 3J) received similar inspections less frequently, around 3–4 times a year. It may be that this partially reflects the more dependent character of captive generic suppliers on higher-tier firm patronage and, conversely, the relatively greater autonomy and client-switching capacity of independent suppliers.

The examples cited above are consistent with a framing of commercial relations between Tier-3 firms and higher-tier firms via relational governance or as a type of inter-firm control. However, these relations have additional characteristics which do not fit as simply into these categories. Besides closely monitoring the product quality and operations of Tier-3 firms, higher-tier firms also regulate the activity of lower-tier firms through control over prices and sales income. This regulation is direct, through price-fixing, and indirect, through design specifications, alterations, and payment frequency that also have an impact on the sales income and profitability of Tier-3 firms.

---

[3] Not all Tier-3 firms receive inspections from higher-tier customers. At Firm 3D, electroplated metal parts were sold to a vendor who transported them to a Tier-2 client in Gurugram for eventual use in MSIL engine and chassis parts. No higher-tier firm regularly visited the company to check on products. At Firm 3B, the owner had previously received frequent visits from a Tier-2 manufacturer, but was no longer producing parts for this customer and focused only on the aftermarket. Information on inspections or visits from higher-tier customers was not available for Firms 3F and 3H.

Price levels for components are, alongside product volume and order frequency, critical to the income, profitability and viability of auto manufacturing suppliers. Ultimately, these prices are heavily dependent upon the market control of OEMs, the branding of motor vehicles within consumer markets, and the capacity of OEMs to compete within these markets or to segment markets with their OEM competitors.

For example, the price and quality levels attached to complex assembled components like engines, transmission systems and automotive electrical systems have a knock-on impact on the Tier-2 firms that manufacture sub-assembled products and, consequently, the Tier-3 firms that manufacture or process the individual, usually simpler, parts and components that are used in higher-tier processing and assembly operations. The survival of Tier-3 firms within global production networks is thus heavily dependent upon the pricing, quality and market strategies of OEMs.

This also means that higher-tier suppliers put great emphasis on lower-tier suppliers meeting product quality and volume requirements within a strict price range. Most Tier-3 firms studied in this research competed primarily on *price*. OEMs, Tier-1, and Tier-2 clients pressurised owners and managers in these firms, through regular factory visits and inspections, to conform to price-driven requirements. For example, the owner of Firm 3C explained that his main client was a Tier-2 manufacturer in Faridabad with about 800 employees who purchased simple engine parts (gaskets and O-rings) from his small factory. This client firm encouraged price competition among parts suppliers: 'They have over 200 suppliers. They will often cut orders or give them to our competitors if they offer a cheaper price. They sometimes change orders without [providing any] notice' (Owner, Firm 3C, interview with author, 9 April 2013).

The owner of Firm 3I complained that his company's single OEM client in the NCR – the company's main client being a local Tier-2 firm – kept prices at a low level: 'They are always here checking [our] axle bearings and they always talk to us. But they haven't increased their prices for [the last] five years' (Owner, Firm 3I, interview with author, 18 April 2013). Many of his firm's 40 employees were aware of this issue.

Workers at this workshop were met with after their shift on three separate occasions and five agreed to be interviewed together. During the interview one skilled worker and one mechanical engineer, complained about the firm's main OEM client:

> There is cutthroat competition among vendors. [The OEM client] hasn't
> increased its parts prices in five years. Consequently, wages cannot go up among

the suppliers. Each vendor competes on low-cost production. Each vendor tries to under-cut others in order to win contracts (Engineer, Firm 3I, interview with author, 18 April 2013).

A worker in the group who has been employed there for 20 years added the following statement: 'There is no way wages can go up in this environment... Buyers cannot increase the rate of parts so wages cannot go up. There is no point moving to a different employer [if you are not happy with these wages]. The employers are united [but] the workers are not' (Worker, Firm 3I, interview with author, 18 April 2013).

Along with price competition among hundreds of lower-tier suppliers and frequent inspection for conformity with design specifications and product quality, higher-tier firms were able to manipulate the activities of Tier-3 firms by unilaterally controlling the frequency of payments. Put simply, Tier-3 proprietors producing for global production networks had little control over the frequency with which they were paid for orders. Their clients tended to make late payments. As the owner of Firm 3E explained:

> [Our customer, a Tier-2 firm in Faridabad,] is here once or twice every month to talk to me. He is checking for the quality of products. We have very good relations [and] they provide ongoing and regular work. But they use about 200 vendors to supply parts. There is a lot of competition. The rates charged by companies are falling due to competition based on low-cost. And [our customer] refuses to pay on time. They are supposed to pay bills in 60 days but usually take 110 days to pay (Owner, Firm 3E, interview with author, 15 April 2013).

As outlined below, these commercial practices have important implications for employment relations within Tier-3 firms. They also suggest that, besides inter-firm control or relational governance, these firms are also engaged in global production network in which characteristics of *market-based* governance are also a prominent feature. As outlined in Chapter 1, market-based governance is based on a high level of dispersal of production across multiple suppliers, and high dependence of both lead firms and suppliers on price-based relations to underwrite the production of finished commodities.

While many small auto manufacturers are able to satisfy the product requirements of OEMs, the much greater relative market value and economic power of OEMs means that their pricing decisions have a profound impact on the operations of these smaller suppliers. This finding is consistent with the claim that value chain governance in auto manufacturing is not fixed and, instead, tends to oscillate between relational and market-based forms (Sturgeon et al, 2008).

A regional casual labour system

As outlined above, most Tier-3 and Tier-4 firms cannot afford to, and often do not need to, participate in the regional contract labour system that dominates employment regulation in OEMs, Tier-1, and Tier-2 firms. Instead, precarious and informal work manifest via a regional *casual* labour system that operates through the intersection of firms' direct hiring practices with circular and seasonal flows of inter-state migrant workers through industrial areas.

Informal work completely dominates economic activities in India, including manufacturing activities. A core claim of this book is that informal work similarly characterises most employment in the Indian auto industry and that the modernisation and regional expansion of auto manufacturing has been predicated upon and, also, expanded the employment of informal workers. In this chapter, we focus on the role of informal work in Tier-3 and Tier-4 firms.

Informal work reflects economic activities in which state regulations are either absent, relaxed or systematically evaded by economic actors. In India, informality is officially defined by the employment size of enterprises, with the 'organised sector' referring to firms with 10 or more workers and the 'unorganised sector' referring to firms with fewer than 10 workers. As outlined previously, most auto work thus appears to be concentrated in the organised sector.

Similarly, the *Contract Labour (Abolition and Regulation) Act 1970* (the 'CLARA') restricts the employment of contract workers in core functions of enterprises on an ongoing basis for firms with 20 or more workers. While this applies to virtually all OEMs, Tier-1, and Tier-2 firms (see Chapter 5), it has mixed application to Tier-3 firms. While the average employment size for Tier-3 firms in Table 6.1 is 29 workers, the CLARA does not apply to five of these firms, or half the sample. An irony of this is that very few Tier-3 proprietors rely on labour contractors' services due to the extra cost pressures of low-margin price competition in the lower rungs of automotive GPNs.

In contrast to Tier-3 firms, virtually all Tier-4 firms fall within the unorganised sector. Tier-4 firms are generally represented by own-account or self-employed operators who work alone, hire a small number of wage workers when required, or operate with assistance from unpaid workers such as family members. While Tier-4 firms are therefore predominantly informal in character, even here, minimum wage laws are meant to apply to all wage workers.

Most workers in Tier-3 and Tier-4 firms are engaged in precarious work with little labour-related security. Other than the seven cases of labour-related security (Standing, 2011), an eighth form of socio-economic security is the concept of 'precarity of place', which relates to the stability of residence for an individual or their family (Banki, 2013).

Precarity of place is a critical issue for the mass of inter-state migrant workers on whom the NCR's automotive global production networks rely. The majority of hired workers interviewed from Tier-3 firms, like those hired by OEMs, Tier-1, and Tier-2 firms, had migrated from inter-state regions for work. Of the 30 Tier-3 employees interviewed for this book, 23 were originally from towns or villages in Bihar, and the remaining seven were from eastern Uttar Pradesh. None were originally from Haryana or Delhi. Of the 11 Tier-3 employers who participated in interviews, five were from Haryanvi families, while three were from Bihar, and three from Uttar Pradesh. Among the Tier-4 proprietors, all were inter-state migrant workers – two from Uttar Pradesh, and one each from the States of Bihar and Jharkhand.

Most Tier-3 workers are aged in their 20s or 30s. Among those (male workers) who participated in this research, most were single; although some were married, and there was also a small minority of unmarried women who had migrated to industrial colonies for work. The term, 'locals', was commonly used by the participants to describe people raised in towns and villages in Haryana or Delhi. For example, the owner of 3D, who migrated with his brother from a village in the Rajapakar area of central Bihar 10 years ago, explained his view about employment trends in small firms: 'Locals are unwilling to do casual labour in industry. We must employ men and boys from Bihar or other places to survive' (Owner 3D, interview with author, 6 April 2013).

Most of the workers who migrated sent a large proportion of their wage income as remittance to relatives in inter-state regions. In most cases, this was to their parents' household although a minority of married workers sent money directly to their spouse. Out of the 30 workers interviewed, 21 remitted income to inter-state regions, ranging from 30 per cent of their monthly wage up to 80 per cent.

The majority of these workers would return to their home village or town once or twice a year for festivals – especially for Diwali in October/November and Holi in February/March – as well as for weddings of relatives or for harvesting rice or grain on their family holdings. However, nine of these workers did not remit any income and rarely returned to their village or town of origin. These workers were more likely to be longer-term migrants who had travelled with their spouse, and often children, for work, and remained in the NCR on a permanent basis.

For migrant workers in Tier-3 and Tier-4 firms, there was no regional contract labour system in operation. As stated above, only one firm in Table 6.1 made regular use of labour contractors (Firm 3A). However, most migrant workers had found jobs via an informal system of labour market intermediation which relied upon workers' social and kinship networks, often through a close relative, such as a sibling who had previously migrated to the area for work.

A 23-year old casual helper at Firm 3B explained how he arrived in the area two years ago: 'My brother was already working here [in Faridabad] before I arrived. He said the boss was looking for helpers and told me to come [from the city of Deoria in eastern UP] for work' (Casual worker, Firm 3B, interview with author, 8 April 2013). At Firm 3D in Mujesar, a 24-year old worker explained:

> I used to work as a tailor in Mumbai. But the company I was working with closed down. Simultaneously, I used to do the same thing as here which is plating of auto parts. I acquired the skills for both the jobs. There were a few people from my village [near the city of Gorakhpur in eastern Uttar Pradesh] who were working here at the time. They suggested I come here and that's when I came to Delhi (Casual worker A, Firm 3D, interview with author, 6 April 2013).

Furthermore, most of the workers interviewed belonged to the official category of Other Backward Classes (OBCs), which is used by the State to record numerous castes classified as socially disadvantaged and, in some cases and in some States, to provide reservations for public sector employment. However, some workers came from Dalit, Scheduled Caste, or Muslim families. Most of the OBC workers came from families with a background in cultivation of small or marginal land holding with fewer than five acres. In some Tier-3 firms, all employees hailed from OBC castes with a family background in small-scale cultivation in inter-state regions (Two casual workers, Firm 3D, interview with author, 13 April 2013; Owner, Firm 3E, interview with author, 15 April 2013; Owner, Firm 3C, interview with author, 15 April 2013; Five workers, Firm 3I, interview with author, 18 April 2013).

Furthermore, the wage gap between different categories of workers in Tier-3 firms often followed regional lines. For example, at Firm 3C, which employed a total of 40 workers across two workshops in Faridabad, the firm's 10 helpers were all OBC workers from Uttar Pradesh or Bihar earning a basic (sub-minimum) wage of ₹4,800. In contrast, the 20 skilled workers employed by the firm as a mix of machine operators and engineers comprised of both locals, and migrants from West Bengal and Uttar Pradesh. Skilled workers' wages were ₹10,000, or over double the wage for unskilled workers.

This does not mean that income differences mirror regional or caste differences in an exact way. While most OBC workers seemed to be hired as helpers, some were also employed in skilled occupations. For example, although all workers at Firm 3B's workshop in the Sururpur Industrial Area in Faridabad were OBCs from Bihar or UP, some had jobs as machine operators and were paid a basic wage of ₹10,000, or nearly double the wage of helpers. While caste differences did not correspond to occupational, skill and wage income levels in an exact way, the prevalence of OBC workers from inter-state regions and the maintenance of a low-wage environment meant that there was often an overlap between workers' caste origins, their work status and income.

The caste and regional ties between workers and their home towns and villages meant that, even though many desired to stay in the NCR on an ongoing basis to earn sufficient income for themselves and their families, workers identified with their home regions and commonly felt duty-bound to provide material support. One 21-year old worker at firm 3D explained:

> I have worked here for one year. This is my first job. ₹4,800 is my basic pay and with overtime I earn about ₹7,000… I work 12 hours a day and 6 days a week with Sundays as holidays… [Since arriving in Faridabad], I have gone home and spent three months there. My father is a farmer [in Gorakhpur district, eastern Uttar Pradesh]. He has about five acres of land. We barely manage to meet our domestic expenses but are unable to make any profit from the produce. I manage to send around ₹4,000 [home per month]. I somehow manage to live here on the money I get on my overtime pay (Casual worker, Firm 3D, interview with author, 6 April 2013).

An electrician and manager for Firm 3D, who was originally from Rajapakar in Bihar, explained:

> There are two types of workers who come from Bihar: workers who come here with their families permanently, and [who] go home occasionally for festivals or weddings. They work in industry. Most of these workers own some land. These are medium-sized plots and are used only for subsistence for families. [Second], there are agricultural labourers who migrate on a seasonal basis to Punjab or Haryana. They are the lower castes. Most of the jobs in local industry are taken by workers from Bihar or UP [Uttar Pradesh]. But this not considered as taking jobs from locals [in Haryana]. Most of the local workers are farmers and they find industrial work to be derogatory. Maybe 60 per cent of workers in this area are from Bihar and about 25–30 per cent from [UP], and the rest from Punjab and other places (Manager, Firm 3D, interview with author, 2 April 2013).

In this narrative, 'industry' and 'industrial work' refers explicitly to small-scale workshops, not large factories. In fact, many workers raised within the region *do* work in larger-scale industry, particularly in OEMs or Tier-1 firms, and a small minority will work in Tier-3 firms although rarely as unskilled labourers and helpers.

While most of the workers interviewed in Tier-3 firms were men, it was possible to formally interview four women (one each at Firms 3B, 3E, 3G and 3H) and to speak informally with several others in the industrial colonies of Faridabad.

A significant minority of women could be observed working in Tier-3 firms. In the nearly 120 small factories and workshops observed in the laneways of Friends Industrial Complex, Welcome Industrial Complex and Suraj Industrial Complex in Sector 23, Faridabad, women were found working in at least 20 firms. In most cases, women appeared to be employed as helpers, undertaking a range of manual tasks such as cleaning, counting and sorting components. This is similar to how, in higher-tier firms, a minority of women were employed in ancillary roles such as cleaning, working in canteens, helping or office jobs (see Chapter 5).

However, a smaller minority of women in some firms were employed as semi-skilled machine operators, including drills, lathes and cutters. While women working in the export garments sector or in informal (especially home-based) enterprises is common and well-established in the NCR, several employers and workers explained that there was growing pressure for married women to seek employment in small automotive enterprises. For example, one male worker at Firm 3I in Sanjay Colony, Faridabad explained that rising living costs and low wages increased pressure at the household level for workers' spouses to find work in local enterprises:

> Most families need ₹8,000–10,000 [about US\$125–160 per month to survive]. We have two options. We can work overtime or we can ask our wives to find work. Sometimes we have to borrow food from shopkeepers. During lean times, we can only pay landlords [rent] when we can. Sometimes we ask our employer for more money [as a wage advance] to keep going (Worker A, Firm 3I, interview with author, 18 April 2013).

His workmate added that: "Now maybe half the families in this area [of Faridabad] have both the husband and the wife working locally and this [proportion] is increasing" (Worker B, Firm 3I, interview with author, 18 April 2013).

This pressure was shaped by the regulation of working hours by employers but also by the work and migratory *preferences of workers themselves*. Low basic wages in Tier-3 firms meant that workers commonly relied upon overtime payments to meet basic living costs such as rent and food. During periods of high customer demand in Tier-3 firms, workers would commonly be required to work 12 hour shifts, six days a week. However, overtime hours fell dramatically during festival and wedding seasons in February–April and October–November as major clients began to cut back orders in response to hundreds of thousands of workers returning to their home villages and towns: 'Most workers leave for festivals or weddings or harvesting. They tell me they will come back and they do. But they come back late. Some workers don't come back for two months. It is very hard to find workers [during these times]' (Owner, Firm 3D, interview with author, 6 April 2013).

While the circular migration of workers has an impact on firms, and the operation of global production networks, it also has a material impact on those workers who live permanently in the NCR or who do not wish to leave temporarily. Between February and May, many newer or younger workers lose their jobs and longer-serving or more senior workers lost overtime hours. For example, at Firm 3A, most workers lost overtime hours as orders fell, even though the company had multiple Tier-2 clients and was not a captive or dependent supplier (Five casual workers, Firm 3A, interview with author, 13 April 2013). During these months, the monthly wage of the workers fell from around ₹7,000, based on 12 hour shifts, six days a week, to their basic wage of ₹5,700. For workers at 3F, wages could fall by over 40 per cent during these months, from around ₹9,000 to ₹5,300.

While some could earn piece rates doing job work for Tier-4 owner-operators, opportunities were limited by inconsistent demand. Workers who lost overtime would often go into debt to meet rent payments or borrow food from shopkeepers (Four casual workers, Firm 3F, interview with author, 2 April 2013). These pressures arguably put greater pressure on married women and other female relatives of male workers to enter paid work, including in the Tier-3 auto workshops clustered throughout Faridabad and Gurugram.

As anticipated, many cases were found in which women in these firms were paid lower wages than men. At Firm 3I, 10 of the 40 workers were women who only worked as helpers or cleaners and earned ₹4,000 for the same work as male workers who earned ₹8,000 (Five male workers, Firm 3I, interview with author, 18 April 2013). In other cases, wage inequality was shaped by different working hours and skill differences between men and women, rather than unequal pay rates. At 3B, five of the 12 workers were women employed as unskilled helpers undertaking sorting, counting, cleaning and washing parts. Male and female unskilled helpers earned the same base wage of ₹5,000–6000.

However, this was lower than the ₹10,000 paid to semi-skilled machine operators who were all men in this establishment. In addition, women tended to work for two hours less per day than male workers, which was justified on the basis of their 'domestic duties' as well as legal restrictions on women's night work (Owner, Firm 3B, interview with author, 8 April 2013). In other cases, female workers were employed in semi-skilled roles. At 3E, four of the 15 workers were women, two of whom were employed as machine operators (Owner, Firm 3E, interview with author, 15 April 2013).

Other than the direct and indirect impacts of labour migration, most of the work conducted in lower-tier auto firms lacked labour-related security. Most workers had no employment security – that is, no legal or institutional protection against arbitrary or unfair dismissal. As has been argued in this chapter, most Tier-3 firms are not covered by the *Industrial Disputes Act 1947 (IDA)* and there are virtually no restrictions on employers dismissing or hiring new workers as and when required. Furthermore, most Tier-4 workers are self-employed and any workers they do hire are often temporarily recruited, with workers fully aware that their employment is ad hoc or temporary.

The only form of security that lower-tier workers seem to *possess* is labour market security because of the abundance of jobs on offer in multiple tiers of the auto industry. However, this security is tempered by circular migration and low-margin business operations. This encourages workers to pursue an exit option in response to conflict at work, rather than attempt to bargain over grievances or disputes at the workplace. With numerous low-skilled and helper jobs available in the region – in the auto industry as well as in other manufacturing sectors like export garments – a 23-year old casual worker from eastern Uttar Pradesh employed in Firm 3D in Mujesar, Faridabad, explained how workplace conflict shaped his personal choices and mobility:

> I am involved in the plating of auto parts [which are sold to] Maruti [Suzuki]... I have been working here for the last four years... I get paid ₹5000 [per month or about US$75–80] for eight hours a day and ₹2500 for the extra four hours of overtime. I work overtime very rarely and it is not a regular affair... [It] is very difficult to keep up [with the cost of living]. I live in a room with two of my brothers for which the rent is ₹1700... I have to go without meals occasionally and go through the day on tea and some snacks, as the employer does not provide us lunch. I eat at night when I go home, but only drink tea before leaving from home.
>
> If there were a problem, I would quit and look for other work. It is not as if this is the only plant in Faridabad which has jobs. There are several other plants. I am confident that I would find work elsewhere. They put up notices for employment...
>
> There was one time that we had also gone on strike demanding an increment in our salaries [for Diwali]. Two hours into the strike our boss gave in to our demands and gave us a pay hike... I would have quit [if we didn't get this increase]... Strikes generally take place in big companies where there are several workers. This is a small workshop. Workshops such as these have small strikes, which last a couple of hours... If the demands are not met, the workers quit the jobs (Casual worker B, Firm 3D, interview with author, 5 April 2013).

This story was typical of the casual workers interviewed from Tier-3 firms for this study. This worker is a young, unmarried man from a cultivating family in a poor inter-state region. He earns wages close to the minimum wage (₹5,330 per month at the time of field research) in the State of Haryana and struggles with living costs in the region. Low profit margins in his firm mean that wages remain low, and there is no formal collective bargaining over wages or the presence of any trade unions. However, conflict was a regular occurrence over *extra*-hourly wage issues such as allowances and festival bonuses. Wildcat industrial action was common, and unsatisfied workers often chose to leave an employer due to existing labour market security in the region.

Despite commonly possessing this exit option, workers had few other forms of labour-related security. Job security through training in new skills and career progression is extremely limited in small firms and the distinction between skilled and unskilled work is largely determined by access to education, or vocational and technical training through ITIs. Similarly, work security is limited through a common lack of appropriate safety equipment. Manufacturing processes such as machine operating is commonly undertaken without protective eye wear. Acid soaking for nickel electroplating was observed without protective clothing or footwear. Even metal casting and forging, involving metalwork at extreme temperatures, was observed being undertaken manually by workers without protective clothing. Although the *Factories Act 1948* was applicable to most of these Tier-3 firms, most workers worked long hours without sufficient compensation as required under this law.

A further major problem for Tier-3 workers was a lack of income security which refers, broadly, to the stability of social income, incorporating real wage rises and household savings, family and community assistance, non-wage enterprise benefits, as well as state benefits such as social security, work-based subsidies and subsidised social services. The low-margin operations of Tier-3 producing parts for clients in global production network and the general absence of collective wage bargaining meant there was no institutional means to guarantee workers' real wage rises or to accrue most non-wage benefits, such as allowances for productivity, transport, clothing and the cost of living. However, it *was* common for employers to grant, and workers to expect, bonuses for major festivals like Diwali and Holi. Since wages tended to hover close to the Haryana minimum wage, maintaining living standards was a major issue for most workers interviewed. Half of the firms listed in Table 6.1 paid at least some of their workers at sub-minimum wages. For two of these firms (3E and 3H), the firm's top rate of pay, including overtime and bonuses, is below the minimum wage.

Furthermore, medical insurance (ESI) and pension contributions (PF) were not always paid. For example, the 10 workers at Firm 3D – comprised of nine men and one woman from different parts of Bihar and UP – could earn up to ₹7,500 based on overtime and also usually received festival bonuses, but were not paid ESI or PF and often endured irregular hours:

> It is very difficult to keep up with living costs… [If] there is a workload we do not have weekends and have to work through the month. I prefer to work 12 hour

shifts to make more money and support a living. If I work for eight hours then I would only have to face more hardship (Casual worker A, Firm 3D, interview with author, 6 April 2011).

The final form of labour-related security denied was trade union representation. Collective wage agreements were largely non-existent and, given the low-margin operations of many Tier-3 firms, arguably impractical at the enterprise level. None of the Tier 3 workers interviewed or spoken to for this book had been a trade union member or ever worked with a trade union member. Thus we can conclude that workers employed in Tier-3 firms tend to lack all forms of labour-related security, with the exception of labour market security due to the abundance of employment opportunities in the region.

Most workers lack protection from arbitrary dismissal, opportunities for a career path, skill development or upward mobility, collective bargaining rights, and are often vulnerable to hazardous working conditions. Wages are low by wider auto industry standards and workers have weak bargaining power to negotiate significant wage rises. Faced with a hostile working environment or a disagreeable or unscrupulous employer, workers are likely to pursue an exit option to seek alternative work in the region, either in auto manufacturing or, often, in garments manufacturing or services-based informal enterprises.

Conclusion

As outlined in Chapter 5, the informalisation of the automotive workforce in the National Capital Region's OEMs, Tier-1, and Tier-2 firms has been underpinned by the entrenchment of a regional contract labour system that systematically undermines most workers' access to labour-related security, including employment, job, skill reproduction, income, and representation security.

The ability of trade unions or labour NGOs to respond effectively to this challenge has been blunted by a range of factors, including the historical relationship between trade unions and state institutions, the party-political orientation of unions, the emergence of plant-level unions focused on enterprise, and, in some parts of the NCR, the role of organised groups of local landowning families influencing the politics of plant-level unions by acting as land market and community-level intermediaries between workers and their principal employer.

In villages like Binola and Kharkari, this has created a situation in which union leaderships have a material stake in the continuing operation of the contract labour system. While workers in higher-tier automotive firms often have tremendous structural economic power, as made evident by the impact of industrial strife on highly-sensitive, inter-firm commercial relations, their associational power, and therefore their capacity to wrest concessions from employers and the state through collective action, has been restricted by these political, social, and institutional factors.

The structural and associational power of workers in Tier-3 firms is quite different to these higher-tier firms. The low-margin, low-wage environment in these firms means that conflict rarely occurs over basic wages. No evidence of union membership or of union efforts to recruit workers in Tier-3 industrial zones in Faridabad or Gurugram was found. This low-profit, low-wage environment encourages many workers to pursue individualised strategies. While labour turnover is a common occurrence among workers seeking higher incomes, conflict is more likely to emerge over working conditions or over *additional* payments such as bonuses.

Conflict over pay and conditions often encourages workers to leave in search of alternative employment in other auto firms, components manufacturers, or workshops and factories of export garment (Two casual workers, Firm 3D, interview with author, 6 April 2013; two casual workers, Firm 3J, interview with author, 13 April 2013). While workers can move between employers with few restrictions, they have very limited chances to significantly lift their income. To increase earnings, workers can follow an individual strategy of pushing for more overtime when available, or taking collective action for bonuses and allowances. The operation of these small firms suggests that there is rarely collective organisation directed against wage rates themselves.

As outlined above, the workforce is predominately young and male, relatively mobile and engaged in circular and seasonal migration between industrial areas in the NCR and their homes in villages and towns in inter-state regions, especially those in Bihar and eastern Uttar Pradesh. This mobility has a major impact on employment relations practices throughout global production networks in the NCR, especially in Tier-3 firms. Of the 11 Tier-3 employers interviewed for this study, six complained that there was a shortage of workers during festival seasons for Holi or Diwali (from Firms 3B, 3C, 3E, 3F, 3H and 3K). The owner of Firm 3C in Shiv Colony, Faridabad, provided a summary that typified this view: 'My main problem is a labour shortage. Some workers from Bihar return home for festivals and don't come back on time or when they agreed. Sometimes I have to find casual workers [to replace them]. Sometimes I have to send work to other companies' (Owner, Firm 3C, interview with author, 9 April 2013).

When interviewed a month after Diwali in 2011, a casual worker at firm 3D in Mujesar, Faridabad explained: 'There are 10 men and 1 woman working here [but] 8 of them have gone on leave and currently only 3 people are working here. Because of Diwali most people are visiting their villages for the festive season' (Casual worker, Firm 3D, interview with author, 6 December 2011).

The proprietor of Firm 3B in the Sarurpur Industrial Area explained how the Holi festival impacted his business each year in February and March: 'Workers go home for one month. So we have to lower production for the whole month. This is not good but we have no choice' (Owner, Firm 3B, interview with author, 8 April 2013). Many Tier-3 firms echoed this view. For example, workers at Firm 3I confirmed that Tier-3 owners and managers adjusted their operations and reduced demand for workers during festival seasons. As one of these workers explained, 'Most companies cut production levels during the festive season. Thousands of workers leave the region and don't return for weeks or months. The employers have no choice [but to do this]' (Casual worker, Firm 3I, interview with author, 18 April 2013).

The circumstances of Tier-3 and Tier-4 firms operating within automotive global production networks in the NCR continue to present labour movement activists with enormous challenges. This chapter has outlined characteristics of just some of the huge number of small Tier-3 firms that cluster in the NCR, particularly in the older industrial colonies of Faridabad which emerged in the 1960s and grew over the subsequent generation as factory production and small-scale industry continued to spillover from New Delhi's southern fringe into Haryana. Despite the presence of some domestic and foreign OEMs, Faridabad remains the regional stronghold for lower-tier auto manufacturing, in contrast to Gurugram's role as the main centre for higher-tier auto manufacturing.

The evidence presented in this chapter suggests that Tier-3 auto firms tend to be small, Indian-owned-and-operated companies that largely reflect a mix of specialised independent suppliers and captive generic suppliers. The chapter has also outlined the role of Tier-4 firms, which primarily operate as informal enterprises and mainly represent the work of self-employed workers who use a combination of family members as unpaid workers or temporary wage workers. Across Tier-3 and Tier-4 firms covered during the field research for this book – from 2011 until mid-2013 – wages tend to hover around the Haryana minimum wage level, with many firms paying workers sub-minimum wages.

It remains to be seen what impact rising wages, following on from major wage concessions offered by OEM and Tier-1 employers in 2012 and rises in the State minimum wage (see Chapter 4), have had on the low wage, low margin business model commonly pursued by local Tier-3 enterprises. This, and the resulting capacity of higher-tier firms to continue relying upon this large network of price-competing small firms, remains an important area for future research

Critically, these low-margins mean that the contract labour system, which has been so important for recruitment and employment relations practices in higher-tier firms, has barely featured in Tier-3 firm because employers cannot afford to use labour contractors' services on an ongoing or regular basis. Lower-tier firms are, instead, populated by thousands of casual, predominantly unskilled labourers. The concept of the 'helper' – the unskilled labourer who is engaged in a variety of manual tasks – is important here. Casual work denotes the reality that, even for workers employed for a long period of time, workers have no employment security – in other words, no legal or social protection against arbitrary dismissal by their employer.

Furthermore, the low-margin operating model of these firms reflects a lot about the structures of inter-firm governance within automotive global production networks. These governance practices have a dual character. On one hand, higher-tier firm and vendor representatives frequently visit and inspect Tier-3 sites. Captive generic suppliers appear to be particularly closely-monitored and inspected by higher-tier clients, including direct inspections by OEMs.

On the other hand, the behavior of Tier-3 firms also reflects a market-based governance structure in which price levels, product quality standards, design specifications, the size and frequency of product orders by client firms, and the frequency of payment for delivery are largely determined by OEMs and Tier-1 firms. Tier-3 employers are compelled to adapt their business models to this power structure and to engage in price competition for ongoing contracts within global production networks. This structure of inter-firm commercial relations reproduces the low-margin, low-wage environment that can be observed in these small enterprises.

These factors also contribute to the reproduction of a highly precarious and largely informal workforce. With the exception of labour market security – due to the abundance of job opportunities in regional manufacturing – Tier-3 workers are generally denied all forms of security through their work. In addition, the circular and seasonal character of migration in the region means that many workers lack permanent roots in the industrial zones of the NCR and, consequently, relatively little local support from social or kinship networks while in these areas.

The individualised strategies of workers, and the difficulties of constructing a collective or union-like response to problems encountered at work, reflect the conflation of these multiple factors: of the high mobility of workers due to their status as semi-permanent or temporary migrants and ongoing familial and financial ties to their place of origin in inter-state regions; high labour turnover; low-margin business making collective bargaining over basic wages extremely rare; and abundant job opportunities in other firms and industries in the region, including alternative global production networks.

7

Driving Down the 'Low Road'?

Leading industrialists in auto manufacturing have made recent, widely-publicised efforts to support Narendra Modi's 'Make in India' initiative, which aims to attract new Foreign Direct Investment (FDI) in Indian manufacturing as the basis for income growth, employment creation and rising prosperity (GoI, 2016; 2016a). For example, India's second Automotive Mission Plan (*AMP-2*), co-produced by the Society of Indian Automobile Manufacturers (SIAM), aims 'to propel the Indian automotive industry to be the engine of the "Make in India" program' (SIAM/GoI, 2015: 3).

CEOs of several global auto manufacturers have visited India during Modi's premiership to reiterate their commitment to Indian manufacturing. High profile examples include Suzuki, Toyota, Hyundai, Renault-Nissan and Ford. Maruti Suzuki India Limited (MSIL) chairman, R.C. Bhargava, has argued that 'nobody wants to miss the opportunity and the size. They don't see the kind of potential growth in any other market like in India' (cited in Thakkar, 2017a).

The scale and intensity of conflict in India's automotive industry presents a radically different side to this elite-driven narrative. Conflict in Indian auto manufacturing has taken many forms, manifesting at a workplace or enterprise-level, at an industry level through solidarity strike action and street protests, and at the level of social and political conflict. Various forms of industrial conflict, including strikes, employer lockouts, factory occupations and hunger strikes, have increased in frequency since the 1990s.

During this period, a gradual process of economic liberalisation has culminated in the opening up of all domestic auto manufacturing to FDI, and the removal of residual restrictions on the investment activities of industrialists – domestic and foreign. Since the mid-1990s, most of the world's leading global automotive lead firms – known as Original Equipment Manufacturers (OEMs) – and their strategic partners and key components suppliers have established operations in different regions of India.

This process of liberalisation, investment, relocation and industrialisation has profoundly shaped the development of Indian regions. It has given rise to new industrial zones and reshaped established ones. Auto manufacturing transplants have resulted in a rise in infrastructure development through road and rail-building, commercial and residential construction and construction of shopping malls to cater for a growing minority of middle-to-high income residents. These strata have intersected with the growing consumer markets for motorcycles, scooters, and passenger cars.

The largest industrial zone remains the National Capital Region (NCR) which surrounds New Delhi, especially the semi-rural districts of Gurugram, as well as Faridabad, Rewari, Alwar, South Delhi and the city of Greater Noida. The next largest industrial zones fall within the Chennai Metropolitan Area (CMA), the Chakan Special Economic Zone (C-SEZ) and Pune. In addition, major industrial zones exist in parts of Gujarat and Uttarakhand, some near Bengaluru (Bangalore), some in Jamshedpur and in some other regions.

As the largest auto producing region, the NCR has also experienced the most significant number of reported industrial conflicts. The NCR is the base for India's largest passenger car manufacturer – MSIL and India's largest motorcycle and scooter manufacturers – Hero MotoCorp and Honda Motorcycle and Scooter India (HMSI). Together with Tata Motors' and Mahindra and Mahindra's domination of commercial vehicles manufacturing from their multiple regional sites, these firms have dominated Indian auto manufacturing since the 1980s. They have the largest market shares, the largest sales volumes and employ the highest number of workers in the industry.

About half of the major industrial disputes recorded since 2000 have occurred in the NCR, with around a fifth occurring in the CMA, and the rest evenly split between key sites in Maharashtra, Gujarat and Karnataka.[1] Of the industrial conflicts that have occured in the NCR, the vast majority have taken place in Gurugram District, with an even split between the townships of Gurugram and IMT Manesar. These disputes have commonly taken the forms of strike action, employer-initiated lockouts, or a combination of the two. A common spark for conflict has been attempts by a conscious minority of workers to unionise. These efforts have generally built upon the perception of the workers regarding their maltreatment by the employers.

There is, therefore, a need to address and explain the character and scale of industrial disputes in Indian auto manufacturing, but also its geographical and regional concentration, particularly in the commercial, financial and industrial hub of Gurugram. This book has attempted to address this problem, mainly through empirical data collection and ethnographic research in Gurugram and Faridabad, which is the base for an older cluster of auto components manufacturers and smaller OEMs based in agricultural vehicles, construction equipment and motorcycles. It has also drawn on documentary analysis of government reports, company reports and secondary source material from India's other key auto industrial zones.

---

[1] See Table 1.1 in Chapter 1

This book has attempted to offer a social-relational explanation for the high levels of conflict which have beset the auto industry in India since the turn of the century. This explanation is, in turn, connected to the imposition of global production networks in Indian auto manufacturing, their interaction with regional social structures of accumulation predicated upon precarious and informal work, phases of gradual economic liberalisation, and changing market structures.

These macro-level changes have had an impact at the firm level through the emergence of two different regional labour control regimes. In high-tier firms, this has led to a dominant role for a regional *contract* labour system. In low-tier firms, this has led to the imposition of a regional *casual* labour system. In each system, combinations of workers in different employment configurations have enabled auto manufacturing to function with a high degree of reliance upon informal and precarious work.

The lack of recognition and social protection for most of these workers belies predictions that a thriving auto manufacturing industry would lead to 'high road' labour standards and employment relations. Drawing upon findings from the previous three chapters, this concluding chapter summarises and substantiates this claim. It focuses on the manifestations and degrees of precarious and informal work among workers in each employment configuration, and explains how the agency of these workers interacts with, reproduces and reshapes the two main regional labour control regimes. Ultimately, it is the refusal of workers to accept the consequences of 'low road' labour standards that underlies the high levels of industrial conflict in the industry.

The book has located explanations for conflict in the Indian auto industry in four main areas. These relate to: the emergence of global production networks in auto manufacturing regions; the role of economic liberalisation in transforming the structure of markets in the auto industry; the impact of changing markets upon employment relations and labour standards; and, finally, the intersection of auto-based global production networks with established regional social structures of accumulation across low-tier as well as high-tier firms. A summary of each of these four core areas is outlined below.

The emergence of global production networks in auto manufacturing regions

The first factor which helps us address the scale and character of conflict in auto manufacturing concerns the emergence of global production networks in the industry. This process began in the 1980s, and radically accelerated in the 1990s and 2000s. These global production networks have been led by domestic OEMs by foreign OEMs in passenger car and two-wheeler manufacturing. Foreign

OEMs have increasingly run fully-owned and directly-managed subsidiary manufacturing operations.

Even within a single industry like auto manufacturing, different lead firms have different strategies of network governance depending upon factors like their product types or product range, production volume, degree and type of market access, national origin, and the degree to which OEMs must accommodate or hybridise with institutional rules, established regional practices and organisational norms and customs. This book has introduced the question of *timing of entry* with relation to market competitors as a critical additional factor that explains the capacity of lead firms to establish and pursue their preferred network strategies (see Chapter 3).

Early-arriving OEMs in the 1980s and 1990s have generally had the greatest capacity to pursue their preferred strategic approach in regional operations, including their preferred models of work organisation. The key examples are MSIL and Hero MotoCorp in the NCR and Hyundai Motor India Limited (HMIL) in the CMA. Modifying the 'Global Production Network 2.0' approach (Coe and Yeung, 2015), this work has argued that the establishment of these firms' global production networks and their shaping of these regions into the largest auto producing areas in the country, has followed a type of *first-mover coupling* in which risk-taking, early-entrants into emerging markets can, if successful, reap value-capture rewards that disadvantage later-entrant rival OEMs.

The concept of first-mover coupling is an adaptation of Coe and Yeung's (2015) concepts of functional and structural coupling between lead firms and regional assets. Under structural coupling, regions are surveyed and explored by external actors – in this case, foreign or global OEMs – who seek to enter regions from the 'outside-in'. In theory, this model incorporates regional firms, institutions, workers, and other regional assets into situations of economic dependency, with a relatively high chance of de-coupling compared to other GPNs and, thus, a higher level of risk-shifting onto these regional actors. Under functional coupling, there is a lower chance of de-coupling, and a more even share of risks as regional actors seek to market regional assets to global lead firms.

In the case of Indian auto manufacturing, the entry of foreign OEMs since the early 1980s has exhibited *some* features of structural coupling. In the 1980s, for example, both the Suzuki Motor Corporation (SMC) and the Honda Motor Company (HMC) represented second-tier global OEMs which, encouraged by high levels of competition and volatile sales in Western markets, pursued an 'outside-in' approach to emerging markets like India. These foreign OEMs aimed to establish local operations which could take advantage of low-cost labour and potential opportunities for rapid sales expansion while minimising financial and institutional risk by importing Complete-Knockdown (CKD) kits with minimal reliance on local manufacturers.

But the pioneering OEMs did not have it all their own way. Through encouragment by state institutions, difficulties in supply chain management and poor regional transport infrastructure, OEMs were generally compelled to establish production networks that became reliant upon local components manufacturers and regional institutions. The OEMs with the greatest capacity to shape this process, and those which emerged with the most favourable market position, were generally the ones who arrived *first*.

In the case of MSIL, Japanese managers were able to pursue an inter-firm partnership strategy by bringing strategic partner firms to the NCR and by co-investing in the operations of foreign and domestic partners and independent suppliers. By March 2015, MSIL had control over seven subsidiary companies operating in the region and other parts of India, as well as controlling equity stakes in six joint venture companies and 12 'associate companies'. In many cases, MSIL leveraged its equity share to establish substantive control over management and operations.

MSIL's dominant position within its global production network also led to inter-mingling with the networks of rival OEMs. For example, MSIL purchased equity stakes in Denso (part of the Toyota Group) and Magneti Marelli (part of Fiat Chrysler Auto NV, or FCA). At the same time, MSIL has pursued a combination of relational and market-based value chain relations among its much larger network of independent and generic suppliers. This has been pursued through a frequent 'hands-on' interaction with suppliers, and process/product inspection in order to meet the requirements of assembly operations, alongside its encouragement of price-based competition between suppliers.

Hero MotoCorp was able to similarly establish numerous controlling equity relations with strategic partners and other auto components suppliers, although this was achieved primarily through its 26-year joint venture with Honda in motorcycle and scooter manufacturing. Unlike MSIL, the Hero Group, as an Indian family-operated conglomerate, preferred to establish equity relations with firms it already influenced or controlled. Differences over the governance of its production network were important in creating commercial conflict within the Hero Honda joint venture. This eventually led to its dissolution in 2010 and the establishment of two rival OEMs as leaders in the national two-wheeler market.

A more MSIL-like approach seems to have been pursued by Hyundai in the CMA, through its partnership with a range of Hyundai Group companies which also supply components to rival OEMs. Late-arriving OEMs like Renault-Nissan, which only established operations in India in 2010, have been more likely to rely upon suppliers that were embedded in the global production networks of already-established, rival OEMs.

Further examples are OEMs like Honda and Ford, which have been operating in India for several years, but whose capacity to pursue their preferred network strategy was constrained through joint venture operations and management structures. In the case of Honda, their focus on the two-wheeler market was shaped by the Hero Group's version of inter-firm partnership. Ford was constrained by its early joint venture with Mahindra and the domination of the commercial vehicle segment, including its preferred 'pick-up' and light-duty truck markets, by Mahindra and Tata Motors.

Like the Hero Group, Tata Motors has also been able to pursue a version of inter-firm partnership based on the Tata Group's inter-industry network of firms and its preference for establishing commercial relations with firms in which it has invested in joint ventures. This strategy has enabled Tata to entrench its preferred network strategy within its key supplier bases at manufacturing sites in Sanand, Pantnagar and Jamshedpur.

In MSIL's case, the company's capacity to control key suppliers in its own global production network, and influence the practices of strategic partners and suppliers to rival OEMs, was critical when the firm began to shift its employment relations practices in the late 1990s (see below). But regardless of the manufacturer in question, foreign managers have had to contend with established domestic and regional institutional frameworks, organisational practices, cultural expectations and norms. These factors have challenged, constrained and forced modifications to firms' preferred employment relations strategies.

Since the emergence of Indian auto manufacturing has also invoked a shift towards global production networks, it has meant that foreign OEMs and their foreign strategic partners and independent suppliers have been compelled to outsource a significant portion of components manufacturing and distribution to domestically-owned and operated firms as well as many foreign-domestic joint venture operations. In doing so, global production networks in auto manufacturing have integrated networks of production based overwhelmingly on practices of precarious and informal work.

Like most other sections of Indian society, domestic manufacturing is dominated by informal work of one variety or another. As the auto industry has expanded and modernised, and as its competitive structure has evolved, OEMs, Tier-1 and Tier-2 manufacturers have increasingly taken advantage of these workforce characteristics and practices. The OEMs with the greatest capacity to influence this process have generally been the pioneering firms which established operations in the 1980s and 1990s before their global competitors arrived.

Economic liberalisation and the transformation of the auto industry

The second key factor that helps to address why Indian auto manufacturing has been beset by industrial conflict is the change to the structure of market competition in different segments of the auto industry and, connected to this, the role of national and regional state institutions in facilitating and liberalising FDI in the 1990s and 2000s. The arrival of new foreign OEMs, with their strategic partners and suppliers, hugely expanded the terrain on which industrial conflict could occur.

In the 1980s, there was only a small group of auto manufacturing OEMs in the country. Although mechanised vehicles had expanded into agriculture since the 1960s, and three-wheeler vehicles were a popular mode of transport in cities, private ownership of motorcycles and scooters was still an emerging consumer pursuit and passenger car ownership was a rare luxury.

By 1985, when the Government of India embarked upon a gradual policy of economic liberalisation and export promotion, passenger car production was limited to MSIL and older Indian OEMs such Hindustan Motors and Premier Limited. Through a policy framework of restricted openness, underpinned by a residual Import Substitution Industrialisation (ISI), most other vehicle manufacturers were prevented from entering the passenger car or two-wheeler markets under the pre-1991 license-permit system.

By the 2010s, industrial licensing was a distant memory. Domestic and foreign OEMs were free to invest in any segment of the auto industry without government obstruction and most of the world's leading OEMs had established operations in the country on different scales. While the underlying framework for industrial policy shifted relatively quickly in the early 1990s from ISI to neo-liberalism, this shift was underpinned by a gradual, decades-long change in industrial policy. It took until the 2000s for liberalisation measures to be fully implemented and the full impacts to be felt in auto manufacturing.

Four main aspects of industrial policy-making shaped the rise of foreign ownership and the subsequent transformation of market competition in the auto industry. First, the Government of India dropped its commitment to segmenting the auto industry. Although Tata Motors was granted a license to manufacture passenger cars in 1985, the government maintained a policy of preventing new foreign entrants in the passenger car and two-wheeler segments from 1982–1993, enabling Maruti Udyog Limited (the forerunner of MSIL) and Hero Honda to establish dominant positions in their respective industry segments. These restrictions were gradually removed from 1993 until their abolition in 2000.

Second, the Government of India gradually dropped the joint venture as its preferred mode of operational regulation for foreign OEMs. The joint-venture model enabled national and regional governments to encourage and manage FDI, which was considered necessary to modernise auto manufacturing operations, without formally violating the terms of India's ISI-based policy framework. For example, a joint-venture policy which limited foreign investors to minority equity stakes and limited the capacity of foreign managers to treat local operations as de facto subsidiaries was still consistent with the *Foreign Exchange Regulation Act (FERA) 1973*, which restricted foreign equity in Indian companies to 40 per cent in the 1980s.

Third, Phased Manufacturing Programs on all foreign-involved OEM operations were gradually lifted. PMPs had been used in the 1980s and 1990s to encourage foreign-led operations to aim for a high level of local content in supply chain manufacturing activities rather than rely upon imported Incomplete or Complete Knockdown kits (IKDs or CKDs) to service regional assembly operations. For example, MUL/MSIL's operations in the 1980s had to aim for a 95 per cent target of local content in components manufacturing, although this policy complemented – rather than contradicted – SMC's desire to establish better-quality supply operations by entrenching its global production network in regional components manufacturing.

Fourth, the abolition of industrial licensing for auto manufacturing (1991–1993) removed residual regulatory constraints on OEMs that wished to diversify assembled products or enter new product markets. This was an important shift, particularly in enabling key domestic OEMs like Tata Motors and Mahindra to excel in the passenger car market as well as light, commercial vehicle segments, and enabling other domestic OEMs like Bajaj Auto, TVS and Premier Limited to develop as Tier-1 components manufacturers for assemblers in the automotive and other manufacturing sectors.

Thus, the relatively sheltered conditions under which industry pioneers like MSIL and Hero Honda were able to establish dominant market positions had been transformed by the mid-1990s and early 2000s. Regulatory changes at the national level – via an end to national market segmentation, the gradual eradication of the joint venture as the prime mode of operational regulation, the uneven implementation of supply chain conditions under PMPs, and the abolition of industrial licensing – transformed the national auto market by enabling much greater levels of competition between OEMs in different market segments.

In the two-wheeler market, Hero MotoCorp and HMSI became key competitors rather than collaborators, and also operated in competition with Bajaj Auto and Piaggio. Though never usurped as the market leader in passenger cars in the nearly four decades of its operations in the NCR, MSIL's domination of the passenger car market nevertheless came under a range of challenges from foreign and domestic OEMs.

Throughout this transition in national government policy, there was a sense of policy continuity at the regional level. Since the 1980s, State governments had continued to offer generous subsidies to attract FDI from global OEMs and their strategic partners and key components suppliers. State governments have emulated a regional model of institutional support and public investment in transport infrastructure that was developed by the Government of Haryana to support the early MUL/MSIL and Hero Honda operations in the 1980s. This model is also similar to the industry support developed for domestic software services and IT-enabled Services (ITES), such as policies in Karnataka, Andhra Pradesh, Maharashtra among others, and supported at a national level by the passing of the *Special Economic Zone (SEZ) Act 2005*.

The continuity of regional policies, in the context of regulatory change at a national level, shaped the transformation of several peri-urban and semi-rural districts and *tehsils/taluks* (administrative divisions) into major industrial zones. As detailed in Chapter 5, town and village life was radically transformed in little more than a generation in Gurugram and, to an extent, in Faridabad, Rewari and Greater Noida. The same can be said for equivalent sub-regions in the CMA, in Pune and Chakan, in the village of Bidadi on the fringe of Bengaluru, and villages and towns in other regions. The conflict that emerged in the NCR and CMA, and in some other regions, was shaped not only by changes in intra-firm management and employment relations but also the intersection of shop-floor life with social relations at a town and village level.

Rise of the regional contract labour system

This leads into the third factor that addresses why industrial conflict has been so widespread in Indian auto manufacturing. The gradual transformation of market competition in the industry, represented by the transition from restricted openness to emergent neo-liberalism, had a dramatic reflexive effect on the management and employment relations practices of leading OEMs. As outlined in detail in Chapter 4, this effect was experienced, above all, at Maruti Suzuki (MSIL) where company responses to changing market competition and the changing national-institutional framework set off a series of events culminating in a radical shift in employment relations and labour standards across the country. In the NCR and CMA, these events led to the gradual displacement of regular workforces in key OEMs, Tier-1 and Tier-2 supply firms in favour of cohorts of 'de facto informal workers' hired through regional contract labour systems.

To briefly reiterate this process, a combination of growing market competition and a less stable global business climate the late 1990s put pressure on MSIL's profitability. In this context, company management moved to restructure the system of wage allowances and bonuses they had previously offered to their regular workers through union-negotiated collective wage agreements. The opposition of the union to these changes at MSIL's Gurugram assembly plant led to a strike and lockout in 2000/01, ending with the defeat and eventual de-registration of the Maruti Udyog Employees Union.

After seeing off the MUEU and successfully implementing a revised wage scheme for regular workers, MSIL moved to significantly draw down its regular workforce through a Voluntary Retirement Scheme (VRS). From early 2001 until mid-2004, MSIL reduced the size of its regular workforce by 42 per cent to levels comparable to operations in the mid-1980s. In order to satisfy ongoing demands for production volume, the company began to recruit new employees by hiring the services of labour contractors. By 2004, MSIL had implemented a policy of hiring nearly all production-line and shop-floor maintenance workers via labour contractors.

In hindsight, the period of instability in employment relations and change at the MSIL Gurugram plant from 1998 until 2004 ushered in a transition from one dominant employment relations strategy to another in the context of emergent neo-liberalism. In 1998, Maruti was still a Public Sector Unit, albeit with significant operational oversight by SMC managers from Japan. Labour standards were based upon a high level of employment security, opportunities for skill advancement and high basic wages which were boosted by a relatively generous system of incentives, bonuses, allowances and enterprise-based benefits.

These benefits were offered in exchange of the consent and active participation of workers and local managers in work organisation based upon lean manufacturing principles like team work, quality management and worker participation in operational improvement. Employment relations were underpinned by MUEU-MSIL negotiated collective wage agreements and an active voice for regular workers on the shop-floor. Under relatively sheltered market conditions from the early 1980s until the mid-1990s, this settlement represented a 'lean manufacturing employment relations compact' that contributed to stability in work organisation and to MSIL's rapid emergence as the leading passenger car manufacturer in the country.

Under the new settlement gradually implemented from 2001 until 2004, the revised terms of this compact were reserved for a minority of regular workers, including some workers in supervisory and lower-level management positions. In order to sustain production volumes, MSIL now relied upon a new, younger core of production-line workers whose integration into the company and ongoing employment was managed by labour contractors.

These contract workers were paid a fraction of the regular workers' basic wage and denied access to the full range of bonuses, allowances and enterprise benefits made available to regular workers through collective wage agreements and union membership. The basis for this system of contract labour was further entrenched by the company encouraging multiple labour contractors to compete amongst each other for contracts. This practice helped to standardise the costs of labour contractors' commission fees and further ensured that labour contractors were unlikely to represent genuine concerns of employees to the company for fear of losing business.

Thus, MSIL can be regarded as a pioneer in the Indian auto industry in two senses: first, as a pioneer of Indian auto manufacturing's modernisation through global production networks and lean manufacturing practices and, second, as a pioneer in the transformation of the industry's framework of employment relations through the imposition of a regional contract labour system. This practice spread across the industry, including to rival OEMs, to OEMs in alternative auto industry segments and product markets, and to many Tier-1 and Tier-2 components manufacturers across the country.

As outlined in Chapter 4 and 5, employers in many large auto assembly and components plants systematically replaced regular workers with contract workers, as well as directly-hired temporary or casual workers. In the NCR, this was true for Hero Honda by the mid-2000s, and later for Hero MotoCorp's Gurugram and Dharuhera plants and for HMSI's Manesar plant. In the CMA, this practice was emulated by HMIL in the 2000s and, from 2010, by Renault-Nissan.

While contract labour has been utilised by most firms in every major regional cluster of auto manufacturing, contract workers are not necessarily the numerically dominant employment configuration for *all* firms. Nevertheless, contract labour is pervasive in the industry and virtually all OEMs make *extensive use* of labour contractors' services, including in 'core' production-line and shop-floor maintenance roles. This occurs despite the restrictions imposed by the *Contract Labour (Abolition and Regulation) Act 1970 (CLARA)*.

While the fieldwork for this book was not conducted for leading domestic OEMs like Tata Motors and Mahindra, corporate information provided by these companies suggests that contract labour forms a central part of their respective workforces. Across Tata Motors' seven Indian plants by early 2016, half of its nearly 53,000-strong workforce was hired on a 'temporary/contractual/casual basis'. The same is true for Mahindra's total Indian workforce of over 39,000 at the time.

However, more research can be conducted to explore how these policies manifest at a regional level; for example, how Tata Motors' employment of contract workers is implemented across its extensive network of assembly sites in Gujarat, Jharkhand, Karnataka, Maharashtra, Uttarakhand and other regions. The same can be said of Mahindra's multiple operations in Karnataka, Maharashtra, Telangana and Uttarakhand, or for smaller domestic OEMs like Bajaj Auto, Eicher or TVS.

So, while a strategy of employing all or most workers through regional contract labour systems is not universal, this strategy *is* present for market leaders in passenger car and two-wheeler manufacturing. Based on the findings in this book, we can conclude that the dominant means of labour control in auto manufacturing involves segmenting workforces between multiple employment configurations. As outlined in Chapter 1, an employment configuration represents a specific link between workers and labour markets and a specific mode of social regulation for their work (Swider, 2015).

Table 7.1 distils this information by focusing on the degree to which each employment configuration separately reflects informal work and precarious work and the main work-based interests that emerge from the author's field research. The left-hand column lists each of the employment configurations identified in this research from no. 1 to no. 8. The table indicates the degree to which each employment configuration represents informal work and precarious work.

Since informality and precarity represent changing sets of attributes, the table uses the phrases 'high', 'moderate' and 'low' to do this. 'High' suggests that all or a large majority of workers are engaged in work that can be described as informal or precarious. 'Moderate' suggests that a significant number – either a small majority or a large minority – are engaged in informal or precarious work, while 'low' suggests that between a small minority and no workers are engaged in informal or precarious work.

Table 7.1 shows that most employment configurations involve work that is informal and precarious in character. This is true for contract workers, casual workers, undeclared workers, workers hired by formal Tier-3 enterprises or informal enterprises and, finally, own-account workers, Tier-4 job workers and industrial outworkers. However, it also shows that some employment configurations (trainees and apprentices) combine work which is relatively formal with work that is relatively precarious. In OEMs and other high-tier firms, trainees and apprentices are generally employed through a process which is formally codified by management or, in the case of apprenticeships, co-regulated by state and training-based institutions. Regular workers, who are employed on open-ended contracts by their employers, are engaged in relatively formal work that has a moderate level of precarity and is, thus, more secure than work in all other employment configurations.

The reason why particular ascriptions of 'high', 'low' or 'moderate' have been chosen are described in detail below for workers in each employment configuration. Informal work is defined in relation to the degree of recognition afforded by state institutions. Precarious work is defined in relation to the degree of protection from socio-economic risk and framed by Standing's seven forms of labour-related security (Standing, 2011).

As Table 7.1 also shows, different employment configurations reflect workers with interests in achieving different forms of labour-related security. In some cases, a form of labour-related security may be absent or lacking in more than one employment configuration with the problem manifesting differently in each one. For contract workers, casual workers, undeclared workers, apprentices and trainees, for example, the need for income security refers to the need to secure higher real wages that reflect the value their work generates relative to regular workers undertaking similar work or in similar occupational roles. But for workers employed in Tier-3 and Tier-4 firms, income security would manifest through general standards for wages, enterprise benefits and social security negotiated at an industry level.

Table 7.1 also shows how employment configurations are broader than occupational groups. The occupational division of labour within auto manufacturing is highly complex. At the level of management, OEMs and other higher-tier manufacturers are led by senior executives and managers, middle-level managers in different business divisions (such as finance, R&D, human resources, supply chains and public relations), highly-paid professionals in industrial engineering, mechanical engineering, product design and business administration, and lower-level managers and supervisors, such as team leaders and 'foremen'.

On the shop-floor, the workforce is generally divided between craft workers and production workers. Craft workers include a range of skilled and semi-skilled occupations such as paint-shop operators, metal workers in press shops, casting technicians, welders, fitters, tool-makers, machinists, as well as skilled workers employed in the maintenance and repair of electrical and mechanical equipment.

Production workers, who constitute the largest macro-occupational group in auto manufacturing, represent a range of semi-skilled and less-skilled occupations like product assemblers, process and plant operators in metal-working, rubber, plastic and textile manufacturing and manufacturing labourers, such as packers and sorters. These manufacturing roles do not include the wide range of 'ancillary' roles such as white-collar occupations in offices, clerical work, sales, marketing, purchasing, product inspection, transport, product testing, finance, insurance, software and a range of less-skilled ancillary roles like cleaning, security and 'helping'.

The findings from this research indicate that employment configurations include and transcend many of these broad occupational groups. For example, as Table 7.1 shows, regular shop-floor workers include some lower-level managers and supervisors. In some Tier-1 and Tier-2 manufacturers, most regular workers perform these roles, creating a clear occupational and status distinction between regular and non-regular workers. More often, however, regular work involves a mix of supervisory and non-supervisory roles which overlap with production-line and craft work undertaken by workers in a range of employment configurations, including contract and casual workers.

Table 7.1: Main work-based problems encountered by employment configuration

Employment Configuration	Occupational groups	Extent to which work is...		Forms of labour-related security which are absent, denied or inadequately applied...							
		Informal	Precarious	Employment	Job	Skill	Income	Representation	Work	Labour market	Other
1. Contract worker	Mainly production workers, some craft workers	High	High	X	X	X	X¹	X			X³
2. Casual		High	High	X	X	X	X¹	X			
3. Undeclared worker		High	High		X	X	X¹	X			X⁴
4. Trainee		Low	High	X	X		X¹	X			
5. Apprentice	Craft workers	Low	High		X	X	X¹	X			
6. Worker in Tier-3 or informal firm	Mainly production, some craft workers	High	High	X	X		X²	X	X		
7. Own-account worker or Tier-4 firm	Mix of production /craft workers	High	High				X²	X		X	
8. Regular worker	Mainly production, some craft workers, some lower-level managers/ supervisors	Low	Moderate	X	X	X		X			

High = all, mainly or large majority; *Moderate* = significantly (either small majority or large minority); *Low* = small minority or none

[1] income security via wage equality for similar work/occupations

[2] income security via industry-wide bargaining and standards

[3] re-regulation of labour contractors

[4] written contracts with enforcement of pension (PF) and medical insurance (ESI) entitlements

Table 7.1 also lists two types of security not directly captured by these seven forms. In the first case, this is the interest that contract workers have in state authorities re-regulating the role of labour contractors in labour market intermediation. The second case refers to the interest that undeclared workers have in securing written contracts that define their entitlements to private pension contributions and medical insurance. Along with the basic characteristics of each employment configuration, these issues have been outlined in detail below.

Within OEMs, Tier-1 and Tier-2 firms – where regional contract labour systems represent the primary regime of labour control – the key employment configurations are: contract workers, casual workers, undeclared workers, trainees, apprentices and regular workers. Based on the findings from Chapters 4, 5 and 6, we can now summarise the key problems faced by workers in these different employment configurations, the degree to which each configuration comprises precarious or informal work, and the key forms of labour agency and types of conflict in which workers in each category have been involved. The remaining employment configurations are discussed in the next section on regional *casual* labour systems in Tier-3 and Tier-4 firms.

The contract worker

Based on observations from field research undertaken in 2011–2013, the most common employment configuration in OEMs, Tier-1 firms and Tier-2 firms is the contract worker. The main occupations and roles taken up by contract workers are manual production-line or assembly-line labour, machine operation, maintenance, and ancillary roles such as canteen work, cleaning and clerical work. Workers in this configuration tend to be young men who have migrated from villages and towns in inter-state areas and are recruited by labour contractors who then regulate their employment on behalf of the primary employer.

Data from Chapter 5 shows how this practice had filtered down to key Tier-1 and Tier-2 components manufacturers. From the chapter's sample of 25 firms in the NCR, it can be concluded that an average of 71 per cent of the manufacturing workforces were employed as contract workers at this level of the industry. While it is not a statistically representative sample of Tier-1 or Tier-2 firms in the NCR, this data gives a strong indication of recruitment, employment and wage practices in the sector.

There are three main pathways into contract work. First, some workers migrate alone or with family members to industrial areas of the NCR. Some workers arrive without any social contacts and little local knowledge, while others are able to take advantage of social or kinship networks established by employed migrant workers. Either way, after enquiring directly with firms for employment, such workers are commonly referred to individual labour contractors or the employee of a labour contracting firm.

Second, labour contractors are hired by firms to source potential recruits from Industrial Training Institute campuses, which are government-run vocational training providers. Third, labour contractors are hired to source potential recruits directly from inter-state urban or rural areas. This pathway can manifest through a relatively formal process in which labour contractors travel to these areas directly or ask a local employee or business contact to source local workers. It can also manifest through a relatively informal process in which employers ask workers directly to source potential recruits through their regional social and kinship networks by convincing relatives or friends to migrate for work. Interestingly, it is common for firms to rely more on this informal mode of labour market intermediation once their operations have become established. In this scenario, the functions of labour contractors shift increasingly away from recruitment towards selection and employment regulation.

Labour contractors offer firms various selection functions, including police and background checks and work orientation courses. But their most significant role lies in the regulation of workers' employment through management of payroll lists and payment of wages, monitoring attendance, punctuality and conformity to workplace standards like appearance and cleanliness, and liaison with firm managers over the performance of individual workers.

This book has also argued that the employment of most of these contract workers is best understood as a type of 'de facto informal work'. This refers to employees whose work is formally-recognised, regulated and protected by laws, government policies or other state regulatory agencies, but who, in practice, have little or no social agency to access institutions that can redress legal violations or provide compensation.

This concept has drawn upon Chang's (2009) idea of the 'in fact informal worker'. This is an unconventional understanding of informal work, which generally refers to economic activities which may be regulated socially but are not formally recognised by state institutions. It is unconventional since contract labour *is* recognised and regulated by the State – indeed, the concept of 'contract labour' is largely a juridical creation of the State via the *CLARA* – but these regulations are mostly inaccessible to the people whose interests they are meant to protect. The evidence outlined in this book suggests that, in practice, the majority of these contract workers do not and cannot access the restrictions and protections enshrined in the law despite widespread violations across the sector.

The *CLARA* was introduced in order to restrict the employment of workers hired by labour contractors – i.e., 'contract workers'– to the ancillary functions of firms that employ 20 or more workers. The *CLARA* also outlaws the employment of contract workers for more than 240 consecutive days. Section 10(1) enables State governments to prohibit contract labour if their work is found to take place in 'core' activities of a firm and if it is found to be continuous in nature, or better-suited to 'workmen' (regular workers) as defined under the *Factories Act 1948*.

In the NCR, most production-line work in OEMs, Tier-1 and Tier-2 firms is undertaken by contract workers. Since almost all of these firms employ 20 workers or more, they are not supposed to employ contract workers in such core business functions. In addition, it is common for contract workers to be effectively employed on a continuous basis. A further violation of labour law appears to be the payment of contract workers at much lower levels and with far fewer non-wage enterprise benefits than regular workers even if they undertake similar work.

In Haryana, where the largest auto manufacturing operations cluster in Gurugram and Faridabad, there is no evidence uncovered in this research that the Government of Haryana has used its power under the *CLARA* to prohibit the employment of contract workers in regional auto operations. To complicate matters further, full application of this law may not deliver justice to affected workers if the outcome is effective 'abolition' of their employment rather than conversion to a permanent or open-ended employment contract with their primary employer (Cox, 2012).

If we apply Standing's concept of labour-related security, we also find that most contract workers are engaged in precarious work. Most lack employment security, job security, skill reproduction security, income security and representation security. Their employment insecurity is closely tied to the de facto informality of the contract labour system. In order to avoid the *CLARA*'s prohibition of continuously-employed contract labour, most contract workers are employed in six or seven month contracts which expire before the law's 240-day limit. It is common for workers to be re-hired on new contracts or re-deployed by their primary employer to another workplace.

These limits to employment security have a knock-on effect on other forms of labour-related security. Most long-term contract workers cannot develop job security since they cannot translate their employment tenure into opportunities for career development and promotion. Nor do they have skill reproduction security through training and access to new roles. Contract workers also tend to lack income security. This income insecurity manifests through similar work undertaken by many regular workers on the shop-floor for much lower levels of pay. Based on the data in Chapter 5, on an average, contract workers received a basic wage that was less than half of the regular workers' basic wage for undertaking similar production-line work in Tier-1 and Tier-2 firms.

Finally, contract workers lack representation security. They have few practical rights and opportunities to join trade unions or form their own unions. Contract workers are excluded from the formal structures of collective bargaining. Their wages and employment conditions are not regulated through collective wage agreements negotiated between regular workers' trade union executives and primary employers. There are no records in the NCR of contract workers successfully joining or forming unions in the auto industry. In addition, these workers have little capacity to request labour contractors to represent any grievances to their primary employer since employers prefer to hire multiple labour contractors and encourage competition among them.

Based on this evidence, we can say that the core work-based interests of contract workers are: for their principal employer to take full and direct responsibility for regulating their employment, entitlements and responsibilities at work; for employment security via ongoing work with their principal employer without breaks, interruptions or arbitrary re-deployment; job security via opportunities to transform work experience into career development; skill reproduction via opportunities to access new roles through training; income security through substantial wage rises to reflect equal pay for equal work to regular workers in similar occupations or roles; and, finally, the right and opportunity to join trade unions.

In this context, it is significant that the MSIL dispute in Manesar in 2011/12 involved a high level of collaboration and solidarity between regular, casual and contract workers. Despite significant company obstruction and state repression, MSIL eventually responded with major increases in wage levels for workers in all employment configurations and the introduction of 'company temps' to replace most of the company's previous contract labour-based workforce.

However, the logic of leaders in key trade unions continues to reflect a position whereby unions should attempt to organise contract workers and temps *only after* formal registration and a collective wage agreement has been achieved for regular workers (Interview, AD Nagpal, National Secretary, HMS, 8 March 2013; DL Sachdev, National Secretary, AITUC, 9 March 2013). Despite this position, no evidence was found of higher wages or better employment conditions accruing to contract workers as a result of wage agreements negotiated for regular workers. Wage rises for contract workers and temps only occurred through unilateral management concessions which usually followed outbursts of intense conflict. Most unions have continued to adapt to the highly restrictive institutional environment and the regional contract labour system by, in practice, excluding contract workers.

A further contributing factor to the weakness of unions relates to the social interests of local landowning families and their intersection with the politics of local trade union affiliates. As outlined in Chapter 5, several semi-industrial villages nearby IMT Manesar are populated by a mix of Haryanvi landowners and migrant workers from inter-state regions. In these villages, a select group of local landowners, who are mainly from the Jat and Yadav communities, act as intermediaries in land asset markets between regional state institutions, industrialists participating in global production networks, and labour contractors who sublet rooms to migrant contract workers. It has been increasingly common for the sons of these local families to gain employment in local auto manufacturing firms and, in doing so, to establish leadership positions in trade unions by leveraging their local connections.

This raises a contradictory role for some local union leaderships: on the one hand, they have a material stake in the operation of the contract labour system due to family links to land ownership and property leasing. On the other hand, they have led campaigns, including often-disruptive mobilisations of local villagers encouraged by *gram panchayats* (village councils), which have created some, albeit limited pathways for workers employed in informal or precarious work to improve their material conditions of life.

The absence of security for workers in multiple employment configurations is important given the shift in MSIL's recruitment and employment relations strategy following the 2011/12 dispute in Manesar. Although MSIL's more recent system of company temps marginalises a formal role for labour contractors in recruitment and human resource management, these workers mostly remain on short-term contracts and, despite major improvements in basic wages since 2011, are still denied the level of labour-related security afforded to regular workers.

Beyond MSIL, there is little evidence that a system of directly-hired company temps has displaced regional contract labour systems, including among key Tier-1 and Tier-2 suppliers that operate within its global production network. Instead, the instability of 2011/12 appears to have influenced a *modification* in employment relations strategy in which the employment of a slightly larger core of workers is regularised, unions are given recognition for this expanded group of regular workers, and unilateral wage concessions are offered.

Even with this shift, industrial conflict has persisted in the NCR, most significantly in late 2015 and early 2016 with the dispute at HMSI's Tapukara plant in Alwar District in the NCR. This dispute has some similarities to the MSIL case, with violent conflict and repression from the company and regional state institutions implemented in response to solidarity between contract, casual and regular workers.

The casual worker

Casual workers – also known as temporary workers or 'temps' – form a smaller group of employees within OEMs, Tier-1, and Tier-2 firms compared to contract workers. They are also employed in smaller Tier-3 firms and, occasionally, in Tier-4 firms. The casual worker is distinguished from the contract worker by the direct manner of recruitment, and employment regulation by firms rather than labour contractors, but are different from the regular worker because they lack a permanent or open-ended contract, or have been hired on a short-term basis.

Although labour contractors are not involved in their recruitment or employment regulation, the pathway of the casual worker's entry into employment can be similar to contract workers. Like contract workers, most are young male migrants from poorer inter-state regions, and many migrate alone to industrial areas in the NCR in search of work, or take advantage of social and kinship networks to find jobs. Like contract workers, casual workers are mainly hired to undertake manual production-line roles although some are also found in craft-work occupations or ancillary roles.

Casual workers are employed in either formal or informal contexts. In OEMs, Tier-1 firms, Tier-2 firms and many Tier-3 firms, their wages, employment conditions and working conditions are subject to the *Factories Act 1948* and relevant State government labour laws. Furthermore, their status as directly-recruited and directly-employed workers means that their entitlement to labour-related security are not subject to the manoeuvring of employers who wish to evade the *CLARA*.

However, many casual workers are employed in Tier-3 and Tier-4 firms which fall outside the regulatory scope of the organised sector. Furthermore, there are those casual workers, employed in either organised or unorganised sector firms, whose employment leans towards informality due to the absence of a written employment contract.

Many casual workers can be described as employed in precarious work with similar dimension of insecurity as contract workers. For example, the regulation of wages and employment conditions of casual workers also tends to be excluded from collective wage agreements.

The undeclared worker

Undeclared or unregistered workers form a segment of the workforce in various tiers of the auto industry that often overlaps with other employment configurations. As a rule, hiring workers without formally registering their employment with the state-based Department of Labour is a common and often, relatively straightforward way for employers to avoid the costs of obeying state regulations on wages, working hours and other employment entitlements. This group can include workers who have not been given a written employment contract, and who do not receive written payslips.

By definition, firms in the agricultural and unorganised sectors do not need to register their workers with the Ministry of Labour and Employment. As such, all wage workers outside the organised sector can be regarded as undeclared and, therefore, engaged in informal work. However, for employers in the organised sector who wish to avoid declaring workers, there are two main avenues. First, employers can avoid paying medical insurance entitlements. The *Employees' State Insurance Corporation Act 1948* applies to all workers who earn ₹21,000 (US$320–330) or less per month in firms in the organised sector. If an employer is able to successfully avoid registration for ESI, then the employment of an affected worker will be undeclared and informal.

Second, employers can avoid registering workers for pension contributions. The *Employees Provident Funds Act 1952* is applicable to all companies with 20 or more workers. By hiding the employment of workers from the Ministry of Labour and Employment, many employers are able to avoid PF contributions.

Based on the field research undertaken for this book, it is found that this practice is common in Tier-3 enterprises. This activity also overlaps with other groups of workers with different work-based interests. For example, some contract and casual workers may be undeclared through the failure of their employer – either the primary employer or a labour contractor – to pay ESI and PF entitlements. While there may be some cases in which this also occurs for regular workers, the overlap between undeclared work, contract labour and casual employment means that most undeclared workers have similar work-based interests in securing employment security, job security, skill reproduction, income security and representation security.

A further core work-based interest is the need to register and pay ESI and PF contributions for those workers who desire it. Some workers may be aware of the undeclared character of their employment and, through conscious inaction, effectively cooperate with their employer in the belief that this minimises their personal costs. However, employers who wish to avoid paying ESI and PF contributions can exploit workers' lack of knowledge about their legal rights or take advantage of inadequate enforcement for these policies.

This avoidance can be further concealed by not issuing written contracts or payslips, by not including ESI and PF as discrete items on payslips, or by lowering the basic wage rate in order to (illegally) absorb ESI and PF costs into workers' wages. There are other cases in which employers tell their workers they are (legally) deducting ESI and PF costs from their wages but (illegally) keep the deductions for their own purposes rather than deposit them with the state.

The trainee

OEMs, Tier-1, and Tier-2 firms commonly employ trainees in entry-level roles. For many firms, most directly-hired recruits are initially regarded as trainees and must enter a process of in-house orientation, training, selection and probation in order to be eligible for a permanent contract. For those firms that offer it, the length of tenure and selection required to achieve permanency can vary between one and three years. Only a fraction of the workers who join as trainees are offered permanent contracts at the end of this process.

Trainees can be regarded as engaged in formal work. Few firms in the unorganised sector have the institutional means for such a formal process of traineeship. Within firms in the organised sector, trainees' wages, employment conditions and working conditions are subject to the *Factories Act 1948* and relevant State government labour laws. Their capacity to seek job security and skill reproduction security is often linked to codified company procedures, including some collective wage agreements.

Depending on the proportion of trainees who are eventually offered permanent contracts, many trainees are effectively employed as temporary or casual production-line staff for extended periods, even lasting for several years, and excluded from trade union membership, since the regulation of their wages and employment conditions often stands outside the terms of collective wage agreements. Thus, many trainees lack employment security and representation security.

For such workers, there is a need to prevent employers from arbitrarily dismissing or re-deploying them, and a need to enshrine their right and opportunity to join unions. In addition, there is a need for *enhanced* job security for those trainees who are not selected for permanent contracts, and income security for those trainees who are effectively treated as regular production-line workers and thus undertake similar work to many regular workers.

The apprentice

Apprentices are generally employed on a formal basis in OEMs, Tier-1, Tier-2, and some Tier-3 firms as skilled maintenance workers or machine operators. The period and terms of apprenticeships are set under amendments to the *Apprentices Act 1961* and, since 2014, have been overseen by the Ministry of Skill Development and Entrepreneurship. Despite these formal regulations, these workers are often treated in practice, like many trainees, as low-cost production-line workers for the duration of their apprenticeship.

A key manifestation of precarious work among apprentices is the lack of a pathway into permanent employment if employers decide to terminate their work on the conclusion of their apprenticeship term. In such cases, apprentices would benefit from enhanced job security and skill-reproduction security. Similarly, if they are being employed primarily as production-line workers in practice, they need income security to lessen the gap with the wage levels of regular workers undertaking similar work, and representation security to enable them to join unions.

The regular worker

This employment configuration is akin to the 'workman' as defined and regulated under the *Factories Act 1948*. Regular workers resemble those employed in the classical 'standard employment relationship' characterised by identifiable employer-employee relations, standardised work hours with ongoing employment, collective bargaining rights and freedom of association (Vosko, 2010). 'Regular' refers to the worker's ongoing, open-ended or permanent contractual status. In India, regular workers are employed in formal work in firms in the organised sector and their employment security is usually protected through the hire-and-fire restrictions in the *Industrial Disputes Act 1947*.

In the auto industry, regular workers, like contract and casual workers, are employed in a range of roles and occupations, including production-line or assembly-line jobs, machine operators and skilled maintenance workers, engineers, supervisors, team leaders, group leaders and lower-level managers. Regular workers are employed on relatively secure terms.

However, changing employment relations in OEMs, Tier-1, and Tier-2 firms over the past two decades has meant that many regular workers would potentially benefit from greater employment security, job security, skill reproduction and representation security. For instance, not every enterprise has a collectively-negotiated wage agreement. There are often no guarantees that regular workers will be able to use their experience or tenure to advance their careers, win promotions, or break into new roles through training. Despite the *IDA*'s restrictions, employers have often succeeded in laying-off large numbers of regular workers.

Finally, representation security is a major issue for many regular workers. Many Tier-1 and Tier-2 firms lack union representation. Although there are legally-enshrined processes for union formation and registration under the *Trade Unions Act 1926*, there is no compulsion on employers to recognise unions under Indian labour law. Employers have often victimised regular workers for attempting to form or register unions, including layoffs. Thus, despite the formal and relatively secure status of their work, many regular workers would benefit from regulatory changes to enhance employment, job, skill reproduction and representation security.

Global production networks and the regional casual labour system

The fourth and final key issue in addressing the character of industrial conflict in Indian auto manufacturing concerns inter- and intra-firm economic and social relations at the bottom of the 'value chain'. The capacity of OEMs and Tier-1 firms to shape work organisation and employment relations is linked to the integration of their global production networks with regional social structures of accumulation predicated upon varieties of informal and precarious work. For auto manufacturing in the NCR, this structure is based upon low-cost, low-wage and labour-intensive work, a high incidence of owner-operation in small-to-medium sized firms, a preference for hiring mobile young men from inter-state villages, towns and cities and a gendered division of labour in which formal work is dominated by men while women occupy a minority of paid positions which are usually regarded as unskilled or low-value.

There is also a contradictory caste dimension to manufacturing work in the NCR, with 'middle-ranking' castes officially referred to as OBCs providing most of the labour supply of young men from inter-state regions in States like Bihar and Uttar Pradesh – albeit with a large number of Dalit and Muslim workers as well – while young men from middle-ranking castes in local areas are socially and culturally conditioned to seek non-manual jobs in family-run businesses, organised sector firms and Public Sector Units (PSUs). While some migrant workers have remained in the NCR on a permanent basis, a circular flow of migrants between regional source and industrial site, and between firms in recipient sites, has strongly influenced employment relations and work organisation in the region.

For the auto industry, this impact is especially felt in Tier-3 firms. Circular migration means that the structural and associational power of workers in these firms is expressed very differently to workers in OEMs, Tier-1, and Tier-2 firms. While basic wages tend to be lower in lower-tier firms, greater emphasis is placed in Tier-3 firms on bonus payments linked to religious festivals and public holidays with potential for conflict to emerge over these 'extra-wage' payments linked to cultural practices and labour mobility.

Auto manufacturing firms whose operations are linked to global production networks have tended to adapt to these social employment practices. But the emergence of global production networks has also *sharpened* these practices. Firms which have been selected to function either partially or completely as Tier-3 enterprises within the global production networks of OEMs have been a mix of specialised, independent suppliers and captive, generic suppliers. One of the prices of network participation is the right of higher-tier client firms to exercise a high degree of control over Tier-3 operations through frequent, close-monitoring of operations and inspection of product quality at the site of production. In addition, OEM control over price levels, product design specifications, quality standards, order volumes and payment frequencies filter down through global production networks to influence Tier-3 operations. These pressures are most acutely experienced in the operations of captive generic suppliers.

This reproduction of inter-firm control or relational value chain governance intersects with market or price-based value chain governance. Tier-3 firms are encouraged to compete to maintain or acquire orders and contracts with higher-tier clients. This combination of price competition and low-margin operations reproduces the low-wage environment characteristic of small-to-medium manufacturing enterprises in India. In Faridabad, wages in Tier-3 and Tier-4 firms tended to move at a level close to the Haryana minimum wage at the time of field research (see Chapter 6).

This low-margin, low-wage working environment means that Tier-3 firms generally lack the same capacity to make transformational investments in their operations as Tier-1 or Tier-2 firms, and also lack the disposable income to spend on commission fees for labour contractors. This, and the experience of a circulating flow of young workers who migrate through industrial areas via social or kinship networks, means that the contract labour system does not operate below Tier-2 of the auto industry.

Instead of labour contractors, the absence of employment security, job security and income security in Tier-3 firms is tied to low-margin operations and susceptibility to seasonal fluctuations in product orders and volumes. Some of these enterprises are informal by virtue of employing fewer than 10 workers – thus, joining the ranks of the unorganised sector – while some are formal enterprises that hire undeclared workers whose informality is shaped by the absence of written employment contracts, payslips or medical insurance (ESI) and pension contributions (PF).

Tier-3 firms are generally populated by casual and predominantly unskilled labourers. The concept of the 'helper' – the unskilled labourer who is engaged in a variety of manual tasks and who is vulnerable to instant dismissal without formal social protection – typifies work in these firms. This is true even for firms that utilise semi-skilled or even skilled occupations alongside lesser-skilled roles.

The low-margin character of these firms also means that conflict rarely occurs between employers and employees over basic wage levels. When conflict does emerge – for example, over perceived maltreatment or the non-payment or under-payment of bonuses during festivals and holidays – it can lead either to short-lived 'wildcat' industrial action in which employers offer basic concessions or to workers leaving in search of alternative employment. The abundance of casual employment in these firms – as well as opportunities in higher-tier manufacturers and OEMs for workers with the required aptitude – encourages many workers to pursue an 'exit' strategy. The mobility of the region's predominantly young workforce means that employers commonly complain about labour shortages. The absence of a basis for ongoing or formal collective bargaining over wages and employment conditions at an enterprise level, combined with the generally hostile legal and institutional environment for labour activism, means that trade unions barely exist or attempt to organise workers below Tier-2 of the industry.

Based on Table 7.1, it is possible to identify and summarise the key employment configurations that dominate these regional casual labour systems. Other than casual workers, regular workers and undeclared workers, key employment configurations include: wage workers in Tier-3 firms and informal enterprises, own-account workers and Tier-4 job-workers. These are outlined below. While some of these employment configurations also appear in higher-tier enterprises, they are a mainstay of employment in Tier-3 and Tier-4 firms.

The worker employed by an informal enterprise or formal Tier-3 enterprise

As outlined above, Tier-3 firms transcend the regulatory division between organised and unorganised sector enterprises. Some Tier-3 firms employ dozens of workers and can also be regarded as small-to-medium enterprises in terms of gross sales. Others employ relatively few workers and can be regarded as micro-enterprises.

The size of these firms generally rules out assembly line work. As a result, most employees undertake work in a range of occupations that can be broadly classified in three ways: as machine operators, as machine maintenance specialists or as unskilled labourers – commonly known in the local industry as 'helpers'. Skilled or semi-skilled work includes machine operating, including Computer Numerical Control (CNC), cutting, drilling, shaping with lathes, as well as the physical processing of parts and components. Unskilled work generally refers to the role of the helper: the worker who is tasked with counting, sorting and checking products, or performs ancillary tasks such as cleaning, running errands, and bringing meals, tea and drinks. In Tier-3 firms, most workers are male. But a significant minority of women are employed, primarily as helpers, but in some firms, also as machine operators. Wage workers in Tier-3 firms can also be a mix of workers with permanent contracts and those employed as casuals.

Like many precariously-employed workers in higher-tier firms, workers in Tier-3 firms commonly express the need for employment security, job security, income security and representation security. However, the manifestation of these insecurities are shaped differently by the character of commercial relations between Tier-3 firms and their higher-tier customers, which also have a strong bearing on employment relations. A combination of factors – OEM and Tier-1 firm regulation of price levels, design specifications, monitoring of product quality and client control over payment frequency – means that Tier-3 firms tend to have cost-oriented, low-margin businesses.

These operations are also highly sensitive to seasonal fluctuations in client orders, which drop especially during the Hindu festival months of Diwali and Holi as large numbers of employees across the industry return to their home cities, towns and villages to participate in family and community celebrations, weddings, and, in many cases, harvesting crops on family-held farms.

During these months, low demand for generic Tier-3 products has a knock-on effect on the workers who live permanently near industrial areas, with casual employees retrenched and many others losing shifts and working hours due to lower demand for workers. Loss of working hours has a major impact on households, as many workers rely upon overtime to cover housing costs and family overheads. These factors mean that the degree of precarious work in Tier-3 firms is very high.

Like people engaged in precarious work in higher-tier firms, most workers would benefit from employment security through longer employment tenure without breaks and interruptions and greater protection from arbitrary dismissal, as well as greater job security via career paths and development. Work security is more likely to be a major issue for workers in Tier-3 firms than in higher-tier firms due to a higher incidence of unsafe or hazardous work practice and a lower likelihood of workplace safety rules and protection.

While income security and representation security are major issue for Tier-3 workers just like workers in higher-tier firms, these forms of labour-related security manifest differently. For representation security, employers commonly lack the agency or capacity to engage in ongoing structures of collective bargaining with a separate bargaining agent due to the financial and organisational pressures of managing highly-flexible, cost-oriented operations with margins squeezed by higher-tier client firms.

This also means that there are few mechanisms at an enterprise-level for workers to achieve income security through negotiated, real wage rises. Whereas income and representation security for people employed in precarious work in higher-tier firms – especially contract workers, but also casual and undeclared workers – could be addressed through their inclusion in established processes of collective bargaining, income and representation security for precarious workers in Tier-3 firms would require the recognition of *new processes of industry-level* bargaining. This might enable basic minimums for wages and social security to be negotiated at a tripartite level between representatives of employers, unions and state institutions.

In other highly-informalised sectors like cigarette (*bidi*) manufacturing and construction, informal workers' organisations have shifted the locus of political conflict from the workplace or enterprise to the state, via demands to establish tripartite welfare boards jointly funded by the state, business-owners, and workers and administered by State governments. Although currently being reviewed by the Government of India, these welfare boards can potentially deliver particular work-based benefits and, especially, welfare benefits outside the workplace such as funding for death and accident insurance, weddings and children's education (Agarwala, 2013). There is potentially a case for extending this model of bargaining to workers in Tier-3 and informal manufacturing firms although, thus far, there is little evidence of this occurring in the Indian auto industry.

The own-account worker, Tier-4 job-worker and industrial outworker

Self-employment plays a significant role in the industry in lower tiers. Whereas Tier-3 manufacturers are often owner-operated, they also tend to employ small numbers of wage workers and, as outlined above, straddle the divide between the organised and unorganised sectors. At Tier-4 firms, self-employed workers are far less likely to hire wage workers, and virtually all work falls within the unorganised sector. Some Tier-4 proprietors hire casual workers on a temporary or seasonal basis, although most work alone or with unpaid 'help' from relatives or friends.

Many work as machinists, having purchased or rented a piece of machinery, such as a drill, lathe, or cutting machine, to manufacture generic parts on order from Tier-3 enterprises in industrial areas. These machines are operated in small workshops which are located in small work-sheds or at workers' homes. In other cases, the machinery is located on the premises of a Tier-3 firm, with the person effectively employed as a sub-contracted piece worker.

This type of work can transcend multiple situations, including: the self-employed, own-account worker who undertakes regular work on order from Tier-3 firms and other clients, either in their own workshop or in the premises of a client firm; the self-employed, own-account worker who undertakes occasional 'job work' for Tier-3 firms and other clients during periods of excess demand from higher-tier firms; or the industrial outworker who undertakes work on order from Tier-3 firms or other clients from their own home with the unpaid assistance of relatives.

Like wage workers in Tier-3 firms, these Tier-4 workers would benefit from income security via industry-negotiated real wage rises and social security benefits. Similarly, they would benefit from representation security at an industry level. In addition, representation security could be enhanced through the formation of cartels to bargain for work and to enforce occupational standards. Cartelisation is linked to a final form of labour-related security which is relatively unique to Tier-4 own-account workers, job workers and industrial outworkers within the auto industry: the need for access to frequent and adequate paid work to cover living costs. Whereas abundant demand for wage workers throughout the industry means that labour market security has rarely been a problem for most workers, this is a major issue for Tier-4 workers. Thus, representation security through cartelisation would be as much about negotiating regular *access* to work as about the social regulation of work and the terms of employment.

Conclusion: Implications of informal and precarious work in auto manufacturing

While remaining cognizant to the concerns of the evolving literature on work, employment and labour agency in global value chains and global production networks, this book has attempted to approach the problem of conflict from the perspective of 'labour-centred' development theory (Selwyn, 2016). The aim has been to use this as an alternative analytical entry point into the framework of 'GPN 2.0', which is required to understand the transformation of domestic industry and domestic conflict by global production networks (Coe and Yeung, 2015).

This book has argued that the high levels of industrial, social and political conflict that have characterised India's auto industry in the twenty-first century can be explained by a combination of four factors: the transformation of commercial relations within the industry by the emergence of global production networks from the 1980s to the 2000s; the conditioning of market conditions and commercial relations by economic liberalisation; the deterioration of labour standards and employment relations in the 2000s under these new institutional rules and market conditions; and, finally, the intersection of these global production networks with entrenched regional social structures of accumulation. At the core of this rising conflict has been the re-fashioning and reproduction of different forms of precarious or informal work.

In the case of the NCR, the transformation of inequality can be seen in the industrialisation of town and village life in Gurugram and beyond. While this process, and the role of state institutions in the provision of mass transport infrastructure, have facilitated new forms of mobility for people moving between industrial zones, the national capital, and cities, towns and villages in inter-state regions, it has also reproduced and expanded inequalities in employment relations within the industry, and inequalities between workers, employers and labour market intermediaries.

Regional industrialisation has also generated new inequalities along small-scale landowners and agrarian families between those who have benefitted financially from land value inflation and those who have not, and new inequalities between landowners as tenants, labour market intermediaries and the migrant workers who have entered these industrial sub-regions in large numbers. This process has intersected with and reproduced the male-dominated character of formal workforce participation, despite growing employment of women as paid workers throughout global production networks and, especially within regional auto manufacturing, as unskilled and semi-skilled workers in Tier-3 enterprises.

Some may conclude that the high levels of commercial, industrial, social and political conflict in the industry since the 1990s show that 'low road' relations have been normalised across multiple tiers and regions. In truth, the pairing of the auto industry's firm diversity and technological sophistication with the two forms of labour control outlined in this book suggest that there is no necessary or automatic binary distinction between 'high' and 'low road' paths of development. It is possible for enterprises – particularly OEMs and Tier-1 firms – to implement lean manufacturing principles and invest in employee development and skills for *some* of their workers, while simultaneously pursuing a flexible, low-cost labour approach for other workers. In this sense, the practices documented in this book come close to the idea of 'labour force dualism' which has been developed for the Chinese auto industry (Zhang, 2015), although the extent to which workers are employed in precarious or informal roles is proportionately much higher in India than China.

At the same time, there are strong grounds for expanding the scope of exploratory and comparative inter-regional studies, including Pune District and the C-SEZ – where Jürgens and Krzywdzinski's study of VWI and Mahindra concentrates – and the emerging role of auto manufacturing in the industrial centres of Gujarat and Uttarakhand where comparatively little empirical work has been conducted. A further line of future enquiry could explore the extent to which the higher-wage model pursued by OEMs and Tier-1 firms in the NCR as a consequence of the 2011/12 industrial conflict has influenced the practices of Tier-3 and Tier-4 firms.

A final question raised by this research relates to the reasons why there has been a relative lack of attention paid to poor labour standards and 'low road' employment relations in auto manufacturing, including numerous violations of workers' rights and legal entitlements. Although struggles like the Hero Honda campaign in 2005 and the Maruti Suzuki (MSIL) conflict in 2011/12 generated national and international media coverage, very little attention has been paid to the conditions of work at the bottom of the value chain where most workers find employment and where trade unions rarely exist. In contrast, there is a large and growing literature on precarious and informal work in labour-intensive manufacturing, construction and home-based occupations in India.

Significant attention has rightly been paid to the new forms of worker's organisations that have challenged preconceptions of policy-makers and many trade unionists in the country. But insufficient light has so far been shed on workers in the low-tier, low-margin and low-wage enterprises on which auto manufacturing's global production networks rely, and the implications for labour agency and activism. Hypothetically, there is a case for an extension of models of social protection and labour organising established in labour-intensive manufacturing or construction to workers in Tier-3 and Tier-4 auto manufacturers. A type of 'cartelisation' among firms and self-employed workers, supported by trade unions and informal workers' organisations, could potentially enhance workers' capacity to secure frequent and ongoing work, to enforce occupational standards and to provide a basis for higher employment security, income security and collective voice.

Overall, this book has tried to challenge preconceptions about the expected impact of auto manufacturing on work organisation, labour standards and employment relations in emerging regional and national economies. Despite its historical role as a crucible for cohesive industrial communities and a lever for trade union-led transformation in work and living standards, the expansion and modernisation of auto manufacturing in India has not led to major advances in socio-economic security, social protection or collective rights.

At the high end of the industry – in OEMs, Tier-1 firms and Tier-2 firms – labour standards and employment relations have been transformed by the imposition of regional contract labour systems that have, to paraphrase Sen and Dasgupta (2009), reproduced an informal work environment within formal institutions. At the low-value end of the industry – in Tier-3 and Tier-4 firms – labour standards and employment relations have been shaped by the intersection of regional social structures of accumulation with the pressures of operating within global production networks. Rather than this intersection engendering an upward shift in social and regional transformation, it has tended to reproduce and expand the conditions of precarious, circulatory labour migration which have long-characterised work and industry in these regions. This is not the picture of social transformation and social reform envisaged by industrial policy-makers past or present, in India or globally.

Appendix

List of Interviews

In total, 157 people were interviewed for the study of automotive manufacturing firms located in the National Capital Region (NCR), which is India's largest auto producing area. This includes 106 workers in different tiers of the industry, 21 employers or managers, four labour contractors, as well as 26 other participants, including landowners, trade union officials, government officials, and some workers employed in other sectors or industries.

For OEMs, 12 workers were interviewed, but no employers. The workers were all employed as regular workers or had recently been retrenched. For Tier-1 firms, 47 workers were interviewed. Of this, 13 were contract workers and 34 were regular workers. In addition, it was possible to interview 4 Tier-1 employers: two plant managers, one senior manager, and a senior company executive.

For Tier-2 firms, 14 workers were interviewed, of which 12 were contract workers and 2 were regular workers. Two Tier-2 employers – a senior executive and a plant manager –were also interviewed. For Tier-3 firms, 33 workers and 11 employers were interviewed, including 6 business owners or proprietors, 3 managers and 2 skilled workers in supervisory roles. Four Tier-4 business owners – all own-account workers – were also interviewed.

Four labour contractors were interviewed. No employer, worker or trade union was willing or able to put the author in contact with a labour contractor. In total, 90 labour contracting enterprises were contacted by mail and over 40 enterprises were physically approached at the cluster of offices in Old Gurgaon. Most labour contractors refused to speak about their work. However, 8 labour contractors were prepared to hold discussions and, of these, 4 agreed to participate in formal interviews to document their activities, functions, and relations with workers and employers in the auto industry.

The interviews are listed by tier or group and in chronological order by the date of interview. In order to maintain the anonymity of participants, most names of most of the firms in this study have been coded. A minority of participants were not adversely affected by having their identities revealed and instructed the author to do so. In these cases, the names of participants and their position and affiliations have been recorded.

In the book, the coding of firms reflects the tier that the firm occupies within the automotive manufacturing industry. For example, if a Tier-1 firm is coded as 'B', then this is written as 'Firm 1B' when referred to in the main part of the book. If a Tier-3 firm is coded as 'F', it is written as 'Firm 3F'. The location, product types, supplier type as well as information about the number of workers, employment conditions, and wages for most of these firms are listed in Table 5.1 for Tier-1 and Tier-2 firms (Chapter 5) and Table 6.1 for Tier-3 firms (Chapter 6). In the list of interview participants below, the minority of female participants are marked with an asterisk (*). In total, six female workers participated in the interviews.

Workers

OEMs

3 regular workers, Honda Motorcycle and Scooter India (HMSI), IMT Manesar, December, 2011.

3 retrenched regular workers, Maruti Suzuki India Limited (MSIL) (IMT Manesar), Old Gurgaon, March, 2013

5 regular workers, Hero MotoCorp (Gurugram plant), Old Gurgaon, March, 2013

1 regular worker (product quality inspector), Firm X, April, 2013

Tier-1

1 regular worker, A, Gurugram, December, 2011

1 regular worker, B, Greater Noida, December, 2011

2 regular workers, C, IMT Manesar, December, 2011

2 regular workers, D, Gurugram, December, 2011

1 regular worker, E, Old Gurgaon, December, 2011

1 contract worker, F, IMT Manesar, December, 2011

3 regular workers, G, IMT Manesar, December, 2011

1 contract worker, H, IMT Manesar, November, 2012

3 regular workers, I, IMT Manesar, November, 2012

1 contract worker, J, IMT Manesar, November, 2012

4 contract workers, K, IMT Manesar, November, 2012

2 contract workers, L, Faridabad, November, 2012

1 regular worker (plant union president), N, Old Gurgaon, March, 2013

1 regular worker (plant union president), O, Binola, March, 2013

3 contract workers, O, Binola, March, 2013

4 regular workers, P, Gurugram, March, 2013

3 regular workers, Q, Binola, April, 2013

1 regular worker (plant union president), R, Binola, April, 2013

2 regular workers, R, Binola, April, 2013

1 regular worker (plant union president), S, Binola, April, 2013

1 regular worker, T, Binola, April, 2013

1 regular worker, U, Gurugram, April, 2013

1 regular worker, V, IMT Manesar, April, 2013

1 regular worker, W, Gurugram, April, 2013

1 regular worker, X, IMT Manesar, April, 2013

2 regular workers, Y, Gurugram, April, 2013

1 contract worker, Z, Faridabad, April, 2013*

1 regular worker, A1, Gurugram, April, 2013

Tier-2

7 contract workers, A, Udyog Vihar, Gurugram, April, 2013

1 contract worker, B, Faridabad, April, 2013

1 contract worker, C, Udyog Vihar, Gurugram, April, 2013

1 regular worker (shop-floor supervisor), C, Udyog Vihar, Gurugram, April, 2013

1 regular worker, D, IMT Manesar, April, 2013

3 contract workers, E, Faridabad, April, 2013

Tier-3

2 casual workers, D, Mujessar, Faridabad, March, 2013

5 casual workers, A, Faridabad, April, 2013

4 casual workers, B, Sururpur Industrial Area, Faridabad, April, 2013 (one female)*

2 casual workers, C, Shiv Colony, Faridabad, April, 2013

2 casual workers, D, Mujessar, Faridabad, April, 2013

2 casual workers, E, Shiv Colony, Faridabad, April, 2013 (one female)*

4 casual workers, F, Sanjay Colony, Faridabad, April, 2013

1 casual worker, G, IMT Manesar, April, 2013*

1 casual worker, H, Welcome Industrial Complex, Sector-23, Faridabad, April, 2013*

5 workers (1 skilled engineer, 4 casuals), I, Welcome Industrial Complex, Sanjay Colony, Sector-23, Faridabad, April, 2013

2 casual workers, J, Welcome Industrial Complex, Sector-23, Faridabad, April, 2013

2 casual workers, M, Shiv Colony, Sector-22, Faridabad, April, 2013*

1 casual worker, N, Welcome Industrial Complex, Sanjay Colony, Sector-23, Faridabad, April, 2013

Employers and managers

Tier 1

1 plant manager, L, Faridabad, April, 2013

1 plant manager, M, IMT Manesar, April, 2013

1 senior manager, O, Binola, April, 2013

1 senior executive (Chief Operating Officer), U, Faridabad, April, 2013

Tier 2

1 senior executive (company vice-president), C, Udyog Vihar, Gurugram, April, 2013

1 plant manager, D, Faridabad, April, 2013

Tier 3

Owner, B, Sururpur Industrial Area, Faridabad, April, 2013

Owner, C, Shiv Colony, Faridabad, April, 2013

Owner, D, Mujesar, Faridabad, April, 2013

Electrician, D, Mujesar, Faridabad, April, 2013

Owner, E, Shiv Colony, Faridabad, April, 2013

Engineer/manager, E, Shiv Colony, Faridabad, April, 2013

Manager, F, Sanjay Colony, Faridabad, April, 2013

Owner, H, Welcome Industrial Complex, Sanjay Colony, Sector-23, Faridabad, April, 2013

Owner, I, Welcome Industrial Complex, Sanjay Colony, Sector-23, Faridabad, April, 2013

Manager, K, Welcome Industrial Complex, Sanjay Colony, Sector-23, Faridabad, April, 2013

Manager, L, Welcome Industrial Complex, Sanjay Colony, Sector-23, Faridabad, April, 2013

Tier 4

Owner, K, Binola, April 2013

Owner, L, Welcome Industrial Complex, Sanjay Colony, Sector-23, Faridabad, April, 2013

Owner, M, Welcome Industrial Complex, Sanjay Colony, Sector-23, Faridabad, April, 2013
Owner, N, Welcome Industrial Complex, Sanjay Colony, Sector-23, Faridabad, April, 2013

Labour contractors

Labour contractor LCA, Old Gurgaon, March, 2013
Labour contractor LCB, Old Gurgaon, April, 2013
Labour contractor LCC, Old Gurgaon, April, 2013
Labour contractor LCD,Old Gurgaon, April, 2013

Trade union officials

AD Nagpal, national secretary, Hind Mazdoor Sabha (HMS), New Delhi, March, 2013
DL Sachdev, national secretary, All-India Trade Union Congress (AITUC), New Delhi, March, 2013
Anil Kumar, Gurugram secretary, AITUC, Old Gurgaon, March, 2013
Jaspal Singh, Gurugram secretary, HMS, Old Gurgaon, March, 2013
AK Padmanabhan, national secretary, Centre of Indian Trade Unions (CITU), New Delhi, April, 2013
Ananya Bhattacharya, Garment and Allied Workers Union (GAWU), Varanasi, April, 2013

Other

5 garment workers, Okhla Industrial Area, Delhi, November, 2012
3 canteen workers, Okhla Industrial Area, Delhi, November, 2012
2 workers, Aliyar Village, Sector-8, IMT Manesar, November, 2012
2 local landowners, Aliyar Village, Sector-8, IMT Manesar, November, 2012
2 local landowners, A & B, Kharkari Village, IMT Manesar, April, 2013
Local landowner C, Kharkari Village, IMT Manesar, April, 2013
Local landowner A, Binola Village, Haryana, April, 2013
2 local landowners, Binola Village, Haryana, April, 2013
Sher Singh, Faridabad Mazdoor Samachar (Faridabad Workers Newspaper), December 2011, November 2012, March/April, 2013
Assistant Director, Automotive Components Manufacturers Association of India (ACMA), northern region, New Delhi, April, 2013

Bibliography

AGC Automotive. 'Profile.' Accessed 17 August 2016. Available at http://www.agc-automotive. com/english/index.html.

Adam, C. and B. Harriss-White. 2007. 'From Monet to Mondrian: Characterising Informal Economic Activity in Field Research and Simulation Models.' In *Trade Liberalisation and India's Informal Economy*, edited by B. Harriss-White and A. Sinha. New Delhi: Oxford University Press.

Agarwala, R. 2013. *Informal Labor, Formal Politics and Dignified Discontent in India*. Cambridge: Cambridge University Press.

Ahn, P. S. 2007. *Organising for Decent Work in the Informal Economy: Strategies, Methods and Practices*. New Delhi: International Labour Organisation.

Ahluwalia, M. S. 2002. 'Economic Reforms in India since 1991: Has Gradualism Worked?' *Journal of Economic Perspectives* 16 (7): 67–88.

Ajay, L. 2016. 'Gujarat Tata Motors Plant Strike: 22 Trade Unions Support Suspended Workers.' *Indian Express*, 12 March. Accessed 3 April 2017. Available at http://indianexpress.com/ article/india/india-news-india/gujarat-tata-motors-plant-strike-22-trade-unions-support-suspended-workers/.

Allirajani, M. 2009. 'Workers Kills Company VP in Coimbatore.' *Times of India*, 23 September. Accessed 6 July 2014. Available at http://timesofindia.indiatimes.com/india/Workers-kill-company-VP-in-Coimbatore/articleshow/5044794.cms.

Anand Enterprise. 2016. 'Company Profile.' Accessed 12 August 2016. Available at http:// www.anandenterprise.com/profile.html.

Anand, N. 2008. 'Renault-Nissan Suppliers to Get 250 Acres.' *The Hindu*, 29 May. Accessed 18 August 2016. Available at http://www.thehindu.com/todays-paper/tp-national/tp-tamilnadu/renaultnissan-suppliers-to-get-250-acres/article1266911.ece.

Anievas, A. and K. Nisancioglu. 2015. *How the West Came to Rule: The Geopolitical Origins of Capitalism*. Chicago: University of Chicago Press.

Anner, M. 2015. 'Labor Control Regimes and Worker Resistance in Global Supply Chains.' *Labor History* 56 (3): 292–307.

Arnold, D. and J. Bongiovi. 2013. 'Precarious, Informalising and Flexible Work: Transforming Concepts and Understandings.' *American Behavioral Scientist* 57 (3): 289–308.

ASAL (Automotive Stampings and Assemblies Limited). 2016. 'About the Company.' Accessed 16 August 2016. Available at http://www.autostampings.com/about.htm.

Ashutosh Rubber. 2016. 'Our Company.' Accessed 16 August 2016. Available at http://www. ashutoshrubber.com/Company-Profile.aspx.

Autor, D. H. ed. 2009. *Studies of Labor Market Intermediation*. Chicago: University of Chicago Press.

Awasthi, D., S. Pal and J. Yagnik. 2010. 'Small Producers and Labour Conditions in Auto Parts and Components Industry in North India.' In *Labour in Global Production Networks in India*, edited by A. Posthuma and D. Nathan. New Delhi: Oxford University Press.

Audi. 2015. *Audi 2015 Annual Report*. Ingolstadt, Germany.

BMW. 2015. *BMW Annual Report 2015*. Munich.

BMW India. 'Sachin Tendulkar Making a BMW at Plant Chennai #SachinMakingBMW.' Accessed 5 September 2016. Available at https://www.youtube.com/watch?v=8HoTRS2jmu0.

Babson, S. 1986. *Working Detroit: The Making of a Union Town*. Detroit: Wayne State University Press.

Baggonkar, S. 2015. 'Honda, Hero Prepare for Final Showdown.' *Business Standard*, 27 July. Accessed 12 January 2017. Available at http://www.business-standard.com/article/companies/honda-hero-prepare-for-final-showdown-115072701408_1.html.

Bair, J. ed. 2009. *Frontiers of Commodity Chain Research*. Redwood, California: Stanford University Press.

Bajaj Auto. 2016. *Ninth Annual Report, 2015–16*. Pune.

Banaji, J. 2010. *Theory as History: Essays on Modes of Production and Exploitation*. Leiden: Brill.

Banerjee-Guha, S. 2008. 'Space Relations of Capital and Significance of New Economic Enclaves: SEZs in India.' *Economic and Political Weekly* 43 (7): 51–59.

Bardhan, P. 1998. *The Political Economy of Development in India*. New Delhi: Oxford University Press.

Barnes, T. 2012. 'The IT Industry and Economic Development in India: A Critical Study.' *Journal of South Asian Development* 8 (1): 61–84.

———. 2015. *Informal Labour in Urban India: Three Cities, Three Journeys*. London: Routledge.

Barnes, T, K. S. Lal Das and S. Pratap. 2015. 'Labour Contractors and Global Production Networks: The Case of India's Auto Supply Chain.' *Journal of Development Studies* 51 (4): 355–69.

Barrientos, S. W., G. Gereffi and A. Rossi. 2011. 'Economic and Social Upgrading in Global Production Networks: A New Paradigm for a Changing World.' *International Labour Review* 150 (3/4): 319–40.

Barrientos, S. W. 2013. 'Labour Chains: Analysing the Role of Labour Contractors in Global Production Networks.' *Journal of Development Studies* 49: 1058–71.

Barrientos, S. W., U. Kothari and N. Phillips. 2013. 'Dynamics of Unfree Labour in the Contemporary Global Economy.' *Journal of Development Studies* 49: 1037–41.

Basile, E. 2013. *Capitalist Development in India's Informal Economy*. Oxford: Routledge.

Becker-Ritterspach, F. 2007. 'Maruti Suzuki's Trajectory: From a Public Sector Enterprise to a Japanese-owned Subsidiary.' Paper presented at the 15th GERPISA International Colloquium, Paris, 20–22 June.

———. 2009. *Hybridisation of MNE Subsidiaries: The Automotive Sector in India*. London: Palgrave MacMillan.

Bernstein, H. 2010. *Class Dynamic of Agrarian Change*. Halifax (California): Fernwood Publishing.

Bhaduri, A. 1983. *The Economic Structure of Backward Agriculture*. London: Academic Press.

Bishnu, S. 2009. 'What Lalgarh Signifies for the CPI(M).' *Economic and Political Weekly* 44 (25) .

BorgWarner. 2016. 'Company Locations.' Accessed 18 August 2016. Available at https://www.borgwarner.com/en/Company/Locations/Locations/Forms/PopForm.aspx?ID=88.

Bo Nielsen, K. and H. Wilhite. 2015. 'The Rise and Fall of the "People's Car": Middle-class Aspirations, Status and Mobile Symbolism in "New India".' *Contemporary South Asia* 23 (4): 371–87.

Bose, A. J. C. and S. Pratap. 2012. 'Worker Voices in an Auto Production Chain: Notes from the Pits of a Low Road.' *Economic and Political Weekly* 47 (33): 46–59.

Boyer, R. 1998. 'Hybridization and Models of Production: Geography, History and Theory.' In *Between Imitation and Innovation: The Transfer and Hybridization of Productive Models in the International Automobile Industry*, edited by R. Boyer, E. Charron, U. Jürgens and S. Tolliday. Oxford: Oxford University Press.

Brass, T. 1999. *Towards a Comparative Political Economy of Unfree Labour: Case Studies and Debates*. London: Frank Cass.

Breman, J. 1994. *Wage Hunters and Gatherers: Search for Work in the Urban and Rural Economy of South Gujarat*. New Delhi: Oxford University Press.

———. 1996. *Footloose Labour: Working in India's Informal Economy*. Cambridge: Cambridge University Press.

———. 1999. 'The Study of Industrial Labour in Postcolonial India–The Informal Sector: A Concluding Review.' In *The Worlds of Indian Industrial Labour*, edited by J. P. Parry, J. Breman and K. Kapadia. New Delhi: Sage.

———. 2004. *The Making and Unmaking of an Industrial Working Class: Sliding Down the Labour Hierarchy in Ahmedabad, India*. Amsterdam: Amsterdam University Press.

———. 2007. *The Poverty Regime in Village India: Half a Century of Work and Life at the Bottom of the Rural Economy in South Gujarat*. New Delhi: Oxford University Press.

———. 2013. 'A Bogus Concept?' *New Left Review* 84.

Burawoy, M. 1985. *The Politics of Production*. London: Verso.

———. 1992. *Manufacturing Consent*. Chicago: University of Chicago Press.

Business Insider. 2016. 'General Motors, Ford and Fiat are Reconsidering their Plans for Investment in India.' *Business Insider India*, 25 July. Accessed 26 August 2016. Available at http://www.businessinsider.in/General-Motors-Ford-and-Fiat-are-reconsidering-their-plans-for-investment-in-India/articleshow/53377868.cms.

Business Standard. 2015. 'Ford India Recognises Workers' Union.' *Business Standard*, 12 March. Accessed 12 March 2017. Available at http://www.business-standard.com/article/news-ians/ford-india-recognises-workers-union-115031200296_1.html.

Business Today. 2015. 'Renault Unveils Kwid in India, to be Priced up to 4 Lakh.' *Business Today*, 20 May. Accessed 16 August 2016. Available at http://www.businesstoday.in/sectors/auto/renault-unveils-kwid-in-india-priced-up-to-rs-four-lakh/story/219575.html.

Callinicos, A. and J. Rosenberg. 2008. 'Uneven and Combined Development: The Social-Relational Substratum of "the International"? An Exchange of Letters.' *Cambridge Review of International Affairs* 21 (1): 77–112.

Campbell, I. and R. Price. 2016. 'Precarious Work and Precarious Workers: Towards an Improved Conceptualization.' *Economic and Labour Relations Review* 27 (3): 314–22.

Carré, F. and J. Heintz. 2010. 'Globalisation, Informality and Non-Standard Employment.' Paper presented at the 12th Annual Conference, Association of Heterodox Economics, University of Bordeaux, 7–10 July.

Carswell, G. and G. de Neve. 2013. 'Labouring for Global Markets: Conceptualising Labour Agency in Global Production Networks.' *Geoforum* 44 (1): 62–79.

Caparo Engineering. 2016. 'Manufacturing Plants.' Accessed 17 August 2016. Available at http://www.caparo.co.in/stamping_manufacturing_plants.html.

Castells, M. and A. Portes. 1989. 'World Underneath: The Origins, Dynamics and Effects of the Informal Economy.' In *The Informal Economy: Studies in Advanced and Less Developed Countries,* edited by A. Portes, M. Castells and L. A. Benton. Baltimore: John Hopkins University Press.

Chang, D. 2009. 'Informalising Labour in Asia's Global Factory.' *Journal of Contemporary Asia* 39 (2): 161–79.

Chaudhary, V. 2016. 'BMW to Increase Localisation Level from 20 per cent to 50 per cent in Chennai.' *Financial Express,* 21 March. Accessed 20 August 2016. Available at http://www.financialexpress.com/auto/news/bmw-to-increase-localisation-level-from-20-to-50-in-chennai/223299/.

Chen, M. A. 2006. 'Rethinking the Informal Economy: Linkages with the Formal Economy and the Formal Regulatory Environment.' In *Linking the Formal and Informal Economy: Concepts and Policies,* edited by B. Guha-Khasnobis, R. Kanbur and E. Ostrom. Oxford: Oxford University Press.

Chibber, V. 2003. *Locked in Place: State-building and Late Industrialisation in India.* Princeton: Princeton University Press.

Chin, G. T. 2010. *China's Automotive Modernisation: The Party-State and Multinational Corporations.* London: Palgrave MacMillan.

Clark, G. and S. Wolcott. 2003. 'One Polity, Many Countries: Economic Growth in India, 1973–2000.' In *In Search of Prosperity: Analytical Narratives on Economic Growth,* edited by D. Rodrik. Princeton: Princeton University Press.

Coe, N. M, M. Hess, H. W. Yeung, P. Dicken and J. Henderson. 2004. '"Globalising" Regional Development: A Global Production Networks Perspective.' *Transactions of the British Institute of Geographers* 29 (4): 468–84.

Coe, N. M. and D. C. Jordhus-Lier. 2011.'Constrained Agency? Re-evaluating the Geographies of Labour.' *Progress in Human Geography* 35 (2): 211–33.

Coe, N. M. and H. W. Yeung. 2015. *Global Production Networks: Theorising Economic Development in an Inter-connected World.* Oxford: Oxford University Press.

Comau India. 2016. 'Company Global Presence.' Accessed 18 August 2016. Available at http://www.comau.com/EN/this-is-comau/global-presence/india.

Cumbers, A., C. Nativel and P. Routledge. 2008. 'Labour Agency and Union Positionalities in Global Production Networks.' *Journal of Economic Geography* 8: 369–87.

D'Costa, A. P. 1995. 'The Restructuring of the Indian Automobile Industry: Indian State and Japanese Capital.' *World Development* 23 (3): 485–502.

———. 2003. 'Uneven and Combined Development: Understanding India's Software Exports.' *World Development* 31 (1): 211–26.

————. 2005. *The Long March to Capitalism: Embourgeoisment, Internationalisation and Industrial Transformation in India*. Basingstoke: Palgrave MacMillan.

————. 2009. 'Economic Nationalism in Motion: Steel, Auto and Software Industries in India.' *Review of International Political Economy* 16 (4): 620–48.

————. 2014. 'Compressed Capitalism and Development.' *Critical Asian Studies* 46 (2): 317–44.

Daimler. 2015. *Daimler Annual Report 2015*. Stuttgart.

Das, G. 2001. *India Unbound: A Personal Account of a Social and Economic Revolution from Independence to the Global Information Age*. New York: Alfred Knopf.

Das, S. 2013. 'Global Vendors Flock to Ford's Plant at Sanand.' *Business Standard*, 31 July. Accessed 11 July 2016. Available at http://www.business-standard.com/article/companies/global-vendors-flock-to-ford-s-park-at-sanand-113072900847_1.html.

Datt, R. 2003. 'Lockouts Dominate Industrial Relations: A Case Study of West Bengal.' *Indian Journal of Labour Economics* 46 (4): 745–56.

Datta, V. C. 1986. 'Punjabi Refugees and the Urban Development of Greater Delhi.' In *Delhi Through the Ages: Selected Essays in Urban History, Culture and Society*, edited by R. E. Frykenberg. New Delhi: Oxford University Press.

De Haan, A. 1999. 'The *Badli* System in Industrial Labour Recruitment: Managers' and Workers' Strategies in Calcutta's Jute Industry.' In *The Worlds of Indian Industrial Labour*, edited by J. P. Parry, J. Breman and K. Kapadia. New Delhi: Sage.

De Soto, H. 1989. *The Other Path: The Economic Answer to Terrorism*. New York: Basic Books.

Denso. 2016. 'Presence in India.' Accessed 17 August 2016. Available at http://www.denso.co.in/Presence%20in%20India.aspx.

Dinhata, A. 2016. *Report on the Ongoing Struggle and Repression at Honda Motorcycle and Scooter Factory, Tapukara*. 5 March. Workers Solidarity Centre, Gurugram/Bawal. Accessed 3 June 2017. Available at http://sanhati.com/wp-content/uploads/2016/03/Honda-Workers-Report_WSC.pdf.

District of Gurugram (Gurgaon). 2016. 'Administrative Structure.' Accessed 17 March 2016. Available at http://gurgaon.gov.in/administrative.php.

Doner, R. F. and Wad, P. 2014. 'Financial Crises and Automotive Industry Development in Southeast Asia.' *Journal of Contemporary Asia* 44 (4): 664–87.

Dongsung Automotive. 2016. 'About Dongsung.' Accessed 18 August 2016. Available at http://dsprecision.net/.

Doval, P. 2010. 'Hero, Honda Split Terms Finalised.' *Times of India*, 16 December. Accessed 11 April 2012. Available at http://timesofindia.indiatimes.com/business/india-business/Hero-Honda-split-terms-finalized/articleshow/7109297.cms.

Dunn, B. and H. Radice. eds. 2006. *100 Years of Permanent Revolution: Results and Prospects*. London: Pluto Press.

Dupont, V. 2008. 'Slum Demolitions in Delhi since the 1990s: An Appraisal.' *Economic and Political Weekly* 43 (28): 79–87.

Dutta, D. and S. De. 2009. 'Political Economy of IT in India: Challenges and Policy Responses.' *International Journal of Interdisciplinary Social Sciences* 4 (9): 201–11.

Dymos Lear. 2016. 'About Us.' Accessed 18 August 2016. Available at http://dymos.co.in/aboutus1.aspx.

Economic Times. 2011. 'Volkswagen's German Suppliers are Still Setting up Production Facilities, Helping the OEM Reduce Costs.' *Economic Times*, 13 October. Accessed 2 September 2016. Available at http://articles.economictimes.indiatimes.com/2011–10–13/news/30275534_1_manufacturing-base-sheet-metal-volkswagen-india.

————. 2012. 'Vendors' Strike Hits Hero MotoCorp's Haridwar Unit.' *Economic Times*, 10 April. Accessed 12 March 2017. Available at http://articles.economictimes.indiatimes.com/2012–04–10/news/31318711_1_component-makers-unions-wheeler.

————. 2015a. 'Maruti Manesar Plant Temporary Workers Too Demand Wage Hike; Around 300 Protest Outside Factory.' *Economic Times*, 26 September. Accessed 12 February 2016. Available at http://auto.economictimes.indiatimes.com/news/industry/maruti-manesar-plant-temporary-workers-too-demand-wage-hike-around-300-protest-outside-factory/49117923.

————. 2015b. 'Maruti Suzuki Hikes Wages of Temporary Workers by 10 percent.' *Economic Times*, 21 October. Accessed 16 February 2016. Available at http://auto.economictimes.indiatimes.com/news/industry/maruti-suzuki-hikes-wages-of-temporary-workers-by-10/49483998.

————. 2017. 'Bajaj Auto Workers to Go on 2-day Hunger Strike on Jan 7.' *Economic Times*, 4 January. Accessed 13 February 2017. Available at http://auto.economictimes.indiatimes.com/news/two-wheelers/motorcycles/bajaj-auto-workers-to-go-on-2-day-hunger-strike-on-jan-7/56338143.

Eicher Motors. 2014. *Annual Report 2014*. New Delhi.

Endurance Group. 2016. 'Company Profile.' Accessed 18 August 2016. Available at https://www.endurancegroup.com/about-us/company-profile.

FMC (Ford Motor Company). 2015. *2015 Annual Report*. Dearborn, Michigan.

FMS (Faridabad Mazdoor Samachar). 2015. 'Wildcat Strike of Temporary Maruti Suzuki Workers in Manesar.' *Faridabad Mazdoor Samachar*, October.

Felipe J., E. Laviña and E. X. Fan. 2008. 'The Diverging Patterns of Profitability, Investment and Growth of China and India during 1980–2003.' *World Development* 36 (5): 741–74.

Fiat (Fiat SpA). 2013. *Annual Report 2013*. Turin (Italy).

Fine, B. 1992. 'Linkage, Agency and the State: The Case of South Korea.' Economics Working Paper, School of Oriental and African Studies (SOAS), University of London.

Fine, B. and Z. Rustomjee. 1996. *The Political Economy of South Africa: From Minerals-Energy Complex to Industrialisation*. London: Westview.

First Post. 2016. 'Strike at Tata Nano Sanand Plant Ends.' *First Post*, 15 June. Accessed 18 November 2016. Available at http://www.firstpost.com/business/strike-at-tata-nano-sanand-plant-ends-2692166.html?utm_source=FP_CAT_LATEST_NEWS.

Force Motors. 2015. *56th Annual Report, 2014–2015*. Pune (India).

Gabriel India. 2016. 'Company Overview.' Accessed 16 August 2016. Available at http://www.gabrielindia.com/overview/index.aspx.

Gallagher, K. S. 2006. *China Shifts Gears: Automakers, Oil, Pollution and Development*. Cambridge, Massachusetts: MIT Press.

Geertz, C. 1963. *Old Societies and New States: The Quest for Modernity in Asia and Africa*. New York: Free Press of Glencoe.

George, S. 2014. 'Deregulation and the Fading Labour Agenda: Evidence from Transnational Automobile Companies in India.' *Economic and Political Weekly* 49 (46): 19–21.

Gereffi, G. and M. Korzeniewicz. 1994. *Commodity Chains and Global Capitalism.* Westport, CT: Greenwood.

Gereffi G., J. Humphrey and T. Sturgeon. 2005. '*The Governance of Global Value Chains.' Review of International Political Economy* 12: 78–104.

Gopalakrishnan, R. 2017. 'The Draft Labour Code on Social Security: Workers' Concerns.' Accessed 28 May 2017. Available at https://kafila.online/2017/05/15/the-draft-labour-code-on-social-security-workers-concerns-ramapriya-gopalakrishnan/.

Gopalakrishnan, R. and J. Mirer. 2014. *Shiny Cars, Shattered Dreams.* New York: International Commission for Labour Rights. Accessed 19 December 2014. Available at http://www.laborcommission.org/files/uploads/2Shattered_Dreams_FINAL_website.pdf.

Gopalakrishnan, R. and K. R. Shyam Sundar. 2015. 'Who Cares for Labour, Anyway?' *The Hindu*, 21 May. Accessed 21 February 2016. Available at http://www.thehindubusinessline.com/opinion/who-cares-for-labour-anyway/article7232069.ece.

Government of Haryana. 2005. *Industrial Policy.* Chandigarh: Department of Industries and Commerce.

———. 2006. *Policy of Special Economic Zones.* Chandigarh: Department of Industries and Commerce.

———. 2007. *Eleventh Five Year Plan 2007–12 and Annual Plan 2007–08.* Chandigarh: Planning Department.

———. 2009a. 'Profile of District of Gurgaon.' Accessed 24 September 2009. Available at http: //gurgaon.nic.in/.

———. 2009b. *The Challenge of Employment in India: An Informal Economy Perspective, Volume 1.* New Delhi: NCEUS (National Commission for Enterprises in the Unorganised Sector).

Government of India. 2010. *Strategic Plan for Department of Heavy Industry.* New Delhi: Ministry of Heavy Industries and Public Enterprises.

———. 2011. *Annual Survey of Industries, 2008–09, Volume 1.* Kolkata: Central Statistical Office, Ministry of Statistics and Programme Implementation.

———. 2013. *Key Indicators of Employment and Unemployment in India, 2011–12: NSS 68th Round, July 2011–June 2012.* New Delhi: National Sample Survey Office, Ministry of Statistics and Programme Implementation.

———. 2016a . *Make in India: Sector Survey – Automobile.* Accessed 30 July 2016. Available at http://www.makeinindia.com/article/-/v/make-in-india-sector-survey-automobile.

———. 2016b. *Make in India: Sector Survey – Automobile Components.* Accessed 30 July 2016. Available at http://www.makeinindia.com/article/-/v/make-in-india-sector-survey-automobile-components.

———. 2017. *Special Economic Zones in India.* New Delhi: Department of Commerce, Ministry of Commerce and Industry. Accessed 19 May 2017. Available at http://www.sezindia.nic.in/index.asp.

Gordon, D., T. E. Weisskopf and S. E. Bowles. 1987. 'Power and Crisis: The Rise and Demise of the Post-War Social Structure of Accumulation.' In *The Imperilled Economy: Macroeconomics from a Left Perspective: Book 1*, edited by R. Cherry, C. D'Onofrio, C. Kurdas, T. R. Michl, F. Moseley, and M. I. Naples. New York: Union for Radical Political Economics.

Groupe Renault. 2015. *Drive the Change: 2015 Annual Report*. Paris.

Guha, R. 2007. *India after Gandhi: The History of the World's Largest Democracy*. New York: HarperCollins.

Gulyani, S. 2001. *Innovating with Infrastructure: The Automobile Industry in India*. London: Palgrave.

GWN (Gurgaon Workers News). 2009. *Newsletter 16*. Accessed 24 September 2009. Available at www.gurgaonworkersnews.wordpress.com.

———. 2011. *Newsletter 45*. Accessed 19 December 2009. Available at www. gurgaonworkersnews.wordpress.com.

———. 2014. *Newsletter 61*. Accessed 15 February 2009. Available at www.gurgaonworkersnews. wordpress.com.

HMC (Hyundai Motor Company). 2015. *Annual Report 2014*. Seoul.

———. 2016. 'Hyundai Motor India – Who Are We?' Accessed 18 August 2016. Available at http://www.hyundai.com/in/en/AboutUs/HyundaiMotorIndia/WhoWeAre/index.html.

Hammer, A. 2010. 'Trade Unions in a Constrained Environment: Workers' Voices from a New Industrial Zone in India.' *Industrial Relations Journal* 41 (2): 168–84.

Harriss-White, B. 2003. *India Working: Essays on Society and Economy*. Cambridge: Cambridge University Press.

———. 2005. *India's Market Society: Three Essays in Political Economy*. Gurugram: Three Essays Collective.

Harriss-White, B. and N. Gooptu. 2000. 'Mapping India's World of Unorganised Labour.' In *Socialist Register 2001: Working Classes, Global Realities*, edited by L. Panitch, C. Leys, G. Albo and D. Coates. London: Merlin Press.

Hart, K. 1973. 'Informal Income Opportunities and Urban Employment in Ghana.' *The Journal of Modern African Studies* 11 (1): 61–89.

Harvey, D. 2003. *The New Imperialism*. Oxford: Oxford University Press.

Hattari, R and R. S. Rajan. 2010. 'India as a Source of Outward Foreign Direct Investment.' *Oxford Development Studies* 38(4): 497–518.

Hensman, R. 2000. 'Organising against the Odds: Women in India's Informal Sector.' In *Socialist Register 2001: Working Classes, Global Realities*, edited by L. Panitch, C. Leys, G. Albo and D. Coates. London: Merlin Press.

Hero MotoCorp. 2015. *Manufacturing Happiness: 2014–2015 Annual Report*. New Delhi.

———. 2016. 'About the company.' Accessed 17 August 2016. Available at http://www. heromotocorp.com/en-in/about-us.php.

Hill, E. 2009. 'The Indian Industrial Relations System: Struggling to Address the Dynamics of a Globalising Economy.' *Journal of Industrial Relations* 51 (3): 395–410.

Hill, E. 2010. *Worker Identity, Agency and Economic Development: Women's Empowerment in the Indian Informal Economy*. London: Routledge.

Hindu Business Line. 2015. 'GM Exit Plan for Halol Unit Irks Workers.' *The Hindu (Business Line)*, 29 July. Accessed 17 July 2016. Available at http://www.thehindubusinessline.com/ companies/gm-exit-plan-for-halol-unit-irks-workers/article7477845.ece.

Hindustan Motors. 2015. *Annual Report and Statement of Accounts 2014–15.* Kolkata.

Hindustan Times. 2016. 'Top Chinese Carmakers like Great Wall, SAIC Motors steer toward India.' *Hindustan Times*, 7 April. Accessed 12 August, 2016. Available at http://www. hindustantimes.com/autos/top-chinese-carmakers-like-great-wall-saic-motors-steer-towards-india/story-ENwdauKFgAhK7lxzzXbdJP.html.

Hogg, R. 2015. 'Skoda: Simple Clever Logistics.' *Automotive Logistics*, 6 July. Accessed 12 August 2016. Available at http://automotivelogistics.media/intelligence/skoda-simply-clever-logistics.

Holmström, M. 1984. *Industry and Inequality: The Social Anthropology of Indian Labour.* Cambridge: Cambridge University Press.

Honda. 2015. *Annual Report 2015.* Tokyo.

Honda Cars. 2016. 'Company Profile.' Accessed 17 August 2016. Available at https://www. hondacarindia.com/about/companyprofile.aspx.

Hopkins, T. K. and I. Wallerstein. 1982. *World Systems Analysis: Theory and Methodology.* London: Sage.

Hwashin Automotive. 2016.'Overview.' Accessed 18 August 2016. Available at http://www. hwashinindia.com/.

International Labour Organisation (ILO). 1972. *Employment, Incomes and Equality: A Strategy for Increasing Productive Employment in Kenya.* Geneva.

————. 2002. *Women and Men in the Informal Economy: A Statistical Picture.* Geneva.

Industriall. 2011.'Workers Call off 51 Days Strike in General Motors India.' *Industriall*, 7 May. Accessed 3 January 2017. Available at http://www.industriall-union.org/archive/imf/workers-call-off-51-days-strike-in-general-motors-india.

————. 2016. 'Appeal Launched against Double Life Sentence for Pricol Workers.' *Industriall*, 12 February. Accessed 2 May 2017. Available at http://www.industriall-union.org/appeal-launched-for-pricol-auto-workers-in-india.

Irawati, D. and D. Charles. 2010. 'The Involvement of Japanese MNEs in the Indonesian Automotive Cluster.' *International Journal of Automotive Technology and Management* 10 (2/3): 180–96.

Irawati, D. and R. Rutten. 2011. 'The Java Automotive Industry: Between Keiretsu and Learning Region.' *Journal for Global Business Advancement* 4(3): 208–23.

Ishigami, E. 2004. 'Competition and Corporate Strategy in the Indian Automobile Industry, with Special Reference to Maruti Udyog Limited and Suzuki Motor Corporation.' Paper presented at the International Conference: 'A Comparison of Japanese Firm and Korean Firm in Indian Automobile Market', Centre for Area Studies, Gyeongsang National University, Jinjyu, South Korea, November.

JBM Group. 2016.'Company overview.' Accessed 17 August 2016. Available at http://www. jbm-group.com/about-overview.asp?lk=Overview.

Jagdambay Forgings. 2016. 'Profile and Overview.' Accessed 18 August 2016. Available at http://www.jagdambayforgings.co.in/crank-shafts-copper-precision-forgings-manufacturer-india.html.

Jaguar Land Rover. 2015. *Annual Report 2014–15.* Coventry.

Jessop, B. 1990. '*Regulation Theories in Retrospect and Prospect.*' *Economy and Society* 19 (2): 153–216.

Joshi, C. 1999. 'Hope and Despair: Textile Workers in Kanpur in 1937–38 and the 1990s.' In *The Worlds of Indian Industrial Labour*, edited by J. P. Parry, J. Breman and K. Kapadia. New Delhi: Sage.

Joshi, V. and I. M. D. Little. 1994. *India: Macroeconomics and Political Economy, 1961–91*. Washington DC: World Bank.

Jonas, A. E. G. 1996. 'Local Labour Control Regimes: Uneven Development and the Social Regulation of Production.' *Regional Studies* 30 (4): 323–38.

Jürgens, U. and M. Krzywdzinski. 2016. *New Worlds of Work: Varieties of Work in Car Factories in the BRIC Countries*. Oxford: Oxford University Press.

Kadokari, P. 2017. 'Maharashtra Government Amends Key Contract Labour Law, Trade Unions upset.' *Times of India*, 13 February. Accessed 13 March 2017. Available at http://timesofindia.indiatimes.com/city/mumbai/maharashtra-government-amends-key-contract-labour-law-trade-unions-upset/articleshow/57117571.cms.

Kalleberg, A. L. 2009. 'Precarious Work, Insecure Workers: Employment Relations in Transition.' *American Sociological Review* 74 (1): 1–22.

Kalleberg, A. L. and K. Hewison. 2013.'Precarious Work and the Challenge for Asia.' *American Behavioural Scientist* 57 (3): 271–88.

Kannan, S. 2016. 'General Motors puts $1 Billion India Plan "On Hold".' BBC News India, 26 July. Accessed 11 August 2016. Available at http://www.bbc.com/news/world-asia-india-36881177.

Khan, N. A. 2014. 'How S K Arya Established One of India's Biggest Auto Components Firms.' *Economic Times*, 11 June. Accessed 17 August 2016. Available at http://economictimes.indiatimes.com/industry/auto/news/auto-components/how-s-k-arya-established-indias-one-of-the-biggest-auto-component-firms-jbm-group/articleshow/36384206.cms.

———. 2015. 'New Wage Deal Promises Maruti Employees a Hike of up to 38 per cent.' *Economic Times*, 26 September. Accessed 13 February 2016. Available at http://auto.economictimes.indiatimes.com/news/industry/new-wage-deal-promises-maruti-employees-a-hike-of-up-to-38-percent/49109187.

———. 2016. 'Renault-Nissan Beats M&M as Third Largest PV Maker.' *Economic Times*, 1 August. Accessed 18 August 2016. Available at http://auto.economictimes.indiatimes.com/news/industry/renault-nissan-unseats-mm-as-3rd-largest-pv-maker-honda-outsells-tata-motors/53492787.

Kidron, M. 1965. *Foreign Investments in India*. London: Oxford University Press.

Kotz, D. M. 1987. 'Long Waves and Social Structure of Accumulation: A Critique and Re-interpretation.' *Review of Radical Political Economics* 19 (4): 16–38.

Kudaisya, M. 2009. '"A mighty adventure": Institutionalising the Idea of Planning in Post-colonial India, 1947–60.' *Modern Asian Studies* 43 (4): 939–78.

Kumar, A. 2008. 'Faltering National and Global Growth Prospects.' *Economic and Political Weekly* 43 (28): 15–19.

Kumar, R. 2014. 'Assembling a Stable Supply Structure.' *Automotive Logistics*, 17 December. Accessed 12 April 2016. *Available at:* http://automotivelogistics.media/intelligence/assembling-a-stable-supply-structure.

Kumari, L. 2008. 'Dismissed Employees beat CEO to Death.' *Times of India*, 23 September. Accessed 12 January 2016. Available at http://timesofindia.indiatimes.com/city/delhi/ Dismissed-employees-beat-CEO-to-death/articleshow/3513395.cms.

Lakhani, T., S. Kuruvilla, S. and A. Avgar. 2013. 'From the Firm to the Network: Global Value Chains and Employment Relations Theory.' *British Journal of Industrial Relations* 51 (3): 440–72.

Lal Das, K. S. and S. George. 2006. 'Labour Practices and Working Conditions in TNCs: The Case of Toyota Kirloskar in India.' In *Labour in Globalising Asian Corporations: A Picture of Struggle*, edited by D. Chang, 273–302. Hong Kong: Asia Monitor Resource Centre.

Le Mons Walker, K. 2008. 'Neoliberalism on the Ground in Rural India: Predatory Growth, Agrarian Crisis, Internal Colonisation and the Intensification of Class Struggle.' *Journal of Peasant Studies* 35 (4): 557–620.

Lee, C. K. 2007. *Against the Law: Labor Protests in China's Rustbelt and Sunbelt*. University of California Press.

Lerche, J. 2007. 'A Global Alliance against Forced Labour? Unfree Labour, Neo-liberal Globalization and the International Labour Organization.' *Journal of Agrarian Change* 7: 425–52.

———. 2011. 'The Unfree Labour Category and Unfree Labour Estimates: A Continuum with Low-end Labour Relations.' *Working Paper No. 10, Manchester Papers in Political Economy*. Available at http://eprints.soas.ac.uk/14855/.

Levien, M. 2011. 'Special Economic Zones and Accumulation by Dispossession in India.' *Journal of Agrarian Change* 11 (4): 454–83.

———. 2012. 'The Land Question: Special Economic Zones and the Political Economy of Dispossession in India.' *Journal of Peasant Studies* 39 (3/4): 933–69.

Lewis, W. A. 1954. 'Economic Development with Unlimited Supplies of Labour.' *The Manchester School* 22: 139–91.

Lumax. 2016.'Company Overview.' Accessed 14 July 2016. Available at http://www. lumaxindustries.com/.

MRF. 2016.'Who We Are – Company Overview.' Accessed 12 August 2016. Available at http://www.mrftyres.com/overview.

MSIL (Maruti Suzuki India Limited). 2015. *Annual Report 2014–15*. New Delhi.

MacDuffie, J. P. 1995. 'Human Resource Bundles and Manufacturing Performance: Organisational Logic and Flexible Production Systems in the World Auto Industry.' *Industrial and Labour Relations Review* 48 (2): 197–221.

Madhavan, N. 2011. 'Nurturing the Family.' *Business Today*, 12 June. Accessed 11 March 2017. Available at http://www.businesstoday.in/magazine/case-study/tvs-group-labour-problem/ story/15784.html.

Magneti Marelli. 2016. 'Company locations.' Accessed 17 August 2016. Available at http:// www.magnetimarelli.com/company/locations.

Mahindra. 2016. *Annual Report 2015–16*. Mumbai.

Mahle Behr India. 2016. 'Company Overview.' Accessed 18 August 2016. Available at http:// www.mahlebehrindia.com/overview/index.aspx.

Maiti, D. and K. Sen. 2010. 'The Informal Sector in India: A Means of Exploitation or Accumulation?' *Journal of South Asian Development* 5 (1): 1–13.

Makino Auto. 2016. 'Corporate Profile.' Accessed 12 June 2016. Available at http://www.makino.in/thecompany.htm.

Maloney, W. F. 2004. 'Informality Revisited.' *World Development* 32 (7): 1159–78.

Mathur, S. 2016. 'Renault Kwid: The Sum of all Parts.' *Auto Car Professional*, 13 January. Accessed 16 August 2016. Available at http://www.autocarpro.in/features/kwid-sum-10137.

Mazumdar, I. 2007. *Women Workers and Globalisation: Emergent Contradictions in India.* New Delhi, Centre for Women's Development Studies.

Mazumdar, S. 2010. 'Indian Capitalism: A Case that Doesn't Fit?' Research Paper, Institute for Studies in Industrial Development, New Delhi. Accessed 10 December 2013. Available at http://mpra.ub.unimuenchen.de/28162/1/MPRA_paper_28162.pdf.

McCartney, M. 2009. *India: The Political Economy of Growth, Stagnation and the State, 1951–2007.* London: Routledge.

Mehta, N. 2016. 'On Likely Closure of GM Halol Plant in Gujarat.' *Centre for Workers Education.* Accessed 24 February 2017. Available at https://workerscentre.wordpress.com/2016/01/13/on-likely-closure-of-general-motor-halol-plant-in-gujarat/.

Menon, N and A. Nigam. 2007. *Power and Contestation: India since 1989.* London: Zed Books.

Mezzadri, A. 2008. 'The Rise of Neoliberal Globalisation and the "New Old" Social Regulation of Labour: A Case of Delhi Garment Sector.' *Indian Journal of Labour Economics* 51 (4): 603–18.

Mezzadri, A. 2016a. *The Sweatshop Regime: Labouring Bodies, Exploitation and Garments 'Made in India'.* Cambridge: Cambridge University Press.

———. 2016b. 'Class, Gender and the Sweatshop: on the Nexus Between Labour Commodification and Exploitation.' *Third World Quarterly* 37 (10): 1877–900.

Mitra, M. 2013. 'How Toyota Brought its Famed Manufacturing Method to India.' *Economic Times*, 5 April. Accessed 27 June 2016. Available at http://articles.economictimes.indiatimes.com/2013-04-05/news/38279447_1_tkm-dealership-toyota-motor-corporation/2.

Monaco, L. 2015. 'Bringing Operaismo to Gurgaon: A Study of Labour Composition and Resistance Practices in the Indian Auto Industry.' PhD Thesis, SOAS University of London.

———. 2017. 'Where Lean May Shake: Challenges to Casualization in the Indian Auto Industry.' *Global Labour Journal* 8 (2): 120–38.

Mondal, D. 2015. 'Aim to achieve 90 per cent Localisation in Long-term: Kodumudi of Volkswagen India.' *Business Today*, 16 June. Accessed 16 August 2016. Available at http://www.businesstoday.in/sectors/auto/aim-to-achieve-90percent-localisation-in-long-term-kodumudi-of-volkswagen-india/story/220626.html.

Mukherjee, S. 2014. 'Maruti to Absorb all Contract Workers in Two Years.' *Business Standard*, 23 August. Accessed 13 November 2014. Available at http://www.business-standard.com/article/companies/maruti-to-absorb-all-contract-workers-in-two-years-114082300031_1.html.

Nachane, D. N. 2009. 'The Fate of India Un-incorporated.' *Economic and Political Weekly* 44 (13): 115–22.

Narayanan, B. G. and N. Vashisht. 2008. Determinants of the Competitiveness of the Indian Auto Industry. *ICRIER Working Paper 201.* New Delhi: Indian Council for Research on International Economic Relations.

Nathan, D. 2016. 'Governance Types and Employment Systems.' In *Labour in Global Value Chains in Asia*, edited by D. Nathan, M. Tewari and S. Sarkar, 479–502. New Delhi: Cambridge University Press.

Natsuda, K., K. Otsuka and J. Thoburn. 2015. 'Dawn of Industrialisation? The Indonesian Automotive Industry.' *Bulletin of Indonesian Economic Studies* 51 (1): 47–68.

Neilson, J. 2014. 'Value Chains, Neoliberalism and Development Practice: The Indonesian Experience.' *Review of International Political Economy* 21 (1): 38–69.

New Indian Express. 2016. 'Tata Motors lifts Lockout at Dharwad.' *New Indian Express*, 7 March. Accessed 16 February 2017. Available at http://www.newindianexpress.com/states/karnataka/Tata-Motors-Lifts-Lockout-at-Dharwad/2016/03/07/article3313963.ece.

Newmans, S. 2012. 'Global Commodity Chains and Global Value Chains.' In *The Elgar Companion to Marxist Economics*, edited by B. Fine and A. Saad-Filho. London: Edward Elgar.

Nippon Seiki. 2016. 'Overseas Companies.' Accessed 18 August 2016. Available at http://www.nippon-seiki.co.jp/global/company/group_company_abr/.

Nowack, J. 2016. 'Strikes and Labor Unrest in the Automobile Industry in India: The Case of Maruti Suzuki India Limited.' *Working USA* 19 (3): 419–36.

Organisation Internationale des Constructeurs d'Automobiles (OICA). 2014. 'Production Statistics.' Accessed 12 November 2015. Available at http://oica.net/category/production-statistics/.

Omr Bagla. 2016. 'About Us: Omr Group and Bagla Group.' Accessed 16 June 2016. Available at http://www.omrbagla.com/about.html.

Padhi, R. 2007. 'Forced Evictions and Factory Closures: Rethinking Citizenship and Rights of Working Class Women in Delhi.' *Indian Journal of Gender Studies* 14 (1): 73–92.

Pandit, V. 2012. 'GM India to Source Components Worth $1 billion from Domestic Suppliers.' *The Hindu (Business Line)*, 23 March. Accessed 23 August 2016. Available at http://www.thehindubusinessline.com/economy/gm-india-to-source-components-worth-1-b-from-domestic-suppliers/article3205745.ece.

Paret, M. 2016. 'Towards a Precarity Agenda.' *Global Labour Journal* 7 (2): 111–22.

Park, A. and F. Cai. 2011. 'The Informalisation of the Chinese Labour Market.' In *From Iron Rice Bowl to Informalisation; Markets, States and Workers in Changing China*, edited by S. Kuruvilla, C. K. Lee and M. E. Gallagher. Ithaca, NY: Cornell University Press.

Pathak, M. and N. Rodricks. 2016. 'General Motors India defers Halol Plant Closure until March 2017.' *LiveMint*, 24 June, Accessed 21 August 2016. Available at http://www.livemint.com/Companies/oyYfR414UpADH5LOPOSlHI/General-Motors-India-defers-Halol-plant-closure-until-March.html.

Patnaik, U. ed. 1990. *Agrarian Relations and Accumulation: The 'Mode of Production' Debate in India.* Bombay: Oxford University Press.

Pattenden, J. 2016. 'Working at the Margins of Global Production Networks: Local Labour Control Regimes and Rural-based Labourers in South India.' *Third World Quarterly* 37 (10): 1809–33.

Pavlinek, P. 2002. 'Transformation of the Central and East European Passenger Car Industry: Selective Peripheral Integration through Foreign Direct Investment.' *Environment and Planning A* 34 (9): 1685–709.

———. 2014. 'Whose Success? The State–Foreign Capital Nexus and the Development of the Automotive Industry in Slovakia.' *European Urban and Regional Studies* 1–23.

Pavlinek, P. and L. Janak. 2007. 'Regional Restructuring of the Skoda Auto Supplier Network in the Czech Republic.' *European Urban and Regional Studies* 14 (2): 133–55.

Pavlinek, P. and J. Zenka. 2010. 'Upgrading in the Automotive Industry: Firm-level Evidence from Central Europe.' *Journal of Economic Geography* 1–28.

Pawar, T. 2009. 'Nashik Strike Causes Production Losses of ₹150 crore to Mahindra's Vendors.' *Business Standard*, 14 May. Accessed 14 August 2016. Available at http://www.business-standard.com/article/economy-policy/nashik-strike-causes-production-losses-of-rs-150-crore-to-mahindra-s-vendors-109051400030_1.html.

———. 2013. 'Workers of Mahindra and Mahindra Call Off Strike.' *Times of India*, 8 March. Accessed 2 February 2017. Available at http://timesofindia.indiatimes.com/city/nashik/Workers-of-Mahindra-Mahindra-call-off-strike/articleshow/18856440.cms.

Perry, G. E., W. F. Maloney, O. S. Arias, P. Fajnzylber, A. D. Mason and J. Saavedra-Chanduvi. 2007. *Informality: Exit and Exclusion*. Washington DC: The World Bank.

Piaggio Group. 2015. *Financial Statements 2015*. Pisa (Italy).

Picherit, D. 2012. 'Migrant Labourers' Struggles between Village and Urban Migration Sites: Labour Standards, Rural Development and Politics in South India.' *Global Labour Journal* 3 (1): 143–62.

Pinglé, V. 1999. *Rethinking the Developmental State: India's Industry in Comparative Perspective*. New Delhi: Oxford University Press.

Portes, A. and K. Hoffman. 2003. 'Latin American Class Structures: Their Composition and Change During the Neoliberal Era.' *Latin American Research Review* 38 (1): 41–82.

Posthuma, A. and D. Nathan. eds. 2010. *Labour in Global Production Networks in India*. New Delhi: Oxford University Press.

Premier Ltd. 2015. *69th Annual Report 2014–15*. Pune (India).

Price, J. 1995. 'Lean Production at Suzuki and Toyota: A Historical Perspective.' In *Lean Work: Empowerment and Exploitation in the Global Auto Industry*, edited by S. Babson, 81–108. Detroit: Wayne State University Press.

Pyke, F. and W. Sengenberger. eds. 1992. *Industrial Districts and Local Economic Regeneration*. Geneva: International Institute for Labour Studies.

Radhakrishna, R. 2009. 'Agricultural Growth, Employment and Poverty.' In *Growth, Employment and Labour Markets: Perspectives in the Era of Globalisation in India*, edited by J. Krishnamurty and R. P. Mamgain. New Delhi: Daanish Books.

Raj. A. 2016a. 'Maruti Suzuki Steps up Hiring of Contract Workers.' *LiveMint*, 17 August. Accessed 17 March 2017. Available at www.livemint.com/Companies/E1c3nEBpJkD8I4YFl1RrPN/Maruti-Suzuki-steps-up-hiring-of-contract-workers.html.

———. 2016. 'India Car Firms Form Consortium for Electric Vehicle Components.' *LiveMint*, 15 June. Accessed 12 March 2017. Available at http://www.livemint.com/Industry/kxHCpLgEYd2L9WBuwJESYJ/Car-firms-collaborate-for-electric-vehicles-cause.html.

Raj, A. 2017. 'Peugeot Coming Back to India in a Humble Way: Carlos Tavares.' *LiveMint*, 26 January. Accessed 3 April 2017. Available at http://www.livemint.com/Companies/LQns43r7vhgzJ5GswzlQNK/Peugeot-coming-back-to-India-in-a-humble-way-Carlos-Tavares.html.

Rajhans Pressings. 2016. 'About Us.' Accessed 18 August 2016. Available at http://www.rajhanspressing.com/about-us.html.

Rakshit, M. 2009. 'India amidst the Global Crisis.' *Economic and Political Weekly* 44 (13): 94–106.

Ram Mohan, T. T. 2009. 'The Impact of the Crisis on the Indian Economy.' *Economic and Political Weekly* 44 (13): 107–14.

Rani, U. and P. Belser. 2012. 'Low Pay Among Wage Earners and the Self-Employed in India.' *International Labour Review* 151: 221–42.

Rao, H. 2016. 'Jat Quota: High Court Dismisses Petition, Decks Cleared for Notifying New Law.' *Hindustan Times*, 16 April. Accessed 14 July 2016. Available at http://www.hindustantimes.com/india/jat-reservation-haryana-govt-set-to-notify-new-quota-law/story-hRwVM9v8jhpbS4jY50tunL.html.

Rasandik. 2016. 'About Rasandik Engineering Industries India Limited.' Accessed 12 August 2016. Available at http://www.rasandik.com/.

Ray, S. and P. K. Ray. 2011.'Production Innovation for the People's Car in an Emerging Economy.' *Technovation* 31 (5/6): 216–27.

Riisgaard, L. and N. Hammer. 2011. 'Prospects for Labour in Global Value Chains: Labour Standards in the Cut Flower and Banana Industries.' *British Journal of Industrial Relations* 49 (1): 168–90.

Rockman Industries. 2016. 'About Rockman Industries.' Accessed 17 August 2016. Available at http://www.rockman.in/about.php.

Rosenberg, J. 2006. 'Why is There No International Historical Sociology?' *European Journal of International Relations* 12 (3): 307–40.

———. 2009. 'Basic Problems in the Theory of Uneven and Combined Development: A Reply to the CRIA Forum.' *Cambridge Review of International Affairs* 22 (1): 107–10.

Ramaswamy, E. A. 1996. 'Wealth and Power Convert into Status: The Impact of Society on Industry.' In *Social Structure and Change: Complex Organizations and Urban Communities – Volume 3*, edited by A. M. Shah, B. S. Baviskar and E. A. Ramaswamy. New Delhi: Sage.

Roy, T. 2008. 'Sardars, Jobbers, Kanganies: The Labour Contractor and Indian Economic History.' *Modern Asian Studies*, 42: 971–98.

Society of Indian Automobile Manufacturers (SIAM). 2016. 'Industry Statistics.' Accessed 15 August 2016. Available at http://www.siamindia.com/statistics.aspx?mpgid=8&pgidtrail=9.

SIAM/GoI. 2015. *Automotive Mission Plan 2016–2026: A Curtain Raiser*. New Delhi: Society of Indian Automobile Manufacturers Ministry of Heavy Industries.

Saket MTC. 2016. 'About Saket Metal Technocraft Private Limited.' Accessed 9 July 2016. Available at http://www.saketmtc.com/our-profile.html.

Sako, M. 1992. *Price, Quality and Trust: Inter-firm Relations in Britain and Japan*. Cambridge: Cambridge University Press.

Saleem, S. Z. 2015. 'After Maruti Suzuki: Honda Motorcycle, Hero MotoCorp Negotiate Wage Pact.' *Financial Express*, 23 October. Accessed 15 August 2016. Available at http://www.financialexpress.com/article/industry/companies/hmsi-hero-negotiate-wage-pact/155394/.

Sampat, P. 2008. 'Special Economic Zones in India.' *Economic and Political Weekly* 43 (28): 25–29.

Saraswati, J. 2012. *Dot.compradors: Power and Policy in the Development of the Indian Software Industry.* Chicago: University of Chicago Press.

Satyam Auto Components. 2016. 'Company Profile.' Accessed 17 August 2016. Available at http://www.satyamauto.in/.

Scania. 2014. *Annual Report 2014.* Södertälje (Sweden).

Scully, B. 2016. 'Precarity North and South: A Southern Critique of Guy Standing.' *Global Labour Journal* 7 (2): 160–73.

Selwyn, B. 2012. 'Beyond Firm-centrism: Re-intregrating Labour and Capitalism into Global Commodity Chain Analysis.' *Journal of Economic Geography* 12 (1): 205–26

———. 2013. 'Karl Marx, Class Struggle and Labour-centred Development.' *Global Labour Journal,* 4 (1): 48–70.

———. 2016a. 'Theory and Practice of Labour-centred Development.' *Third World Quarterly* 37 (6): 1035–52.

———. 2016b. 'Global Value Chains and Human Development: A Class-relational Framework.' *Third World Quarterly* 37 (10): 1768–86.

Sen, S. and B. Dasgupta. 2009. *Unfreedom and Waged Work: Labour in India's Manufacturing Industry.* New Delhi: Sage.

Setco Automotive. 2016. 'About Setco.' Accessed 20 August 2016. Available at http://www.setcoauto.com/about-setco/.

Seth, S. 2010. 'Bajaj Auto Gains from Outsourced Non-critical Manufacturing.' *Live Mint,* 13 April. Accessed 12 August 2016. Available at http://www.livemint.com/Companies/tJEDajAT1nWiRZ9P5ciLxH/Bajaj-Auto-gains-from-outsourced-noncritical-manufacturing.html.

———. 2014. 'Mahindra to Reduce Supplier Base as Part of New Sourcing Strategy.' *Live Mint,* 6 October. Accessed 3 September 2016. Available at http://www.livemint.com/Compampanies/1FOq6BpomNLkmJLIsPLRSK/Mahindra-to-reduce-supplier-base-as-part-of-new-sourcing-str.html.

Sethi, A. 2017. '13 Guilty of Murder in 2012 Maruti Factory Riot that Killed One, 117 Acquitted.' *Hindustan Times,* 17 March. Accessed 2 April 2017. Available at http://www.hindustantimes.com/gurgaon/13-guilty-of-murder-in-2012-maruti-factory-riot-that-killed-one-117-acquitted/story-0OEhWKQplgDVzbkNcS008H.html.

Sharma, K. L. 1997. *Social Stratification in India: Issues and Themes.* New Delhi: Sage.

Shriya, S. 2013. 'Uttarakhand: Report of Workers' Struggle in ASAL and their Arrest.' *Sanhati,* 21 June. Accessed 15 June 2014. Available at http://sanhati.com/articles/7257/.

Shyam, A. 2015. 'Maruti Creates History: Overtakes Japanese Parent Suzuki in Market Value.' 22 July. Accessed 3 January 2016. Available at http://auto.economictimes.indiatimes.com/news/auto-finance/maruti-creates-history-overtakes-japanese-parent-suzuki-in-market-value/48167731.

Shyam Sundar, K. R. 2005. 'State in Industrial Relations System in India: From Corporatist to Neoliberal?' *Indian Journal of Labour Economics* 48 (4): 917–37.

Shyam Sundar, K. R. 2012a. *Contract Labour in India: Issues and Perspectives.* New Delhi: Daanish Books.

————. 2012b. 'Counter-tendencies to Labour Flexibility Regime in India: Achieving Decent Work for Non-Regular Workers.' *Indian Journal of Labour Economics* 55 (4): 551–72.

Singh, N. 2008. 'Services-led Industrialisation in India: Assessment and Lessons.' In *Industrial Development for the Twenty-First Century*, edited by D. O'Connor and M. Kjöllerström. London: Orient Longman/Zed/United Nations.

Singh, N. and M. Kaur Sapra. 2007. 'Liberalisation in Trade and Finance: India's Garment Sector'. In *Trade Liberalisation and India's Informal Economy*, edited by B. Harriss-White and A. Sinha. New Delhi: Oxford University Press.

Silver, B. 2003. *Forces of Labor: Workers Movements and Globalisation since 1870*. Cambridge: Cambridge University Press.

Skoda. 2015. *Skoda Annual Report 2015*. Mladá Boleslav (Czech Republic).

Sogefi Group. 2016. 'The Group's Joint Ventures.' *Sogefi Group*. Accessed 15 September 2016. Available at http://www.sogefigroup.com/en/sogefi-group/joint-ventures/main.html.

Srivastava, S. and M. Handique. 2009. 'Gurgaon Workers Plan Stir After Violence at Rico Auto.' *LiveMint*, 19 October. Accessed 25 June 2010. Available at http://www.livemint.com/Articles/2009/10/19214234/Gurgaon-workers-plan-stir-afte.html.

Starosta, G. 2010. 'The Outsourcing of Manufacturing and the Rise of Giant Global Contractors: A Marxian Approach to Some Recent Transformations of Global Value Chains.' *New Political Economy* 15 (4): 543–63.

Sturgeon, T., J. Van Biesebroeck and G. Gereffi. 2008. 'Value Chains, Networks and Clusters: Reframing the Global Automotive Industry.' *Journal of Economic Geography* 8 (3): 297–321.

Subramaniam, B. 2015. 'BMW Joins Make in India Wagon; Increases Localisation to 50 Percent,' *Business Standard*, 7 May. Accessed 20 August 2016. Available at http://www.business-standard.com/article/news-cd/bmw-joins-make-in-india-wagon-increases-localisation-to-50-percent-115050701212_1.html.

Subramanian, D. 1997. 'Bangalore Public Sector Strike: A Critical Appraisal.' *Economic and Political Weekly* 32 (15/16) .

Subramanian, A. and D. Rodrik. 2008. 'From "Hindu Growth" to Productivity Surge: The Mystery of the Indian Growth Transition.' In *India's Turn: Understanding the Economic Transformation*, edited by A. Subramanian. New Delhi: Oxford University Press.

Subros. 2016. 'About Subros.' *Subros*. Accessed 17 August 2016. Available at http://www.subros.com/about.html.

Sudarshan, R. M. and S. Bhattacharya. 2009. 'Through the Magnifying Glass: Women's Work and Labour Force Participation in Urban Delhi.' *Economic and Political Weekly* 44 (48): 59–66.

Standing, G. 2008. 'The ILO: An Agency for Globalization?' *Development and Change* 39 (3): 355–84.

————. 2011. *The Precariat: The New Dangerous Class*. London: Bloomsbury Academic.

————. 2014. *A Precariat Charter: From Denizens to Citizens*. London: Bloomsbury.

————. 2016. 'The Precariat, Class and Progressive Politics: A Response.' *Global Labour Journal* 7 (2): 189–200.

Sugrue, T. J. 2005. *The Origins of the Urban Crisis: Race and Inequality in Post-war Detroit*. Princeton: Princeton University Press.

Suprajit. 2016. 'About the Group.' Accessed 18 August 2016. Available at http://www.suprajit.com/The-Group.

Sundram Fasteners. 2017. 'About us.' Accessed 12 March 2017. Available at http://www.sundram.com/about-us.php.

Suresh, T. G. 2010. 'Cost-cutting Pressures and Labour Relations in Tamil Nadu's Automobile Components Supply Chain.' In *Labour in Global Production Networks in India*, edited by A. Posthuma and D. Nathan. New Delhi: Oxford University Press.

Swider, S. 2015. *Building China: Informal Work and the New Precariat*. Ithaca, NY: Cornell University Press.

TKSA. 2016. 'Members – Toyota Kirloskar Suppliers Association.' Accessed 12 August 2016. Available at http://tksa.in/members/bangalore.html.

TVS. 2016. *24th Annual Report, 2015–2016*. Chennai.

Takata Automotive. 2016. 'Company History.' Accessed 18 August 2016. Available at http://www.takata.com/en/about/history.html.

Tata Motors. 2016. *Towards Tomorrow: 71st Annual Report, 2015–2016*. Mumbai.

Taylor, P. K. Newsome and A. Rainnie. 2013. 'Putting Labour in its Place: Global Value Chains and Labour Process Analysis.' *Competition and Change* 17 (1): 1–5.

Tenneco Automotive. 2010. 'Tenneco Opens New Manufacturing Plant in Chennai, India.' Accessed 18 August 2016. Available at http://www.tenneco.com/_tenneco_opens_new_manufacturing_plant_in_chennai_india/.

Thakkar, K. 2015. 'Maruti Wins the Majority, Corners Highest Market Share in Over a Decade'. *Economic Times*, 11 August. Accessed 8 September 2015. Available at http://auto.economictimes.indiatimes.com/news/passenger-vehicle/cars/maruti-wins-the-majority-corners-highest-market-share-in-over-a-decade/48438555.

———. 2016. 'Tata Motors Union Awaits Tata Blessings on New Wage Agreement.' *Economic Times*, 20 December. Accessed 12 January 2017. Available at http://auto.economictimes.indiatimes.com/news/passenger-vehicle/cars/tata-motors-union-awaits-tata-blessings-on-new-wage-settle-agreement/56075957.

Thakkar, K. 2017a. 'Half a Dozen Carmakers like Kia, Daihatsu, SAIC Waiting to Enter India.' *Economic Times*, 8 June. Accessed 12 June 2017. Available at http://auto.economictimes.indiatimes.com/news/passenger-vehicle/cars/half-a-dozen-car-makers-like-kia-daihatsu-saic-waiting-to-enter-india/56324300.

———. 2017b. 'Global Auto Companies Heads Drive into India.' *Economic Times*, 15 March. Accessed 6 April 2017. Available at http://economictimes.indiatimes.com/industry/auto/news/industry/global-auto-companies-heads-drive-into-india/articleshow/57639612.cms.

The Hindu. 2011. 'Strike Ends at Caparo Sriperumbudur Unit.' *The Hindu*, 5 December. Accessed 3 December 2016. Available at http://www.thehindu.com/business/strike-ends-at-caparo-sriperumbudur-unit/article2689971.ece.

Thyssenkrupp India. 2016. 'Thyssenkrupp in India.' Accessed 18 August 2016. Available at https://www.thyssenkrupp-india.com/en/startpage.html.

Times of India. 2017. 'Negotiations on with Workers: Tata.' *Times of India*, 5 June. Accessed 16 June 2017. Available at http://timesofindia.indiatimes.com/city/ahmedabad/negotiations-on-with-workers-tata-motors/articleshow/58991441.cms.

Tiwari, S. 2016. 'Jat Agitation Spreads to Gurgaon as Protestors Block Major Roads.' *Indian Express*, 21 February. Accessed 12 July 2016. Available at http://indianexpress.com/article/india/india-news-india/jat-agitation-spreads-to-gurgaon-as-protesters-block-major-roads/.

Trotsky, L. 1922. *1905*. Accessed 20 February 2008. Available at http: //marxists.org/archive/trotsky/works/index.htm.

————. 1934. *History of the Russian Revolution, Volume I: The Overthrow of Tsarism*. London: Victor Gollancz.

————. 1962. *The Permanent Revolution* and *Results and Prospects*. London: New Park.

UNCTAD. 2013. *World Investment Report 2013: Global Value Chains – Investment and Trade for Development*. New York: United Nations.

Umbrajkar, M. 2013. 'Johnson Controls acquires Tata Johnson Controls.' *Times of India*. Accessed 19 August 2016. Available at http://timesofindia.indiatimes.com/business/india-business/Johnson-Controls-acquires-Tata-Johnson-Controls/articleshow/20396228.cms.

Upadhya, C. and A. R. Vasavi. 2006. *Work, Culture and Sociality in the Indian IT Industry: A Sociological Study*. Final Report to the Indo-Dutch Program for Alternatives in Development, Indian Institute of Science, Bangalore. Accessed 12 February 2008. Available at www.iisc.ernet.in/nias/idpadfinalreport.pdf.

Van Wersch, H. 1992. *The Bombay Textile Strike, 1982–83*. Bombay: Oxford University Press.

Varroc Group. 2016. 'Company Overview.' Accessed 16 July 2016. Available at http://www.varrocgroup.com/overview.

Visteon. 2016. 'Company Profile.' Accessed 16 August 2016. Available at http://www.visteon.com/company/profile.html.

Volkswagen AG. 2015. *Moving People: 2015 Annual Report*. Wolfsburg (Germany).

Volvo Group. 2015. *Annual and Sustainability Report*. Göteborg (Sweden).

Vosko, L. 2010. *Managing the Margins: Gender, Citizenship and the International Regulation of Precarious Employment*. Oxford: Oxford University Press.

Wabco. 2016. 'Wabco India.' Accessed 20 August 2016. Available at http://www.wabco-auto.com/wabcoindia/home/.

Williams, C. C., and M. A. Lansky. 2013. 'Informal Employment in Developed and Developing Economies: Perspectives and Policy Responses.' *International Labour Review* 152 (3/4): 355–80.

Williamson, O. E. 2000. 'The New Institutional Economics: Taking Stock, Looking Ahead.' *Journal of Economic Literature* 38 (3): 595–613.

Womack, J. P., D. T. Jones and D. Roos. 1990. *The Machine that Changed the World*. New York: Scribner.

Woojin Automotive. 2016a . 'Corporate Overview.' Accessed 18 August 2016. Available at http://www.woojinengineering.com/aboutus/woojin-overview.php.

————. 2016b. 'About Woory Industrial.' Accessed 18 August 2016. Available at http://www.woory.com/eng/about/abouts1_01.asp.

Wright, E. O. 2000. 'Working-class Power, Capitalist-class Interests and Class Compromise.' *American Journal of Sociology* 105 (4): 957–1002.

————. 2016. 'Is the Precariat a Class?' *Global Labour Journal* 7 (2): 123–35.

Yadav, A. 2015. 'Workers' Problems: The More Things Change at Maruti's Manesar Plant, the More They Stay the Same.' *Scroll.in*, 14 December. Accessed 4 April 2016. Available at http://scroll.in/article/773241/workers-problems-the-more-things-change-at-marutis-manesar-plant-the-more-they-stay-the-same.

Yapp Automotive. 2016. 'Company Profile.' *Yapp Automotive.* Accessed 20 August 2016. Available at http://www.yapp.com/en/gsgk/gsjj/A040101web_1.htm.

Yeung, H. W. 2015. 'Regional Development in the Global Economy: A Dynamic Perspective of Strategic Coupling in Global Production Networks.' *Regional Science: Policy & Practice* 7 (1): 1–23.

Yeung, H. W. and N. M. Coe. 2015. 'Towards a Dynamic Theory of Global Production Networks.' *Economic Geography* 91 (1): 29–58.

Z. F Hero. 2016. 'Chassis Systems.' Accessed 20 August 2016. Available at http://www. heromotors.com/index.php?option=com_content&view=article&id=79&Itemid=80.

Zhang, L. 2015. *Inside China's Automobile Factories: The Politics of Labor and Worker Resistance.* New York: Cambridge University Press.

Index

Aathi Thamizhar Peravai (ATP), 121
AGC Automotive, 50
All-India Central Council of Trade Unions
(AICCTU), 119
All-India Trade Union Congress
(AITUC), 114, 165
American automotive OEMs, 18
apprentices, 218
Apprenticeship Act, 101
Asahi India, 45
Ashok Leyland, 57
Ashutosh Rubber, 53
Asia, auto-producing regions in, 37
auto assembly manufacturing, 9
auto-based global value chains, 15
Automotive Components Manufacturers
Association of India (ACMA), 137
automotive global production networks,
17–23
automotive manufacturers in NCR,
149–158
average proportion of contract labour,
155–156
female labour force participation, 156
hiring and employment relations
practices, 151
wage rates, 156–158
Automotive Mission Plan 2006- 2016
(AMP-1), 96
Automotive Mission Plan 2016-2026
(AMP-2), 96–97, 197
Automotive Mission Plans, 34
Auto Sector Skill Development Council, 97
auto workers, 34
data collection (field research and
interviews), 137–139

Bajaj Auto, 58–60, 123
export share, 58–59
factories, 58
industrial conflict at, 124
motorcycle and three-wheeler
production volume, 59
regular workforce, 58
suppliers, 60
Bellsonica, 45
BharatBenz, 55, 57, 119
Bharatiya Janata Party (BJP), 165
Bharatiya Kamdar Ekta Sangh (BKES),
128
Bharatiya Mazdoor Sangh (BMS), 165
Bharat Seats, 45
Bhargava, R.C., 197
Bidi Workers Welfare Cess Act 1976, 100
BMW, 119
passenger cars and Sports Utility
Vehicles (SUVs), 1
Bosch India, 16, 69
BRIC (Brazil, Russia, India, China)
economies, auto manufacturing in,
10
Building and Other Construction Workers'
Welfare Cess Act 1996, 100
buyer-driven commodity chain, 12–13

Caparo Engineering India, 123
Caparo Maruti, 45–46
captive governance, 13
casual labour system, 32
casual workers, 215–216
Central Trade Union Organisations
(CTUOs), 114, 116, 165–166
Centre of Indian Trade Unions (CITU),
114, 165

Chakan Special Economic Zone (C-SEZ), 39–41, 57–67, 134, 198, 226
  Bajaj Auto, 58–60
  employment relations in, 119–123
  FCA India Automobiles Private Limited (Fiat India), 64–67
  Mahindra and Mahindra Limited, 60–61
  Mercedes Benz India (MBI), 67
  Piaggio, 60
  SAIC Motor, 63–64
  Skoda Auto India Private Limited (SAIPL), 63–64
  Volkswagen India, 62–63
Chakan-Special Economiz Zone (C-SEZ), 10
Chennai Metropolitan Area (CMA), 39–41, 51, 136, 198
  BharatBenz, 55
  employment relations in, 119–123
  Ford India Private Limited (FIPL), 54–55
  Hyundai Motor India Ltd (HMIL), 52–53
  income disparities, 121
  OEMs, 55–57
  proportion of migrant workers, 121
  Renault-Nissan, 53–54
  trade unionism, 121
  trend towards workforce contractualisation, 120–121
  violation of labour rights, 121
China, automotive output, 36
Chrysler, 64
classes of labour, 20
Complete-Knockdown (CKD) kits, 43, 48, 62, 65, 67, 70, 73, 90, 125, 200, 204
contract labour, 9, 28–29. *see also* regional contract labour system
Contract Labour (Abolition and Regulation) Act 1970 (CLARA), 99–102, 140, 164, 207, 212–213
contract worker, 211–215
contract workers in India, 9, 121
  income disparities, 121

Criminal Procedure Code 1973, 117

day labouring, 28
de facto informal work, 29
Delhi
  female labour force participation, 143
  historical structure of manufacturing in, 141
  informal enterprises across, 143
  Okhla Industrial Estate, 142
  proportion of inter-regional migrants living in, 141
  shift of migrating rural families, 143
  slum clearance initiatives, 143
Denso, 46–47
Denso India, 45
Dev, Awanish Kumar, 3
domestic OEMs, 9
Dongsun Automotive, 52

Eicher Motors, 119
Eicher Motors Ltd, 56
emergent neo-liberalism, 9
Employees Provident Funds Act 1952, 27, 170, 217
Employees' State Insurance Corporation Act 1948, 27, 170, 217
employment configuration, 9, 23, 31–32, 199, 207–210
  definition, 26
employment relations at Maruti Suzuki under emergent neo-liberalism, 111–119
  at its Gurugram plant, 114
  under 'restricted openness,' 1982-91, 107–111
  structure of employees' pay and conditions, 112–113
  Voluntary Retirement Scheme (VRS), 112, 206
employment security, 10, 30, 32, 108, 111, 123, 130, 132–133, 163, 190, 196, 206, 213
Endurance Technologies, 59
extra-firm actors, 17–18
extra-firm bargaining, 18

Factories Act 1948, 27, 30, 126, 165, 170, 213, 218–219
FAME policy (Faster Adoption and Manufacturing of Hybrid & Electric Vehicles), 97
FCA India Automobiles Private Limited (Fiat India), 64–67
Fiat Chrysler (FCA), 63
    Fiat Uno CKD kits, 65
    licensing agreement with Premier, 65
    strategic partners, 66
    Tier-1 suppliers, 66–67
Fiat India
    industrial conflict at, 124–125
first-mover coupling, 78–84, 200
first-mover foreign OEMs, 8–9
FMI Automotive Components, 45
Force Motors, 56, 119, 123
Ford, 15
Ford India Employees Union (FIEU), 122–123
Ford India Private Limited (FIPL), 54–55, 68, 119
    market share, 54
    support for independent foreign suppliers, 54–55
    Tier-1 suppliers, 54–55
Ford Motor Company, 94
    apprentices, 120
    percentage of contract workers, 120
    wage rates, 120
foreign OEMs, 8–9, 45, 50–51, 57, 64, 76–79, 81–82, 87, 89–95, 102–103, 106, 111–112, 195, 199–200
formal employment contracts, 27
'form of exploitation,' concept of a, 26
Friends Industrial Complex, 172

Gabriel India, 63
General Motors (GM), 15, 40, 68, 123
    Delphi's relationship, 15
    SAIC Motor as a minority shareholder in, 64
    suppliers, 63
Genpact, 83

Global Commodity Chains (GCC), 10, 12
Global Production Network (GPN), 10, 12, 17–23, 35–36, 42–43, 181
    in auto-manufacturing, 9, 199–202
    definition, 17
    GPN 2.0, 17–19, 22
global-regional integration, 8
Global Value Chains (GVC), 10, 12–17, 19–20, 35, 42, 181
    governance in, 13, 15–16
Graziano Trasmissioni, 106

Halla Visteon, 45
Haryana State Electronics Development Corporation (HARTRON), 83
Haryana State Industrial and Infrastructure Development Corporation (HSIIDC), 82
Haryanvi population, caste status of, 145
helper, 196
Hero Group, 202
Hero Honda, 95, 207
    industrial action at, 129
Hero MotoCorp, 46–49, 68, 72, 80, 83, 129, 136, 149, 198, 200, 207
    assembly factories abroad, 48
    brand and reputation, 48
    conflict between the Munjals and Honda, 48–49
    joint venture partner, 47
    manufacturing and assembly facilities, 47
    partnership with suppliers, 48
    regular workforce, 48
    shareholders, 49
    two-wheeler production, output volume, 47
hierarchy-based governance, 13
Hind Mazdoor Sabha (HMS), 114, 165
Honda
    cars, 49
    core suppliers, 50
    production network, 50–51
Honda Motorcycle and Scooter India (HMSI), 45, 48–51, 58, 95, 150, 198
    protests at, 129

share of national two-wheeler market, 49

Honda Motorcycle and Scooter Limited (HMSI), 136

hostile industrial disputes, 2–6
Asti case, 131–132
in C-SEZ and Pune district, 123–126, 134
dismissal-related issues, 122
in Gujarat, 127–128
in NCR, 2, 106, 116–117
in Pantnagar, 128
wages, issues related to, 123
workforces, issues related to, 129–132

Hwashin Automotive, 52

Hyundai Motor India Anna Thozhilalar Sangam (HMIATS), 121

Hyundai Motor India Employees Union (HMIEU), 121–122

Hyundai Motor India Limited (HMIL), 119, 121–122, 200

Hyundai Motor India Ltd (HMIL), 52–53, 68, 70, 81, 94
global production network, 52
Tier-2 suppliers of, 52–53

Import Substitution Industrialisation (ISI), 28, 77, 85, 87–89, 91–92, 99, 103, 106, 109, 203

income security, 30, 32, 123, 130, 165, 192, 209, 213–214, 217–218, 221–224, 226

Incomplete Knockdown (IKD) kits, 90, 204

India as the global 'destination of choice,' 1

Indian auto manufacturing, 1, 3, 7
contract labour in, 28–29
employment configurations in, 31
gendering of work in, 21
hostile industrial disputes, 2–6
inter-regional competition, 8
key foreign OEMs in, 93–94
list of industrial actions reported in, 4–6
modernisation of, 22
process of global-regional integration, 8–10

role of precarious and informal work in, 23–33
social-relational explanation for conflict in, 12
sub-national territorial unit, 19
supply chain production and distribution, 39
turnover, 2014-15, 36
two-wheelers, production volumes in, 37

Indian National Trade Union Congress (INTUC), 114, 165

Indian OEMs, 11, 16

industrial citizenship, 30

industrial colonies of NCR, 171–174
Aliyar Village, 148
automotive manufacturers in, 149–158
Ballabgarh, 173
Binola, 174
Binola Village, 146, 168
Faridabad, 142–144, 171–172, 181–183, 195, 198
Gurugram, 144–145, 173, 198
Kharkara, 174
Kharkari Village, 146–147, 165
Manesar, 174
Mujesar, 173

Industrial Disputes Act 1947, 30, 163, 219

Industrial Employment (Standing Orders) Act 1946, 101, 115

industrial society, 23

Inergy Automotive Systems, 45

informal work, 24, 27, 29

institutional conflict, 7, 106

inter-firm control, 18, 181

inter-firm coordination, 18

inter-firm partnership, 18, 43, 75–76, 80–81, 90–91, 95, 158, 181, 201–202

inter-firm relations between OEMs and suppliers, 14–15

intermediaries, 18

International Labour Organisation (ILO), 24

IT and IT-enabled Services (ITES) industries, 83

Jagdambay Forgings, 52
Japanese OEMs, 11, 15, 151, 158
   relational governance in, 15
   strategy of inter-firm control, 80–81
Jay Bharat, 45
JBM Auto System, 54–55, 59
job application and recruitment processes,
   31
job security, 30

Kamgar Ekta Premier Sanghatana
   (KEPS), 125
Kirloskar Group, 94
Krishna Ishizaki, 45
Krishna Maruti, 45

labour agency, 20
Labour Code on Industrial Relations Bill
   2015, 101
labour contractors, 28
labour control mechanism, 11
labour control regimes, 23, 25–26
labour market intermediaries, 2
labour market security, 30
labour-related security, 30
labour relations within OEMs, 12
labour standards and employment relations
   in OEMs, Tier-1, and Tier-2 firms,
   105–106
Land Acquisition Act 1894, 97
lean manufacturing principles and
   techniques, 8, 10–11
Lumax Industries, 69

Machino Plastics, 45
Magneti Marelli, 46, 66, 75
Magneti Marelli Powertrain India, 45
Mahatma Gandhi National Rural
   Employment Guarantee Act 2005
   (NREGA), 100
Mahindra and Mahindra, 11, 123, 198, 207
   assembly factories, 61, 124
   exports, 61
   industrial conflict at, 124
   regular workforce, 61
   Tier-1 suppliers, 61

Mahindra and Mahindra Limited, 60–61
Mahindra Sona, 61
Mahindra Ugine Steel, 61
Mahindra USA (MUSA), 61
Make in India initiative, 1, 6, 34
Makino Auto, 59–60
Mando India, 54
Manesar Steel Processing India, 45
manufacturing design, 14
market-based governance, 13, 15, 171, 184
Mark Exhaust, 45
Maruti Suzuki conflict in 2011/12, 2,
   106, 116–117, 131, 133–134, 167,
   205–206, 226
   changes to its employment relations
      practices in, 117
Maruti Suzuki India Limited (MSIL), 43–
   47, 68–69, 74, 76, 80, 105, 136, 200,
   205. *see also* employment relations at
   Maruti Suzuki
   capacity to control key suppliers, 202
   car exports, 2014-15, 44
   equity shares in in associate companies,
      45
   equity stakes in Tier-1 suppliers, 46
   Good Conduct Bond, 115
   hiring practices for temporary workers,
      45
   initial efforts to restructure workers'
      wages, 106
   investment in Tier-1 supply firms, 45
   main facilities, 44
   market capitalisation, 118
   partnerships with foreign companies,
      46
   regular workforce, 44–45, 117–118
   shareholding pattern, 44
   share in passenger car market, 43–44
   strategic partners and joint venture
      firms, 106
   subsidiary companies, 45
   suppliers, 45–47
   transformation of employment
      relations, role of, 107

Maruti Suzuki Powertrain Employees
  Union (MSPEU), 118
Maruti Suzuki Workers Union (MSWU),
  2, 114, 116
  membership, 3
Maruti Udyog Employees Union
  (MUEU), 206
Maruti Udyog Kamgar Union (MUKU),
  112
Mercedes Benz India (MBI), 67, 123
  family-oriented customs at, 125
Minimum Wage Act, 101
Modi, Narendra, 1, 8
modular governance, 13
Motherson Sumi, 68
MRF (Madras Rubber Factory) Limite, 59
Munjal family, 47–48, 72, 95

National Capital Region (NCR), 39–41,
  141, 198
  auto manufacturing and fieldwork sites
    in, 142
  Faridabad, 43
  Gurugram, 43
  Hero MotoCorp, 47–49
  Honda Motorcycle and Scooter
    (HMSI), 49–51
  land acquisition, 144–148
  Maruti Suzuki India Limited (MSIL),
    43–47
  Tier-3 and Tier-4 auto manufacturers,
    174–180
  trajectories of socio-political conflict in,
    128–132
National Capital Region Planning Board
  (NCRPB), 141
national industry policy and auto
  manufacturing
  AMP-1 and *AMP-2*, 96–97
  conditions of trade and investment
    liberalisation, 95
  contract worker law, 99–100
  Daimler-Chrysler-TELCO, joint
    venture between, 92

economic liberalisation and
    transformation of auto industry,
    202–205
  establishment of fully-owned subsidiary
    companies, 94
  first-mover coupling, 78–84, 103
  Ford–Mahindra, joint venture between,
    92, 94
  foreign OEMs, 79, 81–82, 87, 89–95,
    102–103
  Honda–Siel Limited, joint venture
    between, 92
  implementation of lean manufacturing
    practices, 82
  Import Substitution Industrialisation
    (ISI), 28, 77, 85, 87–89, 91–92,
    99, 103, 106, 109, 203
  industrial subsidies and land
    acquisition, 99
  joint venture policy, 92
  labour law framework, 99
  major concessions and exemptions,
    82–83
  model of land acquisition, 83–84
  model of regional state support, 83
  model of state institutional support for
    foreign OEMs, 82
  Modi's 'Make in India' initiative, 95–96,
    101–102
  neo-liberal policy-making after 1991,
    91–102
  offshore services operations, 83
  100 per cent foreign-owned operation,
    94
  restricted openness, 1982-1991, 84–91,
    103
  SEZ Act 2005, 98
  strategic coupling, 78–79
  strategy of inter-firm partnership, 80
  Toyota–Kirloskar Group, joint venture
    between, 92, 94
New Holland Fiat India Private Limited,
  64
Nippon Seiki, 50

Nippon Thermostat, 45

Original Equipment Manufacturers
(OEMs), 7–8, 197

panchayat system, 145–146
passenger cars and commercial vehicles
export profile, 37
production volume, 2000-14, 38
top countries, production volume, 37
Piaggio, 60
employment relations practices, 126
investment in India, 60
Premier Limited, 16
Pricol Limited, 2
Pricol Ltd., 119
producer-driven commodity chain, 13
Punjab Shops and Commercial
Establishments Act 1958, 172

Rajhans Pressings, 51
Rao, Narasimha, 91
regional casual labour system, 9, 32, 35,
171, 185–193, 221
global production networks and,
219–224
in Tier-3 and Tier-4 firms, 185–193
regional contract labour system, 34–35,
140, 171, 180, 199
de facto informal workers, 163–168
labour-related security, 163–165
in NCR, 34, 158–163
relationship with union members, 167
roots of, 141
working conditions, 165–166
regional industrialisation, 104, 141, 144,
168, 225
regional labour control regime, 25
regional social structure of accumulation,
concept of, 21
regions of motor vehicle manufacturing in
India
Bidadi village, 72–73
Chakan Special Economic Zone
(C-SEZ), 39–41

Chennai Metropolitan Area (CMA),
39–41
emerging regions, 42
employment relations in, 119–128
Gujarat, 67–71
Mysuru, 73–74
National Capital Region (NCR), 39–41
of OEMs, 41–42
Uttarakhand, 71–72
regular worker, 219
relational governance, 13, 15, 76, 181–182,
184
Renault-Nissan, 53–54, 119–121, 123, 207
competitors of Renault Kwid, 53
employment relations strategy, 134
market expansion plans, 53
Tier-1 suppliers, 53–54
representation security, 30
restricted openness, 8
Rico Auto, 129
Right to Education Act 2009, 100
Right to Fair Compensation and
Transparency in Land Acquisition,
Rehabilitation and Resettlement
Act (Land Acquisition Act) 2013,
98
Rockman Industries, 72
Royal Enfield, 56

SAIC Motor, 63–64
Satyam Auto Components, 48, 72
Setco Automotive, 56
SEZ Act 2005, 84
Shanghai Volkswagen, 64
Shivam Autotech, 129
short-term contracts, 9
Singh, Manmohan, 91
SKH Metals, 45
skill reproduction, 30, 111, 193, 213–214,
217–219
Skoda Auto India Private Limited
(SAIPL), 62–64
manufacturing base, 62
production volume, 62
suppliers, 63

Society of Indian Automobile
Manufacturers (SIAM), 34, 95–96,
197
Sogefi India, 63
Sona Kayo Steering Systems, 69
Sona Koyo Steering, 45
Special Economic Zone (SEZ) Act 2005,
98, 205
SsangYong, 60
Street Vendors (Protection of Livelihood
and Regulation of Street Vending)
Act 2014, 100
Sunbeam Auto, 129
Sundram Fasteners, 119
Suprajit Engineering, 51, 54, 56
Suraj Industrial Complex, 172

Takata Automotive, 50
Tata, Ratan, 69
Tata Group, 42, 66, 69–70
Tata Johnson Controls, 54
Tata Motors, 8, 57, 68–71, 73, 79, 118, 123,
198, 202, 207
industrial conflict at, 124
Tata Motors Employees Union (TMEU),
124
Tata's investment in Sanand, controversy
over, 8
Tendulkar, Sachin, 1
Tenneco Automotive, 53
Tier-3 firms, 15–16, 31, 105, 123, 137–139,
144, 147–148, 169–170, 174–180
framing of commercial relations
higher-tier firms and, 182
income security and representation
security, 219, 223
inspections of product quality in,
181–182, 184
low-margin operating model of,
195–196
people engaged in precarious work,
222–223
range of occupations, 222
regional casual labour system, 185–193

relational value chain governance, 220
survival of, 183
wage workers in, 222–224
work security, 223
Tier-4 firms, 15, 35, 105, 123, 137–139,
144, 147–148, 169–170, 174–181
job-worker and industrial outworker,
224
job-worker or industrial outworker, 31
low-margin operating model of,
195–196
regional casual labour system, 185–193
work security, 224
'Tier-1' suppliers, 7
Toyota, 11
Toyota Group, 46
Toyota Kirloskar, 94
Toyota Kirloskar Auto Parts Limited
(TKAPL), 73, 126
Toyota Kirloskar Motor Limited (TKML)
industrial unrest at, 126–127
Toyota Kirloskar Motors Employees
Union (TKMEU), 126
Toyota Kirloskar Motors Limited
(TKML), 72–73, 76, 92
Toyota Kirloskar Suppliers Association
(TKSA), 73
Trade Union Act 1926, 30, 99, 126
trainee, 217–218
Trasmissioni, Graziano, 2
TVS, 73

undeclared or unregistered workers,
216–217
United Auto Workers (UAW) union, 123
United Union of Hyundai Employees
(UUHE), 121–122
Unorganised Workers' Social Security Act
2008, 100

value chain governance, 13, 76, 80, 109,
171, 181–184, 220
Varroc Group, 60
VE Commercial Vehicles, 57

Vision 3/12/65, 97
Visteon Automotive Systems India
    (VASI), 54
Visteon Technical and Services Center
    (VTSC), 54
Volkswagen India (VWI), 10, 62–63, 123
    assembly plant, 10
    total sales volume, 62
    'Trainee Development Scheme,' 125
Volvo Trucks India, 57

Wabco India, 57
wage fixing, 30

wage rates
    automotive manufacturers in NCR,
        120, 156–158
    industrial disputes related to, 123
    Tier-3 and Tier-4 firms, 179–180
Welcome Industrial Complex, 172
Woojin Automotive, 52
work security, 30
World Systems Theory, 13, 19
written employment contracts, 27

Yapp Automotive Systems, 54–55